STALKING
THE ACADEMIC
COMMUNIST

STALKING
THE ACADEMIC
COMMUNIST

Intellectual Freedom
and the Firing of
Alex Novikoff

DAVID R. HOLMES

Published for University of Vermont by
University Press of New England
Hanover and London

© 1989 by the Trustees of University of Vermont

Printed in the United States of America

∞

Library of Congress Cataloging in Publication Data
Holmes, David R.
Stalking the academic Communist.

Bibliography: p.
Includes index.
1. Academic Freedom—Vermont—History—20th century.
2. Novikoff, Alex Benjamin, 1913–1987. 3. Communist college teachers—Vermont—Biography. 4. College teachers—Vermont—Dismissal of—History—20th century.
I. Title
LC72.3.V5H65 1988   378'.121   88–40129
ISBN 0–87451–466–5
ISBN 0–87451–469–X (pbk.)

5   4   3   2   1

CONTENTS

Contents

Figures follow page 54.

FOREWORD

More than thirty-five years have passed since McCarthyism swept through the academic community, but we are only just beginning to understand what happened during the late 1940s and early 1950s. Despite their stated commitment to academic freedom, the nation's colleges and universities succumbed to the anti-Communist furor. Hundreds of professors lost their jobs, thousands more shunned controversy in order to retain theirs, and hundreds of thousands of students learned that dissent was dangerous and criticism of the status quo unwise. Nor were the dismissals and self-censorship limited to the nation's campuses; labor unions, movie studios, school boards, and the federal government, among others, took part in the political repression we now call McCarthyism.

The meaning of these events remains unclear. McCarthyism still touches a political nerve; as a result, historical judgments about it often reflect preconceived notions rather than any critical evaluation of evidence. In addition, the old debates about communism and the role of Senator McCarthy still structure our knowledge, diverting attention from fundamental issues and forcing scholars to address irrelevant ones. Yet, changes are occurring. The new materials that the Freedom of Information Act and the development of oral history collections have created are encouraging scholars to ask new questions.

The scope of this new investigation of McCarthyism is broader; we now look at institutions as well as individuals, bureaucratic procedures as well as political ideologies. No longer is it enough to use FBI files, for example, to assess the guilt or innocence of such eminent or notorious figures as Alger Hiss and the Rosenbergs. We must now address the more important questions of the FBI's own role in the anti-Communist crusade. Similarly, we must also reexamine American communism, not only because understanding the Communist movement will help us understand the individuals involved but also because a broader examination will enable us to assess the impact of Mc-Carthyism.

Not surprisingly, this new research is producing a new interpretation that rejects the traditional view of McCarthyism. No longer do historians view it as a populist political aberration identified with the demagogic behavior of "Tail-Gunner Joe." Rather, McCarthyism is seen as an elite phenomenon, designed to eliminate from any position of influence in American life communism and all the people, ideas, and organizations associated with it. Though it began in the federal government, McCarthyism soon spread throughout the nation, achieving its purposes primarily by imposing political tests for employment. When viewed from this perspective, the McCarthyist movement becomes understandable as an institutional, almost bureaucratic, phenomenon rather than a predominantly ideological one. And the most useful scholarship on it turns out to be the study of individual cases that reconstruct the process through which the nation's public and private institutions collaborated with and contributed to the anti-Communist crusade.

This is David Holmes's achievement. By taking a single case, the dismissal of biologist Alex Novikoff from the University of Vermont, and subjecting that case to intensive scrutiny, Holmes has shown us exactly how the mechanism of McCarthyism operated. Using materials from private papers, interviews, FBI files, university archives, and the local press, Holmes offers us both a detailed account of a typical McCarthy victim's political evolution and professional career as well as a thorough analysis of the way in which one university dealt with a professor who would not name names.

In the process, Holmes exposes the bureaucratic rationality of McCarthyism. When Vermont's trustees fired Novikoff, they were simply following the rules. Novikoff, because he had once been a Communist and refused to recant, had by definition violated those rules. Through an almost microscopic examination of the way in which the men who ran the University of Vermont came to their decision about Novikoff, Holmes enables us to understand exactly how so many well-meaning, intelligent, yet essentially uninformed, Americans were able to collaborate with the anti-Communist furor.

The importance of this study lies in its detail, in its dispassionate exposition of the seemingly ordinary procedures through which a liberal institution in a democratic society came to participate in the repression of dissent. Holmes and the other scholars who are investigating similar cases in other institutions and communities offer us a discouraging message. They show us just how fragile our political freedom may be. It is, of course, our task to learn the lesson they seek to teach.

New York City   Ellen W. Schrecker
May 1988

ACKNOWLEDGMENTS

This book reconstructs events that occurred over a span of fifty years and in three cities. Only with the assistance of many individuals has the book become a reality. I am particularly grateful to Alex Novikoff, his family, and his many loyal friends. Phyllis Novikoff, Sonia and Sidney Klein, Kenneth Novikoff, Oscar Shaftel, Frederic Ewen, and Arnold Schein provided materials and support at crucial points in the undertaking.

The final product has benefited greatly from the close reading and commentary of David Oshinsky and Ellen Schrecker, both superb scholars of McCarthyism in American life. They were unstinting in their criticism and in their enthusiasm for the book. Others who commented helpfully on various drafts and sections of the book included Henry Steffins and Alfred Andrea of the Department of History at the University of Vermont; Frederic Ewen, Oscar Shaftel, and Morris Schappes, who were participants in the events of the 1930s and 1940s; and Betty Thurber and Howard Cady, valued friends of the Holmes family.

Edward Ducharme and Robert Arns supported my work and assured that, in the midst of my duties as a professor and as an administrator at the University of Vermont, I had sufficient time to see the project to conclusion. My travels and the acquisition of materials were supported by an Institutional Research Grant from the Graduate College of the University of Vermont and by a Henry J. Kaiser Family Foundation Research Travel Grant from the Walter Reuther Library of Labor and Urban Affairs. At crucial points in the writing of this book, Charles Backus of the University Press of New England and Henry Steffins, a member of the Editorial Board, expressed their confidence and offered their advice.

Primary documents and records were essential to the writing of the book. For help in locating and utilizing these materials, I am especially indebted to Connell Gallagher and David Blow in the Special

Collections Division of the University of Vermont Library; Jordan Kurland, Associate General Secretary of the American Association of University Professors in Washington, D.C.; Linda Kloss, who expedited several Freedom of Information Act requests at the Federal Bureau of Investigation; and several archivists at the New York State Archives in Albany. Their highly professional (and patient) assistance was appreciated at every stage of my work. I am grateful also to the many individuals who agreed to be interviewed by me. Their willingness to talk about the past, including sometimes painful memories, was a gratifying part of the research.

The book was inspired in the first instance by a student of mine, Ann Dumaresq, who did a paper for a course taught by me and who shared her enthusiasm for the Novikoff story. Gail Kemp provided essential typing assistance. My wife, Antonia, read the final draft and fortunately discovered many, many sentences requiring repair. My sons, Chris and Caleb, guard a legacy of the undertaking, an inscribed copy of *Climbing the Family Tree*, Alex Novikoff's wonderful science book written for children. Alex made a gift of this book at a luncheon gathering at our house in Vermont in May 1985.

Washington, D.C.   DRH
March 1988

STALKING
THE ACADEMIC
COMMUNIST

INTRODUCTION

Despite the prediction of rain showers, the morning of graduation day brought a warm May sunshine and the suggestion that summer might eventually come to northern Vermont. Across the raised platform the short, stoop-shouldered man moved forward with uncertain step before an audience of six thousand students and parents. The audience rose to its feet under the blue Vermont sky and applauded, producing a low roar that washed over the old football stadium. Then he turned and faced the smiling president.

In a gesture of the well-schooled public man of the 1980s, the president of the university deftly revised the formal script of the occasion and added his personal touch: "We welcome you back to the campus."

The university marshal read the words of praise, words that described Alex Novikoff's accomplishments as a scientist and as a teacher. Then, in a commanding voice the black-robed president completed the medieval ritual by pronouncing the Latin phrases for the awarding of the honorary degree of doctor of science. The marshal placed the radiant colors of the degree over Novikoff's head.

Always an emotional man, Novikoff had lost some of his old self-control, and his eyes filled with tears. He was overcome by the thought that he had returned in honor to the campus that thirty years earlier had produced so much pain. The four of them—his wife, his two sons, and he—had suffered a searing humiliation, and things were never the same again. The wrong had been admitted for all to hear, and now he had his satisfaction.

His keen eyes, eyes that saw under a microscope things that no other scientist saw until he pointed the way, cleared after a few moments. Later he left the platform to accept the handshakes and hugs of former colleagues, old friends, and smiling strangers. These were moments of exquisite pleasure.

In 1953 Novikoff had faced another president on this same campus. Identified by an informer as a member of the Communist party during the 1930s, he invoked the Fifth Amendment before Senator William Jenner's Internal Security Subcommittee. The University of Vermont brought proceedings against Novikoff to determine his fitness to remain a faculty member. Urged on by the governor of Vermont, who was an ex officio member of the board of trustees, the board overturned the recommendation of its own committee of investigation and voted overwhelmingly for dismissal.

The action against Novikoff in 1953 was the midpoint of a journey into and through the dangerous battlefields of twentieth-century American politics. The journey began in the poverty and upheaval of the Brownsville section of Brooklyn. Novikoff became an academic man and for a few years in the 1930s and 1940s a political activist. This book tells about his turning to the academic world and to politics—in particular to the Communist party—and about the consequences of those choices.

Novikoff was well known among research biologists and on two occasions a subject of newspaper interest because of his involvement in America's campaign against the Communist party. He was not a famous man, however. Certainly, he would have been more widely known if he had received the Nobel Prize that many believed he deserved, but this was not to be. Yet the story of his entanglement in the anti-Communist inquisition needs to be told. For thirty-five years— from an investigation of the House Un-American Activities Committee in 1938 to a loyalty investigation instigated by the National Institutes of Health in 1973—he endured the consequences of his political activities. What his story reveals most vividly is the lengthy duration of the anti-Communist inquisition as well as its comprehensiveness. The board of trustees at the University of Vermont was one actor in a large and continuing cast of characters that included congressional committees, a legislative committee of the state of New York, a state governor, administrators and faculty members on two college campuses, several federal agencies, national higher education associations, and the newspapers. McCarthyism was an interconnected and interdependent web of organizations and people, and Novikoff was trapped in the web for a good part of his adult life.

The McCarthy campaign targeted government employees, entertainment figures, and educators. Only recently, with Ellen Schrecker's important work *No Ivory Tower,* has a comprehensive picture emerged of the campaign against academic Communists. Schrecker's book conveys vividly the anatomy of the inquisition. Once a teacher was identified publicly as a Communist or invoked the Fifth Amendment in response to questions from a committee of investigation, it fell to the faculty member's college to carry out the punishment. Except for the most autocratic colleges, the institution would then commence a proceeding to determine the fitness of the teacher to continue on the faculty. Because on most campuses Communist party membership was judged to constitute unprofessional conduct and because invoking the Fifth Amendment was interpreted to be a lack of candor inconsistent with professional conduct, these proceedings almost always led to dismissal. Whether as a result of a formal proceeding or through more private, quieter means, some one hundred suspected Communists were fired during the McCarthy era. Many other faculty members resigned rather than endure a direct confrontation with their institutions. The firings occurred at public as well as private institutions, at elite as well as unprestigious institutions, at colleges in every region of the country, and among faculty representing virtually every academic discipline. At a minimum we must take cognizance of the scale of the anti-Communist campaign and the energy and resources devoted to carrying it out.

Whereas Schrecker's work is a comprehensive overview of the national scene, the Novikoff narrative traces a single individual's involvement in and path through the history of the anti-Communist inquisition in higher education. There are few studies in depth of individuals and their confrontation with McCarthyism, especially studies of academic Communists. This book aims to capture the complexity and the totality of Novikoff's experience during the extended campaign against Communists.[2]

Although the focus is on a single individual, it is pertinent to note that his life touched events and circumstances that affected hundreds, perhaps thousands, of Americans. These were events that poisoned the academic environment from the early 1930s until at least the 1970s. Novikoff's story is, therefore, another vantage point from which to understand and assess the broader picture.

Until recently, most former Communists were reluctant to talk candidly about their experiences, and many of the telling documents of the period were under seal in government agencies, libraries, and private collections. Earlier studies of the McCarthy era were limited by the inaccessibility of primary sources. Benefiting from the opening of files and the increased willingness of key participants to discuss the past, this book draws on (1) interviews with participants in the events of the 1930–1960 period, almost all of whom were over seventy years of age at time of the research, and (2) files acquired through the Freedom of Information Act and from newly available archives.[3]

Novikoff's life was embedded in three interrelated worlds. First, he was a political activist who joined efforts in the 1930s to improve conditions at Brooklyn College. This brought him into the Communist party and various progressive causes and, in time, produced his troubles with authorities. His immersion in the world of political activism—at least the academic version of political activism—was an important part of his life. Second, because of his political activities Novikoff became entangled in America's anti-Communist campaign. He was pursued by the Rapp-Coudert Committee in New York State, the Senate Internal Security Subcommittee, and the board of trustees of the University of Vermont. His loyalty was investigated by various government agencies, most comprehensively by the FBI, and a massive security file was developed on his case. Through the vantage point of his life we are exposed to the culture and the apparatus of the anti-Communist inquisition. Third, Novikoff was a scientist and a man of the academic world. For fifty-five years, from the age of eighteen, he conducted research, taught students, and participated in the affairs of higher education. He became an outstanding scientist, who made several important discoveries in the field of cancer research. Although Novikoff fought against aspects of the higher education environment, his life was shaped in a critical way by the structure and values of the university. Above all, he was a man of academe.

Novikoff's life demonstrates how the worlds of political activism, anticommunism, and higher education interacted and affected each other. We see, for example, the crucial role played by the FBI in monitoring Novikoff's activities and in supporting and shaping the anti-Communist campaign. We see too the crucial role played by a single investigator, Robert Morris, who worked for two committees investigating Novikoff and energetically assisted the actions against Novikoff in Vermont. On a more general scale, we see the duration, complexity, and consequences of the inquisition.

Ultimately, Novikoff's story centers on the environment, values, and actions of the American university. The concept of academic freedom best exemplifies the special values and ideas that give the university its unique place in American society. With a legacy from the European medieval university and the prototype of the modern research university developed in Germany in the eighteenth and nineteenth centuries, the American university has long asserted and defended the pursuit of truth wherever it may lead. The freedom to inquire and to teach and the protection from unwarranted interference in these activities define academic freedom as it emerged in the late nineteenth century. After 1915 the American Association of University

Professors (AAUP) codified these ideas and elaborated procedural safeguards for protecting the rights of institutions and individual faculty
members. Because academic freedom is not a legislated concept protected by civil law and because most American colleges and universities are governed by an external lay board of trustees, academic
freedom is a fragile concept, vulnerable to shifting political and philosophical allegiances.[4]

The Novikoff affair illustrates the vulnerability of academic freedom to the exigencies of the moment. On the outside, an attitude of
intolerance and an inclination to willful behavior brought pressure on
the University of Vermont. On the inside, the president of the university
acted in ways that were contrary to beliefs that he had articulated many
times and held dear as an academician. Novikoff's faculty colleagues,
except for a small core of supporters, were noticeably silent during the
six months of proceedings against him. Moreover, the AAUP was not
disposed or organized to put up a serious battle on behalf of Novikoff
or other academics under fire across the country. Thus, one of the most
significant aspects of this story is the damage done to the integrity of
colleges and universities, singly and together, and to the principles that
define what is special about higher education in this country.

The deeper problem may be confusion, perhaps disagreement,
about the appropriate role of the university in our society. These events
remind us that deep-set suspicions exist in America about the life of
the mind and about fancy, complex thinking on presumably straightforward problems. Suspicions of this kind go back at least to the time
of Thomas Jefferson. In the McCarthy era simple logic was addressed
to symbolic and easily generalized issues. The attitudes and approaches
of the intellectual, as exemplified by the college professor, were dismissed by many as weak, impractical, and dangerous, and the entire
academic enterprise was brought under suspicion. In this environment
educational leaders operated from a position of political weakness. It
is not surprising that trustees, presidents, and many faculty members
ended up accepting the premises of the anti-Communist program and
cooperating with the effort to purge accused Communists. In the joining of the University of Vermont with the anti-Communist campaign
of national and local political leaders one cannot fail to observe the
gradual compromising of institutional independence.[5]

Honest philosophical conviction as well as human weakness contributed to the behavior of the universities during the McCarthy era.
Moreover, the Novikoff story demonstrates that the success of the anti-
Communist campaign in higher education was based on a series of
misunderstandings. Although the academic Communists were asso-

ciated with a movement intent on reducing the power and defying the will of America's leaders, college teachers were rarely a threat to national security except by the most farfetched logic. Their activities and intentions were mundane and close to home. The Communists on New York City campuses, for example, aimed primarily to reform the functioning of the local colleges. It is evident that most Americans during the McCarthy era and probably most academicians did not understand or did not choose to accept this distinction.

Looking at the issue more broadly, mainstream American society, especially the part of America away from the melting-pot cities, had experienced little and knew little of Jews, immigrant ghettos, and radical politics. Exposed to these phenomena, the inclination of Americans was to suspect the intentions and values of persons of such different backgrounds. The behavior of otherwise well-intended and fair-minded Vermonters suggests that lack of knowledge and worldly experience contributed to the decision to remove Novikoff from the University of Vermont.

Finally, there was frequent confusion and misunderstanding about issues such as invocation of the Fifth Amendment and the meaning of academic freedom. In several instances popular interpretations of the day were repudiated later by legal and professional authorities. Catalyzed by the confusion of motives and fast-paced events of the 1940s and 1950s, limited experience, lack of knowledge, and misunderstanding offer, together, an explanation of what happened to Alex Novikoff and perhaps a hundred other college faculty members.

The proceedings in Vermont against Novikoff were a solitary episode in a campaign that stretched across the country and over many years. From one perspective there was an inevitability to the fate that befell Novikoff and his fellow teachers. Operating from the widely held premise that repression in the cause of liberty or national security is acceptable, the stalking of suspected Communists became largely a technical problem. The committees and agencies that had the files and the privileges of government were not likely to shrink from the task. It was simply a matter of time before public identification, enforced testimony, and actions of dismissal took place.

From a more optimistic perspective, this narrative demonstrates that although the outcomes were eminently predictable, they were not inevitable. There were points of choice at which enlightened and courageous educators could have altered the course of events. The decision to fire Novikoff could well have gone the other way. In this sense the lessons of Novikoff's story have relevance for contemporary higher education. At a time of simplistic statements about higher learning and impatience with the actions and effectiveness of the enterprise, the academy needs strong and enlightened leadership. We needed in 1953—and we need today—leadership that strengthens the traditions of academic freedom. Novikoff's life story provides insights and lessons that may help us move toward this important goal.

Chapter 1

ORIGINS OF POLITICAL ACTIVISM

Academic Life at Columbia University and Brooklyn College

By the age of twenty-two Alex Novikoff was committed to the academic world, both as a place to work and as an avenue of professional achievement. He had considerable experience as a biology teacher at Brooklyn College and was well on his way toward attaining a doctoral degree at Columbia University. What set Novikoff on the path of controversy and trouble, however, was his commitment to political action. In the tumult and political upheaval of Depression-era New York City, he was not unusual in this respect. Although the actual percentage of college faculty members who were politically active was small, he was not on a solitary journey. The local campuses were anything but ivory towers, and hundreds of faculty, including many at prestigious Columbia, mixed politics and academics. Looking back on the 1930s, we see that Novikoff was part of an important activist tradition.[1]

A commitment to political action and to upsetting the status quo, however, was not the typical course for most Americans nor for most academicians. Because Novikoff's political activities and their painful consequences are a central focus of this story, his turn to academics and then to politics is an important part of his life story. It is evident that Novikoff's development was shaped by several interacting forces: his immersion in Jewish immigrant culture with its poverty, its socialist leanings, its worldly ambitions; his role as the first son in the family and his sense of "specialness"; his brilliant mind and its capacity to recognize and value ideas and moral principles; his sense of

8

rejection emanating from an unhappy experience at Columbia University; his coming to Brooklyn College, where politics was in the air and the list of grievances was lengthy. Recent scholarship has shown that political commitment is the result of a complex process that proceeds differently for each individual. So too, the forming of Alex Novikoff proceeded in idiosyncratic ways over many years.[2]

Yet there are important common patterns among members of a generation. Becoming an activist, for instance, rarely involves a fundamental change of core values. Novikoff's emergence as a political activist and a Communist, like that of his contemporaries, was consistent with moral principles and social values that were formed in earlier years. For this reason Novikoff's turn to political activism was not surprising or illogical. The ground was fertile for such a step, and Novikoff's background and personality were strong predisposing factors. Looking at the earliest influences on his life, the story begins with the frustrations and impatience of a young couple living under difficult conditions in a small town in the Ukraine.[3]

A PRECOCIOUS YOUNG MAN

In early 1912 Zelig Novikoff and his wife, Anna, surveyed the circumstances of their existence and arrived at the same conclusion other Eastern European Jews had reached. Zelig was a handsome twenty-four-year-old Ukrainian who had been a Russian soldier on the Japanese front at a very young age. Fortunately, he returned unscathed to his home in Semyonevka, a village near Kiev. Although only slightly over five feet in height, he carried himself with pride and had visions of a career in the theater. He performed in plays with Sol Hurok, his boyhood friend and later a famous Broadway producer, but acting provided little money. He tried his hand at teaching Hebrew and apprenticed as a tinsmith, but none of these undertakings offered any realistic hope of escaping the poverty that pressed on his life. His resources were stretched even more by the birth of a daughter, Sonia; now, Anna was pregnant again.[4]

Zelig and Anna knew well that thousands of others, including many relatives, had left for America. The dream, which was also a source of wry humor in the family, was that in America the "streets were paved with gold." Anna's relatives wrote about the difficulties and the poverty in New York City. The tantalizing prospect, however, was that one could become rich, as had Anna's older brother, a wealthy garment manufacturer. Ambition ran strong in Zelig's blood and, facing few prospects in Semyonevka, the choice was not a difficult one to make. It was decided that Zelig would leave for America that fall, find work, and send money for Anna's passage the next year.[5]

In October Zelig booked passage in steerage on the *Czar*, one of three steamships of the Russian-American line traveling between Kursk on the Baltic Sea and New York. In the final years of the czarist regime these were the only passenger ships sailing regularly between Russia and the United States. Zelig arrived in New York on October 28, 1912, and made his way to relatives. Hearing of work up the coast in New London, Connecticut, he moved there and began work as a tin-smith. With long hours of labor and disciplined saving, he was able to send money back to Anna and in a few months he secured a small dwelling in New London. In the spring he heard that his son Alex had been born.[6]

On September 30, 1913, Anna, Sonia, and six-month-old Alex boarded the steamship *Kursk* with their belongings and two weeks' worth of food. Although the *Kursk* was advertised as a "newbuilt twinscrew" steamer equipped with the "latest maritime improve-ments, wireless telegraphy, submarine signals," steerage accommoda-tions were cold and uncomfortable. Until the end of her life Anna would retell stories about the discomfort and danger of the crossing. Fortunately, Anna and her two babies remained healthy, and the boat arrived on schedule in New York. Zelig, now known by the American name, Jake, met his family, took them to see relatives in New York, and then accompanied them to the house in New London.

For the next five years, Jake struggled, often unsuccessfully, to provide adequately for his family. His novice skills as a tinsmith—he made small animals and other kinds of figures—were not well remu-nerated, and many other lines of work were closed to Jews. Yet, in a manner described by other chroniclers of the Jewish struggle to survive in America, the Novikoff's persevered.[8]

Sonia and Alex started school, and at once Alex was noticed by his teachers as an unusually bright young boy. Before the children got fully settled into their schooling, however, Jake and Anna decided that economic prospects were better back in New York. Anna's brother offered Jake a job as a salesman for his dress company, and this was too good to refuse. The family, now enlarged by a new baby daughter, moved to a third-floor walkup apartment on Sackman Street in the Brownsville section of Brooklyn, where they joined the growing mul-titude of Jewish immigrants. For the first time feeling a degree of se-curity and stability in his new country, Jake applied for American citizenship. On December 10, 1918, he received his certificate of naturalization from the Kings County Supreme Court in Brooklyn, which automatically granted derivative citizenship to his wife and children.[9]

As with so many thousands of newly arrived families, the children knew little of their European origins and psychologically were "second-generation Americans" rather than "immigrants." For Sonia and Alex, the process of Americanization had already begun in earnest, especially in the public schools. The schools offered a solid education, both in providing the basic intellectual skills and knowledge and in imbuing the symbols and values of being an American. Along with disciplined exposure to the academic subjects, every student pledged his or her allegiance to the flag, studied the American revolution and the Civil War, and celebrated the American holidays. During childhood and adolescence, the socialization that took place in the schools and in the streets weaned thousands of immigrant children from the family's native tongue, the old customs and the old—limiting—dreams.[10]

During the early primary-school years Alex was recognized by his family and teachers as a brilliant student. A youngster with boundless energy, he pressed his teachers for explanations and facts and hounded them over and over with the question "Why?" At home he developed a keen interest in nature and at different times kept white rats, mice, and frogs. His drive to understand the workings of living organisms led to skinnings and amateur autopsies. On one occasion his family recoiled from the nauseating spectacle of the cat he had boiled to extinction on the stove in order to study its skeleton. In due course his quick mastery of schoolwork brought grade promotions, and soon he had surpassed his older sister in school. Sonia felt inferiority and embarrassment over this circumstance, especially when her friends would point out that little Alex was already in the upper grades. Looking back, she recalled that Alex rarely stayed in class the whole term and "this gave me a complex and I hated him then." Over the course of his public schooling, he jumped four grades and was graduated from high school at age fourteen.

Despite Sonia's discomfort, Alex's precocity was a constant source of pride for his parents. Everyone in the family, including Alex, knew he was special: he was the only male (until Aaron was born in 1922); he was thought to be "the brains in the family"; and he was noticed by others, including his teachers, neighbors, and other members of the family. Unquestionably, he was Anna's favorite; according to Sonia, she saw him "as God." The Novikoff's, like other Jews, placed a preeminent value on intellectual brilliance as the avenue through which ambitions and dreams could be realized. Although Jake still harbored his own ambitions, the more likely prospect was that their lives—and sacrifices—would be justified by the success of their son. Not surprisingly, Alex became the focus of Jake's and Anna's striving and the instrument through which their hopes might be realized.[12]

During his high school years Alex and his parents came to the conclusion that he should be a doctor. His interest in natural science was evident, and one of his high school teachers encouraged him in this direction. A Brownsville neighbor who was a physician took Alex to see an operation and spoke to him frequently about the profession. Yet the family's poverty meant that this goal was not easily attainable. Day to day, it was understood that the family must live frugally. Except in an emergency Alex and Sonia walked rather than pay for the trolley, and this often meant many extra miles along the Brooklyn streets. After the age of eleven Alex spent most of his holidays painting desks in the schools. Even with these contributions, it was not unusual for Alex to go to bed early with only a slab of bread and a piece of herring.[13]

Alex was graduated from Franklin Lane High School in 1928 with A grades and membership in a senior honor society. The Novikoffs knew that he must continue his education if medical school was to become a realistic possibility, and there was no question that the family, including Sonia, was prepared to make the necessary sacrifices to achieve that goal. The most important decision was where he should go.

END OF A DREAM

The principal college alternatives at the time in New York City were private New York University, private and prestigious Columbia University, and public and free City College of New York. Despite its expense and its well-known policy of limiting the number of Jews enrolling as undergraduates, Columbia's undergraduate arm, Columbia College, was an attractive choice for many of New York's Eastern European Jews. During the early part of the twentieth century Columbia's program to attract outstanding students from New York City public schools brought a flow of Jews to Columbia College. The entering classes at stately, elitist Columbia enrolled over 40 percent from New York's Jewish community. New York's upwardly mobile Jews recognized Columbia's outstanding academic reputation and its utility as a point of entry to the upper social and economic classes of American society.[14]

In the years before World War I, Columbia's top administrators and trustees determined that, in the interest of preserving the social character of the campus and Columbia's reputation among the Protestant upper classes, it was necessary to limit the enrollment of Jews. This decision was made easier by the fact that leaders at other prestigious universities, such as Harvard, Yale, and Princeton, came to the same conclusion. There was a shared concern about the Eastern European Jews, who were perceived to be less cultured and more prone to clannishness than Jews from Western Europe.[15]

Under the leadership of Frederick Keppel, dean of Columbia College from 1909 to 1918, and Herbert Hawkes, who succeeded Keppel, Columbia developed selective admission procedures that succeeded in reducing Jewish enrollments from the 40 percent level to 22 percent in 1921 and to 17 percent in 1934. A 1931 study by Heywood Broun and George Britt described the program of Jewish exclusion:

> Columbia's machine for regulating the flow of Jewish students through its classrooms is one of the most elaborate ever devised. Armed with its eight-page blank, its talk of scholarship standards, its personal interviews, psychological tests, physical examinations, and passport photograph requirements, Columbia can select exactly the applicants it desires, keep the Jewish quota down to a fractional percentage it may determine, and defy anyone to slip through unnoticed.

Another aspect of the Jewish "problem" was that entry to Columbia College was in many ways a ticket to training at the graduate level. During the late 1920s approximately 60 to 65 percent of Columbia's graduating classes went on to one of Columbia's graduate or professional schools. This pattern had the effect of increasing the number of Jews enrolled at the graduate level. Administrative concern about the high percentage of Jews in medicine led to admissions policies that reduced the proportion of Jews enrolled in the College of Physicians and Surgeons from 50 percent in 1919 to less than 20 percent in 1924. There were no major changes in the makeup of law school classes. Graduate training in many of the sciences actually benefited from the policies of the medical school. Jews denied by the medical school or anticipating denial went into related science fields, which had the effect of increasing the number of outstanding students enrolling in these areas.[16]

Despite the near impossibility of gaining admittance to Columbia College, the Novikoffs decided that Columbia represented the best opportunity of reaching medical school. Fortunately, Columbia had opened a two-year college in Brooklyn, Seth Low Junior College, which was the predecessor of Columbia's well-known School of General Studies. Although Seth Low was Columbia's way of deflecting Jews from its doors, the very best students at Seth Low were often admitted to Columbia College as regular degree students. Some of Seth

Low's courses, especially the science courses, were taught on the main campus on Morningside Heights. Despite its nonselective admissions procedures, its lower prestige, and its image as a pressure valve for New York's immigrant "subway students," Columbia's Seth Low was preferred by Novikoff to City College. City College was a predominantly Jewish institution (approximately 80 percent of its students were Jews), did not carry Columbia's academic reputation in the sciences, and was less likely to promote an aspiring doctor's chances of gaining acceptance to medical school.[17]

The unspoken understanding was that the Novikoff family would support Alex's attendance at Columbia. Sonia, a year older than Alex and not yet graduated from high school, quit school at fifteen to take a job. She started at $8 a week and then found work in an employment agency at $15 a week. Her money-saving ritual was to spend no more than 10 cents for lunch by buying a pot of beans and a cup of coffee. Alex continued to work on his holidays, and in a stroke of good luck he found regular part-time work at the famous Roseland Dance Hall on Fourteenth Street and Broadway. In his duties as a hat check attendant he became well acquainted with the clientele, and during slack time he was able to study his books behind the desk.[18]

Alex plunged immediately into a pre-med course of study, achieving six A's and three B's in his science courses. Over three semesters and a summer at Seth Low he took courses in zoology, physics, chemistry, and physiology and came into contact with many of Columbia's outstanding faculty members. During the summer of 1929 he elicited enthusiastic recommendations from his professors and was admitted as a regular student in Columbia College. He was enrolled officially in the pre-med curriculum and received a scholarship to cover part of his tuition and costs. Alex and his family took satisfaction from the fact that his strategy of seeking admission to Columbia, instead of attending City College, had paid off. He set out to sustain his excellent academic performance and to prepare the ground for his application to medical school.

In his remaining science courses at Columbia, Alex attained seven A's and three B's. Although enrolled in one of Columbia's most difficult undergraduate curricula, his only grade below B was a C+ in French. He offset this grade by making an A in Russian the following semester. On June 2, 1931, he received his bachelor of sciences degree at the age of eighteen.[19]

During his junior year (his first year as a regular Columbia student) Alex applied to two medical schools, including the medical school at Columbia, and was placed on the waiting list of each. This was not an unusual consequence for an early application; indeed, it served to raise optimism. Unfortunately, as events ensued, this optimism was misplaced. Prior to his graduation in the spring of 1931 he received the bitter news that he was turned down at the three medical schools to which he had applied in his senior year. His disappointment was profound. It was a blow to his pride and a deep injury to the ambitions that he and his family had sustained for so long. He came immediately to an explanation for the rejection: institutional anti-Semitism. "When I was a junior at Columbia," he later said, "I was put on a waiting list at two places. When I was a senior, I was put on the waiting list at none. There was a quota system. It was well known." What was "well known" to Alex, his fellow students, and many of his professors was Columbia's successful program of exclusion. Columbia had renewed the effort begun in 1909 by Keppel to limit the number of Jews in medicine, and with the severe competition for a shrinking number of places for Jews, Alex was a victim of the numbers. In the fall of 1931 almost 30 percent of the entering class of 115 students in the College of Physicians and Surgeons were Jews. By 1934 the proportion had dropped below 20 percent. Furthermore, in 1931 63 percent of Alex's graduating class went to a Columbia graduate school, but this had dropped to 45 percent by 1934. [20]

Alex had no choice but to look at other options. Confronted by the sustained vigilance of the Columbia administration and of some key faculty on the medical admissions committee ("From the Zoology Department, one was known to be anti-semitic."), he sought the counsel of several of his professors. The alternative of waiting a year and reapplying was thought to be risky, especially since there was no reason to believe that the policy of exclusion would be relaxed. Several of his professors recommended that he stay at Columbia and begin work toward a Ph.D. in one of the sciences. After a few weeks of deliberation that is what he chose to do. He applied for a position in the doctoral program of the department of zoology and was promptly accepted. He recognized that he would be working with an outstanding faculty engaged in pioneering research. As exciting as this option seemed, however, the step represented the abandonment of a long-standing dream. Alex was deeply bitter about the perceived injustice, and he carried his bitterness for the rest of his life. [21]

The immediate effect was to raise the first glimmering of a heightened political consciousness. Although his strong feelings smoldered below the surface for a long while, by the mid-1930s events at Brooklyn College would trigger a more direct response. Then he would turn the sting of rejection and the hatred of injustice toward focused political action. And this turning would take him into the embrace of the Communist party.

Deflected by the medical schools but buoyed by the confidence expressed by his undergraduate professors, Novikoff stayed at Columbia. He knew well the reputation of the Columbia science faculty, particularly the luminaries in the zoology department led by E. B. Wilson, the dean of American zoologists. Wilson's impact on the field of cell biology was unrivaled at the time, and he had drawn other superb zoologists to the Columbia faculty, such as R. H. Bowen, A. W. Pollister, and L. G. Barth. The ambitious Novikoff knew that Wilson, then in his seventies, was still an active presence in Columbia courses and similarly in summer research programs at the Woods Hole facility in Massachusetts. Despite his disappointment over medical school Novikoff's appetite for scientific work was high, and by virtue of his excellent training at Columbia he was well prepared to start serious professional study in the fall of 1931.

His major worry was money. No longer could he call on financial assistance from his sister Sonia or his father. He presented this problem to his professors at Columbia, and shortly he was recommended for a part-time position in the biology department at Brooklyn College. The college was a considerable distance from Columbia's location on Morningside Heights in upper Manhattan but close to his home in Brownsville. Knowing that he would be spending a good part of his life riding the subway, he nevertheless accepted the position of "fellow" at the part-time pay of $300 for the fall semester. His duties were to keep records of student performance on assignments and tests and to monitor lectures in the introductory biology course. With this adequate but not by any means lucrative financial arrangement, Novikoff was able to finance his first year of studies. At the same time he was well aware of his youth—he would almost certainly be younger than many of his students—as well as his inexperience in teaching. He was not at all certain whether he would enjoy or do well at his new teaching duties. With these immediate worries at the forefront, he had no idea of the extent to which Brooklyn College would become the focal point of his personal and professional life in the years ahead.[22]

Brooklyn College in 1931 was a stepchild of the City College and Hunter College extension campuses that had existed in Brooklyn for several years. The City College program was started in 1917 at Boys High School, and the Hunter facility was opened in 1925. During the

1920s Columbia's leaders recognized the merits of a college in Brooklyn to divert Jewish students away from its undergraduate college. An important aim was to diffuse pressure from " 'undesireables' residing in the Brownsville section," as Dean Keppel phrased the matter in a 1912 letter to the Columbia president. One response was to open Seth Low Junior College in Brooklyn, offering a two-year curriculum, as one means of addressing the situation. Finally, in order to reduce admissions pressures from Jews and to head off the threat of a proposed state university that might actually compete with Columbia, the university lobbied, with others, for the creation of a separate City College branch in Brooklyn. These pressures coalesced in 1930, and Brooklyn College was formed and located in five office buildings scattered throughout Brooklyn. The new college inherited students from the City College and Hunter campuses and attracted new ones, producing at once an enrollment of twenty-eight hundred in the day session and five thousand in the evening session. Students could pursue a degree in either division. The evening students, however, were older and were mostly men; they worked full-time jobs during the day and felt the burden of family responsibilities and perpetual fatigue. Regardless of these differences, Brooklyn College in the early 1930s was a hothouse of ambitious immigrants, of seething resentments directed against various authorities, and of heightened political consciousness.[23]

Studies undertaken by Thomas Coulton, a Brooklyn College administrator at the time, disclosed that the vast majority of the college's students perceived higher education as an avenue to attaining a job, whether choosing a job directly from college or taking a job after advanced professional preparation. This clear vocational goal was offset, however, by wide-ranging intellectual interests and an aversion to focusing too narrowly in one's coursework. The humanities disciplines were popular areas for major study, especially for many of the college's most capable students.[24]

Despite its status as a municipal institution with low tuition, Brooklyn College, especially the day division, was not by any means an "open admissions" institution. Facilities and teaching staff were limited in size, and there was not enough room for all who wished to attend. One fall semester, for example, there were thirty-five hundred applicants for nine hundred openings in the freshman class. Admissions standards and procedures were developed that focused on high school academic achievement. When a student presented less than exemplary high school credentials, entrance examination scores were also considered. Although a health examination was required, an interview was not, and as a result, such factors as personality, personal appearance, and family background were ignored. This neglect of the "gentlemanly virtues" was in stark contrast to the admissions procedures of most other colleges. A process that the college called "democratic" was indicative of a meritocratic impulse that did not take hold in American higher education until the 1960s.[25]

A consequence of this admissions situation was that on several measures Brooklyn College enrolled a highly capable student group. Compared with scores of 317 other institutions on a test of general intellectual ability, Brooklyn College freshmen consistently ranked in the highest six percent. The college's freshmen consistently ranked in the top quarter of a national sample. Although the intellectual prowess and later academic successes of Brooklyn College students of this era may not have matched the performance of their contemporaries at City College (City College has produced more Nobel Prize winners than any other public institution, including three winners from the class of 1937), the intellectual potential was considerable.[26]

Brooklyn College's students commuted to school from home, on the average were a year younger than students nationally, and with few exceptions held part-time jobs to support themselves and their families. The vast majority were Jewish and first-generation Americans. Coulton's most provocative observations were addressed to the social characteristics of the students.

> They lacked as a group many of the opportunities afforded most students on other American campuses to acquire social poise and broad cultural experiences. They were mostly living at home and undergoing parental supervision over their time, friends, and money; their record of high school achievement and home pressure to succeed scholastically emphasized the importance of intellectual values.

He found that the college's students were immature, tended to engage in "argumentative conversation," offended others by their persistence and competitiveness, and "were inclined in their thinking to depend too greatly on verbalizing." The greatest weakness, Coulton reported, was "their incompetence in easy, courteous, persuasive human relations." While this profile of the typical Brooklyn College student may be fundamentally accurate, one discerns the discomfort and disapproval of the older generation. The 1930s soon brought severe conflict between the administrative leaders of the college, with their ideals of appropriate collegiate behavior, and hundreds of these argumentative, demanding students, with their ideals of equity, democracy, and political involvement.[27]

THE SHAPING OF A NEW COLLEGE

Opposed to the more formal Columbia environment, where anti-Semitism was still a force, the Jewish student population and leftist political atmosphere of Brooklyn College presented a comfortable social and political fit for Novikoff. This sense of fit was reinforced by the number of staff members who were Jewish. Most of the teaching staff had been educated at City College and had been teachers at one of the City College campuses. In addition, many at the lower ranks were, like Novikoff, beginning their academic careers with the most tenuous possible tie to the institution. As the college matured, however, academic responsibilities expanded, and many sought and attained permanent appointments.

The biology department that Novikoff joined was chaired by Earl A. Martin, who assumed this responsibility at the time Brooklyn College was formed in 1930. He had begun teaching at City College in 1920 and had gone on to City College's new Brooklyn extension in 1926. It was Martin who had hired Novikoff on the recommendation of the Columbia professors. The small department also included B. R. Coonfield and Ralph C. Benedict, who had taught in the earlier extension units and now, with a newly merged institution, were involved in the challenging task of building a new, larger department.[28]

Novikoff's first assignment was to serve as Professor Martin's lecture assistant in the introductory biology course: "My first job was to go down the length of the room in the old building and tap a guy on the shoulder. If Benedict was lecturing, they were terrible lectures and the guys would read the newspaper, so my job was to tap them on the shoulder . . . keep them awake." He also had responsibility for various logistical duties such as maintaining the student records for the course. Whether it was boredom with his responsibilities or a failure to appreciate the importance of accurate student records, Novikoff's "carelessness in the preparation of records" incurred Martin's displeasure. Fortunately, Martin found redeeming qualities in Novikoff's performance and attributed the bookkeeping errors to "inexperience." He reappointed him to the course for the spring semester and, additionally, gave him responsibility for teaching one of the biology laboratories. Novikoff's full-time appointment for the spring 1932 semester carried a $500 salary. The annual salary rate of $1,000 was less than the regular salary for the same duties. He was told that he was paid less because of his youth, a circumstance he resented.[29]

The two most junior members of the department were Novikoff

and Harry Albaum, who was completing his undergraduate degree in biology at the college and was hired as an assistant during the spring semester. The two young instructors became close friends. Albaum, born in Odessa in the Ukraine, had attended Boys High School in Brooklyn until a family crisis forced him to leave school and take a job as a bank clerk. While continuing work, he took courses at Brooklyn Evening High School and graduated in 1927. He began taking evening college courses at the City College branch in Brooklyn, switched to day courses after finding a night job, and with a change in academic major from Latin to biology, finally completed his degree in 1932. He acquired a master's degree from New York University two years later and then, as Novikoff had done already, went into the Ph.D. program in biology at Columbia. Eventually, Albaum and Novikoff moved to the same apartment building in Brooklyn, and as the years passed, their professional and personal destinies became closely intertwined.[30]

Teaching at Brooklyn College was sometimes disconcerting, especially for a nineteen-year-old who was given responsibility for teaching the laboratory section of the comparative anatomy course: "There were also boys but they were kept separate in those days. I taught comparative anatomy for girls. And the girls were older than I and they would do naughty things!" Novikoff remembered the girl in the front row who repeatedly folded and unfolded her legs for him to see. The girls embarrassed him on a trip to the zoo when they repeatedly pointed out the masturbating monkeys. Novikoff's classroom was enlivened too by students such as Arthur Miller, the playwright, and Irwin Shaw, the novelist. After a few upsetting experiences Novikoff developed the skills and fortitude to cope successfully with the challenges of teaching Brooklyn College undergraduates.[31]

A compensating reward for the discomfort he felt in the classroom arose that first spring. It was the usual practice for many of the biology faculty members at Brooklyn College and at Columbia to carry out research programs at Woods Hole during the summer. He was encouraged by both groups to participate in these research endeavors. During the summer of 1932 he went to Woods Hole and returned every summer during the 1930s, except for 1938 when he was recovering from a serious illness. The Woods Hole summer program presented an important opportunity for Novikoff to establish himself as a scientist. On the most practical level he was able to work directly with the Columbia faculty to mold a research program that would lead to his master's and doctor's degrees. Of longer-term significance, he had the opportunity to meet and interact with the many outstanding biologists who came from around the world to work at Woods Hole during the summer.[32]

The biology department that Novikoff returned to in the fall of 1932 was at first a close-knit entity. The teaching staff worked together closely in developing the course of study for the department, in organizing the annual summer sojourns to Woods Hole, and in supporting the student biology club. Faculty and students joined in supporting dances to raise funds for a Woods Hole student scholarship. Albaum remembered "one summer at Woods Hole around 1935 or '36, when the entire department was engaged in planning the new buildings [for the college]. . . . It was quite an exciting time and all of us were involved every day and late into every night."[33]

For seven years, 1931 to 1938, Novikoff commuted by subway from Brownsville to Columbia in the morning to take classes, rode back to Brooklyn in the afternoon to teach in the lab at Brooklyn College, returned to Columbia at night to study, and went home around midnight to Brownsville. He spent more than three hours a day on the subway and frequently slept through the Brownsville stop. On such occasions the conductor would wake him, and he would board the next train back to Brownsville. He wrote most of his Ph.D. thesis during these hours of commuting.[34]

Despite the excitement that surrounded the enterprise of shaping new careers in a new institution, some serious difficulties for Novikoff and for the department began to surface in the early 1930s. The problems grew out of personnel decisions affecting the younger faculty and an increasing tide of political action on the part of students and faculty. By the end of the decade, these forces engulfed the biology department, throwing the names of Martin, Coonfield, Novikoff, and others into the public spotlight.

A hint of problems to come was that Novikoff did not take enthusiastically to the mundane details of classroom management or to suggestions from his colleagues that he should repair his ways. In his first years at the college he was assigned to teach laboratory sections of the vertebrate zoology course, which was under the supervision of Professor Coonfield. His responsibilities involved arranging materials for demonstrations, setting out dissection materials before class, and cleaning up the lab after each session. Coonfield reported that he had to warn Novikoff several times about "his failure to carry out these duties," especially about cleaning up after the labs. Over several semesters the relationship between the two deteriorated, and eventually Coonfield asked the chairman to transfer Novikoff out of the course. This was done, but Coonfield's assessment did not improve: on another

task at a later date he found that Novikoff "absolutely failed to cooperate with me."[35]

Another biology professor, Paul Orr, found that Novikoff's work in
the physiology lab under his supervision during 1935 was unsatisfactory. He too asked that Novikoff be transferred out, which was done.
Leonard Worley, a colleague who had become a close acquaintance of
Novikoff's during the summer sojourns to Woods Hole, supervised his
work in the embryology course from 1934 on. Worley's criticisms of
his work were relatively minor—a tardy return of student quizzes on
one occasion and a reluctance to evaluate student work on a clay model
exercise—and in each case the problems were rectified. His most serious complaint was that although Novikoff would eventually get his
work done, he "frequently will not perform his duties without being
argued into it." The department chairman, Professor Martin, was dis-
tressed by Novikoff's relationship with Worley.

> The first time that I seriously doubted my judgment in bringing Mr. No-
> vikoff into the department resulted from a conference with him at
> Woods Hole, Massachusetts, which occurred after Dr. Worley succeeded
> Dr. Waterman as head of the Embryology courses. Mr. Novikoff asked
> me to take the Embryology course away from Dr. Worley and give it to
> him. He informed me that he had a more up to date knowledge of the
> subject and felt that it would be best for the course if I made the
> change. At this time he had not completed his work for the Ph.D. This
> conference left me with a very discouraged opinion of him. The only
> way I could interpret his move was an effort to displace Dr. Worley and
> obtain the course for himself.[36]

In many respects the conflict that arose between Novikoff and his
colleagues between 1931 and 1935 was not peculiar to Brooklyn College. Since the emergence of the modern university—a phenomenon
of the twentieth century—and the turn toward academic specialization, a departmental structure has prevailed. The academic department
is both a bureaucratic entity, with an appointed leader and discrete
educational and organizational responsibilities, *and* a community of
scholars trained in a particular academic discipline (e.g., history, eco-
nomics, biology). At almost all institutions of solid academic reputation
the staffing of a department is shaped by a sharply defined promotional
ladder and a system of tenured appointments. This arrangement as-
sures careful assessment of candidates for promotion and tenure and,
with tenured appointments, considerable continuity of membership.
The overlapping of organizational authority and academic expertise is
the essence of departmental organization.

Departments are characterized by close face-to-face relationships,
concern about academic priorities and philosophy, sensitive egos, and

a schedule of decisions about staffing and curriculum that have the potential for bringing underlying conflicts and animosities to the surface. Traditionally, decisions are made in a consensual fashion, with the chairman being perceived as the "first among equals." The situation is ripe for disagreement and conflict. Departments rarely function in the absence of tacit, if not overt, conflict.[37]

The senior members of the biology department worked closely with Novikoff, whose professional fate they would ultimately decide. In the early 1930s his performance and cooperation were perceived to be unsatisfactory, and this caused resentment and disapproval. Within this small community of scholars, his lack of civility when confronted was his worst sin. At least two of the faculty simply did not want to associate with him.

Looking at the other side, Novikoff was an ambitious young man, barely in his twenties, with rough edges socially, and he already had a sense of his gifts as a scientist. He found the laboratory duties to be menial, distracting, and beneath his intelligence. He was impatient to get on to bigger things, particularly the exciting research carried out by the scientists at Woods Hole and Columbia. Furthermore, he came quickly to the belief that his colleagues at Brooklyn College, especially the older veterans of the City College extension, were lacking as scientists. For Novikoff, *this* was the worst sin.[38]

As circumstances evolved, Novikoff's behavior was a nagging but not serious concern for the department for the first several years. The department, like the college as a whole, was growing, forming its own identity, and planning for the move to new buildings. Novikoff was reappointed each year as a fellow, with an annual $100 salary increment. In 1935 he was promoted to tutor, with a $200 increment, which brought his salary to $1,400 a year.[39]

The position of tutor at Brooklyn College was still a junior position without eligibility for a tenured appointment but at twenty-two Novikoff was nevertheless doing well for himself. He was making headway on the academic career ladder at Brooklyn College. He was an excellent student who, according to his academic advisor at Columbia, "was outstanding in his ability to grasp the subject matter of an advanced course and to organize facts into an orderly array for presentation to other people." He had gained his Columbia master's degree in 1933, and he was well on his way with his research for the Ph.D. degree. In the arena of greatest interest to Novikoff, he had established among the scientists at Woods Hole a reputation for "careful thought and untiring application in the laboratory." His investigations of the seaworm, *Sabellaria*, were highly regarded by his more senior colleagues.

During the summer of 1936, at the still tender age of twenty-three, he received the signal honor of an invitation to participate in a seminar to discuss the work of the prominent Swedish zoologist Sven Horstadius, a Woods Hole investigator.[40]

By the middle 1930s Novikoff's ambition, his capacity for long periods of concentrated work, and his skills as a scientist were evident to important members of the scientific community. At Brooklyn College, however, his difficulties in the department were becoming more complex and more serious. Soon incidents and grievances of a political nature were tugging strongly at his attention and his time.

Chapter 2

CONSEQUENTIAL ACTS

Communism and Crisis
at Brooklyn College
in the 1930s

In the first years of its existence Brooklyn College was the stage for a struggle over what kind of institution should be sculptured from the remains of the old extension campuses. Considering that people felt at once a sense of ownership and pride over the borough's first authentic four-year college, it is not surprising that there were competing visions of the college's future among those involved in shaping its destiny. Officially, the task of molding a new college went to William A. Boylan, a former public school superintendent with no previous leadership experience at the collegiate level. Boylan, a favorite of Mayor Jimmy Walker, was appointed president of the college in 1930 and served until illness forced him into retirement at the end of the decade. Like his counterpart, Bertrand Robinson, at City College, he brought conservative instincts to his duties, placing high value on bureaucratic authority and orderly top-down decision making. Given the dispersion of the college buildings around Brooklyn and the need to build a single institution from a staff hired from many sources, the drive for order had an organizational logic. Boylan hired a leadership team that shared his goal of building a well-organized, respectable college.[1]

What Boylan soon discovered, however, was that an academic institution could be sharply resistant to traditional styles of school management. This was especially true of a college of ambitious Jewish immigrants set in the tumult of 1930s Brooklyn. Depression-era poverty, socialist impulses inherited from the old country, perceptions of

25

anti-Semitism, and an almost frantic push to step upward economically enveloped the neighborhoods of the borough. The chaos, conflict, and striving meant that few aspects of existence were accepted as "given." This inclination to question and pressure for change was particularly true of what constituted politics in Brooklyn. Within the largely leftist orientation of the Jews, every gradation of point of view existed, and debate went on incessantly in the papers, on the stoops, and at the dinner table. Jake Novikoff, Alex's father, was typical in many respects: he was a self-styled socialist who read the *Freiheit*, the Jewish left-wing paper. Termed a "likable blowhard" by one relative, he despised the *Forward*, the Jewish paper on the right, and urged his leftist views, including the merits of the Young Communist League, on Alex.[2]

Brooklyn probably exhibited the most leftist political orientation of any large community in the United States, particularly in its openness to the appeals of the Communist party. A Communist was elected by the borough to sit on the city council during the 1930s. Half of the circulation of the Communist paper the *Daily Worker* was in Brooklyn. As the Party expanded its reach in membership and its impact within organized labor in the 1930s, Brooklyn was a focal point for these organizational efforts. In an era when it appeared to many that America was coming apart at the seams and that dire threats—especially fascism—existed nationally and internationally, the Communist party offered a platform with wide appeal and a ready organization for channeling one's efforts. Of course, beginning in 1934 and 1935, a source of the Party's popularity was the Popular Front policy that led the party to identify with, support, and frequently control issues and programs of mass appeal. Issues that had broad appeal to progressives included antifascism, the union movement, and various forms of discrimination such as anti-Semitism.

President Boylan's Brooklyn College was immersed in this leftist-oriented, rambunctious "political ghetto." Before long the students and the staff of the college, almost all of whom were products of the borough, began to assert their views about what kind of society and what kind of college they wanted. During Novikoff's first years at the college, the financial limitations of the college helped to produce an organized response from the faculty. In order to staff the college from a narrow financial base, almost 80 percent of the teaching staff was appointed at the lower ranks, with low pay and no job security. This meant that 400 of approximately 525 faculty members were "below the ladder." The faculty argued that this situation bred favoritism, inequities, and arbitrary personnel decisions. A popular example of the dangers of the system was Boylan's hiring of a retired barber to serve as a laboratory assistant in biology. The retiree, whose attraction was that he was related to the chairman of the Board of Higher Education, had no appropriate academic credentials and was relegated to running errands and sharpening knives for the histology course.[3]

The younger faculty in the lower ranks, who were the most insecure in their positions, organized the faculty to resist and alter the college's personnel system. Led by Frederic Ewen, Howard Selsam, and Bernard Grebanier, an Association of Tutors, Fellows and Instructors was formed. Novikoff was an active member but not a leader of the group. The association, like a similar entity at City College, pressed for the hiring and promoting of faculty based on merit, the "election" of department chairs, a clearly defined schedule for promoting faculty from the lower ranks, a tenure system at the higher ranks, and procedures to protect the rights of faculty under threat of dismissal. A special problem for those in Novikoff's circumstance was the need for a reduced teaching load in order to have time to complete the requirements of a doctoral degree; this too was one of the association's demands. As most faculty knew and Boylan came to realize, several of these conditions of employment, such as promotion based on meritocratic criteria and a tenure system, existed at other campuses, particularly at colleges of substantial academic reputation. With academic precedent (which appealed to those imbued with academic values), a logical platform and shrewd tactics behind it, the association achieved official recognition and limited progress on several of these issues. At least on paper, the college now had a regular system, with faculty involvement, for making personnel decisions. As it turned out, the association's modest successes merely set the scene for a period of more aggressive pressures on the administration.[4]

During the time that the faculty were working within the confines of the college to improve working conditions, two other developments were occurring that would profoundly affect faculty politics at the college. The first was an attempt by the Communist party to take control and expand the influence of the New York Teachers Union. The second was the effort by the Communists to mobilize college students on New York City campuses of the City University. To a considerable extent the Communists succeeded on both counts. Because these developments were a precursor of commitments among the faculty, including Novikoff, it is helpful to examine the status of the Communist party at this time and its capacity to shape events at Brooklyn College.

THE COMMUNIST PARTY BECOMES A POLITICAL FORCE
ON CAMPUS

In 1917, less than four years after Novikoff sailed from Russia, Czar Nicholas abdicated. Trotsky, Bukharin, and Lenin returned from exile and in October shocked the world with their revolution. As Theodore Draper and others have suggested, the Bolshevik revolution, in a single stroke, brought the American Communist party into existence. "The impact of the Bolshevik revolution on the American Left Wing was stunning," Draper wrote. "It was as if some Left Wing Socialists had gone to sleep and had awakened as Communists. The Bolshevik revolution had a dazzling, dreamlike quality, all the more glamorous because it was far away, undefiled by any contact with the more recalcitrant American reality." The contagious enthusiasm of American radicals for the revolution was enhanced by Lenin's view that the Bolshevik success was only a preliminary step to revolution in Europe and America. Within months several Americans made their way to Russia to observe developments, meet with Lenin and other Bolshevik officials, and write glowing tributes. John Reed's *Ten Days That Shook the World* was read by both potential revolutionaries and the general public.[5]

The intoxicating events of 1917 tugged for a long time, perhaps still do, on the American left. Ensuing events, however, were less exalting for those endeavoring to build an effective Communist party and revolutionary movement in America. Radical groups, including the two competing branches of the Communist movement, were harassed by U.S. Attorney General A. Mitchell Palmer and an aggressive committee of investigation in New York State headed by State Senator Clayton Lusk. Raids, arrests, indictments, and jail sentences forced the Communists to go underground and adopt the tactics of an illegal group, including the use of pseudonyms to protect their identities. Despite these various difficulties in the early 1920s, the Communists replenished their supply of leaders, maintained direct ties to the new Soviet regime, and in September 1922 melded into a single, legally constituted entity, the Workers Party.[6]

The new party, influenced by Lenin's directives to build a united front with other organizations and to publish a Communist daily paper in English, set out to broaden its base. For the first time the educational field became a focus of effort, and the Workers Party made a tentative and unsuccessful effort in 1923 to mobilize grade-school children in fifteen cities against the "Capitalist educational system." A year later the Communists turned their attention to teachers as the crucial force for change in schools. In July 1924 the American Communists were directed by the Profintern Congress in Moscow to concentrate on a mass movement strategy, with an acceleration of effort in the trade unions. This began a twenty-year effort to penetrate and control the only trade union in education, the American Federation of Teachers (AFT). Local 5 of the AFT, the New York Teachers Union, was the AFT's largest local and was vulnerable to Communist influence for many reasons, not the least of which was that New York City was the locus of Party headquarters, almost half its membership, and various Party news organs. During 1924 and 1925 a small group led by Scott Nearing, Alfred Brooks, and Benjamin Mandel—all later to declare themselves Communists—acquired considerable influence in the union. This early Communist threat to the union was soundly turned back, however, and it was ten more years before the Communists mounted another serious offensive. During the remainder of the 1920s internecine battles within the Communist movement, a new round of attacks by authorities aimed at radicalism in New York City, and self-incriminating testimony by Communist leaders about their ties to the Soviet Union limited the Party's ability to influence the AFT.[7]

With the onset of the Depression, Communist activity increased on several fronts, and at this time the Party made public a new name, "Communist Party of the United States of America, Section of the Communist International." The name denotes accurately the establishment of Soviet direction over Communist party tactics and policies, a development that in the 1930s had favorable as well as dire consequences for the Party. The first priority of the Communists in the early 1930s was to organize and mobilize American workers toward Party goals. Because so few American workers were unionized, the Communists had a ready supply of recruits. The posture of a "united front" with existing organizations and political factions was a successful tactic that produced an expansion of the membership rolls of the Communist party. By 1934 Party membership had risen to twenty-six thousand from the seven-thousand figure of 1930. In 1935, abetted by the Nazi threat and its Popular Front strategy, the Communist party garnered more than fifty thousand votes in New York City, a twenty percent increase over the previous year and rivaling the vote totals of the Socialist party.[8]

As the Communist party grew in membership, voting strength, and exposure through its multitude of newspapers, renewed efforts were made to gain control of the AFT's New York Teachers Union. The union, which included public school teachers as well as teachers at the city colleges, had only about thirteen hundred of New York's thirty thousand teachers on its membership rolls in the early 1930s. The union's ties to the labor union movement—it was affiliated with the American Federation of Labor—and the growing attraction of organized labor during the throes of the Depression represented a significant potential for growth. At first a factional dispute among the Communists damaged Communist efforts to seize the union. When the union leadership attempted in 1932 to expel the Communists on the grounds of attempted minority control of meetings, Communist efforts finally coalesced. A committee of investigation led by John Dewey, the well known Columbia University philosopher, documented many of the charges, but nothing decisive occurred, especially when a broad-based committee of defense collaborated on behalf of the accused union members.[9]

Continuing agitation and headway by the Communists in Local 5 came to a head at the August 1935 national convention of the AFT. A motion was made to revoke the charter of the "subverted" Local 5 and to create a new union led by the moderate forces. Due to the effective lobbying of a united front of Communists and Socialists, the motion was defeated, and the opposition to Communist influence was in complete retreat. Communist opponents resigned from Local 5 and organized the Teachers Guild as a competitor. Meanwhile, the Communists orchestrated the election of Communist sympathizers, including Charles Hendley as president and Bella Dodd as legislative representative, to lead the New York local. Over the next four years the Communist party maintained its united-front strategy, helped expand the membership of the union, and systematically tightened its control over the activities of the local. A major area of success was the effort to mobilize and activate college faculty at City College and Brooklyn College.[10]

While the Party was consolidating its power in the Teachers Union, it was also insinuating itself among college students. Sensing that there existed many potential recruits to political activism among students, the Communist party created the National Student League in 1932. The League drew its impetus and leadership from the Social Problems Club at City College but also attracted students from Columbia and Brooklyn College. Organized by the League, Brooklyn College students participated in citywide protests against proposed retrenchment in the City College system, especially the imposition of fees for part-time students and for educational items such as textbooks. A protest drawing one thousand students was held on the Brooklyn campus during the spring of 1933. The New York chapter elicited nationwide publicity when a group of about eighty set out on an expedition to study the conditions of coal miners in Harlan County, Kentucky. Although turned back by an angry mob at the Kentucky border, they took their case to Washington. During April 1934, thirty-five hundred students from the college left classes to hold a rally for peace in downtown Brooklyn, an event that drew the criticism of President Boylan and several faculty members. One cause of the criticism was the participation of some college faculty members in the march. A peace strike and May Day demonstration the following year again drew large numbers of students, and members of the campus Young Communist League were instrumental in organizing these demonstrations. Over the next three years the National Student League continued aggressive recruitment and agitation on campuses in New York and elsewhere.[11]

During 1934 and 1935 the Communists broadened their efforts by throwing their support behind the American Youth Congress, a federation of student groups across the country. Party representatives played an important role in guiding the organization, which claimed to represent four million American students, and elicited the support and patronage of Eleanor Roosevelt. In December 1935 the largest and most influential student group, the American Student Union (ASU), was formed from the merger of the Communist and Socialist groups. The ASU, which may have had as many as twenty thousand members nationally, was prominent on the City College and Brooklyn College campuses. Communists—usually also members of the Young Communist League—controlled the leadership positions of these two chapters until 1941. To the consternation of many staff members at Brooklyn College, the ASU and its various publications remained officially authorized aspects of campus life through these years. As Robert Iversen reported in his 1959 book on Communist activities in education, Brooklyn College and City College "were unquestionably the two greatest concentrations of student communism in the United States . . ." At the height of Communist influence in the late 1930s about one third of the students who participated in student elections on these campuses voted for known Communist candidates.[12]

By 1935, then, the Communist party had gained a foothold at Brooklyn College. The Party controlled the New York Teachers Union, which was now beginning to assert itself more strongly on the campus. The Party held sway over various student groups, including the Young Communist League and the American Student Union. On a more narrow ground, the Communist party itself was a force by virtue of the fact that a modest number of students on campus were committed to the Party. As the Depression hung on and political agitation increased, members of the staff began to listen more attentively to the political messages from these sources. Fatefully, the Party and its instruments of political pressure, particularly the union, were well poised to take advantage of this growing political consciousness.

During the expansion of student agitation on the Brooklyn campus, several of the younger faculty members became close acquaintances of the student activists. Novikoff developed close relationships with the students, especially in the informal atmosphere of his science labs, and expressed his support for their political activities. When the American Student Union was formed, Howard Selsam of the philosophy department agreed to be faculty sponsor for the Brooklyn College branch. This latter step soon led to the first important move by the faculty to join forces with the Communists. In early 1953 the students helped persuade Selsam, a man with strong Marxist leanings, to join the Communist Party.[13]

The recruitment of Selsam and the subsequent organizing of a Brooklyn College faculty arm of the Party followed by several months the creation of a Party unit at City College. Morris Schappes, a tutor in English at the college since 1928, had formed the unit in 1934. The City College unit agitated on behalf of the lower academic ranks and increased its influence in the college's Instructional Staff Association. The Party unit began publishing a "shop paper" in March 1935 that displayed on its masthead its sponsorship by the "Communist Party Unit of City College." The paper was published anonymously—the names of its writers and staff were not identified—and was an avenue for Schappes and others to attack the policies of various administrators at the college. Over the next few months the City College Communist unit became the largest on any campus in the country and served as a model for Communist initiatives at Brooklyn College. Selsam met with the City College Communists and borrowed their tactics.[14]

Selsam talked with faculty members that he thought might be willing to join the Party. In all likelihood Novikoff was approached at this time, but it is evident that the first group of faculty to join did not include him. Rather, in the early months of 1935, Henry Klein, a history instructor, Isadore Pomerance, a philosophy instructor, Frederic Ewen, an English instructor, and perhaps one or two others joined Selsam in the Brooklyn unit. Taking their lead from City College, they started plans in April 1935 to issue an underground newsletter. Bernard Grebanier, a member of the English department, was invited to a meeting to provide advice about the proposed publication. Grebanier urged them not to publish. On May 1, however, the Brooklyn College

Communist group took its first overt move by distributing to faculty mailboxes the first edition of *The Staff*, purported to be a regular paper addressing the problems of teachers and students at the college. The paper was unsigned, except for the note that it was issued monthly by the "Brooklyn College Unit of the Communist Party of America." An editorial on an inside page of the four-page paper expressed the intentions of the sponsors.

> We are members of the Communist Party of the United States of America. We are not "outside agitators" but persons who have worked in Brooklyn College for years. . . . We have become Communists because we have found that the Communist Party alone has a clear realistic program through which not only our present problems can be solved, but by means of which a new and better society may be realized. At the same time that we are Communists we are Americans.

The editorial went on to identify budget retrenchment, unemployment, and salary inequities in New York colleges as problems to be addressed by the paper and the Party. The paper, which appeared regularly until March 1939, was written by college faculty, printed at a small Communist publishing house on New York's East Side, and then distributed early in the morning to the campus mailboxes.[15]

Shortly after the publication of *Staff*'s first issue, Grebanier wrote a letter to President Boylan protesting the publication. Succumbing to intense pressure from Party members, however, Grebanier soon overcame his reluctance to identify with Party causes and joined the Party. In 1941 Grebanier recalled his decision to join:

> . . . when the *Staff* first came out it was thought by many people, though I had nothing to do with it, that I had written it myself entirely. I think that came from the fact that I never concealed my opinions and that I had had that episode some years ago with the American Legion. And I suppose I was, after all, in a kind of panic, and I think that if, as I have said several times, there had been any possibility in the college for a liberal movement distinctly right of communism, I probably would have been glad to join it, and never have had anything to do with the Communist Party. . . . I guess in the college I was mostly sympathetic [to the aims of the Party], because I think I stressed the fact that these people seemed to be the only people who had the decency to stand up against the very palpable corruption that the College was full of, the political influences.

Grebanier's less than wholehearted commitment to the Party returned to haunt the Brooklyn party unit in 1941 when he testified to a New York State legislative committee about Party activities and identified the other teachers who had been members.[16]

Although the recollection of Novikoff and other Brooklyn Communists do not establish the precise date, it appears that Novikoff joined the Communist party within several months of the publishing of the first issue of *Staff*. His turn in this direction started during his annual summer visit to Woods Hole. "It was [when] I went to Woods Hole that this guy stuck Daily Workers on my bed. . . . He used to give me the Daily Worker under my pillow and I kept reading it. . . . My father had tried to convert me but I reacted against him but this guy awakened my feelings." Novikoff was invited to hear a Communist speaker at a town near Woods Hole and engaged his colleague in discussions about politics. Novikoff did not identify the person who exerted this influence, except to indicate that he was a scientist affiliated with another university. When Novikoff returned to campus in the fall, he was importuned again by Selsam and others; that fall he joined the Brooklyn College party unit. At about the same time, Samuel Kaiser (chemistry), Elton Gustafson (hygiene), Herbert Morais (history), Solomon Asch (psychology), and a few others joined the party.[17]

In light of the repercussions that haunted him for almost thirty-five years, Novikoff's decision to join the Communist party is central to this story. There are several important questions that pertain to his joining. In behavioral terms, was it a decision to accept concrete commitments and responsibilities, or was it a "nominal" membership? Equally important, why did he decide to join? Of course, these inquiries raise other fundamental questions pertaining to the wisdom of the decision (was it an unwise decision that, on balance, harmed his life?) and the morality of the decision (did his joining harm others?). These latter questions, however, are best postponed until the broad sweep of Novikoff's life is before us. At this juncture it is important to assess what he did and why he did it.

It is evident that joining the Communist party meant something quite concrete. He signed the Party register, began a schedule of weekly meetings of the Brooklyn College faculty unit, was given a pseudonym, Norwood, and took on a commitment to pay monthly dues. He participated in discussions of Marxism and world affairs. Like the others he kept secret his identity as a Communist. Secret actions and undeclared motives were a requisite condition of joining, and although Novikoff never spoke directly about this aspect, his going "underground" was a significant step. In each of these ways his decision to join the Party implied a conscious choice of specific actions. He knew what he was doing and what his decision implied. While his joining the Communist party was not as momentous as suggested later by the adjudicators of the McCarthy-era inquisition, the decision was certainly not a trivial one.[18]

Novikoff's motivation for joining the Party, like most human behavior, was a product of multiple, interacting forces. Based on Novikoff's own comments and on what we know about the 1930s at
Brooklyn College, several motivations and dimensions stand out. First,
the decision had a philosophical aspect. Joining the Party was a matter
of carrying out his Marxist convictions, which were essentially evo-
lutionary and "scientific" in nature. What Marxism did was explain
in objective, empirical terms the world that he saw around him, and
this was highly congenial to his scientific bent of mind. He said many
times, "communism wasn't revolutionary," and what he meant was
that Communism, as an organizational expression of Marxism, offered
a practical way to achieve important political goals. As such, his turn
to communism was an extension of his Marxist convictions and his
ambitious, but not altogether radical, political agenda.[19]

Second, Novikoff's political agenda in 1935 as well as his most
hotly felt grievances were local in scope, and the college's Communist
unit held promise for addressing these issues. For four years he had
struggled with the problems of being a poorly paid teacher "below the
ladder." The union had not yet come into its own, and the Party was
committed to move aggressively on the agenda raised initially by the
Association of Tutors, Fellows and Instructors. In addition, his dis-
agreements with his colleagues in the biology department were a
source of resentment and frustration. Whether rightly or not, he felt
unjustly criticized for his performance. Like others at the college, he
attributed some part of his problems to anti-Semitism, and he pointed
to Martin, his chair, on this score.[20]

A third factor pertained to the political air that he breathed during
these years of a lingering Depression, the rise of Hitler, the joining of
progressive forces into a united front of political action, the Socialist
and Marxist inclinations of his immediate community, and the growing
"romance" of communism to more and more people. In this environment the turn to the Communist party was not far-out or unrespect-
able. Indeed, as many pointed out, it was an "honor" to be a
Communist in the 1930s. Novikoff, only twenty-two years old, was an
idealist (and remained so the rest of his life) and was prepared to carry
out actions consistent with his beliefs, especially if an avenue of perceived honor and principle existed close at hand.[21]

The final factor was the existing left-wing presence on the Brooklyn
College campus. Many potential academic Communists were isolated
on campuses outside New York, where only a few others shared their
convictions and their inclination to action. In these circumstances it
was much more difficult, psychologically and practically, to join the

Communist party. Novikoff, on the other hand, mingled with students and faculty who had already committed themselves to the Party. Organizational mechanisms, zealous advocates, and enticing propaganda (such as the *Staff* paper) were close at hand. Clearly, peer pressure made Novikoff's decision much easier. In a sense, his joining the Party was a decision to join his friends.[22]

Once Novikoff decided to join the Communist party in the fall of 1935, he plunged into it with great energy. In short order, as he admitted in an interview in 1984, "I was a leading figure." One area of activity was Local 5 of the New York Teachers Union. The Communist unit at Brooklyn College set out to strengthen and energize the campus chapter of Local 5 of the Teachers Union by directing the Communists to join the union. Novikoff joined the union and as a member of the Communist "fraction" participated in its meetings and publicly supported its activities. In 1937 he assumed a prominent role in leading the union defense of an ousted Brooklyn professor and Communist, Henry Klein. He was active also in the internal activities of the Communist party, particularly the Party paper.[23]

Novikoff played a central role in the publishing of *Staff* by taking responsibility for printing the paper and for distributing the paper to mailboxes. For several months he and Elton Gustafson were, in effect, the editors. According to Novikoff, "Others were involved too but we were the primary ones. . . . He was the writing guy, but he had help from other people. But we spent a good deal of the night at the thing. . . . It was very hard work, because in addition to what I did at night, in the morning I was stuffing all these into everybody's mailbox." Articles for the paper were frequently discussed at Party meetings: the editors would seek ideas for articles, assign articles to be written, and present drafts for criticism. Party meetings were also the occasion for the mundane task of sealing envelopes for distribution of the paper. Grebanier, who testified about these activities in 1940, remembered once accompanying Novikoff with the finished text in hand on his way by subway to the printer in lower Manhattan. The printer, who was located on West Twenty-third Street, printed materials for several Communist groups in New York, including the Party paper at City College. Novikoff paid approximately $30 in cash for the printing of each issue and made return visits with corrected proofs.[24]

Novikoff was assisted in these duties by Alan Lifshutz, a Brooklyn College undergraduate and a member of the Young Communist League. Lifshutz often accompanied Novikoff to the printer and helped distribute the paper to faculty and students. Although the faculty unit of the Party did not include students, Novikoff's acquaintanceship with Lifshutz was not unusual. Several faculty members served as advisors to Party-dominated student organizations, and fraternization was common. Lifshutz served on the Brooklyn College Student Council, which was dominated for several years by Communist students; he was president of the Karl Marx Society and was a member of the American Student Union. Novikoff and other Party members spoke enthusiastically about the intelligence and political commitment of students such as Lifshutz, and many of the students went on to be active Communists. After graduation Lifshutz was sent by the Party to Oklahoma, where he became secretary of the Party's Oklahoma City branch. In 1940, at a time Novikoff was under investigation in New York, Lifshutz was convicted by an Oklahoma jury on a charge of "criminal syndicalism."[25]

Because *Staff* was a considerable undertaking for Novikoff and his colleagues, the paper's effectiveness is a pertinent issue. Simply put, was it worth the effort? For four years this anonymous, well-written paper ranged across a long list of grievances and political topics. It was read widely by faculty and students, including nonsympathizers, and elicited emotional reactions. Unfortunately for those defending a position attacked by *Staff*, rebuttals could not be sent to an anonymous editor at an undeclared address. (Actually, the paper did invite financial donations and inquiries about the Communist party at an address in Brooklyn, but letters and outside commentary were not a feature of the publication.) A rereading of the paper recaptures the chronology of issues that sustained the attention of the Communists: governance of the college, grievances about staffing decisions, anti-Semitism in the college, criticism of the Board of Higher Education for funding levels for the city colleges, Red-baiting in New York and Washington, Hitler and fascism, the wisdom of Soviet foreign policy, parades and demonstrations. In assessing the content of the paper, a sampling of the writing is educative.[26]

The publication's first edition supported in its lead story the participation of the lower academic ranks—instructors, tutors, and fellows—in academic decision making. The paper editorialized as follows:

> Under the present system, approximately 75% of the teachers in our college are utterly and completely excluded from any participation in the formulation of college policies. This is in striking contrast to the great majority of American colleges and universities where at least the semblance of democracy is preserved by having all members of the staff constitute the Faculty or giving them membership after from one to three years of service. Our system not only violates all democratic principles, but tends to inculcate in the younger men and women a feeling that they do not "belong" to the college, that they are only paid em-

ployees of the Faculty instead of co-partners in an important educational enterprise. . . . In this stratification our college reflects the economic set-up of our capitalist society.

A story in the June 1935 edition reported that Millicent Ellis of the biology department had been dismissed after three years of service and went on to comment on the situation in her department: "The Biology Department is well known for its treatment of teachers in the lower ranks. Two of its members have been promoted only this year to the rank of Tutor, having been kept as Fellows for three years. More Fellows are employed in this department than in any other of the College." In the first anniversary edition of May 1936 the editors of *Staff* reviewed the first year and concluded that they had been "a liberalizing and progressive force in the College."[27]

Although the writing in some articles was sarcastic or exaggerated, it was clear and forceful on the bread-and-butter issues of faculty welfare. There is no question that many articles struck a responsive chord with the faculty at large. The paper may not have brought any people into the fold of the Communist party but it did expand the quantity—and probably the quality—of information about college issues. In an institution governed by a traditional, top-down managerial style, this served the purpose of the Communists as well as, many would argue, the larger faculty. In assessing the publication, it is also interesting to note that it received occasional words of praise from the executive committee of the Communist International in Moscow. It was widely recognized, too, that the Brooklyn paper was of consistently higher quality than the paper at City College.[28]

Party work for Novikoff and the others was time-consuming and for several years demanded constant attention and political vigilance. The Party unit met weekly, either as an entire group or in small groups of five or six persons. Every six months the Communist party district headquarters checked up on the unit at a meeting of the whole membership. The typical meetings, especially when the unit was organized in small groups, occurred at members' residences. The large group meetings were chaired by Ewen, Novikoff, and others over the years. Party members paid regular dues, calculated as a percentage of one's salary. Meetings of the Party were devoted to setting strategy and tactics and delegating responsibility for carrying out tasks. Members of the unit were in regular contact with Party headquarters and other Party functionaries in New York City, and several members attended leadership training schools sponsored by the Party.[29]

In contrast to some Party members, there is no evidence that Novikoff found his Party duties unnecessary or particularly onerous. This was mainly because of the considerable independence that the college branches had in managing their own affairs. Despite occasional actions from headquarters that were perceived to be authoritarian or irrational, the Brooklyn members were usually able to set their own agenda and devise their own tactics. Within the unit there tended to be open discussion and consensus decisions typical of the academic model of collegiality; the hard-nosed democratic centralism of many Party units was not typical of academic communism. Since Novikoff, like most academics, thrived on the freedom to act out plans that had relevance to *his* goals, these internal arrangements reinforced his commitment to organizational details. One suspects also that his conscientiousness derived from his tendency, once having determined a course, to see it through.[30]

Members of the Party were involved with campus student groups, both as advisors and as speakers. At different times Novikoff, Grebanier, and Klein served as the Party link to the Young Communist League. Novikoff and Alan Lifshutz of the League worked closely in publishing and distributing *Staff*. Howard Selsam was day division faculty advisor to the Karl Marx Society, an official campus organization, and assisted in locating speakers for its meetings. Speakers included the educational director of the New York State Communist party and a member of the executive committee of the Kings County Communist party. The Brooklyn College *Vanguard*, the campus student newspaper, was edited by a member of the Young Communist League and provided extensive coverage of activities of interest to the Party. A sampling of *Vanguard* stories involving Party members includes the following:

> (3/6/36) Herbert Morais, faculty advisor to the History Club, says that the club will have as the topic of its term project, "American Imperialism Since 1914."
> (3/13/36) Howard Selsam is speaking at a symposium to be held at Lincoln High School to consider Germany, Russia, Japan and "Who's on the Warpath Today?"
> (3/20/36) Harry Slochower, Frederic Ewen and Paul Gipfel address an anti-war rally and urge united student action.
> (4/3/36) Salomon Asch will preside at a seminar on "War and Education" at the Third Brooklyn Intercollegiate Anti-War Conference.
> (10/2/36) Herbert Morais spoke on the Spanish Civil War, which he witnessed.
> (4/9/37) A symposium on "War and Peace" sponsored by the Psychology Club, drew 300 students and included Alex Novikoff and Howard Selsam as speakers. Novikoff refuted those scientists who believe war is good for mankind.
> (4/30/37) Frederic Ewen, speaking for the Teachers Union at the Fourth

Student Peace Strike, affirmed the unity of teachers and students in the struggle for peace.

(5/14/37) Frederic Ewen addressed the American Student Union on "The Results and Implications of the Klein Case."

(5/21/37) Henry Klein, addressing the American Student Union, denounces R.O.T.C.

(1/14/38) Elton Gustafson, chairman of the Student Relations Committee of Local 537, suggests that the union seeks program of faculty-student cooperation and desires to be of the utmost assistance to the American Student Union.

(9/19/38) American Student Union leaders train in five day session during registration week. Alex Novikoff lectured on 1938 elections and Howard Selsam traced the development of American education.

Between early 1936 and the end of 1940, the *Vanguard* covered more than ninety events of the kind identified above.[31]

This list indicates that influencing students and propagandizing on behalf of political issues was an important priority of the Party chapter. Once it became known that these faculty members were available to speak at public gatherings, invitations came regularly from on and off campus. Ewen remembered that for several years he spoke "all over town." Obviously, the recognition that came with public speaking had its personal gratification but the practice was also an effective vehicle for disseminating the Communist point of view.[32]

Novikoff's extensive involvement in Party activities raises an important question about deleterious effects on the quality of his teaching and research. One possibility was that the classroom had become for the Communists another vehicle for propaganda and Party recruitment. There is no evidence, however, that Novikoff or other Party members ever directly utilized their classrooms for these purposes. Although, as Grebanier pointed out, "the view that some of these people undoubtedly had of their subject was entirely colored by their political philosophy," there was a marked reluctance to politicize the classroom. One factor was the sensible fear that the first place their foes would look for evidence of irresponsibility was the classroom. Indeed, later investigations demonstrated that this was one of the first accusations. Probably the most critical element was that almost all of the Party members were committed scholars, with deep-seated respect for the search for truth in their academic fields and for methods of dispassionate inquiry. Many of the Communists had reputations as outstanding teachers and scholars, and they were not inclined to undermine their hard-earned accomplishments. For this reason, several Communists took great care to hide their Party membership from students.[33]

Although it is evident that the Communists did not compromise their integrity by inserting politics into their academic work, it seems likely that the time devoted to political activities diverted time from teaching and research. If this was the case, then the quality of academic work certainly suffered. Novikoff was adamant in denying such a consequence in his research: "I never at any point diminished my work in science." His ability to sustain his effort was due, he said, to the fact that he "worked like a horse" and "didn't sleep much." Indeed, he sustained his momentum toward completing his Ph.D. thesis and in 1936 began to publish the findings of his summer research at Woods Hole. His first journal article, "Transplantation of the Polar Lobe in *Sabellaris vulgaris*," appeared in *Anatomical Record* in 1936. He followed with one publication in 1937 and two in 1938. Two additional articles were submitted for publication in 1938. His doctoral thesis was finished and defended in early 1938. Novikoff's ability to function on little sleep, which was noted frequently by his acquaintances, and his impressive publications record corroborate Novikoff's claims. At the height of political activity and turmoil at Brooklyn College, he continued and even expanded his research endeavors.[34]

Novikoff's teaching, it appears, was another matter. The problems that surfaced in his first years in the biology department became more serious—and threatening—when he came up for promotion in 1938. An assessment of his teaching is complicated, however, by the fact that by 1938 judgments of his performance had become intertwined with his reputation as a political activist. This situation—the intertwining of the academic and political—warrants analysis. The events at Brooklyn College in 1937 and 1938, including the Novikoff promotion case, provide useful insight into the problems that arise when academic decision making and aggressive political action converge. What we find is that Brooklyn College was in a constant state of conflict and stress, with the academic community strained to the breaking point by the public airing of grievances and by the repeated turning to ad hominem attacks. All in all, it was not a good time for a college only six years into its existence.

STOKING THE POLITICAL FIRES
AT BROOKLYN COLLEGE

The initiatives of the Communists and other progressives did not go unchallenged during the 1930s. The first issue of *Staff* in May 1935 reported that Howard Selsam had been replaced as president of the Association of Instructors, Tutors and Fellows by a candidate supported by the administration. Noting that the "conservative group now has a majority of the Executive Committee," the paper charged that department chairmen had urged conservative faculty to attend the meeting and vote in new leaders. As the months passed, several of the department chairmen, led by Earl Martin of Novikoff's department, became more energetic in resisting the reform program of the Communists.[35]

The reshuffling of influence in the association may have been one reason why, after 1935, the Communists took more interest in the union. The union was hampered, however, by the fact that Local 5 was stronger in the public schools and was not effective in influencing the city colleges' staff associations. The ineffectiveness of the union's college subcommittee and the weakness of the local chapters of the American Association of University Professors, which was dominated by the upper ranks, were seen as serious impediments. Seeking a stronger central coordinating body, the Communist-led Local 5 decided in 1937 to organize under the AFT umbrella a separate citywide union for college teachers. Local 537 immediately became an effective instrument for the Communists. Novikoff's union membership was transferred to the new local, and after this time he became more active and visible in union activities. The union published the *College Newsletter,* which reported developments on each of the New York campuses and agitated on issues pertaining to the welfare of faculty. Because of the union's inside knowledge of decision processes affecting its members, it was able to point its finger in a specific way. Its effective agitation (and naming of alleged culprits), combined with the suspicion that it was Communist-dominated, elicited bitter reactions from administrators and some teachers, especially faculty in the upper ranks.

The political activities of Novikoff and his colleagues were receiving more open criticism, and events came to a head in May 1937. In a move that indicated the deep divisions that had now arisen in the college, the faculty moved by a vote of 70 to 19 to "disassociate" itself from an "anonymous group of the staff of Brooklyn College, calling themselves the Brooklyn College Unit of the Communist Party . . . wherein by innuendo, half truth and direct attack . . . have vilified the character and questioned the honesty of certain of their colleagues, of the President, and of members of the Board of Higher Education." The one-sidedness of the vote suggests that one segment of the faculty, the upper ranks, had lost patience with the continuing upheaval caused by the Communists. The "faculty" at this time included about 125 teachers at the full, associate, and assistant professor levels, which represented less than a quarter of the total number of teachers at the college. The approximately four hundred teachers at the instructor, tutor, and fellow ranks were not eligible to vote. Nevertheless, this vote among the most powerful element in the college is telling. Unquestionably, the secrecy behind the *Staff* paper and the Communist organization was deeply resented.

One surmises, too, that the identities of many of the Communists were now strongly suspected, and this put matters on a more personal level. Many faculty in the upper ranks felt, not unreasonably, that secret political activities and unattributed accusations were anathema in an academic community, an environment that by necessity depends on trust, collegiality, and a reasonable degree of civility. In short, the Communists were doing something to the college that was destructive to what a college should be. From this time forward, the battle lines were drawn more sharply.[36]

As Hitler began his move across Europe, events on the Continent produced alarm and anxiety among faculty and students. A majority of the college community probably was both antifascist and antiwar in attitude; certainly, the Communists were. One member of the Party unit, David McKelvy White, took up the antifascist cause by resigning from the college and joining the Abraham Lincoln Brigade in Spain. He returned in October 1937 to testimonial dinners and celebratory parties, one of which was held at Howard Selsam's home.[37]

Another form of response to the world situation arose among conservative elements on campus. A group of students and faculty, supported by off-campus organizations such as the American Legion, pushed for creating a Reserve Officers Training Corps (ROTC) unit on campus. The debate reached a first decision point in November 1937 when the faculty curriculum committee voted unanimously against the idea. The acting chairman of the chemistry department, Martin Meyer, then agreed to advise students working for an ROTC "club." Meyer became the subject of a leaflet campaign by the Communists and acid articles in *Staff*. The movement suffered another setback in January 1938 when the Board of Higher Education specifically prohibited any clubs that were "military" in character. Eventually, accompanied by regular coverage by the local newspapers and intense argument within the college, the club was approved by the Board of Higher Education. Things did not die down at that point, however. The left-wing students, organized by the Young Communist League, succeeded in disrupting a mass meeting to celebrate the ROTC victory.[38]

The most public controversy of 1937 arose from the decision to dismiss Henry Klein, a tutor in history at the college and a member of the Communist party. The Communists assumed, probably correctly, that the decision was motivated in no small part by Klein's activities on behalf of the union and by the assumption that he was one of the

Communists. The ostensible grounds addressed the poor quality of Klein's teaching. As a member of the union, Novikoff was named to lead Klein's defense. It was this case that created Novikoff's reputation as a political activist, especially among the college's administrative staff. The campaign included a barrage of leaflets, articles in *Staff* and Local 537's *College Newsletter,* sit-down strikes, and marches punctuated by the chant "We want Klein." The shrewdest and most successful tactic was to mobilize the students in considerable numbers on behalf of Klein. At one point, seventy female students held a sit-in at President Boylan's office. Speaking several years later, Novikoff emphasized that his activities at the time were not "revolutionary" in nature. "Let me make clear what "active in politics" meant. I didn't go around politicking in the streets. This was . . . on campus. And I wasn't advocating bombings or anything. I was no Bolshevik, as they make me out to be. It's the kind of thing that, nowadays, you find very respectable." The campaign had mixed success. Klein was rehired without the normal salary raise for the 1937–1938 academic year but was dismissed for good the following year. He was able to find work as a substitute teacher at P.S. 163 in Brooklyn. As for Novikoff, his newly acquired notoriety had a price: the following year he found himself under a similar threat.[39]

1938: THE CLIMACTIC PHASE

During 1938 fears of Nazi and Communist subversion brought into being the Special House Subcommittee on Un-American Activities (HUAC), headed by Congressman Martin Dies of Texas. During the same span of time political controversy at Brooklyn College reached its zenith. In February the Communists mounted an attack against two department chairs, Martin of biology and Meyer of chemistry. The lead article of *Staff,* headlined "Martin uber alles!," accused Martin of orchestrating the demise of physiology as a required science course and the absorbing of the teachers of the course into his own department. The extent to which the Communists ranged in their interests is indicated by the following: "From the point of view of the students this would constitute a definite limitation upon their choice of sciences, and would deprive them of a course they now apparently find very profitable. As Communists, we have always stood for expansion and enrichment of the curriculum, and therefore opposed to such curtailment." The following issue of *Staff* attacked President Boylan for his appointment of Meyer as acting chair of chemistry and presented a litany of criticisms of Meyer's record, including his "untiring cultivation" of the dean, his alleged mishandling of student athletic funds, his lack of scholarly publications, his support of ROTC, and his policy of staffing his department with "the best men at the lowest possible price." The singling out of Martin and Meyer soon had repercussions for the Communists.[40]

In March the *Brooklyn Eagle* began a series of articles, entitled "Peril to Freedom," on "un-American propaganda and activities in the United States as obtained from government and other sources." Over six weeks the paper carried twenty stories, usually placed on page one, about Communist penetration of the armed services, Nazi propaganda and espionage, and subversive activities in organized labor. The articles evoked many letters, usually in support of the stories. In early May, Martin and one of the biology faculty, B. R. Coonfield (who in 1936 had removed Novikoff as his laboratory assistant), packaged a collection of Communist literature and sent it to the editor of the *Brooklyn Eagle* with a note requesting the *Eagle* to write a series of articles on communism at Brooklyn College. Martin stated a few months later that he took this step because of "the heckling" and the interference with carrying out his duties. The initiative of Martin and Coonfield was seized upon by the *Eagle,* and in its Sunday, May 15, edition a bold front-page headline appeared: "Bare Red Plot to Gain Control of Boro College." The article ran several columns and quoted Martin at length. He reviewed the physiology controversy and "the efforts of the radical element to make a political and administrative issue out of a purely academic controversy which has arisen among the faculty." He also described in detail the activities of the communists and the union. The article noted that Martin and Coonfield "are the first faculty members to come out in the open against the radical goings on at the college which have become a matter of common knowledge and evoked resentment of a large body of Brooklyn citizens."[41]

The article provoked rejoinders from the union as well as the presentation of additional "evidence." The *Eagle* followed with front-page articles on May 16, 17, 20, 21, 22, and 24 as the college's problems became a matter of wide public interest and exposure. Whether because of laziness or editorial policy, the paper helped the Communist cause by quoting lengthy letters and position papers written by the union. The union documents were well written and presented plausible explanations for the past events on campus. The Communist tactic of employing the union to defend events at the college and to deflect attention from themselves made good political sense and was utilized whenever the Communists came under public attack. Although the Communists were defended effectively by the union, the *Eagle*'s editorial attitude came through in its headlines and in the rhetoric that seeped into the "news" stories. A passage from the May 22 issue is typical: "These are the weeks [*sic*] developments in the efforts of conservative members of the faculty to 'smoke out' the anonymous Reds among both students and the teaching staff to correct a situation which many citizens of the borough have declared to be disgraceful and symptomatic of conditions in other of the city's higher institutions of learning." The basis for the assertion about public opinion in Brooklyn was not presented in the article.[42]

The significance of this series of articles was that the conflict at the college was changed qualitatively by the public airing. Now many faculty members and organizations at the college were known to the general public. Any future event would draw the interest of news reporters as well as public figures. Every future action would have to be evaluated for its consequences among a much broader audience. Although this changed situation had some advantages for the Communists (e.g., a larger audience for its point of view), pressure on the Communists and the union was mounting, and it was necessary to assess more carefully the wisdom of each political step.

In June the New York City Board of Higher Education approved changes in faculty organization, signifying a victory for the Teachers Union and the activists at Brooklyn College. The board broadened membership in the faculty, entailing full voting rights, to include the rank of instructor. Although this was disappointing to the union leadership, who had pushed for inclusion of tutors and fellows, the compromise solution did reflect a significant broadening of membership. The other important change involved "democratizing" the selection of department chairs. Although the president still approved the selection, new chairs would now be elected by a vote of the department's faculty. In terminology and spirit this was a radical departure from the prevailing approach to selecting chairs in American colleges and universities. Typically, the designation of chairs—even when faculty "advice" was sought—was seen to be a prerogative of the dean or president in his role as chief executive officer of the college. When a new president, Harry Gideonse, took office at Brooklyn College in 1939, the revision of this new clause was a condition of his agreeing to take the job.[43]

It is germane to Novikoff's situation that these bylaw changes followed by several months another significant change. After effective lobbying by the union, the board had approved the granting of automatic tenure at the end of three years of full-time teaching at the college. This meant that in hiring someone for the third year, the college had to decide whether to grant permanent tenure. This too was a considerably more liberal tenure clause than existed on most campuses; typically a faculty member came up for tenure in the fifth or sixth year of service. With the implementation of this clause, Novikoff, who had already been teaching for six years, was granted tenure. This meant that Novikoff and others with tenure had permanent positions at the college, subject to a future determination of unprofessional conduct, moral turpitude, or demonstrated incompetence. On the face of things, the union had achieved significant changes in the conditions of faculty employment, even to the point of surpassing the degree of "democracy" on other campuses.[44]

Political scientists have observed that forceful political actions eventually have countervailing political consequences. Indeed, in the spring of 1938 as the counteroffensive against the Communists continued, the noose tightened around Novikoff. His attitude toward his duties had incurred the displeasure of his colleagues in biology; he had led the defense of Klein; he was believed to be a Communist. To make matters worse, with the *Eagle* articles Martin and Coonfield of his department had taken a public stance against the Communists. It was not surprising, therefore, that there might be some trouble when the question of Novikoff's promotion to the rank of instructor came up in early May. Unfortunately, Novikoff was weakened at this time by illness. Following a bout with tonsillitis, he had become seriously ill with acute hemorrhagic nephritis, which was sufficiently debilitating to put Novikoff in bed from February until early June. As a result, he was absent from the college for the entire spring semester.[45]

Novikoff wrote in May to Coonfield, then acting chairman of the department, to inquire about his fall teaching schedule and about his promotion. The letter conveyed his expectation that the promotion would be routine: he inquired whether the promotion had yet "gone through." He asked whether it was necessary to send the department official notification of his new Ph.D., which he was to receive in two days. Coonfield replied two weeks later with a letter stating that "I believe you should discuss this with me during the next two weeks or when you return to the College in September." The vagueness of the letter impelled Novikoff to phone Coonfield and press for more information. At Novikoff's insistence Coonfield revealed that the department had voted against his promotion and to relieve him of his teaching duties in the embryology course. The department also recommended that his present rank be "continued for one year" with a normal salary increase on the grounds that his work on his doctoral thesis might have hindered his performance and that teaching in two different courses might have made it difficult "to do either course justice." On the same day the Brooklyn College Administrative Committee, which was charged to make recommendations to the president on personnel matters, endorsed the department's recommendations. Although he was not under immediate danger of dismissal from the college, this turn of events was a shock to Novikoff, and he saw at once that the decision was a serious threat to his career. The negative decision would be a permanent blot on his record and, once it became known, would damage his reputation with his colleagues at Woods Hole. Also, with severe competition for every teaching position at the college, the decision would make him vulnerable to dismissal at a later time. In fact, this had happened to Henry Klein, who had survived the first effort to fire him but succumbed the next year.[46]

With his energy gradually returning after his long illness, Novikoff moved into action. The next day, June 15, he met with the biology department's committee on appointments, chaired by Coonfield, and found that he had been charged with "dilatory cooperation" and "independability" by Professor Leonard Worley, with whom he had worked for several years in the embryology course. His most recent difficulties with Coonfield and Worley went back to the previous year. In April 1937 Coonfield called Novikoff to his office to express his concern about Novikoff's involvement as a speaker at a symposium on the bearing of biological research on war. Coonfield offered advice about the "worst consequences" of his involvement in the event, including the possibility that he might jeopardize his position in the department. Novikoff's notes on the conversation are indicative of the wide gap in thinking between himself and the conservative Coonfield.

> [he said] I should try to see things as others would, and also, I must remember that I was not merely an individual, that I was a member of the Biology Department, and my actions reflected on the department. It was better not to discuss such controversial issues with students. I replied that I felt quite differently, that the best way to prevent what happened in the last war was to educate—by such and other discussions before the war. . . . Professor Coonfield then said that he, too, thought he could change the world's ills when he was young, but that he learned that there was little one could do, and one had other obligations. I replied that it would be very unfortunate if nothing could be done about such matters as war. . . . Professor Coonfield cautioned me to be very careful not to say anything that could be misinterpreted by persons hearing me. I told him I had written out what I planned to say and it could hardly be misinterpreted. Yes, he said, but you may slip and, moreover, "you know how newspapers write up things." I replied that one always had to run that risk when he said anything.

Allowing for some distortion due to Novikoff's taking notes as they spoke, what comes through is a subtle threat to his professional position and a not so subtle violation of precepts of free speech and academic freedom. Coonfield's opinion of Novikoff surely worsened when he went through with the symposium and in a few months took on the visible role of defending Klein.[47]

The disagreement with Worley occurred in early June 1937 at the time that the biology department moved into its new building. Worley wrote a letter to Martin indicating that Novikoff had refused to cooperate in moving boxes, a task that all of the faculty undertook. Although Novikoff and Worley patched up their differences at the time (Worley sent a telegram from Woods Hole saying, "Don't worry I think you're a swell guy"), the letter led to discussions among Coonfield, Martin and Novikoff and remained in the file.[48]

These two incidents, combined with his problems in working with other faculty, did not help Novikoff's case. On June 19 he sent an eight-page letter of appeal to Acting President Mario Consenza, who had replaced the ailing Boylan, in which he detailed his scholarly record and defended his actions in the department. Having disposed of the overt issues, he addressed what he felt were the more insidious reasons for the department's recommendation:

> I believe that in the light of the preceding statements, the only grounds for discrimination against me must be sought elsewhere. I have been an active Teachers Union member, have been secretary of the Brooklyn College Charter, and co-chairman of the Union Klein Defense Committee. Professor Martin's and Coonfield's antagonism toward the Union is well known, and the other members of the Department Committee have been in general agreement with them in matters involving the Union; e.g., the proposed by-laws dealing with reorganization and tenure. On at least two occasions Professor Coonfield warned me at length concerning my activities on campus. I have additional reason to believe that in the case of Dr. Worley racial considerations played a part in his general attitude toward me.

Novikoff's raising of the twin specters of antiunion bias and anti-Semitism anticipated his request to the Teachers Union to take action on his behalf. The union quickly accepted the case and sent a letter to the Brooklyn College Administrative Committee asking that the case be reopened and that the union have an opportunity to show why Novikoff should be promoted. A subcommittee of the administrative committee reviewed the case, with a union representative attending, and submitted a report to the New York City Board of Higher Education.[49]

In late June, Novikoff sent a letter to his Columbia advisor, Professor L. G. Barth, at the Marine Biological Laboratory at Woods Hole, setting forth what had happened. He indicated that "somebody is trying to put something over on me in the Department" and "I have decided not to take it lying down." He asked Barth to write a letter testifying to his scholarship and research, a request he had made to several other Woods Hole colleagues. What followed was an exchange of letters that set forth the dilemma facing Novikoff as a serious scientist also engaged in political action. Barth's first letter, addressed "Dear Novikoff," reflected a serious misunderstanding of Novikoff's situation. He urged Novikoff not to "get all excited over this thing" and to avoid a departmental "row" by trying to "play ball with Worley." Novikoff's response set forth in detail the charges against him, including the implication of "incompetence" in the department's letter to the college committee. He pointed out that, though he had tenure, "incompetence is grounds for dismissal." Believing that he was a victim of a vendetta, he enumerated examples of unjust treatment by the biology faculty, antiunion bias and anti-Semitism. His emotional distress was evident from an episode he related:

> . . . they have said that my introductory remarks at the [Ph.D.] oral exam (remember?, thanking you and the other members of the Zoology Dept. for what you had done for me) had "embarrassed the Committee to death since it was so obvious that I was doing it to insure my passing." (Now, damn it!, did I *need* that to pass? Can't they conceive of an honest and sincere person?)

Barth, an influential scientist and sincere advocate of Novikoff's career, answered with a classic defense of the academic and political status quo. Barth's five-page handwritten letter was also an uncanny anticipation of Novikoff's future problems.

> You have ideals and want to work toward their realization. At the same time you want to fit in with your department to develop your scientific career. My advice is this. Take the long term view of the matter. Establish yourself first as a teacher and scientist and during this time keep your social activities secondary. . . . I would go to Coonfield and tell him that I understand his viewpoint and that in order to keep the Biology Department from being involved I am severing all official connections with Unions and other progressive organizations and devoting all of my time to teaching and research. I would tell him that since I can't very well do both, the first consideration is my career. The reason I would take this step is this. As long as you are young and unknown you can do very little. You can fight hard but it will result in your becoming an outcast where you will be powerless. . . .
>
> First get some effective weapons. Respect of your colleagues, influence in scientific events and a reputation for good judgment in a known field like zoology. People are more apt to respect your opinions in a new field if they respect your judgment in a field they know something

about. . . . Let these older and established men take the lead in any
cause until you yourself are really able to do so effectively. . . .
    If you put your change of activities to Coonfield, Worley et al. on
the basis of a sort of departmental loyalty you will keep their friendship
and respect. . . . You have as good chance as any of us of becoming an
outstanding biologist. . . . We all do it and it's worth while in the long
run.

Of course, what Barth did not appreciate was that the battle had been
joined long before and that the parties were committed to seeing the
appeal through to its resolution. Novikoff acknowledged Barth's advice
but emphasized that it was now absolutely critical to have a letter of
support from him. A few days later he acknowledged Barth's "glowing" letter on his behalf but indicated that he was not prepared to drop
his political activities: "I want to demonstrate to you that one can
really do good scientific work along with some 'social' work." Still
only twenty-five years old, Novikoff had resolved decisively and self-
confidently his need to incorporate science *and* social change into his
life. It is clear too that he was prepared to accept the personal risks
outlined so cogently by Barth.[50]

On July 27 the board sustained the original recommendation of
the biology department and endorsed Novikoff's reappointment as tutor for the academic years 1938–1939 and 1939–1940. During October
1938 the question of Novikoff's rank for both 1939–1940 and 1940–
1941 was reopened. A union brief on the case was sent to the board
and disseminated to faculty and staff at Brooklyn College on November 14.[51]

Meanwhile, the *Staff* paper and the *College Newsletter* brought the
case to public notice. *Staff* stated:

> There seems to be no limit to the steps professor Martin (newly ap-
> pointed chairman of Biology) will take in his attempt to dominate the
> affairs of the College and keep his control of the Biology Depart-
> ment. . . . [Novikoff] has differed with his chairman on matters of trade
> unionism, faculty reorganization, and the broader issues of fascism and
> war. . . . [A]nti-semitism, whose existence at the College has been
> sensed by all of us, is brought inescapably to our attention. The Biology
> Department is notorious for its discrimination against Jewish teachers.

The November 11 edition of the *College Newsletter* restated sections of
the union brief on the case and referred to letters of support from
professors addressing Novikoff's scientific work. Indeed, Novikoff had
elicited impressive support from scientists at Columbia, Woods Hole,
Cal Tech, Stockholm, and Munich. Barth's letter stated that Novikoff
"has a brilliant future and will go far in scientific work if given the
proper opportunities for carrying on."[52]

Nevertheless, on November 23 the biology department again recommended against Novikoff's promotion and reiterated its charges. The union responded with a second communication to faculty and staff at Brooklyn College, pointing to "irrelevant" issues raised by the biology department. *Staff*'s December issue offered a comparison of the "academic records of Martin—Full Professor and Novikoff—Tutor." Martin, it was noted, had published one paper over a career spanning twenty-four years. *Staff* pointed out that "Unlike his Chairman, who is known in the scientific world as head of a large department offering job possibilities . . . Novikoff has already established a reputation as an experimental embryologist." *Staff*, of course, did not acknowledge the importance of Martin's department as an avenue of employment during the Depression for budding scholars such as Novikoff.[53]

The case dragged on for four more months as memoranda and reports flowed to the personnel subcommittee of the Board of Higher Education. Finally, after persistent public pressure by the union and continuing public attention, the case was settled in Novikoff's favor in April 1939. He received his appointment as instructor and the corresponding raise in pay, and the union claimed an important victory.[54]

The rationale of the Board of Higher Education's decision to overrule the original recommendation was not made explicit. It appears that Novikoff's scholarly credentials and the possibility of bias due to his union activities were factors in his favor. It appears too that the board resisted the rising winds of anti-Communist sentiment and rejected the considerable evidence that Novikoff had performed poorly in his department duties. All in all, it appears that the decision was a close one and that Novikoff was fortunate in the outcome. The further conclusion is that the union and the academic left in general still carried considerable influence, even as the mood of the country was taking a sharp turn to the right.

It is worthy of note that, during the months of struggle over his promotion, Novikoff's political activities were undeterred by the controversy. During September 1938 Novikoff was a lecturer at a five-day training school for campus leaders of the American Student Union. In December he was a speaker at a forum sponsored by the College Teachers Union on "Society and Higher Education." The forum was held at New York University and featured Harold Laski, the British socialist, and Ordway Tead, chairman of the New York City Board of Higher Education. Novikoff's seminar, entitled "What Is Scholarship?," was chaired by Harry Carman, a Columbia professor and a member of the Board of Higher Education. Novikoff's remarks addressed the question of whether a "social conception of scholarship" should replace the pursuit of "objective truth" as the basis of the scholarly ideal. It is very possible that the favorable decision on Novikoff's promotion case was helped by the fact that two influential members of the board, Tead and Carman, met Novikoff at this forum. Certainly, his presentation belied any suggestion that he was unserious or unthoughtful about the scholarly enterprise. In addition to his public speaking, the minutes of the Brooklyn College chapter of the Teachers Union show that Novikoff continued to play an active role in the union. In 1939 and 1940 he served as a member of the chapter's executive committee.[55]

A particularly significant action was his effort during 1938 to recruit his close friend, Harry Albaum, to the Communist party. Albaum told an investigating committee in 1952 how it happened.

> In the summer of 1938, I went to the country, I took a bungalow up somewhere in New York near Lake Mahopac. Someone wanted to share a bungalow with me because he was really interested in me—he was my friend. When we got to the country, it was apparent that this was part of this whole scheme to, what I conceive of now, is sucking me in or inveigling me into this deal. . . . Well, the *Worker* arrived by mail. There were pamphlets . . . about fascists in this country, about Gerald L. K. Smith. Finally, at the end of the summer, I capitulated. I mean that is what it really was. It was capitulation.

Albaum was one of the last of about thirty Brooklyn College faculty members to join the Party. His commitment to the Party was less than wholehearted, and later, in a pattern similar to the "turning" of Bernard Grebanier, the recruitment would have unfortunate consequences for other Communists. Novikoff in particular would regret his decision to go after Albaum.[56]

Novikoff's victory in the promotion case was the last important success of the Brooklyn College activists before the shadow of legislated anticommunism descended on the college and on the Communists. The *Brooklyn Eagle* stories led in October 1938 to a brief but well-publicized investigation of the Brooklyn Communists by the Dies Committee. In a few months Grebanier defected from the Party and took a public stand against the Communists. Finally, with Grebanier as a key informant, a New York State legislative committee began a highly efficient investigation that brought the Communists out from under their cloak of anonymity.

Novikoff's first seven years at Brooklyn College, spanning ages eighteen to twenty-five and the period of greatest Communist influence in this country's history, saw his emergence as a highly regarded young scientist as well as a committed political activist. He proved himself to be an idealistic young man, passionate in his convictions,

often truculent to a fault, prodigious in his capacity to work, and prepared, it seems, to accept the risks associated with his political commitments.

We know too that his political activities did not arouse the disfavor
of his family. Because he did not volunteer information, the Novikoffs
did not know much about his political involvements; and on the occasions when his name appeared publicly, they instinctively assumed
that Alex, the special son, was in the right. Surely, the solid confidence
and trust of his family was a sustaining factor in this period, even as
he came under attack. The summary effect of these years was that by
1939 he was an experienced political animal, had followed his own
heart in his science and politics, and had no serious regrets about his
actions.[57]

Alex and Sonia, his older sister, with parents shortly after settling in Brownsville section of Brooklyn in 1917. *Courtesy of the Novikoff family.*

Alex at his graduation from Columbia College in 1931. *Courtesy of the Novikoff family.*

The first campus of Brooklyn College, shown in 1937, was built on old circus grounds. *Courtesy of Brooklyn College Library, Special Collections.*

Faculty of the Department of Biology at Brooklyn College in 1934, showing Alex in middle back row (with mustache). Alex's chairman and antagonist Earl A. Martin is in the middle of first row. Harry Albaum, Alex's friend and later an informer, is second from left in back row. *Courtesy of Brooklyn College Library, Special Collections.*

The Workers Bookshop and other Communist party offices at 50 E. 13th Street in New York. Alex's book, *Climbing Our Family Tree,* was sold at this bookstore. *Associated Press Photo.*

This cartoon appeared in the *Brooklyn Eagle* on December 4, 1940. *Courtesy of the Brooklyn Public Library.*

Alex and Rosalind two days before their marriage in 1939. *Courtesy of the Novikoff family.*

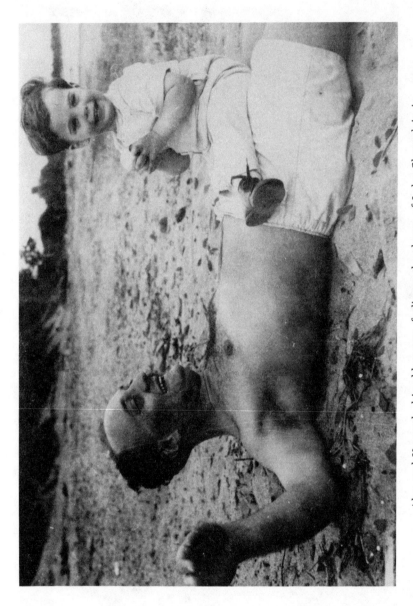

Alex and Kenneth, his oldest son, frolic on the shores of Lake Champlain in 1952, a few months before Alex is called to Washington to testify. *Courtesy of the Novikoff family.*

The family in Vermont, 1950 (from left, Rosalind, Alex, Kenneth, Larry). *Courtesy of the Novikoff family.*

A few months after Chief Counsel Robert Morris interrogated Alex at the Jenner Committee hearing, Morris was appointed a Municipal Court Justice. Morris is shown in January 1954 with his three mentors (left to right): Frederick Coudert, chairman of the New York State Communist hearings in 1940 and 1941; Pat McCarran, chairman of the Senate Internal Security Subcommittee until 1952; and William Jenner, who replaced McCarran as chairman in January 1953. *Associated Press Photo.*

Alex and Francis Peisch, his attorney, before final hearing in August 1953.
Burlington Free Press Photo.

University of Vermont President Carl Borgmann after Alex's dismissal in 1953.
Courtesy of the University of Vermont Archives.

Alex at electron microscope in 1955, the first of its kind at Albert Einstein College of Medicine. *Courtesy of the Novikoff family.*

With Father Joyce, the sole trustee to vote to keep Alex, and Phyllis, Alex's second wife, on honorary degree day, 1983. *Courtesy of the Novikoff family.*

Alex holding back tears after receiving his honorary degree from the University of Vermont in May 1983. *Courtesy of the Novikoff family.*

Chapter 3

CONFRONTED BY THE ANTI-COMMUNISTS

Legislative Committees in Washington and New York

In 1938 an episode in Washington, D.C., touched Novikoff's life at Brooklyn College. During the previous twenty years Congress had conducted numerous investigations of radical politics in the country. As political events heated up during the 1930s, House committees headed by Hamilton Fish in 1930 and by John McCormack and Samuel Dickstein in 1934 assumed active roles. These were mild predecessors, however, to a more aggressive undertaking chaired by Congressman Martin Dies of Texas. Sparked by concerns about subversion from the political right, especially the Nazi-inspired German-American Bund, the Special Committee on Un-American Propaganda Activities was created in early 1938. Under the leadership of its volatile chairman, the Dies Committee soon turned its attention to threats from the political left. Dies targeted "left wingers and radicals," using the committee's subpoena power to conduct raids, acquire documents, call witnesses, and accumulate files. Although his methods were sufficiently extreme to distress even fellow anti-Communists, he honed many of the investigatory techniques of the McCarthy era, including the public identification of hundreds of suspect organizations and individuals.[1]

At the start Dies was not particularly successful in his efforts to put together an effective staff of investigators or to secure a relationship of mutual benefit with the Federal Bureau of Investigation (FBI). The committee was efficient, however, in its systematic collection of information from already available sources, including the newspapers and previous congressional investigations. The committee read and clipped from the *Daily Worker* and other Communist sources as well as from the mainstream press. It is not surprising, therefore, that the Dies Committee learned early on about the charges of Communist infiltration at Brooklyn College. The front-page stories in the *Brooklyn Eagle* caught the attention of Dies and his investigators, and plans were made to subpoena Brooklyn faculty to tell their stories to a national audience.[2]

The committee's initial hearings occurred during eleven days in August and featured the testimony of John P. Frey, who told at length about Communist infiltration of the unions, and Walter S. Steele, a magazine editor, who drew on his files to name hundreds of individuals as Communists. On August 15 the *Brooklyn Eagle* reported on page one that three Brooklyn College "aides" had been subpoenaed. The college staff called to Washington as witnesses were Earl Martin, Novikoff's chairman and the initiator of the *Eagle* series; Martin Meyer, chairman of the chemistry department and the target of *Staff* articles; and Edward Fenlon, a faculty member in the philosophy department. For reasons that are not completely clear, Fenlon took on the leading role in these events.[3]

Daily *Eagle* stories heightened anticipation of the scheduled testimony. An *Eagle* story on August 16 indicated that the men were preparing their answers to three questions posed by the committee: Is there communism in Brooklyn College? What is its extent? Do you consider it a menace and is there a remedy for it? Fenlon was interviewed at length for an August 18 story that included his picture on page one and his comment that his fourteen-page report didn't name any Communist teachers, "but I am ready with names. My report concentrates on the *Staff* and I know the identity of five or six who are the main contributors." If there had been any doubt previously, Fenlon's veiled threat to name Brooklyn College Communists told Novikoff and the others that the Dies Committee testimony represented yet another escalation of the conservative counteroffensive. Suggesting that he had a direct line to the committee, Fenlon went on to say that after the Washington hearings the Dies Committee would come to New York "for a more extensive hearing into radical activities throughout the city and the state . . . and more faculty will be subpoenaed."[4]

For almost two hours on the morning of August 23, Fenlon, Martin, and Meyer read their reports to the committee and answered occasional questions of clarification. The presentations were almost academic in tone as they systematically addressed the committee's inquiries. Fenlon's report was the longest and most comprehensive, covering *Staff*, infiltration of the union, the Klein case, and Communist-

dominated student organizations. Martin presented a detailed scholarly analysis of the content of *Staff*. Meyer discussed his efforts to get
the ROTC established on campus. This public testimony did not include
the names of any Communists and did not provoke any colorful interactions with members of the committee. Indeed, in comparison to the
Eagle series in May, the Dies testimony was anticlimactic. It contained
few new revelations and lasted only a day.[5]

There were, however, reactions back in New York. Ordway Tead,
chairman of the Board of Higher Education, told the *New York Times*
that "If there are Communists in the faculty of Brooklyn, that, too, in
the first instance is a matter of their personal and private convictions."
He expressed his belief that the allegations before the Dies Committee
were "grossly exaggerated." In response Fenlon wrote a letter to the
Eagle saying that he was "forced to disagree with Dr. Tead." Under its
cloak of anonymity, *Staff* responded in vituperative fashion, accusing
the "three reactionary professors" of stopping "at nothing in their
efforts to crush democracy and liberalism, even if it means the complete
vilification of Brooklyn College." The December *Staff* printed a long
satirical poem about Dies and Fenlon, typified by the following passage:

> These Reds are a plague and a pest, Mr. Dies?
> In my hair why will they nest, Mr. Dies?
>   The Faculty's dumb
>   And under their thumb.
> Why, the Reds carry bombs in their vest, Mr. Dies!
>
> What's the number of the Reds, Mr. Fenlon?
> Do they creep under beds, Mr. Fenlon?
>   Have you searched every drawer?
>   Have you ripped up the floor?
> Can you blast them in several heads, Mr. Fenlon?

The college chapter of the Teachers Union passed a resolution suggesting that the testimony "could be easily construed as an attempt to
intimidate the present and future membership and to lessen the effectiveness of the New York City College Teachers Union." Novikoff, in
his role as secretary of the chapter, was the person who mailed the
referendum to union members.[6]

Although the controversy over the Dies testimony raged for several
weeks on the Brooklyn campus, news coverage waned quickly as attention turned to the expanding war in Europe and to Thomas Dewey's
prosecution of a Tammany Hall figure. What is evident, however, is
that the accusations about Communist activity at Brooklyn College
were remembered by legislators and investigators in Washington and

New York. A file on Brooklyn College was opened, and suspect campus organizations were identified. As we well know, files of this kind develop a life of their own. This was confirmed twenty-four months later when a New York State committee made good use of the Dies information. Moreover, the FBI and the Dies Committee were testing a cooperative relationship, and it is probable that the Brooklyn College material was transmitted to the FBI.[7]

A significant question is whether the names of suspected Communists were given to the committee. Novikoff and his colleagues were not named publicly, but it is possible that their identities were mentioned in off-the-record interactions with the committee staff. The committee put high value on "Red lists" and pressured witnesses to provide names. Given Fenlon's readiness to mention names and his claim to know the Communists most active in *Staff*, it is entirely possible that Novikoff was identified. If this was indeed the case, the Dies affair signaled the beginning of Novikoff's history as a "security case" in Washington's files. To put things in perspective, we know that the last entry in the FBI file on Novikoff was thirty-five years later, at the time that the National Institutes of Health deliberated about taking Novikoff off the NIH "blacklist." Unfortunately, available documents do not confirm whether Novikoff's name was presented to the Dies Committee investigators.[8]

THE COMMUNISTS CONTINUE TO LOSE MOMENTUM

Although it seemed that political trouble was now cropping up on all sides, one development was a decidedly happy one. During 1936 Novikoff had become friendly with an undergraduate English major at Brooklyn College. Rosalind Shaftel was eighteen at the time, the youngest child of a successful garment manufacturer. The Shaftels were Jewish and had come from Kiev; her father was one of eight brothers. After a few years as a salesman for a small business, her father had progressed to ownership of his own business in the 1920s. His factory was in Brooklyn, where his children worked during the summers. A mark of the family's economic progress was the move to the "White Line" at the border of Brooklyn and Queens. One of Rosalind's brothers, Oscar, had graduated from City College and had gone on to doctoral study in philosophy at Harvard. During these years of intense political activity on the campus Alex became closer to this quiet, dark-haired young woman. Although Alex's persistent energy and verbosity contrasted sharply with Rosalind's sweetness and dignified intelligence, marriage was discussed seriously.[9]

Since the contrast in age between the students and the lower-ranked staff at Brooklyn College was often small, it was natural for teachers and students to socialize. Outside the classroom the involvement of Novikoff and other faculty members in political organizing on campus brought the two groups in close consort. Moreover, the 1930s at Brooklyn College were a time of social experimentation, especially for those imbued with progressive ideas. It was well known that some of the faculty "slept around" with students. Novikoff had an affair with the wife of a colleague. Selsam married Millicent Ellis, a teacher in the biology department; Ewen married a former student.[10]

Rosalind and Alex married on June 1, 1939. The brief *New York Times* announcement reported that the couple would spend the summer at Woods Hole, where Novikoff would do research at the Marine Biological Laboratories. For Novikoff the marriage represented a step up socially and economically. The Shaftels were less Yiddish, less Jewish than the Novikoffs and were more successful in business; in a sense they were more "American." The fact that each child, not only the first son, had gone to college reinforced the distinction between the families. Rosalind and Alex started their lives as a faculty couple at Woods Hole and took their own apartment when they returned to Brooklyn in the fall. For several years they lived in the same building as Harry Albaum and his family. Inevitably, Rosalind was drawn into the orbit of Alex's professional and political life. In 1939 she joined the Communist party and remained a member until she and Alex left the Party in 1945.[11]

Two events during the course of 1939 created serious problems for the Communists at Brooklyn College. The first was the defection of Bernard Grebanier from the Communist party. Grebanier had joined the Party at Selsam's urging in 1935 but almost at once had second thoughts about his decision. In an interview in 1974 he remembered feeling that he had joined a "band of conspirators" living in "a country as foreign as Abyssinia." He decided to get out, but it was three years before he was ready to take the decisive step. Finally, in June 1939 he wrote a letter to the Party announcing his intention of resigning. He attacked Party policies in the United States and the Soviet Union and indicated that he was resolved to stop being an "intellectual prostitute." In response the Party officially expelled him, charging that he was a "Trotskyite" and a "counterrevolutionary enemy of the working class." His exile was sealed by the declaration that "we consider any personal and social connections with such an individual as incompatible with the honor and self-respect of a conscious and politically developed revolutionist." Although Grebanier wanted nothing further to do with the Party, it is true also that the Brooklyn College Communists refused henceforth to have dealings with him. He was a pariah, but that was perfectly satisfactory to Grebanier.[12]

Grebanier began to speak and write regularly on international issues and the detrimental effects of the policies of the Soviet Union. His activities produced bitter reaction from the Communists and other leftists. An edition of the *Vanguard*, the student newspaper, printed his "open letter" to Brooklyn College students. A subsequent edition accused him of being a "red baiter." The Young Communist League responded by distributing a circular entitled "General Grebanier—Dies Stooge." A theme of the document was that a favorite technique of the Dies Committee was to exploit the defection of individuals such as Grebanier. The document attacked his "slander": "Professor Grebanier made the most slanderous attacks, the most lying statements at his 'anti-communist' meeting. He dared to accuse the Soviet Union of Anti-Semitism. The Soviet Union, the only country in the world which makes Anti-Semitism a crime punishable by death. The only country free of minority repression . . ." Grebanier withstood reactions of this kind and remained an implacable foe of the Communists, capped by his testimony before the Rapp-Coudert Committee in 1940 and 1941. The acrimonious response to his departure, his decision to take a public stance against the Communists, and the resulting open conflict prepared the psychological ground for his becoming an informer. If the Party had let him go quietly, it is possible that he would not have turned against them, an event that had devastating results for Novikoff and the other Brooklyn Communists.[13]

Actually, Grebanier's position was strengthened by the second important development of 1939, the signing of the Hitler-Stalin Non-Aggression Pact. For several years the American Communist party, under the guidance of the Comintern, had pushed for an antifascist alliance of political forces in the United States. They pressed for strong military action to contain Hitler and urged American intervention. When Chamberlain made his bargain with Hitler at Munich in the fall of 1938, *Staff* wrote a long article accusing England of appeasement and of a "long series of capitulations before the Fascist warmakers." In March 1939, however, Stalin, who had urged a collective security alliance against Hitler's expansionism, hinted that the Soviet Union would not be drawn into a conflict with Germany and suggested that any impending war pertained to the affairs of other countries. A trade agreement on July 22 led finally to a nonaggression pact between the Nazis and the Soviets on August 23.[14]

The Germans invaded Poland on September 1; the Russians seized

Estonia, Latvia, and Lithuania and invaded Finland. The American Communists reacted at first by trying to maintain their ties with anti-Hitler progressive groups but soon moved toward the Soviet line. The shift of Soviet foreign policy and the corresponding shift of position by the American Communist party dealt an immediate blow to the credibility of the Communists. In his study of the Communist party of the 1930s, Harvey Klehr noted that membership declined, important relationships with individuals and groups were curtailed, and the Party's goodwill achieved in the Popular Front period was significantly reduced. The obvious lesson, in Klehr's estimation, was that "loyalty to the Soviet Union took precedence over any and every other consideration." While the Party remained a powerful political entity with influence in many areas, the nonaggression pact marked the end of the most successful era in the Party's history. The direct consequence for the Communists at Brooklyn College was that the Party's moral position was weakened by the pact, which seriously eroded support from progressive, noncommunist allies. This shift of political forces helped Grebanier, the Dies Committee, and others keep up—and increase—their pressure.[15]

It was more than a coincidence that the Communists absorbed bad news from other directions too. After a year's search the Board of Higher Education turned to Harry Gideonse as the new president of Brooklyn College. Gideonse, an experienced administrator who had broken with Robert Hutchins at the University of Chicago, presented several conditions for accepting the position. In addition to getting board approval for turning back some of the "democratic" bylaw changes pushed through by the union, he demanded permission to pursue the Communists on campus in an aggressive manner. Gideonse was a shrewd, strong-willed leader. He served as president for twenty-seven years, and from the start of his tenure in June 1939 he was a formidable opponent of the Communists.[16]

There were other indications of the changing political tide. On the order of the New York district of the Communist party the publication of *Staff* was discontinued:

> The action is taken at a time when *The Staff*'s popularity is undimmed, when it is still the accepted voice of the most progressive members of the Brooklyn College staff. However, at the College and elsewhere in the nation, the enemies of labor miss no opportunities to split the unity of working men and women. They point to the existence of anonymous Communist shop papers as evidence that a hidden faction plots secret and subversive aims. . . . So that there shall be nothing to divide workers, the Communist party has decided to abandon shop papers wherever they are now published.

In December the American Student Union lost its first important election on campus when representatives of a moderate party were elected to class offices. Meanwhile, the New York Teachers Union lost its dominant position in the national AFT, which led in 1941 to the expulsion from the AFT of the Communist locals. Following announcement of the Hitler-Stalin pact, the Dies Committee reopened hearings with leaders of the American Communist party.[17]

The early months of 1940 continued in the same vein. An effort to ban the American Student Union from the Brooklyn College campus was fought by the Communists, most vocally by Howard Selsam and Frederic Ewen. The rupture between Communist organizations on campus and those supported by more moderate factions produced numerous controversies. The Communists, under siege from President Gideonse and several department chairmen, were conducting a holding action on several fronts, and the situation only worsened. As it turned out, the most ominous development was that several legislators in Albany had decided the time had come to do something about the Communist problem in the schools.[18]

THE RAPP-COUDERT COMMITTEE

Growing public concern about alleged Communist influence in public education, an incident over a professorial appointment at City College, and ongoing discussion of education financing in New York State moved the state legislature in early 1940 to examine various perceived problems in education. The immediate impetus was the appointment of Bertrand Russell, the eminent British philosopher, to the faculty of City College. Russell, who was sixty-eight at the time, could serve for only two years because of the college's retirement regulation. Noting this fact, Harry Gideonse opposed the appointment on the grounds that it did not meet the long-term needs of the municipal colleges. Despite Russell's unconventional views on social and political issues, a majority of the New York Board of Higher Education and most of New York's higher education community saw the appointment as a unique opportunity to secure the services of a world-renowned scholar. Nevertheless, announcement of the appointment produced a storm of protest in the media, in the legislature, and among Catholic and Protestant leaders. In Brooklyn the newspaper of the Catholic diocese attacked the appointment and called for an investigation of the Board of Higher Education. Russell's socialist views led the paper's editor to conclude that the appointment might "awaken some of the citizens of this city to the danger presented by the City Colleges." In due course the state senate passed a resolution protesting the appointment, and the Board of Higher Education decided to review the matter. The political instincts of Mayor Fiorello LaGuardia showed through when he told Gideonse, "Doc, I'm an Episcopalian and my Bishop in all these years has never made a peep about anything that I've done, and he's entitled to one little peep." For all practical purposes, LaGuardia ended the affair when he removed the line in the school budget that funded the position.[19]

The Russell controversy and the continuing media coverage of campus controversies involving New York City Communists reinforced the idea in the minds of many legislators that something was seriously amiss in New York City schools. After a period of refining various proposed resolutions to investigate New York City schools, the legislature passed a resolution on March 26 calling for a joint legislative committee to investigate procedures and methods for allocating state money for public schools. This resolution of Senator Herbert Rapp was amended on March 29 to include a new subsection, and the complete package was passed again by both chambers. The new subsection made specific reference to subversion in New York City and directed that there be study of "the extent to which, if any, subversive activities may be permitted to be carried on in the schools and colleges of such educational system." It was agreed that Senator Frederick Coudert, the only Republican senator from New York City, would chair a subcommittee with a mandate to carry out the provisions dealing with alleged subversive activities in New York City. Governor Lehman approved a $30,000 budget for the work of the committee, and Senator Rapp, as chairman, began to organize for the study of school financing. Suspecting an impending witch hunt, many leftist organizations, unions, and prominent academicians attacked the committee. Most newspapers and many educational leaders, however, supported the investigations. President Gideonse, who was personally acquainted with Paul Windels, the chief counsel, observed that the Coudert subcommittee had hired a first-rate staff and expressed his optimism about the likely outcomes of the investigation.[20]

Senator Coudert's subcommittee began work in September 1940. Windels, a prominent attorney and former corporation counsel to Mayor LaGuardia, was an active and efficient committee counsel. At Windels' insistence Coudert agreed that the investigation would be left entirely to the professional staff and that political influences on the work of the subcommittee should be prevented. The committee set up headquarters in a spacious building at 165 Broadway in New York City, which allowed witnesses to come and go without being seen by observers in the corridor. In preparation for taking testimony, Windels trained his staff of six lawyers in techniques for interrogating witnesses. Windels believed that the major public concern was the "disorderly conditions" on the campuses and the prevalence of strikes, picketing, and harassment of teachers and administrators. As such, it appears that Windels' actions were driven more by a desire to return "law and order" to the campuses than by an ideological commitment to eradicate communism or other left-wing movements. He was legalistic, shrewd, and occasionally ruthless in carrying out his mandate.[21]

During the next three months the subcommittee reviewed documents and records, interviewed various citizens, and conducted private hearings with witnesses. Public hearings began on December 2 and continued for three days. Further public hearings were carried out on an intermittent basis between March and June 1941. Overall, the subcommittee heard 88 witnesses at public sessions, interrogated 503 witnesses at private hearings, and conducted 712 interviews.[22]

Not surprisingly, the committee staff took advantage of the research done by various government agencies. On October 29, 1940, one of the Rapp-Coudert investigators arrived in Washington to examine the files of the House Un-American Activities Committee—the Dies Committee—and met with Benjamin Mandel. In the 1920s Mandel had left the Teachers Union in a dispute and had taken up full-time work as a Communist party organizer. He left the Party in 1929 and gradually assumed a position of active anticommunism. He joined the staff of the Dies Committee in 1938, which drew greatly on his expertise about Party organization and procedures. The investigator from the Rapp-Coudert Committee reported that he received excellent cooperation from Mandel:

> After I had been in the office for ten minutes I was introduced to Ben Mandel, who is assistant to Mathews (Chief Investigator of the Dies Committee). Mandel then proceeded to give me all the facts that he knew from his own personal files and guided me to the files of the Dies Committee. He secured permission from Mathews for me to go through the files and I spent most of the day (Tuesday) in checking the list of about 150 people in the Dies files.

At Mandel's urging the investigator contacted an official in the Division of European Affairs of the Department of State. He was permitted to inspect the passports of suspected New York City Communists, including Frederic Ewen, Howard Selsam, and Harry Slochower. These inspections revealed that Ewen was born in Poland and had visited Russia during 1936. Selsam had visited Europe and the Middle East on three occasions between 1924 and 1936. Slochower was born in

Moldavia, Bukovina, and was naturalized as an American citizen in 1920. The files of the Rapp-Coudert Committee do not make clear how this kind of information aided their efforts to expose Communists in New York City education. It is telling, however, that Benjamin Mandel was soon thereafter hired away from the Dies Committee to assist the investigation in New York City. It is likely that Mandel sensed that for the moment the more important anti-Communist program was that of the Rapp-Coudert Committee.[23]

The first important breakthrough for the committee came in November when Bernard Grebanier testified in a private hearing about Communist activities at Brooklyn College. Although Grebanier had broken with the Communist party unit at Brooklyn College and had made public attacks on the Communists, he did not at first intend to name other Brooklyn College Communists. Believing that he was the first Brooklyn College teacher to be subpoenaed, he turned to several individuals for advice.

> It was on a Monday night that I was handed the subpoena to appear at a private hearing, for the first time, before the Coudert-Rapp Committee. That same evening I sought the advice of several lawyers. They were unanimous in the opinion that I had no choice other than to answer the questions of the Committee.
> The next day, Tuesday, I showed the subpoena to several of my colleagues at college for this reason: A number of weeks before, there had been a rumor spread in my department (a rumor which I was able to trace to Prof. Ewen) that I had already appeared before the Coudert-Rapp Committee voluntarily; I felt that if I showed my subpoena around I would be doing something to dispel the evil light which Ewen's lie would naturally cast upon my appearance before the Committee.

Striving to handle his appearance in a way that would prevent his becoming an "informer," he then attempted to contact William Mulligan, who had been retained as counsel by the College Teachers Union. He took this step despite his "fears of seeing any lawyer retained by the Union, which I knew to be dominated by members of the Communist Party." After trying all of one day to reach Mulligan, Grebanier finally received a call from Mulligan at home at 1:30 A.M. According to notes made by Grebanier in early 1941, the conversation proceeded as follows:

> "I am sorry," he said, "but I shall not be able to see you today." I protested that it was very important that he see me. So far as I knew, I was the first Brooklyn College teacher to be subpoenaed, and it seemed to me, I said, highly necessary for the Union lawyer to have a talk with me. "I am sorry," he repeated, "I can't make it." This I thought was

strange enough. Nevertheless, I asked him for advice. "I am a member of the Teachers Union," I told him, "and while I have no desire to protect or help the Communist Party, I have a dread of having to identify members of the Communist Party at Brooklyn College. I was once a member of that Party myself, and I broke with it some two years ago. If I am under oath, I do not see what I shall be able to do to avoid appearing in a very odious light. Worst of all, no other former member of the Communist party at Brooklyn College has left it, as I have good reason to know, so I shall be in a terrible position, and all alone."

Mulligan declined to give any direct advice other than to tell Grebanier that if he did not wish to talk he should ignore the subpoena and be ready to accept any legal consequences. If he were to abide by the subpoena, he had to answer the committee's questions. Grebanier's suspicion and paranoia at the time are indicated by his conclusion that "Mr. Mulligan was working in harmony with some Communist strategy to bring me to grief, despite my honorable desire to be in no way connected with any personal harm to them." He noted that Mulligan's advice to the other Brooklyn College teachers was to accept the subpoena, take an oath, and refuse to answer any questions on the grounds that the proceedings were illegal. He noted also that the union later claimed that he had refused to join the union in fighting the committee and therefore was a "traitor." The plan of the union to isolate him, he concluded, was "perfectly conceived and executed."[24]

Grebanier, a dark-haired, somewhat portly man, went to his private hearing intent on telling the committee, if necessary, about his own Communist activities but refraining from naming other Communists. According to his later recollection, he was pressured to confirm others as Communists but resisted by stating that he did not remember. Finally, the investigator produced a list of names of Grebanier's six-man cell and enumerated the pseudonyms of Party members and the times and places of meetings. Grebanier was "staggered" by the information. He gave in to the committee's pressure and confirmed what the committee already "knew." Then, once he began to talk, the flood gates opened. He described his experience in the Communist party, the Party's ties to the College Teachers Union, and the inner workings of the Party organization. In all, he named more than thirty Communists, including Novikoff. On the basis of this testimony, the committee subpoenaed each of the faculty named by Grebanier and called them to testify in private hearings.[25]

On November 13 the confidential phase of the committee's work came to an end when a front-page story in the *Brooklyn Eagle* announced that "ISM Quiz Calls Boro Teachers." For the first time, enabled by Grebanier's private testimony, faculty were named in public.

Novikoff was not mentioned, but the names of Grebanier, Howard Selsam, Frederic Ewen, Harry Slochower, Herbert Morais, Murray Young, and Elton Gustafson appeared. The story pointed out that each of the subpoenaed faculty was a member of the Teachers Union.[26]

Like Grebanier, the Brooklyn College Communists turned to the Teachers Union for guidance on how to respond to the subpoenas. Bella Dodd, the union's legislative representative and a Communist, was determined to fight the committee's procedures, with particular attention to the committee's prohibition against testifying with a legal counsel present and against providing witnesses with transcripts of their own testimony. In addition, it was the common practice for Senator Coudert to open a private hearing and then depart, often leaving the proceeding to various committee staff members without a single legislator present. Under Dodd's leadership and guided by Mulligan's legal strategy, an action was brought in the New York State Supreme Court to request a declaratory judgment on whether the committee had the authority to proceed. In his excellent study of the Rapp-Coudert investigation, Lawrence Chamberlain suggested that the committee's stubbornness on these procedural issues was shortsighted.

> In its insistence that the Brooklyn staff members appear at private hearings on its own terms, the committee chose to stand upon its legal rights and was fully supported in the courts. One doubts that the victory was worth the price. Not one of the points which caused so much criticism—honest or otherwise—bore vitally upon the committee's capacity to discharge its function. In each instance it could have yielded, yet gained the information it sought.

Although, with its victory in the State Supreme Court, the committee was able to proceed as it wished, its tactics elicited the criticism of the American Civil Liberties Union (ACLU) and several prominent liberals. Utilizing a strategy orchestrated by the Teachers Union, the subpoenaed Brooklyn College staff cited the pending court case and refused to cooperate with the committee.[27]

Novikoff was served a subpoena at 6 P.M. on November 26, 1940, in the science building at Brooklyn College. He was ordered to appear the next morning at 11:45 A.M. for a private hearing with the committee. No matter how prepared one may be, the subpoena, with the force of law and the power of the police behind it, is an unsettling event. For the first time in his life, Novikoff was confronted by an unfriendly act of his government. Like his fellow Communists, he felt a sense of exposure and a creeping paranoia. Fortunately for his psychological state, he could turn to his allies in the union and the comfort of an agreed strategy.

The next morning Senator Coudert, accompanied by two assistant counsels and a stenographer, conducted the brief session. The core of the interaction went as follows:

Mr. Shea: Mr. Novikoff, will you tell us whether you have ever been or are now a member of the Communist Party?

Mr. Novikoff: Before I answer questions, I should like to put a few questions to the committee.

Mr. Shea: Go right ahead.

Mr. Novikoff: To begin with, I would like to know who the members in the room are.

Mr. Shea: Senator Coudert is the only member of the Committee present.

Mr. Novikoff: Secondly, will I get a transcript of the proceedings this morning?

Mr. Shea: I am sorry, that is not the practice.

Mr. Novikoff: Well, then, I should like to make a statement. Since the union of which I am a member . . .

Mr. Shea: Will you answer the question?

Mr. Novikoff: Since the union of which I am a member is litigating the propriety of these proceedings, and on advice of counsel, I should like to refrain from answering the question until such time as the propriety of the proceedings have been established.

Mr. Coudert: Mr. Novikoff, I must nonetheless direct you to answer the question.

Mr. Novikoff: You have heard my statement.

According to the transcript of the session kept in the committee's possession, the exchange with Novikoff took four minutes.[28]

Novikoff left the committee's headquarters and returned to Brooklyn to confer with the other Communists under subpoena and to wait out the litigation raised by the union. The final report of the committee, released in April 1942, indicated that the parade of witnesses refusing to testify reinforced suspicions about the union. The committee charged that the teachers used a "carefully prepared legalistic formula, in which they had been rehearsed by the Teachers Union." The singular response of the Brooklyn faculty, with the exception of Grebanier, merely strengthened Windels' resolve to expose Communist infiltration of the union. At an early stage the committee's research into the union was aided by John Dewey, who helped the committee get a copy of the 1933 report of alleged attempts by a "minority" to take control of the teachers union. Once Windels identified the most important members of the union, he "started a line of witnesses rolling toward our offices."[29]

While the committee held forth in downtown Manhattan, President Gideonse was working to shore up the reputation of Brooklyn College. His public statements in support of the work of the committee were reinforced by an action of the college's faculty council on November 14. By a vote of 42 to 7, the faculty council endorsed the following resolution: "The Faculty Council of Brooklyn College endorses the position of the College Administration in cooperating fully with the Rapp-Coudert Investigating Committee in all proper efforts to discover the truth, in so far as Brooklyn College is concerned, with respect to the purposes for which the Committee was established by the Legislature of the State of New York." Gideonse made it known to the Coudert Committee that he would be willing to testify at the committee's public sessions scheduled for early December.[30]

The behind-the-scenes maneuvering of the committee ended on Monday, December 2, when the Rapp-Coudert Committee held its first public session at the County Court House on Foley Square in New York City. The afternoon *Eagle* reported Windels' opening remarks with a bold headline across the top of page one: "Red Teachers Accused of Plot." Windels stated that "nothing could be more despicable than to urge teachers to stand before children as the conscious advocates of a political doctrine, while pretending to be something else." The irony of Windels' opening comments was that this accusation—that the Communists used their classrooms to indoctrinate students—was the *one* accusation that was ultimately shown to be without foundation in fact. He did succeed, however, in creating an atmosphere of suspicion and presumed guilt.[31]

Following Windels' remarks Grebanier was called to the stand. As the committee's first public witness, he lived up to their expectations. Grebanier described his involvement in Communist party activities at Brooklyn College, his second thoughts about his involvement in the Party, the workings of the *Staff* newspaper, the structure of the Party cell, and the role of the Party in the Teachers Union. He showed the committee the exchange of correspondence with the Party at the time of his resignation and pointed out that after his "expulsion" the Communists attacked his reputation among students and teachers and attempted to organize a boycott of his classes. All in all, Grebanier's testimony was detailed, lengthy, and replete with revelations about a life unknown to most Americans.[32]

Although he had named Communists in private, he did not expect that the committee would ask that he do so in public. To his surprise, eight names were presented, and he was asked whether they were members of the Communist party. He objected to the question, but at Windels' insistence he then proceeded to confirm these Brooklyn College people as active members of the Party, including Selsam, Ewen, Young, Slochower, Maurice Ogur, Henry Klein, David McKelvy White, and Selsam's wife, Millicent. Going further, he described the Communist activities engaged in by each. Novikoff was not named. It is not precisely clear why only eight of more than thirty staff members identified in the private hearings were named in public. It appears, however, that the eight named were at that time the only teachers for whom there existed corroborative evidence. The practice of the committee, which anticipated the proceedings of the McCarthy era, was to name in public only those individuals who had been identified as Communists by at least two people.[33]

Grebanier's testimony was a page-one story in *The New York Times* and a blaring headline on the *Eagle*'s front page. There was an immediate storm of reaction on the Brooklyn College campus. However, the week of accusations and publicity had only begun. When Grebanier finished his testimony on December 4, President Gideonse took the stand to express his support of the work of the committee: "Outside forces are leading the Communist groups in the colleges, I am certain of that. They supply the money, leadership, ideas, and sometimes phraseology. I can't prove it. But I'd like to have evidence, evidence that would stand up in a court of justice." He went on to explain how difficult it was to remove a faculty member, citing the many levels of the educational structure that had to approve a firing. However, with evidence in hand he was prepared "to act on it." Other comments by Gideonse suggested to observers, particularly the leadership of the College Teachers Union, that he would support the elimination of academic tenure as well as a reduction in the size of New York's public colleges. The union noted that Gideonse's recommendation for a reduction in size "dovetails nicely with the recommendation of the *Educational Signpost* that free public higher education be made available only to those students who attain a secondary school average of 95 percent."[34]

A backdrop for the public hearings was the continuing controversy over the manner in which the hearings were conducted. Prior to the opening of the hearings, the Teachers Union was told by Windels that witnesses could be heard only at the invitation of the committee, witnesses could not have counsel present, and only the committee could ask questions of the witnesses. William Mulligan, attorney for the Teachers Union, presented a brief to the Appellate Division of the New York State Supreme Court protesting these rules. Mulligan argued that the public probing of witnesses such as Grebanier amounted to an attack on the union and on all teachers and that the union should be heard at the hearings. He addressed a letter to the members of the Coudert subcommittee:

> Your counsel has denied that the Teachers Union is entitled to take part in any public hearing directed at that body of 7,500 members. He has done this without asking you. He has done it without precedent, for while it is true that every witness may not have counsel, these teachers are no mere witnesses before your Committee. They are the very subject of inquisition. . . . Whatever Mr. Coudert has done in his secret hearings, we cannot assume that in public you will adopt the method of a kangaroo court.

Mulligan sensed correctly that the union, alleged to be dominated by Communists, was a primary target of the probe. Mulligan's efforts to alter the ground rules failed both in the courts and in the committee. Windels opened the public hearings on December 2 by reiterating the rules of procedure.[35]

At the end of the final public session on December 4, Windels was authorized by the subcommittee to institute contempt proceedings against twenty-five individuals who had refused to testify at private hearings. The list included sixteen current and three former Brooklyn faculty members, two clerks at the college, and four individuals not affiliated with the college, including Morris Schappes, a leader of the Communists at City College. Windels indicated that those listed would be able to "purge" themselves of the contempt charge by testifying voluntarily at private hearings. Novikoff's name was on the list presented by Windels and published on December 5 in newspapers throughout the city. This was the first time that Novikoff's name was mentioned publicly in connection with the probe.[36]

The airing of the contempt charge and of Novikoff's name altered his situation in a substantive way. He could no longer ride out the proceedings under the assumption that he could not be harmed legally or professionally. There was the further danger that his family, from disapproval or embarrassment, might lose their trust and confidence in him. On this score, however, he could rest secure. Alex's parents and siblings believed that the publicity was a case of massive "distortion" and that furthermore Alex worked too hard to be any kind of "rabble rouser." With his socialist leanings, Jake was especially disposed to believe that his son's political activities, whatever they may have been, were necessary and laudable.[37]

On December 6 students at Brooklyn College and at other New York City colleges held the first meeting of a group formed to protest the activities of the Rapp-Coudert Committee. The meeting was held in two classrooms on the Brooklyn campus. The group, called the Committee of 6,000 to Defend Free and Higher Education, heard Novikoff as its first speaker. The afternoon edition of the *Brooklyn Eagle* reported that Novikoff spoke "in a light vein." The paper quoted him as saying "I was not interested as much in the secret proceedings, where every form of illegality was practiced, as I was in the stenotype machine . . . I never had seen one before." The following morning *The New York Times* reported that one thousand Brooklyn College students had attended the meeting and had heard "several of their teachers [cited by the Rapp-Coudert Committee] discuss their attitude in refusing to testify." The *Times* noted that "among those who addressed the students and urged them to fight against the activities of the committee [was] Dr. Alex Benjamin Novikoff, Instructor in Chemistry."[38]

Novikoff objected to the *Brooklyn Eagle* story and sent a letter to the editor requesting that his rejoinder be published. He also requested "a retraction of its December 6th report within the next three days." Novikoff charged that the story had misquoted and misrepresented his remarks.

> I am not a "chemistry professor." I did not speak "in a light vein:" nothing could be further from the truth. The sentences enclosed in quotation marks were not made. . . . In reference to the stenotype machine, your report is untrue. I had remarked that as a scientist, I was impressed with the machine which I saw for the first time. The operation of the machine distracted me at times. . . . [The report] is a downright distortion.

His response was printed in a subsequent edition of the *Eagle*.[39]

The political response to Grebanier's disclosures and to the pending contempt proceedings was led by the Teachers Union. The December 9 edition of the union's *College Newsletter* blared in its headline that "Coudert Red Scare Falls Flat" and charged that "Prof. Grebanier's testimony followed the by now classic pattern of wild allegations and unsubstantiated charges against a background of exploited innocence and theatrical contrition." The paper reserved considerable venom for President Gideonse: "But Brooklyn College was honored with the initial brunt of the attack by the Coudert Committee not only because it had acquired a finger-man but also because it had as president a Dr. Gideonse, who came riding out of the West bent upon emulating, it would seem, Nicholas Murray Butler." The paper noted also that Windels had requested the membership lists of the Teachers Union. The story reported that the recent CIO convention had condemned the step as leading potentially to a blacklisting of union members and further had approved a resolution to fight what would be a "tremendous blow to labor throughout the entire country." The *Newsletter* announced that a mass meeting of locals 5 and 537 and other trade unions would be held on December 18 to answer charges made by the Rapp-Coudert Committee.[40]

Grebanier returned to the subcommittee on January 30, 1941, to provide further information about Communist activities at Brooklyn College. In this private hearing before Assistant Counsel Shea, Grebanier identified Novikoff by name in connection with several Party activities. The subcommittee displayed a keen interest in Novikoff's role:

> *Mr. Shea:* Did you ever see Mr. Novikoff's party card?
>
> *Mr. Grebanier:* Well, I had no reason to see people's cards, except that—I presume you mean party book, rather than card. The card was simply something you signed when you joined. I had no particular reason to see anybody's card in particular, except as an individual went up to pay his dues he would take out his book normally, and have his stamps pasted in, which the secretary's duty was to do. Mr. Novikoff was chairman on some occasions of the large group [of Brooklyn College members].
>
> *Mr. Shea:* Dr. Grebanier, how did you know that Professor Novikoff was a member of the Communist Party?
>
> *Dr. Grebanier:* I met him often in closed unit meetings of the Communist Party.

Grebanier identified numerous instances of Novikoff's involvement in Party meetings. Also, he described Novikoff's role in producing the *Staff* paper and as a link with the student Communist organization. He confirmed that Norwood was Novikoff's Party alias.[41]

Harry Albaum, Novikoff's long-time friend and fellow biologist, testified the following day, January 31, and denied that he was a member of the Communist party. He implicated no one at Brooklyn College and denied knowing a Mr. Norwood. Eleven years later, before another committee of investigation, Albaum would not be so kind to Novikoff.[42]

The public identification of alleged Communists—through Grebanier's public testimony and through the public listing by Windels of those who were subject to contempt proceedings for refusing to testify—led to the second crucial phase of the anti-Communist program. As Ellen Schrecker emphasized in her study of McCarthyism in academe, the investigatory phase in an "inquisition" of this kind is necessarily accompanied by steps of the employing agency to dismiss its Communist staff members. Thus, with the Rapp-Coudert disclosures exerting public pressure, the New York City Board of Higher Education was impelled to take action. After a mild response by the board in

November and December 1940, the board responded more actively to a call from the Rapp-Coudert Committee to "exercise their [the Board's] disciplinary powers in aid of any subpoena." On January 20, 1941, the board endorsed a resolution recommending action against teachers refusing to respond to subpoenas or refusing to give requested testimony. The resolution contained the following provisions:

> RESOLVED, that it will be the policy of the Board to take disciplinary action in accordance with law and its by-laws, for any failure to comply [with subpoenas or requests to testify].
> RESOLVED, that a copy of these preambles and resolutions be sent to the Joint Legislative Investigating Committee (Rapp-Coudert), and that the Committee be requested to advise the Board of any persons under its jurisdiction failing to testify before it.

As did others who refused to testify before the Rapp-Coudert Committee, Novikoff received by registered mail a copy of the resolution.[43]

Privy to the public records of the Rapp-Coudert Committee, the board's Special Committee on the Joint Legislative Investigation began at once to investigate those under suspicion. In a letter from the committee's chair, Lauson Stone, Novikoff was "requested to appear before the Committee" on February 11. The interview was postponed, and Novikoff was subsequently called to testify on February 22 at Hunter College. The thirty-five-minute session included inquiries about Novikoff's political activities, with specific references to the *Staff* newspaper, the Communist party, the Young Communist League, and various political action committees. He denied any involvement with Communist activities or with activities that could be termed "subversive." The committee's unproductive probing ended with the following exchange:

> *Hirschman:* Do you wish to make a statement?
> *Novikoff:* No, but perhaps you can tell me why I was called?
> *Hirschman:* We are trying to get all the information we can.
> *Novikoff:* I suppose you called me because I was subpoenaed by the Coudert Committee. But I'd like to know why I was subpoenaed. I'd appreciate whatever information you could give me at this point.
> *Stone:* We have no information about that.
> *Bucci:* That will be all.

For the moment, the board's action against Novikoff and others was confined to an accumulation of information and the carrying out of similar interviews.[44]

In March additional public testimony before the Rapp-Coudert

Committee about Communist activity at City College influenced the board to take a more aggressive stance. On March 6 and 7 William Canning, a history instructor at City College, identified thirty-four members of the City College branch of the Communist party. The committee also evidenced an interest in what Canning knew about the Brooklyn Communists. Canning told about seeing several Brooklyn members at a large meeting of the Communist "fraction" in the Teachers Union. The meeting occurred in 1937 at the time that a separate college local was created. He indicated his surprise at how few Brooklyn members Grebanier had named in his public testimony and indicated that he knew of at least ten. He noted that Selsam, Ewen, Slochower, Klein, Morais, White, Belle Zeller, Isadore Pomerance, and Samuel Kaiser were "generally assumed" to be Communists. Almost as an afterthought, he mentioned that he was "morally certain" that Novikoff "was in the know."[45]

Canning's testimony about City College, part of which was corroborated by other witnesses, increased public pressure to move against the Communist teachers. On March 17 the Board of Higher Education resolved "not to retain as a member of the collegiate staff members of any Communist, Fascist or Nazi group or society; or to retain any individual who, or member of any group which, advocates, advises, teaches or practices subversive activities." In addition, the board suspended those named by Canning and began removal proceedings. Those not on academic tenure were dismissed. Morris Schappes, the best-known City College Communist, was dismissed after he was convicted of perjuring himself before the Rapp-Coudert Committee.[46]

As for Brooklyn College, the Board of Higher Education conducted private hearings with a total of fifteen members of the staff. Although no action was taken against the Brooklyn College group during the spring of 1941, three staff named as Communists had left the college before the December hearings (Klein, White, and Milicent Selsam), and three staff resigned while the hearings were in progress (Howard Selsam, Kaiser, and Morais).[47]

Meanwhile, the Rapp-Coudert Committee did not relent in its efforts to induce corroborative testimony about the individuals named by Grebanier. Novikoff was subpoenaed again to appear before the committee on July 1, 1941. The fifty-five-minute session addressed Novikoff's union activity, his attitude toward Germany and Russia, and the *Staff* paper. Again he denied that he was ever a member of the Communist party, that he had used the name of Norwood, or that he had assisted in putting out *Staff*. In response to a request he did not give permission to the committee to send a transcript of the testimony to the Board of Higher Education.[48]

Twice now, under oath, Novikoff had left himself open to a charge of perjury by directly denying his involvement with Communist activities. Like so many of the other Brooklyn Communists, the denials caused Novikoff great discomfort. Although he believed he was forced into his actions by an "illegal" proceeding, he felt a loss of pride and a sense of compromised principles. These feelings became sharper in the 1950s, when invoking the Fifth Amendment emerged as a morally acceptable middle ground between informing on others and untruthful denial. The discomfort of those who perjured themselves in 1941 is reflected by the fact that among former Communists this group has been the most reluctant in later years to talk openly about political activities and affiliations in the 1930s and 1940s.[49]

The Coudert subcommittee continued its activities through 1941. It issued an interim report on December 1, 1941, and a final report on April 23, 1942. In March 1941 the Rapp-Coudert Committee reorganized itself and returned to its original assignment to study financial aid to education in the state of New York. A direct result of the subcommittee's work was that the Board of Higher Education, utilizing revelations contained in public testimony before the subcommittee, ousted twenty persons affiliated with City College. Several others resigned. However, the legal counsel to the Board advised that no charges be brought against Brooklyn College staff. As the subcommittee reported, the board was not in as strong a position in the Brooklyn College situation.

> The Brooklyn College unit was apparently more strictly organized and had fewer defections. As a result, the Committee obtained less evidence concerning the unit, and its exposure of conditions was consequently less complete than in the case of City College. . . . Suffice it to point out that the evidence in the Committee's possession, but not publicly presented, leads the Committee to conclude that the Brooklyn College unit comprised not less than thirty members of the faculty and the administrative staff at the College.

The procedures of the subcommittee required that an individual be named by at least two others before putting such testimony into the public realm. It appears that although Novikoff was named by Grebanier, there was no confirming testimony from other Brooklyn College Communists.[50]

Writing a few years later, a staff member at Brooklyn College observed that "fifteen persons whose names had been publicly listed, plus some who had been investigated in private hearings, remained for many years in a state of limbo on the campus—objects, at once, of suspicion for some of their colleagues, objects of sympathy for others, and centers of attention for all." President Gideonse knew that Communists remained on his faculty and wished to have them removed, but he did not believe he was in a position to take action. According to Novikoff, Gideonse called him into his office one day and told him that he was the only one of the Rapp-Coudert people he wanted to keep. Nevertheless, the accused faculty and the Rapp-Coudert investigators knew that in time someone was likely to come forward and become the second person to name names. Although the onset of World War II brought the Coudert investigation to a halt, many of the faculty looked for a way to leave Brooklyn before the vise closed again.[51]

In many respects the Rapp-Coudert investigation—along with the Dies Committee in 1938 and 1939—laid the groundwork for the anti-Communist crusade of the late 1940s and early 1950s. First, the public naming of alleged Communists was initiated on a broad scale. Second, the committee inspired a two-phase punishment process, whereby the committee named names in public and the Board of Higher Education stepped in to bring ouster proceedings against the accused. Third, the official agencies adhered to a surprisingly rigid requirement that an individual had to be named by two people before the full array of sanctions could be applied. Fourth, affiliation with any kind of Communist activity—whether it was fomenting political dissent on a college campus or plotting to steal atomic secrets for the Soviet Union—was judged to be "subversive" and warranting punishment. Chamberlain's study notes the complete lack of evidence that membership in the Communist party and involvement in its typical activities constituted in themselves subversive activity. Fifth, the Coudert investigation brought the star informer, later a *paid* informer, to the forefront of anticommunism. Grebanier and Canning provided the fuel for sustaining the campaign. Finally, the Rapp-Coudert Committee had the practical legacy of training the personnel and creating the files that were inherited by McCarthy and his allies a few years later. All in all, the investigation established many precedents for the motives and methods of the McCarthy era.[52]

Equally significant was the willingness of those in authority in higher education—board members, presidents, and other administrators—to adopt the mentality and methods of the politicians, even when the sanctity and independence of their institutions were under threat. In the cases of the accused Communists, political criteria replaced educational criteria in making decisions about who should teach in the classrooms of New York City. While political questions were raised previously in New York education, the Rapp-Coudert investigation made political inquisition a matter of public policy. For those concerned about the traditional precepts of academic freedom and committed to the special status of those in our society charged to pursue truth, the Rapp-Coudert period should have raised extreme concern. Whether it was the sudden absorption of the nation in a world war, an obliviousness to the threat to academic freedom, or fear of a public backlash, few educational leaders spoke out forcefully. In due course, the events of 1940 and 1941 slipped from public consciousness. It was the accused and the various authorities of investigation who remembered. There was unfinished business, and in a few years many of the same actors would be back.

Another aspect of the Rapp-Coudert investigation deserves notice. Chamberlain studied the academic credentials of the accused faculty and concluded that the group, with only a few exceptions, displayed outstanding quality and stature.

> . . . the impressive and inescapable fact is that the *only evidence presented by either side* points to: (1) outstanding scholarship, (2) superior teaching, and (3) absence of indoctrination in the classroom . . . their records of training, achievement, and advancement are so impressive that they should raise serious doubts as to the relevancy of party membership. If Party membership made the heavy time demands that committee's informers alleged, and if these people were yet able to compile records of achievement such as those presented, either these people could not be practicing Communists or they were so outstanding that the mere fact of their party membership was of minor importance.

On the basis of what is now known about Novikoff's political activities and his work as a scientist, it seems evident that Novikoff was a prime example of Chamberlain's observation.[53]

An important consequence for Novikoff's future was the accumulation of information about him in the committee's 614 separate files. The committee staff kept topic files (e.g., Brooklyn College, College Teachers Union), transcripts of private and public hearings, correspondence files, and digests of pertinent information. One of the digests, "Summary of Evidence Secured against Individuals Now in the Educational System," contained several hundred entries. Entry 418 included the following information about Novikoff:

ALEXANDER B. NOVIKOFF
3115 Avenue I, Brooklyn
Brooklyn College–Biology Instructor

Listed as Communist suspect by Griffin, formerly of Brooklyn College.

Also listed by Ben Mandel as a communist.

Earl Martin, of Brooklyn College, believes him to be a C.P. member. Member of C.T.U.

Grebanier said that he was chairman of unit, a strong C.P. leader, with party name of Norwood.

Grebanier testified that Novikoff was a contact man between the Y.C.L. and the C.P. unit of the college; that he was active on the Staff; that he attended C.P. meetings at Doris Bernadette's house.

Paul Gipfel testified that a Novikoff discussed questions asked of previous witnesses before coming before the committee.

The files of the committee were sealed in the possession of the New York State Police in the early 1950s, until released to the New York State Archives Library in the 1980s. Long before the release of the files to the library, however, the essence of the files—the accusation of Communist membership—was relayed to other agencies. Eventually, entry 418—the Rapp-Coudert Committee's handy summary—would find its way to the U.S. District Attorney for the Southern District of New York State, the Senate Internal Security Subcommittee in Washington, and the FBI.[54]

Chapter 4

DISENGAGEMENT AND RETREAT

The War Years and the Rise of McCarthyism

The end of the Rapp-Coudert investigation coincided with the full-scale entry of the United States into World War II. A deceptive calm settled on Brooklyn College as it moved from the public eye and as the pressure from the anti-Communists diminished. In other ways, however, the old tensions persisted. President Gideonse remained committed to eradicating Communist influence and kept up the pressure on those accused by the Rapp-Coudert Committee.

One strategy of Gideonse was to take away a major source of Communist support: the students and their organizations. He concluded that the Communists had exploited the "bleak" climate of the college by adjusting their tactics to the interests of the students. Thus, "if they found that a social evening with a guitar and singing folk songs was an effective way of promoting Stalinism, which doesn't have much to do with guitars, well, that's what they do." Gideonse's response was to introduce a highly professional program of student guidance and support. He created a substantial budget line, hired professional counselors, and worked collaboratively with student groups. On educational grounds, these were badly needed steps and did much to bolster the quality of student life outside the classroom. On political grounds, these steps were highly effective in turning students and student organizations away from the Communists.[1]

Gideonse's greatest challenge was in dealing with the Communists who remained on the faculty. He believed that secrecy and "conspiratorial behavior" were destructive to academic life and created "an atmosphere of distrust all over the place as to everybody's motives." In turn, this "skulduggery" produced a demoralized faculty. Although Gideonse had strongly supported the Rapp-Coudert investigation and the effort to dismiss Communist faculty, the changed circumstances softened his stance somewhat. Gideonse was prepared to forgive faculty who "were genuinely now repentant of the conduct they had engaged in. . . . [W]e were not taking a position . . . that anyone who had at one time committed perjury was therefore forever condemned. If I got good and clear conclusive evidence that this was conduct that had taken place in the past but was now regretted and that there was now an open and *bona fide* commitment to a free society, I defended such a person." As a result, an individual's status at the institution depended to a considerable extent on the personal judgment formed by Gideonse. Over several months he met with many of the individuals he knew to be Communist and discussed their situation.[2]

According to Novikoff, Gideonse told him that he was the one faculty member he wanted to keep. Looking back on these events a few years later, Gideonse described a situation that might have pertained to Novikoff. He remembered discovering

> . . . a very brilliant and very young member of our science faculty who undoubtedly and perhaps still was at that time a member of a Commu-nist-related group. . . . And I paid special attention to him because he was very good. Most of these people are not, but he was very good. And as time went on, he convinced me that he had totally broken with this group. . . . I'm not concerned really with the ideas of these people, I'm concerned with their professional conduct. I can accept a member of the staff who is a complete intellectual Marxist.

Another possible subject of this passage was Harry Albaum, Novikoff's friend and fellow biologist. Although Albaum went on to promotions and a deanship at Brooklyn College, he did not have Novikoff's brilliance as a scientist and was not, like Novikoff, a self-professed Marxist. Although the evidence is not conclusive, it appears that Gideonse was referring to Novikoff.[3]

Practical man that he was, Gideonse called on the best source of information about the Communists on campus, Bernard Grebanier. On several occasions Grebanier told Gideonse about the past Communist connections of fellow faculty members. Not surprisingly, Grebanier's life was extremely stressful, exacerbated by continuing acts of derision by students. Although the factual basis for the statement is unclear, he apparently told his classes that he thought Frederic Ewen would push him onto the subway tracks. The most painful repercussion of the period was the breakup of his marriage in 1942 after twenty years.[4]

Ewen, who was initially a good friend of Grebanier's, had a hard time of things too. Although he was recommended annually by his department for promotion to the rank of associate professor, Gideonse always vetoed the promotion. In Ewen's estimation Gideonse was a "son of a bitch." Obviously Ewen never offered the proper acts of repentance. Despite the cloud that loomed over his future, Ewen was a popular teacher and became as well one of the outstanding scholars at the college. He published works of highly regarded literary criticism until well into the 1980s. Because he was forced to leave the college in 1952 during a new investigation, much of his writing was done as an independent scholar. In Grebanier's view Ewen was a "tragic figure" whose career was seriously damaged by his politics.[5]

Although the Brooklyn College Communists were for the time being beyond the reach of legislative committees and the Board of Higher Education, several sought to escape the suspicion that hung over them. Avenues of escape included an enhanced commitment to scholarly accomplishment and reputation, academic positions at other— preferably more prestigious—institutions, and participation in the war effort. Harry Albaum found refuge at the University of Wisconsin.

> I was recruited into the Party sometime around 1939. In 1940, when the Rapp-Coudert investigations came up, I never was called to testify [publicly], but was frightened to death that I might be. I tried to get out at that time, but as I indicated earlier, I was not permitted to. I realized that the only way I could get out of the Party was to break contact with the cell at the college. I therefore sought an outside fellowship, and in 1942 left the campus to accept a National Research Council Fellowship at the University of Wisconsin. That was the point at which I formally broke with the Party.

Albaum interrupted his fellowship to engage in war work at the University of Chicago and at the Edgewood Arsenal in Maryland; he returned to Brooklyn College in 1945.[6]

At about the time that Albaum left for Wisconsin, Novikoff began an attempt to gain a commission in the military. His first application was to the Bureau of Medicine and Surgery of the U.S. Navy. He was notified on October 27, 1942, that there was no opening "for one with your particular qualifications." At the recommendation of the navy's Surgeon General's office, he contacted the Office of Naval Procurement to see whether an opening existed in any other bureau of the navy. He received a standard form letter indicating that his preliminary application for a commission should not be pursued since "your vision does not come up to the minimum requirements" and "all men must be qualified for sea duty." What the navy did not tell Novikoff was that a security review had been undertaken. Documents acquired through Freedom of Information Act procedures reveal that the Office of Naval Intelligence conducted a review in June 1942 and prepared two reports for ONI files. The first stated that "Subject's name appears on a list of persons who are in varying degrees associated or sympathetic with the Communist Party." The second reported that a "confidential informant, Rating A, reports that Subject was a member of the Communist Party in 1938." The report added that "there is nothing to indicate that Subject has ever lost sympathy with the Party or that Subject has left the Party." Copies of these brief reports were transmitted to the FBI and to the Military Intelligence Service. Despite the navy's statements to Novikoff about no openings and poor eyesight, the truth of the matter was that Novikoff's rejection for a commission was a product of a negative security review.[7]

In his naivete Novikoff turned next to the army air forces. On November 12 he received an encouraging letter—actually, an invitation—from the Altitude Training Program. Displaying a tone that suggested that his appointment was an almost certain event, the letter attempted to convince Novikoff of the attractiveness of the work:

> It is realized that the terms of employment may not offer any financial incentive but we believe that by doing this work you will have an opportunity to make an important contribution to the war effort. Much of the work will be routine in character but it will be an excellent opportunity to demonstrate to Air Forces personnel the importance of many physiological considerations in accomplishing effective flight operations. This work would also provide opportunities for imaginative and intellectually aggressive men to do some practical investigative work in the field of aviation physiology.

In his letter the chief of the Research Division of the Air Surgeon's Office asked Novikoff to report for a "final type physical examination" and offered to request a leave of absence on Novikoff's behalf from Brooklyn College. Enthusiastic about the opportunity to apply his scientific expertise to the war effort, Novikoff filed his application for a commission a week later. He arranged with his Brooklyn draft board so that he could be inducted and commissioned during January 1943.[8]

In making application for a commission Novikoff listed the Rapp-Coudert Committee as a reference. On December 18 the Second Service Command at Governors Island, at the direction of the War Department, wrote the Rapp-Coudert Committee to "investigate his references." The letter inquired about Novikoff's "loyalty, integrity and general reputation" and indicated that a phone call would be made to the committee on December 22. Novikoff's motive for listing the Rapp-

Coudert Committee as a reference is unclear. He may have assumed that since there had been no attempt to fire him the committee's assessment would not be negative. More likely he assumed that the army would hear about his problems and would contact the committee anyway, so it made sense to present the impression that he had nothing to hide. In any event, the army's communications with the Rapp-Coudert Committee had immediate consequences for Novikoff's efforts to gain a commission.[9]

According to military intelligence files, a representative of the Second Service Advisory Board, a Colonel Cosby, learned of Novikoff's Communist background from the Rapp-Coudert committee. He then interviewed two of Novikoff's references, both colleagues at Brooklyn College, who vouched for "his outstanding qualifications as a teacher, research worker, and also his ability as a scientist" and indicated that his "loyalty could not be questioned." The investigator interviewed a Brooklyn College administrator, probably Gideonse, who stated that after the Rapp-Coudert proceedings Novikoff "settled down and was a good teacher." As things developed, the Rapp-Coudert information was much more influential than the testimony of Novikoff's colleagues.[10]

Meanwhile, Novikoff learned on January 12 that his draft board had notified the headquarters of the Army Air Corps that he was scheduled for induction on January 27. The draft board wanted to know whether his application would be processed by January 18, the date his orders for induction were to be mailed. On the day he was due to be inducted he received a jolt. Instead of his commission, Novikoff received a letter from the War Department that stated that "no appropriate vacancy could be found for your assignment." The letter went on to say that "the existence of a suitable vacancy and recommendation by a chief of branch are requisites for appointment."[11]

This was a disturbing and demoralizing turn of events. For one thing, the dashing of his hopes at the last moment was difficult to absorb. Of greater consequence for the long term, it raised for the first time the nagging fear that his political troubles would have a serious effect on his reputation and his prospects. He now suspected that more was at issue than the objective review of his qualifications. After a flurry of phone calls and consultations, Novikoff went to Washington to find out what had happened. He learned from an officer of the Army Air Corps that the commission was denied on the recommendation of Army Intelligence. "From what he said, it appeared to me that my activities in the Teachers Union, as related by one person (probably my Department Chairperson), were the basis for this recommendation.

After a long and pleasant conference, Captain West agreed to reconsider the application if I were to get one or two other persons to write him concerning the matter." At Novikoff's request, letters were sent on February 9 to the Army Air Corps headquarters by L. G. Barth of the Columbia University zoology department, his Ph.D. advisor, and by Harry Carman, professor of history at Columbia and a member of the New York City Board of Higher Education. Professor Carman's laudatory testimony attempted to explain Novikoff's reputation as a radical.

> I have known Dr. Novikoff for a number of years and hold him in high regard. On the basis of his character he is A-1. As you may know, he is very presentable in personal appearance, is cooperative and high-minded. He is outstanding in his chosen profession and is a frequent contributor to learned journals dealing with biology. While a loyal person, he is no yes-yes man. He does his own thinking, is a person of high principle, and sticks to his principles. Largely because of this fact he has very wrongly been labelled a radical. As a member of the Board of Higher Education of the City of New York which has jurisdiction over Brooklyn College, and as a member of the Conduct Committee of that Board which is particularly charged with the conduct of members of the staff, I am in a position to know that Dr. Novikoff is a loyal, conscientious citizen. Were he otherwise he would have been proceeded against by the Rapp-Coudert Committee of the State of New York and the Conduct Committee of the Board of Education long before this. Mere membership in a teacher's union should in no way count to his discredit.

Although Carman's letter glossed over the fact that being named by a second witness would have initiated removal proceedings against Novikoff, the letter nevertheless was a very strong endorsement of Novikoff by a prominent, respected New York educator. At this point, faced with conflicting information from two politically well-connected sources (the Rapp-Coudert Committee and Carman), the army determined that it needed to make very sure it was taking the right action in the Novikoff case. A special agent of the Counter-Intelligence Corps (CIC), a special branch of Military Intelligence, was assigned to make a further investigation.[12]

Until he went to Washington, Novikoff did not realize the degree to which the military took an interest in national security issues on the domestic front. His lack of knowledge was probably typical of most Americans at the time. Over the previous twenty-five years the military had established and legitimized its role in domestic intelligence. The first director of the Military Intelligence Division, Colonel Ralph H. Van Deman, moved the army into alliance not only with federal agencies but with private networks, such as the American Protective

League, bent on combating any form of "un-American" activity. Van Deman, later made a major general, accumulated extensive records on alleged subversives, even after he left the military in 1929. His private files on subversives, which were legendary in the intelligence community, drew on information from federal agencies as well as his own agents. When he died in 1952, his files went to the army and later to the Senate Internal Security Committee. Van Deman's legacy included a sophisticated intelligence operation as well as military involvement in monitoring domestic political activities.[13]

Army G-2, the military intelligence branch, was active during the tumultuous Depression years and then strengthened its role during World War II. Wire taps, surveillance, and the use of informers were standard practice at the time that questions were raised about Novikoff's past. Thus, when Special Agent Smith of the CIC set out to assess the loyalty of Novikoff, he was operating in well-charted territory. His first move was to contact Colonel Cosby, who had conducted the first review. Cosby relayed his findings, including the judgment that the supportive recommendations of Novikoff should be looked at skeptically because "Brooklyn College is known to be a cell for spreading communism, as is Columbia University." Smith visited the Rapp-Coudert Committee and looked closely at Grebanier's testimony about Novikoff. In a memorandum to his supervisor he concluded that the "information obtained from the Coudert Committee is reliable." With the army operating from the premise that affiliation with the Communist party, no matter what the nature of the circumstances, was evidence of disloyalty, the conclusion of the investigation was in little doubt. On March 16, 1943, Novikoff received a letter from the air corps informing him that "information furnished this office by Military Intelligence Service precludes favorable action on your application for commission."[14]

Despite his failure to gain a commission, Novikoff resumed his attempt to join the war effort following spring semester classes in 1943. He volunteered for unpaid full-time work on a project sponsored by the Office of Scientific Research and Development at the Aviation Research Laboratory at Columbia University. Novikoff played a prominent role in the project during the summer, and on September 1 he began to draw a half-time salary for his work. He continued his full schedule of classes at Brooklyn College. On September 28 his work was brought to a sudden halt when he was told that he was not approved for employment on the project and that his connections with the project were terminated. On the same day he learned that his name would be removed from the list of authors of a report that had been accepted for publication. He had participated as a member of the research team and as an author of the report. Novikoff sent off letters requesting an explanation, including one to the executive secretary of the Office of Scientific Research and Development. The executive secretary's response provided no information whatsoever: "The contract involved is confidential in character and accordingly it would not be appropriate for me to correspond with you concerning any aspect of it." As a last resort Novikoff wrote Kirtley Mather, a Harvard professor and chairman of the American Association for the Advancement of Science. Mather and Novikoff had worked together on progressive causes, including work for the American Association of Scientific Workers. Mather's inquiries brought Novikoff the following information:

> You certainly have been up against it! Evidently your entire difficulty arises with the Military Intelligence Service, and that is the hardest of all nuts to crack. I am reminded of the insistence of federal investigators upon knowing whether or not certain of my colleagues who were under consideration for governmental appointments had been sympathetic to the Spanish Loyalists during the Spanish Civil War. If so, a heavy black mark was evidently placed against their names, despite the fact that everybody now knows the consequences of our official policy with regard to Spain.

In a final lament Novikoff indicated to Mather that he found it "hard to believe that they would approve taking my name off the list of authors of a paper I helped write, even if they should not agree to put me back on the project." Faced with government intransigence, Novikoff let the matter drop.[15]

After all of his efforts to gain a commission, the final insult to Novikoff was that he was called for induction into the regular army. On October 27, 1943, he was examined by doctors at the induction center in New York and was found unfit for military duty. According to documents obtained through the Freedom of Information Act, three neuropsychiatrists examined Novikoff and concluded that he was "afflicted with psychoneurosis severe." Army records included the following information:

> The examination . . . reflected that the registrant was the victim of sexual maladjustment since early manhood as a result of which he never had complete sexual satisfaction. This fact created a feeling of insecurity which became a great influence in his life, causing him to worry over family and public relationships. This subject's feeling of insecurity gave rise occasionally to ideas of suicide. The physicians recommended rejection of NOVIKOFF because in their opinion the Army offered too many opportunities for vicarious emotional outlets.

The medical file also included a letter, dated October 19, from Novikoff's physician indicating that Novikoff had been under his care for six months for treatments to "overcome psychoneurosis." Although it is possible that Novikoff had serious psychological problems at this time, these documents are the only evidence of this condition unearthed by this research. In any event, a confidential informant of the FBI questioned the medical judgment and brought his doubts to the FBI's New York field office.[16]

The FBI was aware that "a number have malingered by feigning psychoneurosis to avoid induction." Thus, an investigation was undertaken to determine whether Novikoff should be prosecuted for having made false statements to the army. The subsequent report, which was twenty-one pages in length, went well beyond the immediate charge and reviewed Novikoff's problems with the Rapp-Coudert Committee, his failed attempts to attain a commission, and recent reports of several confidential informants. The report drew extensively on earlier FBI inquiries about Novikoff. As for the matter at hand, the FBI concluded that a prosecution might be called for and took the findings of the investigation to an Assistant U.S. Attorney in New York City. The Assistant U.S. Attorney concluded that "no further investigation should be conducted in this matter inasmuch as the original determination of the reputable neuropsychiatrists had been verified and inasmuch as one of those physicians had determined that his original conclusion should not be changed merely because of the additional information developed." FBI documents do not disclose whether the other two doctors were ready to revise their opinions about Novikoff's psychological condition. If Novikoff had known of these events, we can be sure that he would have been grateful for the professional ethics of the third doctor. The summary result of the investigation was that Novikoff avoided induction as an army private and averted prosecution on the grounds of perjury.[17]

Unfortunately, the paper work that resulted from Novikoff's interactions with the military raised new questions about his loyalty to his country. With agent reports in hand from ONI, the army, and the FBI and apparent evidence of "communist tendencies," the FBI decided to undertake a full field investigation. The FBI's investigation was in keeping with a program going back to at least 1936. Director J. Edgar Hoover had developed an emergency detention program to deal with the "grave danger" represented by subversives at the time of a national emergency. The core of the program was the indexing of persons and groups such as "known espionage agents, known saboteurs, leading members of the Communist Party, and the bund." As Athan Theoharis demonstrates convincingly in his book on domestic political surveillance, *Spying on Americans*, the standards used to identify dangerous persons loosened considerably at the outbreak of the war. On September 2, 1939, Hoover directed his special agents to prepare reports on persons "whose interest may be directed primarily to the interest of some other nation than the United States." The FBI looked for persons with German, Italian, and Communist sympathies, subscribers to suspect newspapers, members of suspect organizations, and subjects of agent reports. Of course, as world affairs evolved, Japanese and Russians were targeted also. The Custodial Detention Index included two broad classifications: persons who should be detained immediately at the outbreak of war and persons who should be watched carefully but had not yet demonstrated that they were dangerous. The unreliability of the information in the Index and its questionable statutory basis led in July 1943 to an order from the U.S. Attorney General to eliminate the Index. Hoover merely renamed it the Security Index, told his agents to keep its existence confidential, and proceeded on a similar course.[18]

The FBI had sufficient information in its files to suspect that Novikoff was a candidate for the Index. The FBI investigation that began in 1943 was carried out over two years and drew on informants, drop-in visits, phone inquiries, and liaison with other agencies. In February 1945 Novikoff was placed on the Security Index. This meant that in the event of hostilities with the Soviet Union he was a prime suspect for arrest. It meant also that America's primary agency of internal security, after a comprehensive investigation, had designated Novikoff a "security risk." The label was unofficial because there was no statutory basis for the Index (indeed, it had been expressly forbidden), but the label had practical consequences. The FBI was the central repository of security information about American citizens, and other agencies and organizations looked to Hoover's FBI for guidance. Whether out of fear of the FBI's power or respect for its professionalism, the FBI's files and classifications had considerable influence over decisions made elsewhere. In Novikoff's case the next few years would demonstrate the accuracy of this observation.[19]

For the first time Novikoff had faced a direct consequence of his entanglement with the authorities in New York State. The Rapp-Coudert episode led to new allegations, investigations, and documents linking him to Communist activities, and this information was in Washington's files. Although it is difficult to see how Novikoff's political activities were dangerous to the security of the United States, his military career died aborning. During the remainder of the war the disappointed Novikoff carried out his teaching and research responsibilities at Brooklyn College.

SCIENTIFIC AND POLITICAL ACTIVITIES

From 1936 to his death in 1987, Novikoff authored or co-authored almost three hundred scientific publications. The only gap over this fifty-year span was the war years 1941 to 1944. As we have seen, his publications up to 1940—nine articles in respected journals—marked him as a promising young scientist. On the face of it, the four-year hiatus during the war is startling. Journals were still publishing, and professors remaining on campuses continued to conduct research and write. With his political problems in New York and Washington and his setback on the Columbia project, it is possible that his verve as a scholar lagged during the period, which under any circumstances is a dangerous development for a research scientist. It appears, however, that the gap was only in published work, the finished product of the scholarly enterprise. During the war years he continued to teach and do laboratory research, though at a reduced level. Equally important, he began an important period of cogitation about conceptual issues pertaining to the field of biology.[20]

By 1945 Novikoff was ready to publish the outcomes of a remarkable period of thinking. Indeed, it was thinking that ranged well beyond the limits of laboratory science and into the realms of philosophy and metaphysics. The March 2 edition of the prestigious journal *Science* contained an article by Novikoff entitled "The Concept of Integrative Levels and Biology." His conception of integrated levels ("the evolution of matter through successive and higher orders of complexity and integration") was the special contribution of the article, but it is sufficient to know that overall he described a modern scientific view of evolution. In so doing Novikoff dismissed explanations of evolution resting on "volitional or purposive" behavior or other such "mystical" attributions of causation. The fundamentally humanistic orientation of his thinking is indicated by his rejection of the thesis that "man's biology decides his social behavior" and of the idea that the "ruthless oppression of certain groups of people is justified because these groups are for all times fixed as 'inferior' by their biology." Significantly, his acceptance of both the biological and social dimensions of evolution helps explain how, and why, Novikoff could be a man of both science and politics: "A sharp separation of the two levels—biological and social—must precede a fruitful discussion of how man's society can be kept free and democratic. That discussion must be based on a study, by means appropriate to the level, of the social forces making for change. Only a scientific analysis of these forces will enable man to speed social progress." He was a Marxist in the broadest sense of the term. At the heart of things, his rigorous standards for discovering scientific truth were consistent with the Marxist attempt at an "objective" analysis of society. Moreover, Novikoff saw in Marxism the idea that society is perfectible; likewise, he saw a rationale for taking political action. Philosophically, then, the biological and the social dimensions, which he interpreted in Marxist terms, were easily accommodated in his thinking.[21]

Since good writing is as important to biologists as it is to other researchers, it is relevant to note that the essay was clearly and succinctly written and forceful in its logic. It was also, as it turned out, provocative. *Science* printed a critique of the article by two scientists, and Novikoff followed in a succeeding issue with a rebuttal entitled "Continuity and Discontinuity." The highly erudite journal *ETC.: A Review of General Semantics* thought well enough of the essay to reprint it for its audience. All in all, the article was a significant achievement for Novikoff. He received a glowing letter of praise from the secretary of the American Association for the Advancement of Science, who said that the article was "written so soundly and so well" that he wondered whether Novikoff would contribute to another journal. The wide circulation of *Science* reached an important audience. The essay enhanced the reputation of Brooklyn College, which was still struggling to gain a foothold in the academic world.[22]

Novikoff's other publication in 1945 was equally intriguing. In April 1945 he contracted to publish a manuscript about evolution for a children's audience. The book, entitled *Climbing Our Family Tree*, was published by International Publishers, which for many years was a vehicle for Communist-inspired works and was managed by Alexander Trachtenberg. Trachtenberg had been active in left-wing politics since 1906 and became a Communist in the 1920s. The book was written in an engaging manner and was superbly illustrated. Intended for those twelve years old and older, the book evoked the drama and excitement of evolution:

> With their furry bodies and long flat noses, these small new creatures looked like a cross between a dog and a lizard. They were not well suited to life in the swamps, so at first they did not prosper. . . . These little animals could hardly compete for existence with the mighty dinosaurs. . . . But then the great change came. It was these creatures—called *mammals*—who survived and the dinosaurs who died out. Their

fur and their warm blood protected them when the cold winds blew. Because they had better developed brains and sense organs, they were cleverer at finding food after the swamps dried up.

The book brought enthusiastic reviews from several scientific journals as well as *The New York Times, The New York Herald Tribune,* and the *Saturday Review of Literature.* President Gideonse at Brooklyn College wrote with congratulations on "an altogether delightful publication." Henry Carman, the dean of Columbia College who had supported Novikoff's application for a commission in the military, sent his compliments. One of the book's reviewers, Bentley Glass, later played an important role on behalf of the American Association of University Professors when that organization looked into Novikoff's firing from the University of Vermont. Glass, a prominent biologist at Johns Hopkins University, wrote his review for the *Quarterly Review of Biology*: "It would indeed be difficult to praise such a book as this account of evolution for the ten or twelve year old too highly, particularly since there has been nothing of its kind before. . . . The author is hereby nominated for the award given for the best children's book of the year." In November 1945 Novikoff was invited by the New York Public Library to attend its thirty-fifth annual exhibit of children's books, which displayed Novikoff's work as one of the books of the year.[23]

International Publishers issued Novikoff's second children's book, *From Head to Foot,* in 1946. The book was an introduction to anatomy and physiology and also received enthusiastic reviews. Glass nominated this book too for the award of children's book of the year. Novikoff's turn to scientific writing for children was successful but shortlived. Although several publishers over the next five years tried to get him to do more writing of this kind, he did not again try his hand. Not only did this form of writing fail to provide much income, but he realized that his future in the academic world depended on writing for the scholarly journals in his field. Returning to more conventional avenues, Harry Albaum, Maurice Ogur, and he published two scientific articles during 1946. These articles reported investigations of chemical processes in the developing chick embryo.[24]

While continuing to teach at Brooklyn College, Novikoff took on additional teaching responsibilities from 1944 to 1946 at the Jefferson School of Social Science. His connection to the Jefferson School (and with International Publishers) indicates that despite his brush with authorities he was not reluctant to associate with suspect organizations. The director of the school was Howard Selsam, who had been fired after the Rapp-Coudert investigation. Government investigators considered the school a "communist training school" and in 1947 listed it on the Attorney General's list of organizations judged to be "Totalitarian, Fascist, Communist, or Subversive." Its ideological bent was suggested by this excerpt from its 1944 catalog of courses: "Forged out of the people's war has come a weapon as important as plane and gun, food and factory. The classroom and public forum, the book and pamphlet, the radio and town meeting have become mass weapons against fascism. These critical times have emphasized the need for education." A House committee concluded that the Jefferson School offered courses "which were designed to soften up and condition the students and to develop prospective material for training as hard-core Communists."[25]

A careful inspection of the school's course offerings, however, reveals that the curriculum looked much like the educational program of today's adult or continuing education center. The courses were offered at night and ran the gamut from the humanities to the sciences, with course titles similar to any typical course. The popularity of the school is suggested by the fact that an astonishing fourteen thousand students took courses in the nine-story building in lower Manhattan during 1946 and 1947. Novikoff's two courses were listed in the catalog as "Introductory Biology: The Nature of Living Things" and "The Origin and Evolution of Life." The courses were featured prominently in advertisements for the school in the *Daily Worker.* In addition to his teaching, Novikoff was a prominent speaker at a book fair at the school in November 1945. The *Daily Worker* commended the talk and noted his comment that one could find excellent children's books "in the Soviet examples." Except for Novikoff's presentation of an "objective" view of evolution (and rejection of divine intervention), there was little of a controversial or suspicious nature in his courses at the Jefferson School. Despite this fact, his affiliation with the place would become in 1953 a source of damaging accusations.[26]

During these years Novikoff allied himself with various progressive organizations, including the American Association of Scientific Workers and the National Council of Scientific, Professional, Art and White Collar Organizations. These groups lobbied for higher wages at a time when several strikes were in progress. On March 2, 1946, Novikoff was a featured speaker at the Tenth Annual Educational Conference of Local 555 of the Teachers Union, a CIO affiliate. U.S. Representative Helen Gahagan Douglas, later to lose to Richard Nixon in a bitter senatorial campaign, was the keynote speaker. Novikoff spoke in a session on "Teaching Science for the Atomic Age."[27]

It is apparent that Novikoff continued to associate with leftist organizations and causes during the years after the Rapp-Coudert investigation. An important question pertains to his involvement with the Communist party. He stated that he separated from the Party in "approximately 1945." If this is indeed the case, it is interesting to surmise what the nature of his Party activities were between 1941 and 1945. Moreover, since he wanted badly to gain a commission in the military and to keep his job at Brooklyn College, one wonders why he stayed in the Party and risked unpleasant consequences. Unfortunately, there is little information available to help answer these questions. Perhaps then, the more pertinent question is why he chose to leave the Party when he did. Here too the information is sketchy but there are some clues.[28]

Oscar Shaftel, Novikoff's brother-in-law and a former Party member at Queens College, suggested that the changed political environment and new professional goals influenced Novikoff to separate from the Party. Indeed, as time went on, the nature of the progressive struggle changed, especially as the political environment on campus became less vulnerable to Communist initiatives. In contrast to its experience in the turbulent 1930s, Brooklyn College settled into its own "cold war," pitting the conservative leadership against a weaker and quieter radical element. Consequently, the Party was a less active and less potent force for change, and for a person like Novikoff this eliminated much of the appeal. On the wider front, there was no escaping the fact that the American Communist party was tied to Stalin's brutal policies of repression. Still, Novikoff did not, like Grebanier, leave the Party in a burst of self-righteous indignation. Rather, the Party gradually lost its priority, and Novikoff drifted away to different involvements. Politically, he stayed close to the Party through the Jefferson School, International Publishers, and progressive scientific organizations, but after 1946 the Party was no longer a focal point of his life. More and more, his absorbing involvement was his work as a scientist.[29]

The critical development on this score was his decision to follow in Albaum's steps and accept a one-year fellowship in cancer research at the University of Wisconsin. Funded by the American Cancer Society, he spent the 1946–1947 school year in Wisconsin. During his sojourn there—the longest time he had ever spent away from New York City—he reconsidered his personal priorities, especially his commitment to political activities: "This separation from any of these activities occurred slowly. It didn't occur all at once and it occurred before I took my job here [at the University of Vermont]. I would say that the most important single factor was the experience at Wisconsin where I was in a new life entirely, and I decided that this was the kind of life I would like to have, if I could have that choice." A "new life" devoted to science appealed to him because he knew that his troubles in New York City were not over. He feared that the testimony against him might lead ultimately to his dismissal and that "my days at Brooklyn College were numbered." Thus, the year at Wisconsin not only expanded his horizons as a scientist but opened up the possibility of taking permanent leave from New York.[30]

RETREAT FROM NEW YORK

Novikoff's work in Wisconsin marked his first serious commitment to cancer research. Working with Professor Van R. Potter, he produced five scientific papers reporting laboratory investigations of cellular processes in the chick embryo and the liver of the rat. The *Journal of Biological Chemistry* and *Cancer Research* published the findings. During this productive year of scientific work the Novikoff's first child, Kenneth, was born.[31]

Another undertaking was his work as a consultant to the Armed Forces Institute of Pathology on the production of two films on enzymes and on carbohydrate metabolism. After all of his troubles during the war, the military had finally called on his talents. He continued his work until October 3, 1949, when he wrote a letter of resignation to the commanding officer of the Institute: "I have been hoping that the serious illness of my young son would improve sufficiently to permit the continuation of my extra-curricular work. But his condition has been steadily deteriorating. In addition, my responsibilities here at the College of Medicine have been continually increased." Both statements about his personal situation were accurate. His son Kenneth had developed a serious case of chronic nephrosis, which at that time had no known cure. Novikoff faced the terrible prospect of watching his son slowly die of the disease. Also, his work had grown in significance and quantity. What this letter didn't say, however, was that in May 1948 the Civil Service Commission, aware of his employment with the military, requested the FBI to investigate Novikoff's loyalty. In his letter to J. Edgar Hoover, the chief of the Investigations Division of the Civil Service Commission, James E. Hatcher, described Novikoff's work with the army and reported that during the investigation of another person Novikoff was "reported to be a Communist." In July the FBI initiated a "full field loyalty investigation," which they curtailed in August because they found that Novikoff was employed at the University of Wisconsin and not by the army. Hatcher wrote again in December to report that in fact Novikoff was employed by the army at $40 per day on a "when actually employed basis." He argued that "his case is one which falls within the incumbent phase of the Federal Employees Loyalty Program." This time the FBI carried out a complete investigation, and in early fall 1949 reported its derogatory findings to the Civil Service Commission. On September 30, 1949, four days *before* his letter of resignation, the army terminated Novikoff's appointment on the film project.[32]

The correspondence that followed Novikoff's resignation included a commendation from the commanding officer of the Institute of Pathology, General Raymond Dart, who stated that he regretted that Novikoff's "splendid contribution" would come to an end. He expressed his distress about the illness of Novikoff's son. The chief of the Medical Illustration Service was equally complimentary. Available documents do not explain the curious discrepancy between the dismissal and this correspondence. Influenced perhaps by the exemplary quality of Novikoff's work on the films, it seems likely that the army decided to offer Novikoff the face-saving option of resigning. There is no doubt, however, that Novikoff was fired. The army reported this fact to the FBI on November 2 and again on December 14 under the heading, "Disposition of Subversive and Disaffected Personnel." Novikoff's contributions to the film project demonstrate, as did his children's books, his ability to translate scientific information for a wide audience. Unfortunately for his career, the episode demonstrates also the impossibility of evading the attention of security-minded investigators in Washington. He would learn again and again that he was a marked man.[33]

Unaware of how his work on the film project would end but buoyed by his exciting research with Potter at Wisconsin, Novikoff returned to Brooklyn College for the 1947–1948 academic year. In early 1948, on the recommendation of Potter, he was approached by the University of Vermont about a position in the Medical College. Vermont was seeking a researcher to begin work in its Cancer Research Laboratory in the fall of 1948. Novikoff communicated his interest in the position and agreed to prepare his papers for review by the faculty in Vermont. The credentials that Novikoff presented to the chairman of the department of pathology included eighteen scholarly papers, several years of research at Woods Hole, Massachusetts, membership in several scholarly associations, the army film project, and a recently awarded grant from the American Cancer Society. The new grant was scheduled to run for a year beginning in July 1948 and would include summer research at the prestigious Biological Laboratory at Cold Spring Harbor on Long Island.[34]

Novikoff was invited for an interview in Vermont, where he met with the department chairman, Bjarne Pearson, and the dynamic new dean of the Medical College, William Brown. The Medical College at that time was small, with a dozen full-time faculty members, and Brown was intent on building up the research program of the school. The credentials that Novikoff presented responded nicely to this goal.[35]

During his visit to the Medical College he was spotted by an old acquaintance from his political days in New York. Arnold Schein, a faculty member in biochemistry, had worked in New York during the early 1940s and was a member of the American Association of Scientific Workers. Schein and Novikoff met when both became officers of the organization. According to Schein's recollection, Novikoff was "already famous as a fabulous biology teacher at Brooklyn College," and Schein's wife remembered him as one of her best teachers. During Novikoff's visit to Vermont, Schein happened to pass a laboratory room and recognized Alex. Over the next few days he "enthusiastically praised" Novikoff to the Vermont staff and urged him to take the position.[36]

Before Novikoff departed from Vermont, he was offered the position, and he decided he wanted to take it. He knew, however, that his wife, Rosalind, was apprehensive about the move. Fortunately, Schein was going to New York on business, and he visited Rosalind and helped persuade her that Vermont was a good place to raise a family. Once the decision was made, Novikoff wrote his new chairman, Pearson, indicating that "I am confident that our association will be a happy one for both of us." Schein found an apartment for the Novikoffs, and they moved to Vermont in August 1948. Just five years later Novikoff's association with Pearson deteriorated, and Schein became his most vocal defender before the University of Vermont board of trustees.[37]

Novikoff was hired as a professor of experimental pathology in the Medical College and as an associate in the Cancer Research Laboratory. He brought his $6,000 American Cancer Society grant to Vermont and with the assistance of several lab technicians set up a laboratory in a Quonset hut on campus. In short order he settled comfortably into his teaching and research and into the community life of Burlington. In the years between 1948 and 1953 Novikoff's work received regular support from the American Cancer Society ($5,000 annual awards) and the Medical College's cancer research program received recognition on the national and local fronts. A lengthy article in the *Vermont Sunday News* on May 1, 1949, prominently displayed a picture of Novikoff and noted that he was the "right hand man" to Bjarne Pearson, chairman of the pathology department and director of the lab. His new grants were regularly reported in the *Burlington Free Press*. An American

Cancer Society certificate of recognition for his research endeavors was presented to Novikoff at a statewide cancer symposium in April 1951. Speeches by Novikoff were subjects of news stories, including a speech to the Disabled Veterans Auxiliary. Nationally, he spoke at various professional meetings, including those of the Histochemical Society, the American Association for Cancer Research, and the Biological Laboratory at Cold Spring Harbor.[38]

Despite Kenneth's continuing struggle with his disease and Novikoff's run-in with army security in 1949, these were happy and satisfying years. A second son, Larry, was born to good health. Alex and Rosalind socialized to a limited extent, usually with Medical College colleagues, and neither wished to do more. Mainly, his life revolved around his work. According to his associates, he radiated enthusiasm and single-mindedness in his research and teaching. He gave his time generously to his students, who respected his gift for visualizing pathology as a dynamic process. Schein found that he "had no weaknesses as a scientist and turned out to be a great one." He published seventeen papers between 1949 and 1952.[39]

Unquestionably, he was a dynamic person with a strong belief in his ability as a scientist. As might be expected, a few individuals were made uncomfortable by the strength of his personality and perceived a self-centeredness in his actions. On occasion, he was sharp-tongued and ill-mannered with colleagues and family. Indeed, there is no doubt that he overpowered the quiet, pleasant Rosalind. However, Alex and Rosalind were in agreement on one area of life: child-raising. According to Schein, they

> . . . tried to outdo each other in permissiveness. . . . The children were being raised by modern methods which meant talking them to death when what they needed were a few swift whacks. A more unruly, selfish, loud, demanding, misbehaving pair of brats can't be imagined. . . . All this the Novikoffs endured with superhuman patience. We and others simply had to withdraw our kids as their playmates.

The Novikoffs' permissiveness may have resulted from the deep pain they felt for Kenny. He fell more seriously ill in 1952, as his body filled with fluids and his body weight went up thirty pounds. Periodically, he had to be punctured in order to release the pressure. For two years Alex searched frantically around the country for a medical treatment with some hope. Finally, he found a center in New York City that was experimenting with the use of cortisone. The treatment worked, and Kenny gradually pulled away from mortal danger.[40]

Thus, by 1952 Novikoff was firmly established in Burlington. He had acquired several close professional and personal acquaintances. His work was proceeding successfully, and he had been made a full professor with tenure. A job as a consultant on a cancer project at nearby St. Michael's College and a four-part series on the university's cancer program, published in the *Burlington Free Press,* served to reinforce his reputation. From all appearances, he had escaped the political controversies of Brooklyn College and the lingering suspicions of authorities in New York State. We know, however, that the ground was shaky. America was moving into the darkest chapter of the McCarthy era. The fear of Communism was rising, and before long committees would begin to call witnesses to Washington.[41]

A warning to Novikoff of his vulnerability occurred in April 1952 when he received a letter from the New York district office of the Immigration and Naturalization Service, an arm of the U.S. Department of Justice. The letter, which was stamped with the signature of the acting chief of the Investigations Section, requested that Novikoff appear at the district office in New York City on April 16 "in connection with an official matter." Novikoff went to New York and met with an Inspector Kent, who indicated that Novikoff's name had been given to the Investigations Section and they wanted to know about Novikoff's citizenship. Novikoff explained that he had "derivative citizenship" through his father, who had been naturalized as a U.S. citizen in 1918. He mentioned that he had his father's citizenship papers and his passport. He described the circumstances of his arrival from Russia in 1913, noting that he had forgotten the name of the ship. Inspector Kent asked whether Novikoff was a member of the American Association of Scientific Workers. Novikoff, who made notes on the meeting, recorded the following: "I asked why he was asking. Reply—We want to know if you are the person reported to us. I then said, 'Yes, I was a member.' He said that was all. Since I was a citizen I did not fall under their jurisdiction." Since the American Association of Scientific Workers was thought by government authorities to be a Communist-front organization, it is apparent that the purpose for calling in Novikoff pertained to his alleged Communist background. In any event, he did not hear again from the Immigration and Naturalization Service.[42]

Despite his newly found prosperity and comfort, Novikoff began to watch events in Washington and New York with increasing trepidation. His security rested on the continuing steadfastness of the suspected faculty at Brooklyn College. No one could be sure that the feared second witness would not come forward.

THE McCARTHY ERA DESCENDS ON HIGHER EDUCATION

Novikoff's life in Vermont was influenced to a significant extent by political events on the national front. Three interrelated developments were significant: the rise of McCarthyism in national politics, the actions of state legislatures and governors to combat communism, and the actions of the higher-education community to accommodate the national mood. In each of these areas there was a pervasive sense of urgency, reinforced by—and symbolized by—the actions and rhetoric of Senator Joe McCarthy.

Joseph McCarthy emerged as the leading figure in America's fight against communism after his famous speech in Wheeling, West Virginia, in February 1950. His message, his methods, and the forces that he released were soon identified as "McCarthyism," a term of esteem for the right wing and a term of revulsion for liberals. Although the McCarthy era cannot be separated from the man who symbolized it, aggressive anticommunism had a deep legacy in American politics. Various arms of government had been investigating alleged subversive activities since 1919, and at the national level the Dies Committee provided the prewar prototype for the modus operandi of the McCarthy years. Then, with the end of World War II, a series of events returned the Communist "bogey" to center stage and provided the circumstances that McCarthy exploited so deftly.[43]

In a shift that has dictated the course of national as well as international politics for over forty years, the United States and the Soviet Union locked themselves into cold war in the months after the defeat of Nazi Germany. Aided by the crumbling of Eastern Europe before the Soviet military might and by the ready charge of "appeasement" against the Democrats, the Republicans made significant headway in the 1946 off-year elections. The Republicans won fifty-four House and eleven Senate seats and gained control of Congress for the first time since 1928. The "Class of 1946" brought conservatives such as Richard Nixon and William Knowland of California and William Jenner of Indiana to Washington. As one scholar of the period observed:

> They were determined to rid the government of Communists, perverts, and New Dealers, get tough with Joe Stalin, crack down on labor unions, and dismantle the Office of Price Administration. Some observers compared them to small-town rotarians; others joked about the resurrection of Calvin Coolidge. But all agreed that it was quite some time since this many like-minded conservatives had massed at the capital gates.

Although his politics were not yet sharply defined, Joe McCarthy was elected also. He used the communism issue against his Democratic opponent, Howard McMurray, which was in keeping with many other Republican campaigns. The prominence of the anticommunism issue notwithstanding, it appears that McCarthy won primarily because of his prodigious appetite for campaigning, which was especially important in his primary run against Wisconsin's senior senator, Robert LaFollette, Jr., and because he was fortunate enough to be running in an overwhelming Republican year.[44]

While McCarthy rambled forth into the Senate, oblivious to Senate rules and customs and looking for issues that would move him into the limelight, outside developments created the conditions for his later prominence. The linking in the public mind of the perceived Russian threat to the evils of communism had an immense impact on American politics and shaped the perspective with which Americans interpreted issues and events. Communism—any form of communism, domestic or international—was linked with a Russian threat to national security. As a result, it is difficult to exaggerate the extent to which anticommunism consumed the attention of both parties and the time of legislators during McCarthy's first term in the Senate. At the start, the assertions of the Dies Committee about Communist infiltration of government, labor, and education were returned to center stage. Legislators were well aware of *Appendix Nine,* which was the 1944 Dies Committee listing of almost twenty-two thousand Communist "fellow travelers." As Congress got serious about finding Communists in government after 1946, investigatory committees relied extensively on the prewar spadework of Dies and his colleagues.[45]

During 1945 and 1946 the anticommunism issue was fueled by the discovery of classified documents in the offices of *Amerasia* magazine and by the charges of espionage against six persons affiliated with the journal. The disposition of the case by the Justice Department brought a congressional investigation. Among the thirty-five projected investigations of Democratic "abuses" following the 1946 elections, one of the most important was a probe of the Department of State by a House appropriations subcommittee. The State Department permitted a team of congressional investigators to examine the loyalty files of the Department. The so-called Lee List contained information on 108 suspect individuals and was printed as an appendix to a congressional report in 1950. Meanwhile, the House Committee on Un-American Activities (HUAC), benefiting from the energy and skills of Richard Nixon, carried out investigations of communism in the labor unions and in Hollywood. Shifting its sights to government, the committee wrangled with the Truman administration over congressional access to the confidential loyalty files of employees of the executive branch. Regretting the earlier decision to open files to the House Appropriations Committee, Truman ordered all government officers to decline such requests.[46]

The anti-Communist movement took a major step during the summer of 1948 when HUAC heard testimony from two former Communists, Elizabeth Bentley and Whittaker Chambers. Bentley's naming of thirty former government employees as Communists had few consequences until the Jenner Internal Security Subcommittee pursued this line of inquiry in 1953, but Chambers's naming of Alger Hiss, the highly placed former State Department official, produced a storm. With many New Deal liberals coming to Hiss's support, the Hiss case became a lingering public issue. For Republicans, such as Richard Nixon, it was a political godsend. As Robert Griffith points out in his superb book on the McCarthy era, the charges against Hiss, followed by his conviction for perjury in January 1950, vindicated the Republican position: "Here at last was meat and substance for the Republican charge of communism in government. Here was confirmation of their worst suspicions and their fondest hopes. Here was proof positive of treason in high places and perfidy at the vitals of government." With charges of Communists-in-government in the public mind, the 1948 elections found both major parties taking strong stands against subversion. The third-party candidacy of Henry Wallace, who associated with alleged Communists and advocated peaceful coexistence with the Russians, was a convenient occasion for Democrats and Republicans to attack a confirmed left winger. Wallace expressed the view that American radicals were being persecuted and took positions on foreign policy questions that were often similar to the public views expressed by the Soviet Union. Doomed to an overwhelming defeat, the Wallace candidacy nevertheless attracted the active support of many liberals, including faculty on college campuses.[47]

Following Truman's surprise reelection in 1948, events unfolded in a way that heightened the communism issue. Mao-Tse-tung and his Communist-led army took power in China in 1949. The Soviets exploded a nuclear bomb for the first time. Revelations came forth about the passing of atomic secrets to the Russians by Klaus Fuchs and allegedly by several American accomplices, including Julius and Ethel Rosenberg. The Korean conflict came to a head in June 1950 and drew American soldiers to Asia for two years of bitter fighting and a final stalemate. A year later Douglas MacArthur, advocate of an all-out effort to defeat the Communists in Asia, was relieved of command by Truman. The tense months of 1950 also brought McCarthy's speech in Wheeling, the passage of the McCarran Internal Security Act, and congressional elections characterized by red-baiting by members of both parties. The McCarran Act, which included provisions for the registration of "communist organizations" and the strengthening of the espionage laws, was passed over the veto of President Truman. If there was any doubt beforehand, the McCarran Act established that anticommunism had become the official policy of the American government. The legislative branch was firm in its commitment; the executive branch, despite occasional doubts about specific aspects of the anti-Communist campaign, was aggressive in its efforts to enforce the laws and demonstrated with its loyalty investigations that it was not "soft" on communism.[48]

During the two years leading to the 1952 presidential election, McCarthy's charges against alleged Communists in government produced continuing controversy, congressional investigations, and countercharges. McCarthy, the accuser, was himself a constant subject of investigation as he presented a stream of invective against all, including prestigious senatorial figures, who challenged his charges or his methods. During this period intellectuals and academic organizations became for the first time featured targets of accusation and investigation. The charges of Communist infiltration of the Institute of Pacific Relations and McCarthy's accusation against Owen Lattimore, then director of the Walter Hines Page School of International Relations at Johns Hopkins University, brought a number of Communists and former Communists to the witness stand. One of the witnesses was Bella Dodd, former legislative representative of the New York Teachers Union, who had left the Party in the late 1940s and would soon testify again with greater consequence. Although the congressional investigation of McCarthy's charges did not bring evidence that Lattimore had been a Soviet spy as charged by McCarthy, he was indicted for perjury.[49]

The circumstances that brought academe into the line of fire of congressional anti-Communists were varied and interconnected. Certainly, liberal political thinking and reformist tendencies had long been equated in the public mind with the activities of college faculty, especially those academicians, such as John Dewey and Robert Hutchins, who were well known and widely published. According to Richard Hofstadter, deeper strains of anti-intellectualism have run through American history and have fluctuated in a cyclical fashion. McCarthyism brought this popular tendency back to the forefront:

> Primarily it was McCarthyism which aroused the fear that the critical mind was at a ruinous discount in this country. Of course, intellectuals were not the only targets of McCarthy's constant detonations—he was after bigger game—but intellectuals were in the line of fire, and it seemed to give special rejoicing to his followers when they were hit. His

sorties against intellectuals and universities were emulated throughout the country by a host of less exalted inquisitors.

Reinforcing these general factors were the accumulated accusations against academics of Communist affiliation going back to the Dies Committee investigation and the Rapp-Coudert investigation in New York State. Given the tenor of the times, the ready availability of names and documentation may have been the most telling factor of all. Furthermore, many of the actors in these previous investigations were still on the scene, including both the accused and the accusers. The probability was high that eventually one or more of the congressional committees would target directly alleged Communist connections in education.[50]

PROCEEDINGS AT THE STATE LEVEL

During the 1948–1952 period, as the McCarthy era in Washington led to the targeting of academicians, several state legislatures and institutions of higher education followed a similar path. The model for state initiative on the anticommunism issue was set by the state of Washington. Following several weeks of intensive investigation and preparation of materials, a Joint Legislative Fact-finding Committee on Un-American Activities opened hearings in July 1948 under the leadership of State Senator Albert Canwell. Canwell had prepared for the hearings by conferring with HUAC staff members and by acquiring information from their files. Intent on tracking down long-standing rumors of a Communist presence on the University of Washington campus, the committee interrogated forty faculty members in private hearings and emerged with the names of ten alleged Communists. Of these ten, the board of regents filed charges against three who had refused to testify and three others who had admitted Communist connections but would not discuss other faculty. A faculty Academic Tenure Committee conducted hearings into the charges, with eight of eleven members concluding that the accused should not be dismissed from the University of Washington. President Raymond Allen, however, recommended that two of the group be dismissed. Finally, the board of regents acted to fire the two individuals cited by President Allen (Herbert Phillips and Joseph Butterworth) plus a third (Ralph Gundlach). Each was fired without severance pay.[51]

The University of Washington case established two important ideas, each of which was accepted by other universities over the next few years. First, it was asserted (and sustained by the decision against Phillips and Butterworth) that membership in the Communist party disqualified an individual from holding a faculty position. Although reputed to be excellent teachers, Phillips and Butterworth admitted their Party ties, and that was the overriding issue in reviewing their fitness to keep their positions. Second, Gundlach's case established that refusing to testify about one's political activities was evidence of "lack of candor," which in turn was an indication that the individual was unfit to remain a faculty member. Although the firings—and particularly the rationale behind the firings—elicited protests by a group of Washington faculty and by commentators in other parts of the country, the political consensus in the state of Washington was sufficiently strong that such dissenting views did not raise a serious response by university or legislative authorities.[52]

The Wallace campaign in 1948, tainted by allegations of following the "communist line," brought trouble for several faculty members in institutions across the country. Faculty who were active in support of Wallace and the Progressive Party often came under fire by their administrations. Two faculty members fired from Oregon State University were vigorous supporters of the Wallace campaign. A faculty member at the University of Evansville in Indiana, chairman of a county Wallace campaign, was fired for "political activity." The University of Miami was especially vigilant when it dismissed three faculty members in the spring before the 1948 presidential campaign. The three people, each active in support of Wallace, were ostensibly fired for "budgetary reasons." There was a brief mobilization of support for the faculty by the student senate, including a rally attended by three thousand students, but the uproar subsided quickly and the board of trustees sustained the administrative decision. Moreover, Wallace supporters were dismissed from Oglethorpe University, Atlanta; Lycoming College, Williamsburg, Pennsylvania; Lyndon State Teachers College in Vermont; Columbia University; the University of Georgia; and the University of New Hampshire. It is likely also that other faculty were compelled to end their pro-Wallace activities or face dismissal. For example, it was reported that two conspicuous Wallace supporters at the University of Miami quietly dropped from political activity after warnings from administrators. Although most of these cases were camouflaged by the citing of causes other than pro-Wallace politics, it is evident from studying several of the cases that politics was the triggering factor. Liberal politics, especially politics identified with Communist "fellow-traveling," was an invitation to trouble on many campuses.[53]

The regents of the University of California passed a motion in 1949 requiring faculty to pledge that they were not Communists or face dismissal. The oath requirement produced a bitter reaction throughout the California system, but by 1951 twenty-six faculty had been dismissed and thirty-seven others had resigned in protest. Although the oath was declared unconstitutional by the California Supreme Court in 1952, California remained an active site for anti-Communist initiative when twenty-eight colleges agreed to cooperate with the legislature's Un-American Activities Committee. The colleges agreed to employ a former FBI or military intelligence officer on each campus to help the committee identify security risks. It was reported that by early 1953 more than one hundred staff members had been dismissed or forced to resign.[54]

In July 1951 the chairman of the art department at Fairmont State College in West Virginia was fired by the board of trustees for casually remarking that she was a socialist and for denying at an American Legion forum that liberals and Communists were the same. The president of the college, who defended his employee at a later court trial for slander, was dismissed shortly thereafter. During 1949 a mathematics professor at the Massachusetts Institute of Technology was named as a Communist. In 1951 he was indicted under Massachusetts law and suspended with pay from his MIT position; he remained in limbo for five years until his indictment was dropped. In order to deter an investigation in 1951 by the Republican-controlled legislature, the University of Colorado instigated a "self-investigation." The board of regents employed two former FBI agents to question faculty and collect information from other sources. Morris Judd, an untenured philosophy instructor, refused to answer questions about his political activities, and his annual appointment was not renewed. An assistant professor of chemistry, Irving Goodman, then on leave to conduct research in Paris, had previously admitted to his president that he had been a member of the Communist party until 1945. A letter of dismissal, which contained no reasons for the action, reached Goodman in Paris. In the case of Robert Hodes, a tenured professor of physiology at Tulane University, it was difficult to distinguish left-wing politics from other factors as the basis for his firing. Initial discussions in 1952 with his department chairman focused on a dispute about a personnel matter and Hodes's handling of it, but according to Hodes, the chairman then raised the question of Hodes's political activities: "He said that the Dean and the Board of Trustees had gotten wind of the fact that I was a 'red.' . . . The most I could gather about my crimes was that I seemed too interested in negro-white relations and that somebody in the Medicine Department had complained . . . that I was a red." Shortly, Hodes was given what the dean stated was a "terminal appointment" for the 1952–1953 academic year. Although Hodes protested his dismissal to the American Association of University Professors (AAUP), a hearing panel at Tulane upheld the decision to dismiss him. Yet the situation remained murky. On the one hand, it is evident that Hodes had Communist connections. On the other hand, though an outstanding scientist, Hodes was evidently a constant source of friction in the university and probably acted unprofessionally on more than one occasion. Still, one suspects that in the absence of the Communist issue he would not have been fired.[55]

Steps by other institutions to dismiss suspected Communists grew out of hearings held in New York City in late 1952 by the Senate Internal Security Subcommittee. Faculty at Rutgers, Columbia, Brooklyn College, and New York University took the Fifth Amendment and were then subject to institutional sanctions. The Rutgers case took on special significance because of the argumentation presented by the Rutgers president, Lewis Webster Jones, in support of the dismissal of the two accused Rutgers faculty. A faculty review committee recommended no action, but the board of trustees, supported by President Jones, took the position that invoking the Fifth Amendment was "incompatible" with the standards of behavior required of college faculty. A lengthy justification of the decision by President Jones was endorsed by the Rutgers board in January 1953 and printed for distribution to institutions around the country. A few months later, trustees at the University of Vermont would rely on Jones's pamphlet in their deliberations over the Novikoff case.[56]

Developments around the country between 1948 and 1952 demonstrate that what would shortly ensue in Vermont was not an unusual occurrence. On a scale unappreciated until recently, congressional committees, state legislative committees, local boards of higher education, statewide regents, and colleges and universities attempted to root out Communists. Because so many of the firings were done quietly (especially the nonrenewal of contracts for untenured faculty,) done ostensibly for other reasons, or were not reported to the AAUP, we may never know the actual numbers of faculty dismissed during the late 1940s and early 1950s. It is probable, however, that the total number of faculty dismissed for political reasons during the McCarthy era surpassed one hundred. This estimate does not include the many faculty who, under threat, resigned or chose to take early retirement.[57]

Catalog statements and commencement speeches about academic freedom notwithstanding, logic suggests that dismissals of faculty in such numbers required the willing cooperation of the institutions themselves. Indeed, as one surveys events during 1952 and 1953, one finds the educational establishment struggling with how to respond to the popular mood and to the persistent pressure of legislative committees. Procedurally, institutions either turned to existing avenues of due process, such as faculty tenure committees, or created special panels to hear the charges of Communist affiliation. Cornell, New York University, MIT, The University of Miami, the University of Michigan, and the University of Vermont established special procedures. The more crucial issues for higher education, however, were substantive and dealt with academic freedom, the Fifth Amendment, and standards of faculty conduct. Was invoking the Fifth Amendment grounds for dismissal? Was evidence of past Communist party membership grounds for dismissal? Did perceived threats to national security override traditional precepts of academic freedom? To what extent should—and could—universities have ignored the national political consensus about the perceived Communist threat?[58]

Although America had long granted universities a special status, the universities of the 1950s were inextricably tied to the larger society and responsive to contemporary political realities. The makeup of most boards of trustees assured a responsiveness at the level of institutional mission and policy. The dependence on outside sources of income, including gifts, legislative appropriations, and grants, tied institutions to business and government. Furthermore, with the emergence of the university as an important collaborator in the military effort during World War II, higher education was now a partner with government on many fronts. Research grants in the defense and medical fields and the G.I. Bill, with its tuition contribution for veterans, enhanced the mutual dependency. A consequence of these developments was that institutional leaders and many faculty members were ever more attentive to political imperatives in the larger society. It is not surprising, then, that institutional leaders were inclined to seek solutions that would not put themselves or their institutions in dangerous opposition to the national mood. As Ellen Schrecker emphasized in *No Ivory Tower*, this inclination had historical precedents:

> [Academic freedom] is a limited protection, and anyone who ventures beyond the mainstream risks losing whatever benefits academic freedom can confer. As we shall see, this has always been the case, especially with regard to political dissent. Moreover, during times of stress, when the acceptable limits of political discourse narrow, the academic community has responded by redefining academic freedom so as to ensure that it remains within these new limits.

Thus, with a prevailing consensus of opinion—among Americans in general and probably among most faculties—that Communists should not serve as faculty, there was little chance that a present or former

Communist would remain long in employment. By late 1952 many cases had confirmed the effects of this proposition. The thornier problem concerned the Fifth Amendment issue. Again, the instinct was to accommodate the prevailing political consensus. According to Schrecker:

> ... the academic community—trustees, administrators, and professors—addressed itself to the task of trying to redefine academic freedom so that the dismissal of Fifth Amendment witnesses would not result in a violation of it. If the academy could draw up and enforce a code of behavior that would redefine taking the Fifth before a congressional committee as professionally unacceptable, then the academic profession might be able to avoid a confrontation with its employers and those outside forces that were trying to purge it of its unacceptable members. It would do the job itself and in that way insure, procedurally at least, that academic freedom would be preserved.

Although many argued for the inviolability of the constitutional right not to incriminate oneself, the higher education establishment soon asserted that invoking the Fifth Amendment was behavior incompatible with serving as a faculty member.[59]

In January 1953 two distinguished legal scholars, Zechariah Chafee of Harvard and Arthur Sunderland of Cornell, published a statement that served to undercut the legal justification for faculty taking the Fifth Amendment. A premise of the statement was that if an accused faculty member was not under danger of *criminal* prosecution he could not justifiably invoke the Fifth Amendment.

> The underlying principle to remember in considering the subject is the duty of the citizen to cooperate in government. He has no option to say, "I do not approve of this Grand Jury or that congressional committee; I dislike its members and its objects; therefore, I will not tell it what I know." He is neither wise nor legally justified in attempting political protest by standing silent when obligated to speak ... the Fifth Amendment grants no privilege to protect one's friends.

In most cases, faculty were indeed not likely to be prosecuted in a criminal court. They were, however, very likely to be prosecuted by their institution, with a definite danger of losing their jobs. Whether or not a suspected faculty member's rationale for invoking the Fifth Amendment included moral and political arguments, he or she knew for certain that taking this step was tantamount to inviting a dismissal proceeding. Later commentators found that the interpretation of the Fifth Amendment by Chafee and Sunderland was overly narrow, but at this crucial time in the McCarthy era their statement reinforced the inclinations of trustees, presidents, and faculty panels across the country.[60]

Later in January 1953 President Jones of Rutgers had five thousand copies made of his justification for the dismissal of the two Rutgers faculty who had invoked the Fifth Amendment. He argued that "negative attitudes of non-cooperation constituted unacceptable professional behavior. . . . Under all the circumstances of our relations to world communism, a minimum responsibility would seem to be that members of the University state frankly where they stand on matters of deep public concern . . . as membership in the Communist Party, even when by a straightforward statement they believe that might incur certain personal risks." Jones went so far as to say that "public investigation of the universities is legitimate, and should be frankly met." For all practical purposes, Jones had both condoned congressional investigation of the political affiliations of his faculty and equated avoidance of such inquiry—the invoking of the Fifth Amendment—with unprofessional conduct warranting dismissal from academe. Jones's arguments were appealing to institutions faced with the political dilemma faced earlier by Rutgers.[61]

In March the position of the higher-education establishment was confirmed without any doubt. After lengthy haggling about the language of a statement on "The Rights and Responsibilities of Universities and their Faculties," the Association of American Universities (AAU) finally agreed on a statement that addressed, among other issues, the Fifth Amendment problem. The thirty-seven presidents of the nation's most prestigious universities had appointed A. Whitney Griswold of Yale to chair a committee to bring the task to conclusion; by March 24 the AAU had endorsed the work of Griswold's committee and released the document for general circulation. The following section pertained directly to the situation of faculty who had taken the Fifth Amendment: "In this respect, invocation of the Fifth Amendment places upon a professor a heavy burden of proof of his fitness to hold a teaching position and lays upon his university an obligation to reexamine his qualifications for membership in its society." Congressional committees, editorial writers, and other higher-education administrators were pleased by the statement. It was distributed widely, aided by an original circulation of fifteen thousand copies and supplemented by thirty-five thousand additional copies financed by the Rockefeller Foundation. Schrecker pointed out that although the statement restated the position of President Jones on the obligation of candor, it went beyond Jones "by attempting to offer a specifically professional rationale for that obligation: its insistence that because the academic profession had a special need for freedom of speech, its members must, therefore, literally speak up."[62]

Thus, by March 1953 precedents and rationales were in place for handling a professor who had not cooperated with a congressional committee. The national political consensus was still firm with respect to the evils of communism; simultaneously, there was a solid consensus among colleges and universities about how to respond to the Communist menace in their own backyards. As such, the definition of academic freedom had indeed narrowed, and the commitment nationally to take action against faculty transgressors was uncompromising.

THE VISE CLOSES ON NOVIKOFF

As McCarthyism expanded its reach and infected higher education, Novikoff's situation became more precarious. The predictable occurred during late 1952 when the Senate Internal Security Subcommittee of the Senate Judiciary Committee, headed by Pat McCarran, decided to look into the unresolved charges against teachers and faculty in New York State. The move in this direction was probably instigated by Robert Morris, who had been on the legal staff of the Rapp-Coudert investigation and had served as legal counsel to the SISS in its investigation of the Institute of Pacific Relations (IPR) during 1951 and 1952. The round-faced Morris had a pleasant, clean-cut look about him, but this exterior hid a hard-nosed commitment to root out Communists. He was a sharp investigator and an aggressive, calculating interrogator, qualities that inspired the confidence and gratitude of his superiors. Morris served as counsel to a succession of anti-Communist legislators: Frederick Coudert in New York State, McCarran, and William Jenner, who in a few months would interrogate Novikoff. His singleness of purpose and his instinct for the jugular made him a dangerous foe of those under suspicion.

Morris left the SISS after the IPR investigation but with the defection of Bella Dodd from the Communist party, he saw that it might now be possible to finish the work begun by the Rapp-Coudert committee in 1940 and 1941. It rankled Morris and others involved in the earlier investigations that many faculty who stood accused as Communists remained in their jobs. At the height of the McCarthy era Morris recognized that the necessary second witnesses might be induced to come forward.[63]

During September and October 1952, Senator Homer Ferguson of Michigan and key committee staff visited the scene of the Rapp-Coudert investigation, the Foley Square courtroom in Manhattan. Morris, serving as chief interrogator, led Bella Dodd through a recapitulation of her activities in the Party and in the Teachers Union. Dodd

Stalking the Academic Communist

named a small number of teachers as Communists, each of whom was subpoenaed and each of whom invoked the Fifth Amendment. In due course, staff members at the city colleges, including faculty at Brooklyn College, began to receive subpoenas. Harry Slochower and Frederic Ewen, both named in 1940 by Grebanier, appeared on September 24 and invoked the Fifth Amendment. Ewen, who feared the worst when he heard that Bella Dodd had become a friendly witness for the committee, retired as a faculty member shortly before he appeared to testify. Harry Albaum, Sarah Riedman, and Melba Phillips were other Brooklyn College staff called to testify. Each of the Brooklyn College faculty members, except for Albaum, invoked the Fifth Amendment. The consequences for refusing to testify were immediate and decisive. Each individual received a standard letter from the chairman of the New York City Board of Higher Education:

> It is the opinion of the Corporation Counsel that Section 903 of the New York City Charter operates automatically to remove any employee who, on the grounds of self-incrimination, refuses to answer a question addressed to him by a duly authorized legislative committee regarding his official conduct.
>
> In the light of your refusal to answer certain of the Committee's questions on grounds of self-incrimination, it is therefore my duty to advise you that you are hereby suspended without pay, effective at the close of business today . . . and that I am placing the matter before the Board of Higher Education.

Section 903 of the city charter was enacted in 1936 during the La Guardia administration with the expressed purpose of dealing with city employees accused of graft. The provision provided that city employees who refused to testify about official business were subject to dismissal. Recognizing that Section 903 applied conveniently to city teachers who refused to talk about their involvement in alleged Communist activities, the superintendent of New York City public schools utilized this provision to dismiss twenty-four teachers during the early 1950s. When Slochower, Ewen, Phillips, and the others invoked the Fifth Amendment before Senator Ferguson's committee, the Board of Higher Education was already on record in pledging "full cooperation" to the committee. The board now called these faculty members to testify, knowing that if they continued to remain silent, Section 903 was a ready means to remove them from the city colleges.[64]

Slochower received this letter of suspension one week after his appearance before the committee. He appeared before the Board of Higher Education three days later, refused to change his testimony, and was fired. Riedman's and Phillips's situations were handled in a similar fashion.

The Albaum case proceeded along a different line. Novikoff's former colleague recalled later the circumstances of his testimony:

> I was subpoenaed one day after a lecture in Ingersoll Hall to appear before that committee the following day. Shortly afterwards President Gideonse called me in, told me that he knew that I had been a member of the Communist cell at Brooklyn College, and encouraged me to testify freely. He informed me that if I did, he would stand behind me and support me. I agreed to testify . . . President Gideonse, as he promised, supported me and my career at the college continued.

Influenced by Gideonse's promise of support, Albaum surprised Senator Ferguson the next day by indicating his readiness to talk. Delighted by this turn of events, the committee in private session took Albaum through his story. The following day, September 25, Albaum made his obligatory appearance in public.[65]

After a string of witnesses who had refused to talk under the provisions of the Fifth Amendment, Albaum's public testimony was a major news story. The *New York Herald Tribune* displayed Albaum's picture on page one under the heading, "Drama at McCarran Red Hearing: Three in Top Roles." Actually, a part of the day's drama was the appearance in the audience of an "alleged agent, a tall burly man" who came to intimidate the witnesses. Albaum's testimony contained information about his recruitment to the Communist party, his participation in Party activities, and his later dissatisfaction and attempts to leave the Party. He described the manner by which he was recruited to the Party by a "friend" during a summer stay at Lake Mahopac in 1938. After resisting the "inveigling" of his friend for several weeks, he finally "capitulated" at the end of the summer. Albaum was asked when he had decided to admit his Communist past and replied: "I have been dreaming about it for a long time. I have had nightmares about it. I finally decided when the subpoena came." Albaum named no other Communists during his public testimony before the subcommittee. Since there was no pressure from the subcommittee to present names, it is clear that prior agreement had been reached on this point.[66]

Albaum's executive session testimony had important consequences for Novikoff. Although Albaum's vague reference to a "friend" who had recruited him to the Party was not pursued by the interrogators in the public session, we know that Albaum was recruited by Novikoff. He probably gave this information to the committee. From documents obtained from SISS and the FBI, we know also that Albaum named several colleagues and former colleagues as Communists, including

Novikoff. When he returned to campus after his testimony, Albaum told a mutual friend that he "had to name Alex."[67]

In accordance with the protocol firmly established by that time in the McCarthy era, the sole route to exoneration was the naming of other Communists in private testimony. Having done this, witnesses were either excused from public testimony or, if required to testify publicly, were asked to testify only about their own Communist activities. Albaum's public testimony proceeded along the latter lines. Furthermore, Albaum received the commendation of Senator Ferguson:

> . . . I want to say that you are to be complimented by the Chair this morning in coming here and explaining what has happened to you in the past, how communism had dominated you, your soul and your spirit, for a considerable time; and it is very refreshing to realize that there has finally been a place that you could come to where you could unload the burden for the good of what we believe is the good of not only America, but, if it is understood by other peoples, of the world. That man who can come in and testify and free his soul and become a free man should be told this, and I think that it is only just that I should say that I appreciate what you have done for the people of the United States this morning by coming in here and becoming a free man again.

At hearings the following spring, Morris took the opportunity to mention Albaum in a favorable vein, and he pointed out that Albaum "appeared before this committee and gave full, frank, and candid testimony, and in executive session even gave additional testimony about his participation in the Communist organization, and therefore did considerable damage to the Communist organization." Thus, it is apparent that Albaum played by the rules of the McCarthy era, named names, and escaped the consequences suffered by so many of his colleagues.[68]

President Gideonse kept his pledge to Albaum. Shortly after Albaum's testimony, Gideonse put his name through for academic promotion. Gideonse was well versed in the protocols of the McCarthy era, especially the "informer principle," which, according to Victor Navasky's 1981 study, "held not merely that there was nothing wrong with naming names, but that it was the litmus test, the ultimate evidence, the guarantor of patriotism." When Gideonse testified before the SISS in early 1953, he was asked whether any of his faculty had ever "repented and recanted" their Communist activities.

> You had one of those before you in this committee, Professor Albaum. The lunatic fringe . . . thought this man should be fired, and they thought, to make it more serious, that this man should not be promoted. He happened to be on my promotion list just at the time your

committee called him in. I put him through for promotion on the stipulated time just about six weeks after he testified.

Gideonse explained that the door should not be closed to those who "repent." Consequently, Albaum went on to a successful career as a scientist and as an academic administrator at Brooklyn College.[69]

As for Novikoff, the 1952 presidential election intruded on the proceedings of the SISS, and the committee adjourned until the new year. Although he had been named by the long-feared second witness, it would be several weeks before the committee would resuscitate its investigation of Communists in higher education. Nevertheless, the ground had been set for the next round of the inquisition. With Albaum's revelations, Novikoff became an active suspect in the files of the committee, especially for Robert Morris, who had twice heard the accusation of Communist party membership: he heard from Grebanier in 1940 and now he had heard from Albaum. Equally significant, Novikoff's FBI file had another damaging entry. Consistent with a practice that had begun in February 1952, Morris sent Albaum's private testimony to the FBI on October 7. The FBI made a copy and duly returned the document two weeks later.[70]

Chapter 5

INQUISITION AND THE UNRAVELING OF A LIFE

The Jenner Committee Reaches
into Vermont

Vermont of the early 1950s was a great distance culturally from the New York known by Novikoff. Although it would not be accurate to label Vermont a "backwater," it is true that many of the traditional myths about Vermont were closer to the truth during this period. The population of this small state was about 380,000 dispersed among 250 small villages, towns, and cities. Influenced by the many hills and mountains that separate one community from another, Vermont's small communities were quite self-sufficient politically and socially. Although tourism was important to the Vermont economy, the ski boom had not yet developed. Agriculture and small business and industry were the backbone of the economy.

Vermont's overall population had not grown significantly over the previous sixty years (a 14.5% growth from an 1890 population of 332,422), but there was a gradual pattern of population concentration in the state's largest towns and cities. As a proportion of Vermont's overall population, its ten largest towns and cities represented 35 percent of the total population in 1950 in comparison to 15 percent at the time of the Civil War. Burlington, located on Lake Champlain in the northwest corner of the state, had almost doubled in population since the turn of the century, reaching 34,000 in 1953. Burlington, the location of the University of Vermont, was Vermont's largest city and was almost twice the size of Rutland, the next largest city.[1]

Vermont was an entrenched Republican state, having elected only Republican governors since 1855. State offices as well as Vermont's congressional seats were virtually always taken by Republicans. Though, practically speaking, a one-party state, Vermont traditionally tolerated liberal-minded and independent public officials. As scholars of Vermont political history have demonstrated, "Republican" and "conservative" were not necessarily synonymous terms. In this vein Nicholas Muller and Samuel Hand have commented on the difficulty of classifying Vermont politics.

> The apparent fluctuations between "liberalism" and "conservatism" and Vermont's atypical behavior as a one-party state led observers to label it a land of political paradox. Comparisons of Vermont with one-party states of the south frequently cited numerous differences including the lack of demagogic appeals, the lack of outright corruption, and an extent of political participation comparable to two-party states. Most difficult to explain, however, was a persisting strain of liberalism.

Anomalies under the Republican banner included former governor George D. Aiken (1937–1940), who moved on to the U.S. Senate, and Ernest Gibson, Jr., who served as governor from 1947 to 1950. Both leaders fostered progressive social programs during their tenures in the State House.[2]

At the height of the McCarthy era, Vermont's two senators were Aiken and the independent-minded Ralph E. Flanders, who had been elected in 1946. By 1948 newspapers were featuring stories of Flanders's propensity to speak his mind and to take positions at odds with the Republican leadership. Flanders, a successful businessman and seventy years old at the time of his reelection in 1952, was an early opponent of McCarthy within the ranks of Senate Republicans. In March 1954 he broke publicly with his colleagues and spoke against McCarthy on the Senate floor. In June he introduced the resolution that led a few months later to the Senate's censure of McCarthy. Both Vermont senators were living evidence that Vermont politicians were not likely to fall unthinkingly into step with any party or conservative position or, moreover, with the sweeping anti-Communist posturing of McCarthy.[3]

Back in Vermont, however, the governorship in the early 1950s was in more conventional Republican hands. Governor Lee E. Emerson had come to office by the traditional "stepladder" pattern, by which he had served in the Vermont House, in the Vermont Senate, and as lieutenant governor before running for governor in 1948. He lost his primary run against Ernest Gibson in 1948 but survived a bitter primary struggle in 1950 and went on to an easy victory in the 1950 general election. Raised in the northeast Vermont town of Barton and trained as a lawyer, Emerson served two terms before stepping down in 1954. Emerson's primary battles against the Gibson forces and his opposition to Gibson reform measures before the legislature caused considerable anti-Emerson feeling among Republicans. By 1953 Emerson had staked out political ground to the right of the more liberal Republicans of the Gibson faction. In the midst of internal divisiveness Emerson was firmly committed to more typical Republican positions on social legislation and anti-communism. Emerson served as an ex officio member of the board of trustees of the University of Vermont and brought his conservative Republican point of view to the problem of a suspected Communist on the faculty of the university.[4]

As the cold war fever rose during the late 1940s, Vermont appeared to respond in ways typical of the rest of the country. On the front pages, the daily newspapers covered national and world news primarily through dispatches from the national news services; on the back pages, editorial writers and readers' letters decried Soviet aggression and the rising Communist threat. In Burlington the *Free Press* assumed an editorial position close to the Eisenhower brand of Republicanism. The *Daily News* (and its Sunday version, the *Vermont Sunday News*), reflected its tie to the William Loeb chain of papers and conveyed a virulent right-wing perspective. Some of Vermont's many weekly newspapers, along with Rutland's *Herald*, were more circumspect in their reactions to Soviet actions and the anti-Communist movement but, on the whole, reflected Vermont's special brand of Republican politics. All in all, the first instinct of the papers and of Vermonters in general was to accept the messages from Washington and elsewhere about the state of world affairs, particularly about the Communist threat.

The Wallace candidacy in 1948 exemplified how Vermont reacted to sentiments that ran counter to the accepted view of the Communist threat. During early 1948 Vermont papers carried an increasing number of stories about the Wallace third-party initiative, featuring Wallace's statements about seeking peace with Russia and his view that the conflict with the Soviet Union was a "false crisis." The overwhelming majority of editorials and letters attacked Wallace's views.[5]

One local incident is noteworthy in this regard. Representatives of three county groups met in Rutland on February 29, 1948, to form a statewide Wallace-for-President organization. This meeting followed earlier meetings in Barre, Burlington, and Brattleboro. A visit to Vermont by Wallace may have helped move planning forward. Seventy-five persons convened in Rutland to vote on several resolutions and to pick officers of the state group. One of the newly elected vice-chairmen was Luther K. McNair, academic dean of Lyndon State Teachers College. Vermont newspapers carried coverage of the meeting and identified the leaders of the Wallace organization. Shortly, McNair's position as an administrator at a state college became publicly known, and several newspapers criticized his keeping his position while at the same time pushing the Wallace candidacy. Pressure mounted on state college administrators and on McNair. On March 18 he submitted his resignation, and on March 26 the president of the college issued a press release announcing his resignation. The release noted that he had served "ably." McNair told reporters that he had resigned to be able to "work more effectively" for Wallace and that he planned to work with Wallace groups in New England or New York State. Although McNair left without causing a public controversy, the evidence suggests that he was forced out for his Wallace views and for his public role as a leader of the Wallace-for-President organization.[6]

Although the contretemps at Lyndon State over radical politics may have surprised some Vermonters, few were surprised that suspicions were raised about Bennington and Goddard colleges. These small private institutions manifested the progressive educational tradition of John Dewey and Columbia's Teachers College. The liberal politics and sometimes unconventional behavior of the faculty were noticed by Vermonters and on occasion reported to authorities. In July 1950 a maintenance worker at Goddard wrote the FBI to report the existence of Communist sympathies on campus and to suggest that the FBI "have a little investigation up there." After a flurry of correspondence and background checks (including several interviews with the maintenance employee), the FBI concluded a few months later that "there is at least an effort being made by the Communist Party to recruit members at Goddard College." The most suspicious finding was an open letter to a Vermont official signed by the "Communist Party of Vermont." Apparently, the suspected organizing effort at Goddard made little headway; FBI records show no further correspondence about Goddard after July 1951.[7]

Although Wallace represented a dangerous force for many Vermonters, he faded quickly from the political scene. In contrast, in the months after the 1950 Wheeling speech McCarthy came to symbolize hard-nosed anticommunism. It is likely that there was a connection between the rhetoric of McCarthy anticommunism and the call by the janitor at Goddard to destroy the "communistic cell" on the campus. Moreover, Governor Emerson was urged to take up the banner. An Emerson political ally wrote the governor in November 1950 to suggest that "we know we have Communists here in Vermont" and to express his confidence that "you will do all in your power to help stem this flow of Communists into Vt. and do something about those we now have here—at least in having them watched closely during this trying period." There is no evidence that Emerson ever undertook any steps to identify or watch Communist suspects, but he did urge in his January 1951 inaugural addresss that Vermont take a "firm stand on communism."[8]

Two years later, following Eisenhower's election and on the eve of Novikoff's confrontation in early 1953 with William Jenner's Senate Subcommittee on Internal Security, McCarthy was still riding high. News stories critical of McCarthy's tactics had been appearing sporadically for several months, but the focus of news coverage in Vermont remained the threat of world communism and the specter of Communists in high places in government.

Although the newspapers of the time overwhelmingly supported the anti-Communist campaign, it is difficult nevertheless to assess with confidence Vermont public opinion during the McCarthy era. Fortunately, a scholarly study was carried out during this period that sheds some light on where Vermonters stood on McCarthy. Martin Trow, a political scientist, conducted research on McCarthyism in the town of Bennington during the first half of 1954. Although this research took place about a year after the Novikoff affair, McCarthy was still much in the news with the Army-McCarthy hearings, though beginning to lose support across the country. Trow's research team interviewed 771 adult men, representing several job categories and income levels derived from lists of employees in various firms and professional groups. All subjects were residents of Bennington, the third largest town in Vermont with a population of 13,000. The high representation of Roman Catholics in the population (about 40%), the existence of an institution of higher learning in the town (Bennington College), the stability and overall profile of the economy, and the existence of a widely read daily newspaper (the *Bennington Banner*) with an editorial slant similar to the *Burlington Free Press* indicate that Burlington and Bennington had many characteristics in common. As such, it is probable that Trow's findings have considerable applicability to the Burlington setting.[9]

Trow sought to find out the level of support for McCarthy by determining, as a proxy, the level of support for McCarthy's methods. His question read as follows: "Just speaking of Senator McCarthy's methods of investigation, how do you feel about them?" The optional responses included: strongly favor (his methods), mildly favor, mildly oppose, and strongly oppose. Combining the two favorable responses, 42 percent of Trow's sample reported that they favored McCarthy's methods. In addition, Trow found that the level of support for Mc-

Carthy was associated with the amount of formal education attained by his respondents.

TABLE I. Support for McCarthy by Educational Level

Formal education	No. of respondents	% Favoring McCarthy's methods	% Opposing McCarthy's methods
Grade school	169	58	42
Some high school	134	46	54
High school graduate	182	47	53
Some college	85	29	71
College graduate	157	21	79

Trow looked also at the level of support for McCarthy among various occupational categories. He found that the highest level of support came from among self-employed small-business owners and merchants with less than a college education. About 70 percent of these small-business owners favored McCarthy's methods, in comparison to the 52 percent level of support among manual workers with the same educational attainment. All white-collar workers, especially those with a college education, tended to be anti-McCarthy.[10]

Another line of inquiry concerned the level of political tolerance of Vermonters, as indicated by an index measured by the following three inquiries:

In peacetime, do you think the Socialist Party should be allowed to publish newspapers in this country?

Do you think newspapers should be allowed to criticize our form of government?

Do you think members of the Communist Party in this country should be allowed to speak on the radio?

As might be expected, Trow found higher levels of political tolerance among those with higher levels of educational attainment. He found the expected relationship between political tolerance and levels of support for McCarthy's methods: those with high political tolerance and high educational attainment tended strongly to oppose McCarthy's methods and vice versa. However, when he held constant the level of educational attainment (i.e., compared only those respondents with similar educational attainment), he found that this relationship between political tolerance and support of McCarthy virtually disappeared. Trow commented as follows:

In other words, the apparent relationship between attitudes toward free-

dom of speech and approval or disapproval of McCarthy's methods . . .
is largely a spurious one, which almost wholly disappears when the factor of formal education is introduced. While support of McCarthy and
support of freedom of speech for unpopular views are both related to
formal education, they are very little related to each other. . . . The implications of this finding are many. In its simplest terms, it means that
whatever the character and content of the *public* fight between McCarthy
and his more prominent opponents, the sources of his support and popularity (and of his opposition) in the population at large appear to have
had little or no relation to how strongly people support the principles of
free speech.

The extent that McCarthyism was *not* an issue of political tolerance (or
free speech) may explain the apparent inconsistency in the behavior
of otherwise enlightened trustees at the University of Vermont who
voted to dismiss Alex Novikoff.[11]

If we can assume that Bennington and Burlington were indeed
largely similar communities in 1954 and that there was little significant change in public sentiment between 1953 and 1954, Trow's research provides a useful backdrop for assessing the forces at play at
the time of the Novikoff affair. First, it is important to recognize that
over 40 percent of the male population favored the methods of investigation employed by McCarthy. In the absence of a vociferous opposition, this helps explain the existence of energetic initiatives against
an alleged Communist. Second, the relationship between lower educational attainment and certain categories of occupation (small-business owners and merchants) and positive attitudes toward McCarthy
help explain the behavior of key participants in the Novikoff situation.
On the basis of these findings, we will see that individual trustees acted
in predictable ways. Third, the lack of relationship between political
tolerance and political methods provides a useful avenue of interpretation. This finding helps explain the actions of the president of the
University of Vermont, a man articulate on the subject of academic
freedom but a collaborator in the proceedings brought against Alex
Novikoff.

In sum, as one looks at Vermont of the early 1950s, one finds a
political environment shaped by the Republican party. It is a party that
features a fundamental conservative tradition, influenced by a strong
liberal and independent strain. The leadership of former Governor Gibson and Senators Aiken and Flanders are testimony to this countervailing influence. In 1953, however, the governor's chair was filled by
the conservative and conventionally anti-Communist Lee Emerson,
who had staked out political territory to the right of the previous administration. For most newspaper editors and probably most Vermon-

ters, world communism was perceived to be a genuine threat to national security, and the goals of McCarthy's anti-Communist campaign were looked on with favor. A solid minority of Vermonters probably approved of his methods of investigation. There was ample evidence from the Wallace campaign that Vermont's political environment was not tolerant of actions and affiliations that indicated sympathy with the policies of the Soviet Union. All of this suggests that, like most of the rest of the country, Vermont was not likely to treat kindly anyone named as a Communist or one who had refused to answer questions about his past. Shortly, Novikoff would be plunged into these circumstances.

THE UNIVERSITY OF VERMONT

By today's standards the University of Vermont in 1952 was a small college, enrolling a total of 2,885 students dispersed among four major academic units. The College of Arts and Sciences, exemplifying the liberal arts tradition of the New England small college, was the largest unit, representing about 40 percent of the undergraduate population. The university was experiencing some growing pains, by virtue of having almost doubled in enrollment since 1940. Sixty percent of the students were male and about 40 percent came from out of state. Except in two or three units of the university, scholarly research had not yet become a significant activity. Principally, it was a teaching institution, exhibiting the typical campus culture of the 1950s. Indicative of the times, four students were arrested in May 1952 for a panty raid on a women's residence hall. The culprits denied riot charges but nevertheless went to trial. The major social event of the school year was Kake Walk, a dance competition in which representatives of fraternities and other student organizations blackened their faces and carried out elaborate routines in hopes of winning the "Kake." It would be several years before the racial stereotypes implicit in the event would dawn on enough people to bring a serious effort to eliminate the competition.[12]

Although chartered in 1791 as Vermont's state university, the University of Vermont functioned in many ways as a private institution. An 1828 legislative act provided that the university would operate with a self-perpetuating board of trustees. Following acceptance of provisions of the Land Grant Act of 1862, however, a new corporation was established that included trustees elected on a self-perpetuating basis, on the basis of selection by the state legislature, and on an ex officio basis. Prior to the 1950s the state legislature did not assume significant fiscal responsibility for the operations of the university, except for regular funding to the College of Medicine and the College of Agriculture. Overall, state support of the institution was limited, especially in comparison to other state universities, and the university functioned quite autonomously. The governor of Vermont sat as an ex officio member of the board of trustees but rarely attended meetings or asserted himself in setting the direction of the institution.[13]

When the board of trustees set out in early 1952 to select a new president, it agreed to seek an individual able to "develop the relationship between the University and the People of Vermont" and able to continue efforts to "raise standards educationally within the University." Carl Borgmann, dean of faculties at the University of Nebraska, was selected over a dean of humanities and social sciences at the Massachusetts Institute of Technology. Borgmann brought to Vermont a background as a chemical engineer and training at the University of Colorado and several European universities, including Cambridge University. Suggestive of the less formal and less comprehensive search procedures of this era, Borgmann was immediately disillusioned by what he found upon his arrival in July 1952: "I arrived in Burlington naively believing that I had accepted a job at a state university which had relationships with the legislature similar to those I had known in the West. I asked to see the biennial budget request and found that none had been prepared." He set out at once to prepare a budget request and to elicit political support for the requested appropriations.

> You can imagine my surprise, as I moved from Rotary Club talk to Chamber of Commerce talk, to find that Vermonters didn't realize that UVM was a state university. They seemed to know that they had some fiscal responsibility for the agricultural college and an emotional tie (convertible into cash) to the medical college and they hoped that the balance of the university would go away and be somebody else's responsibility.

Influenced by the state university and land grant model of Nebraska and the Midwest, Borgmann set as a first priority a revision of the relationship between the university and the state of Vermont. His goals were to establish the University of Vermont as an "instrumentality of the State" and to provide lower tuition for Vermont students enrolled in any program of the university. He perceived that such a revision of the university's relationship with the state would require a charter revision, along with a change in the point of view of Vermont citizens and political leaders. As such, he knew that a major political campaign was needed, one that would bring the governor and the legislature to accept his vision. As a new president, soon to be embroiled in the situation of an alleged Communist faculty member, he was constantly attentive to relationships with the politicians of his adopted state. Much was at stake, and as the Novikoff case unfolded, he did not forget these political issues of strategic importance to the university.[14]

NOVIKOFF IS CALLED TO WASHINGTON

The election of Dwight Eisenhower in November 1952 created an immediate political dilemma within the Republican ranks. Republicans across the country, including Eisenhower, had drawn on Joe McCarthy and the popularity of his anticommunism crusade in carrying out their campaigns. However, McCarthy's controversial behavior as well as his vitriolic attack on Secretary of Defense George Marshall, Eisenhower's former military comrade, led Eisenhower to step cautiously around McCarthy. Meetings between the two figures during the campaign were awkward and colored by Eisenhower's opposition to McCarthy's tactics. Although later analyses suggest that McCarthy's influence on the 1952 electoral success of the Republicans was greatly exaggerated at the time, the widely held perception was that McCarthy had been a crucial political force and that his anticommunism campaign had been vindicated by the American people.[15]

Ambivalence among Republicans about McCarthy surfaced when the new Congress convened in January. McCarthy had been reelected easily, along with several allies in the fight against communism. Although McCarthy, by virtue of seniority, could have taken the chairmanship of the important Senate Appropriations Subcommittee, he chose instead to become chairman of the Committee on Government Operations and to make a bid for exclusive responsibility for investigating communism on a broad front. His plan was to create three investigatory subcommittees and to chair personally the one targeted against Communists in government. Senator William Langer, the new chairman of the Judiciary Committee, resisted McCarthy's attempts to reduce the authority of the Internal Security Subcommittee (SISS). He resisted also McCarthy's attempt to induce Robert Morris, the SISS's chief investigator, to join McCarthy's Government Operations Committee. A compromise settlement was reached whereby the anti-Communist field was divided into three jurisdictions.[16]

It was agreed that the SISS would retain primary responsibility and that the new chairman of the subcommittee would be William Jenner, a virulent anti-Communist, who had called for President Truman's impeachment at the time of General MacArthur's dismissal, had opposed the Marshall Plan, and had elicited the distaste of Eisenhower during the 1952 campaign ("I felt dirty from the touch of the man"). McCarthy had campaigned for Jenner's reelection and could take some credit for his appointment as chairman. Republican leaders, including Eisenhower, were glad to see Jenner, rather than McCarthy, in official charge of the anticommunism effort. They knew that Jenner would be more cooperative with other Republicans and would be less likely to cause embarrassment. The Jenner Committee was charged to investigate alleged Communist subversion at the United Nations and in education.[17]

The House Committee on Un-American Activities was headed by Congressman Harold Velde of Illinois and concentrated most of its efforts on the arts and media, with special attention to the movie industry. McCarthy's Committee on Government Operations targeted the Department of State and the army, aided by Roy Cohn in the role of chief counsel. Cohn had been a prosecutor in the successful case against Ethel and Julius Rosenberg, soon to be electrocuted for conspiracy to commit espionage.

Without losing a beat, Jenner followed in the tracks of Senator McCarran, who had started but not finished his probe of communism in education during September and October of the previous year. Jenner took his subcommittee to New York City in February and to Boston in March to begin his work. Utilizing findings from investigations going back to 1938, Jenner and Chief Counsel Morris subpoenaed professors from numerous institutions in the eastern United States, including Harvard, M.I.T., and Boston University.

There was an inevitability to the surfacing of Novikoff's name. Morris had been an interrogator of Albaum the previous fall. He had played an active role in eliciting the incriminating information from Grebanier before the Rapp-Coudert Committee in 1940–1941. Now he took the precaution of requesting information about Novikoff from the Rapp-Coudert files in New York City. The answer came on March 16 from the Office of the U.S. District Attorney for the Southern District of New York State. It came in the form of entry 418, a summary of evidence against Novikoff. Morris had more than enough information on Novikoff to convince Jenner that a subpoena should go to Vermont.[18]

By chance, Louis Lisman, the counsel for the University of Vermont, happened to be in federal court in Burlington on the morning of March 19. He overheard the Vermont deputy U.S. marshall, John Breen, mention that he had to serve a subpoena on a University of Vermont professor. In response to Lisman's inquiry, Breen told him that it was a Professor Novikoff. Thus, as Marshall Breen arranged to go up University Hill to see Novikoff, who was at home with an acute case of bronchitis, Lisman called to give President Borgmann warning of the subpeona. The subpoena, which ordered Novikoff to appear in Boston on March 26, was served to him in bed at 10:30 A.M.[19]

Actually, Borgmann had already heard about the subpeona from Morris, who had "called the University out of courtesy to let them know." As described by Novikoff, an important meeting then occurred: "I received a phone call from the president in the afternoon of that day. He asked could he come and see me. I said, 'certainly,' if he didn't mind seeing me unshaved and in pyjamas. He came over within the hour and he was with Mr. Lisman, whom I had not, to my knowledge, met prior to that day." The content of the discussion on March 19 and of subsequent discussions involving Borgmann, Lisman, and Novikoff became a matter of disagreement later. Morris recollected being told the following:

> Mr. Lisman told me that he had discussed the matter with the president of the university and that he would have no trouble because this man would be a cooperative witness. I said, "Do you mean he is going to admit that he had been a Communist?" He said, "Well, this man has never been a Communist; he has told us so. He has given us every assurance that he has never been connected with the Communist organization in any way."

Novikoff's representation of the conversations was markedly different: "I never told Mr. Lisman that [I had never been a Communist]. . . . I discussed with him some of the activities I had been engaged in at Brooklyn College. From what I said they may have gained certain impressions, but I was extremely careful . . . not to state whether I had or had not been, whether I was or was not."[20]

In an interview in 1986, Lisman maintained that Novikoff was asked "more than once" during the afternoon meeting whether he had been a Communist and "flatly" denied he had been. On the basis of these assertions, according to Lisman, he and Borgmann concluded that Novikoff was "being falsely accused," and they decided to assist Novikoff in defending himself against the committee's charges.[21]

Discussions during the days following the issuing of the subpoena focused also on Novikoff's potential use of the Fifth Amendment in his testimony. Novikoff told Lisman that his initial impulse was to invoke this "one privilege granted to a witness under my circumstances."

> Finally, after some deliberation and during a second conversation with my president, I decided to compromise with what I considered at that

time to be my principles solely for the sake of lessening the embarrassment to the University of Vermont, which is right now in the process of
asking for money from the State Legislature, and only for that reason
did I suggest that I might be willing not to use the privilege of the fifth
amendment for the time that I had been associated with the university.

Thus, Novikoff's likely strategy with the subcommittee was developed
shortly after the arrival of the subpoena. Because Borgmann was a
participant in the discussions and knew of Novikoff's likely course of
action, Borgmann was in a position to anticipate problems for the
university.[22]

On the basis of advice given by Borgmann and Lisman at the
meeting on March 19, Novikoff decided to secure legal assistance from
a Boston firm, Ropes, Gray, Best, Coolidge and Rugg. Novikoff's letter
to the firm on March 21 stated that "both of them [Borgmann and
Lisman] would be happy if your firm would act as my counsel at the
hearing." Novikoff asked for an appointment on Wednesday morning,
March 25, the day before his scheduled hearing with the Jenner Committee. He indicated that he hoped that he would be well enough from
his bout with bronchitis to travel to Boston. As it turned out, Novikoff's
illness lingered, and he wrote Boston to seek a postponement of the
hearing. On March 25 Lisman tried unsuccessfully to reach Chief
Counsel Morris to arrange for a postponement and to find out what
kind of an affidavit would be necessary to assure the committee that
Novikoff's illness was genuine. So Lisman traveled to Boston on
March 26, to intervene personally on Novikoff's behalf. He returned
on the night of the 26th with the news that the committee had accepted Novikoff's illness as genuine. Furthermore, Lisman told Novikoff that he planned to travel to Washington to urge the committee to
"drop the entire proceeding."[23]

Given the subsequent course of events, especially the later prosecutorial role played by the university attorney, the apparent cooperative relationship between Borgmann, Lisman, and Novikoff is an
interesting sidelight. Lisman, a graduate of the University of Vermont
and Harvard Law School, was a member of a prominent family in
Burlington's small Jewish community. As the weeks passed, he assumed an increasingly crucial role in shaping the University of Vermont's response to Novikoff's troubles in Washington. At this early
stage he was committed to finding a solution that served both the
university's and Novikoff's interests. Lisman was instrumental in post-
poning the Boston hearing, in arranging for Novikoff to appear voluntarily in Washington on April 2, and in getting Novikoff additional
time before appearing in a public session later in April. While these

events were taking place, however, Borgmann and Lisman were looking ahead to how the university would handle the affair if it were to
surface publicly. On March 26, at a scheduled meeting of the University
of Vermont Faculty Senate, Borgmann announced the policy of the
university regarding individuals called to testify before congressional
investigating committees. The connection between the new policy of
March 26 and Novikoff's subpoena was affirmed by Borgmann, who
told the senate that "something had occurred that made it necessary
for him to get from the Board of Trustees a guiding policy under which
he could act in case of necessity." The provisions of the policy were as
follows:

> 1. No known Communist will be permitted on the staff of the Uni-
> versity.
> 2. Any faculty member claiming privilege under the Fifth Amend-
> ment will be immediately suspended. A faculty-trustee committee will
> be set up to investigate the circumstances of the case, and upon its rec-
> ommendation appropriate action will be taken.
> 3. A faculty member who admits previous membership in the
> Communist party, but who now claims that he is no longer a member,
> will be investigated by a faculty-trustee committee who will make rec-
> ommendations on his fitness to continue on the staff of the University.
> 4. A person who is charged with being a Communist and denies
> under oath any such connection will be investigated by the faculty-trus-
> tee committee should evidence be presented to indicate the possibility of
> perjury.

Borgmann indicated to the faculty senate that he had elicited unanimous support for the policy from the University Council and the Senate
Policy Committee. He indicated also that the executive committee of
the board of trustees had approved the policy, subject to a "slight
liberalizing" of the second provision. The trustees had urged that a
faculty member claiming the Fifth Amendment not be "suspended"
but be "relieved of his teaching duties." Following the senate meeting,
Borgmann took the policy to the April 11 board of trustees meeting,
where it was approved with the revision recommended by the executive committee.[24]

The first public disclosure that the university might be facing problems connected with the congressional investigation was a university
news release that appeared in the *Burlington Free Press* on the same day
as the March 26 senate meeting, headlined. "UVM Would Investigate
Some Cases of Faculty Members Accused as Reds." The article itself
did not indicate that a university faculty member might be under investigation: "President Borgmann will point out [at the Senate meet-
ing] that this is the policy now in effect and that the policy is being

restated at this time because many persons interested in academic freedom on American campuses have made inquiries about the attitude of the university toward this current problem." Borgmann and several faculty members found the headline misleading, which led Borgmann to apologize to the senate and explain that "it was a matter over which he had no control." Regardless of how the *Free Press* or the public interpreted the university's policy statement, the media at this time reflected a quickening of interest concerning the congressional probes. Indeed, over the next several days, the Vermont newspapers carried prominent stories on the hearings in Washington and in Boston and the persistent use of the Fifth Amendment by witnesses. A story on March 31 reported the position adopted by the Association of American Universities indicating that "invocation of the Fifth Amendment places upon a professor a heavy burden of proof of his fitness to hold a teaching position and lays upon his university an obligation to re-examine his qualifications for membership in its society."[25]

THE JENNER COMMITTEE AND THE FBI

While events in early 1953 ensnared Novikoff and the University of Vermont in the anti-Communist campaign, the Jenner Committee was active on another front with implications for Novikoff. Robert Morris, who was on excellent terms with the FBI, turned to them for help in building cases against university faculty. On February 11, Assistant FBI Director Louis B. Nichols reported that Morris wanted to "get a hold of a good case" at one of the eastern colleges and "wondered if we could give him any leads." Nichols gave Morris the names of three faculty members and wrote that "I think if we could get a good Communist Party Professor at Harvard, Sarah Lawrence and Bennington, this would be a worthwhile venture." FBI Director J. Edgar Hoover approved this idea by writing on Nichol's memorandum: "Yes. Help if we can. H." Consequently, after contacting its Albany, Boston, and New York offices, the FBI gave Morris the names of two faculty members at Sarah Lawrence and two at Harvard. Each of these people were listed on the FBI's Security Index. No Security Index subjects were found at Vermont's Bennington College.[26]

Transactions of this kind confirmed for both parties the mutual benefit to be derived from a close working relationship. As the behind-the-scenes partner, the FBI chose not to assign its personnel to cover the hearings. Instead, as set forth in a January 26 directive from Hoover to the Washington field office, the Bureau would obtain "through available sources as soon as possible" the transcripts of public and private testimony. The "available source" for the Jenner Committee was Robert Morris. Once a name surfaced, a search of FBI files was to be carried out, to be followed by a full-scale investigation. Hoover wrote: "You should contact confidential informants and confidential sources to determine that all information pertinent to individuals in the educational field has been reviewed and that appropriate investigation has been undertaken. . . . The Bureau desires that all cases involving persons in the educational field be brought at once into a current status." The names that surfaced in the Jenner hearings as well as in the hearings of the House Un-American Activities Committee (HUAC) provided the FBI with a perfect opportunity to expand its files on possible subversives.[27]

In return, the FBI was obligated to provide names and information to Morris. FBI files acquired through the Freedom of Information Act show that the FBI responded regularly to requests from Morris. Indeed, in an effort to keep up with the requests from Morris and the names that surfaced in the hearings, the FBI decided on March 25 to undertake a general survey of "subversive information" available on faculty at fifty-six universities around the country. Over the next several weeks reports flowed in from FBI field offices. The report of the New York office arrived on April 20 and, as one would expect, was the largest nationally. The Brooklyn College survey included data on thirteen persons, two of whom—Elton Gustafson and Melba Phillips—were listed on the FBI Security Index. The information on Phillips, a friend of Novikoff's, suggests why the Jenner Committee showed a special interest in Novikoff's contact with her at his public hearing on April 23: "Her name was found in the address book of Israel Halperin when he was arrested in Canada in 1946 on charges of violating the Canadian Official Secrets Act as a Soviet espionage agent. In 1946 she was found to be unlawfully in possession of top secret information concerning the construction of the atom bomb." The report on Harry Albaum indicated that he had been interviewed by the FBI on April 15 "at which time he affirmed the statements he had made to the McCarran Committee." The report also stated that Albaum "is presently furnishing this office with the names of numerous associates which he knew while he was in the Communist Party."[28]

The report of the Albany office on the University of Vermont arrived in Washington on April 30, several days after Novikoff's confrontation with the Jenner Committee. The Novikoff summary contained four brief paragraphs on his past, mentioned his listing on the Security Index, and noted that there existed "No pertinent [communist] contacts or activities since NOVIKOFF came to Vermont in 1949."

Interestingly, another University of Vermont faculty member, Lewis S. Feuer, was identified as a member of the Security Index. Feuer, a philosopher, had been subpoenaed and interrogated privately by the Rapp-Coudert Committee in 1941 while a teacher at City College. His membership in the Teachers Union at Harvard and at City College caught the interest of the committee, but his name never surfaced publicly in the New York investigation. Feuer, who developed an international reputation as a scholar, was not a close associate of Novikoff at the University of Vermont.[29]

Although available documents do not establish the full picture of the FBI-Morris collaboration, it is evident that there were regular transactions producing mutual benefit. The FBI consistently held back information but provided enough leads to fuel the probe for several weeks. In July, Morris submitted drafts to the FBI of the Jenner Committee's public report. Morris accepted several suggested changes affecting the "Bureau's interests." Operating within this cooperative relationship, the FBI and the Jenner Committee were positioned to share information about the Novikoff case. As we will see as Novikoff's ordeal unfolds, both the Jenner Committee and the FBI exploited the information emanating from the arrangement.[30]

TESTIMONY IN EXECUTIVE SESSION

As a result of Lisman's discussions with Counsel Morris, Novikoff went to Washington on April 2 to meet privately with the Jenner Committee. He spent about four and a half hours with members of the committee, including important off-the-record meetings with Morris and Senator Herman Welker of Idaho. Morris, who was well informed and strong-willed in his role as chief prosecutor, clashed repeatedly with Novikoff. Welker, a committed anti-Communist, was reputed to have a drinking problem and was despised by many of the witnesses who passed through his clutches during 1952 and 1953. His "disheveled" personal appearance was the subject of an FBI report in March 1953 after a local teacher had berated him at a talk at the Charlotte Hill Prep School in Washington. Despite the strained circumstances, Novikoff seemed to get along well with Welker.[31]

Later in the summer Novikoff recalled his conversations with Morris and Welker:

> Within the first five minutes with Mr. Morris, I was told that the only way I could convince the committee that I was sincere in asserting that I have had no connections with communist activities for the time I had been in Vermont was to give them the names of colleagues at Brooklyn

College whom they said I knew to be communists. Mr. Morris said all
he wanted was for me to name Mr.——, "whom you know we know
was the head of the Brooklyn College group" and the name of one other
person "whom you know we know was a member of the group."

Later in the off-the-record session, Senator Welker said that he
would have insisted that I name "all the names," not just two, but
"since counsel had already committed himself," he was "ready to go
along."

During the course of the morning Novikoff scribbled notes on the conversations that were held. His record reveals that Morris at the outset
asserted that the committee knew that he had been "an important
member of the cell at Brooklyn College." He was asked whether his
wife was a Communist and was the one keeping him from testifying
openly. Novikoff answered that it was not his wife; his stance was a
matter of his own "heart." Harry Albaum's name came up in discussion, although it is not clear whether the committee indicated that
Albaum had named Novikoff. Morris told Novikoff that Albaum is the
"happiest man in the world now." Morris revealed that he had recently
seen Albaum, and Albaum had told him that he had been promoted.
According to Novikoff's notes, one of his comments about Albaum led
Morris to "blow up" and accuse Novikoff of a "slur." Morris and
Welker proceeded to praise Albaum's "patriotic behavior." Welker attempted to convince Novikoff of the committee's good intentions by
pointing out that they were not after people like Novikoff; rather, they
were after those "plotting to kill boys in Korea" or "your two little
boys in some future Korea."[32]

At 10 A.M. the committee convened formally in Room 457 of the
Senate Office Building, with Welker presiding and joined by Senator
Robert Hendrickson, Morris, and Benjamin Mandel, the committee's
director of research. The transcript of this confidential hearing has been
obtained through the Freedom of Information Act. Morris and Welker
took Novikoff through an array of allegations going back to his political
activities at Brooklyn College in the 1930s: his relationship to Howard
Selsam, his involvement with the Jefferson School of Social Science,
his leadership position with the American Association of Scientific
Workers, and his contacts with Communists during his tenure at the
University of Vermont. Morris pressed Novikoff repeatedly to admit
that he had told Lisman and Borgmann that he had never been a
Communist. Obviously, Morris wanted to establish that he had lied to
the people in Vermont. Morris asked several questions about Novikoff's
contacts with Communists after leaving Brooklyn College.

Mr. Morris: Have you, since you have been in Vermont, seen any of the people who, to your knowledge, were members of the Brooklyn unit of the Communist Party?

Novikoff: That, sir, to me is asking me whether I was or knew who the members of the Brooklyn College unit were, and I therefore decline to answer the question.

Morris persisted:

Mr. Morris: Who are the people from Brooklyn College you have seen?

Mr. Novikoff: I have seen so many.

Mr. Morris: Will you tell us who they were?

Mr. Novikoff: Why is it necessary for me to tell the names of people I have seen?

Senator Welker: Just a moment. It isn't up to you to cross-examine the counsel and ask why . . . it is necessary. He phrased a perfectly legal, valid question to you, and once again you start evading.

Mr. Novikoff: . . . My only hesitation was not to involve other people. I don't like to give a reason for you to ask other people. But if you insist, I will tell you.

Finally, Novikoff began to discuss his contacts:

Senator Welker: Just answer the question.

Mr. Novikoff: I have seen Melba Phillips.

Mr. Morris: When did you last see Melba Phillips?

Mr. Novikoff: I don't remember, sir. I have probably seen—I undoubtedly have seen Albaum. I have seen my chairman of the department, Professor Martin. I have seen Professor Tulich, I have seen Dr. Ogur.

Morris evidenced a special interest in Melba Phillips:

Mr. Morris: Senator, so that you will have the full understanding of this, Melba Phillips is a scientific professor, or was a scientific professor at Brooklyn College, on whom we had evidence was a member of this same unit. We called Miss Phillips in to testify, and she declined right down to date on whether or not she was a member of the Communist Party. Then I asked Mr. Novikoff if he had seen Dr. Phillips since he has been in Vermont, and he has knowledge that he has seen her.

The most Novikoff would admit was that "I may have very well seen her." There is no indication that Morris had seen the very serious allegations against Phillips held in the files of the FBI. It is entirely possible, however, that the FBI suggested to Morris that it would be fruitful to press this line of inquiry.[33]

Novikoff refused to discuss his Communist past, was adamant that he had not been active as a Communist since 1948, and eventually invoked the Fifth Amendment. The exchanges with Morris were testy and sarcastic. Near the end of the seventy-five-minute session, Senator

Hendrickson entered the discussion for the first time and asked an awkward question: "Whatever led you to involve yourself in Communism?" Novikoff saw this as a "loaded question" and refused to answer but did proceed to say that "my membership in the Union, and my activities in the Union, and the like, certainly stemmed from economic conditions . . . I was a poor boy."[34]

At the close of the hearing, the question was raised by Morris as to whether the committee intended to go ahead with the planned public hearing with Novikoff at 1:30 that afternoon. The committee decided to postpone the public hearing in order to give Novikoff more time to ponder whether he could be more forthcoming in the future. Novikoff agreed to return to Washington at his own expense on April 23, at which time it was "hoped" by Senator Welker that he would eventually agree to give names. That afternoon Novikoff boarded the train for his return to Vermont. On April 6 Novikoff's testimony in private session was transmitted to the FBI.[35]

The pressure on Novikoff increased on his return to Burlington when Borgmann confirmed to the *Burlington Free Press* that a UVM faculty member had been subpoenaed to testify before the Jenner Committee. "UVM Professor Called to Testify in Probe of Reds in Universities" was a *Free Press* headline for a front page story on April 4. The story indicated that President Borgmann had handed the case over to the university attorney. Lisman, who did not reveal Novikoff's name, was quoted as saying that "they may already have given him a clean bill of health." According to the story "Lisman made it clear that the university will not begin any action unless positive proof is presented that the professor has any Red ties. . . . 'This man may be perfectly innocent of any charges,' the lawyer said. 'He may have been called to give information about other people. He may have been cleared before he was due to appear.'"[36]

Over the next ten days the attention of the Burlington community focused on the inaugural festivities for Borgmann, who had taken the presidency of the university the previous academic year. A *Free Press* editorial praised his qualifications and noted that he had "caught the spirit of the people of this state." Borgmann's April 13 inauguration address stressed the meaning of freedom and citizenship, and his comments were praised in the column.[37]

Unaware of Novikoff's difficulties in Washington, the April 15 *Free Press* contained a picture of Novikoff and reported that Novikoff had received a $5,000 cancer research grant from the American Cancer Society. The brief story noted that "Dr. Novikoff will experiment on rat livers, hoping to shed light on why cancer cells grow on without restraint." On the same day Novikoff sent a letter to Senator Welker indicating that he would not testify about activities at Brooklyn College.

> I have gone over all aspects of the situation in my mind time and time again. I find myself unable to follow the course of action you suggest. I know that your suggestion was made in all sincerity, but it is psychologically impossible for me to follow it. . . . In view of my feeling, do you still want me to come to Washington on April 23rd? I am sure that you do not doubt that I have no connections whatever with any activity in which your committee is interested, and that science, especially cancer research, has been my entire concern at the University of Vermont College of Medicine. National and local publicity may do incalculable harm to the University, not to speak of the cancer research program which we have worked so long and so hard to establish, and which is on the verge of important results.

Novikoff's letter alluded in several places to Welker's concern for his situation:

> I wish to express my appreciation to you for the time and friendly advice given me in this difficult time. . . . I deeply appreciate the interest that you have taken in me, as a scientist and a person. I hope that you will not feel that the time and sympathy you expended in my behalf were wasted in the light of my subsequent decision, and I am sure, from your attitude, that you can understand, if not agree with, that decision.

He closed the letter by asking for "one further indulgence" and requested that "you inform me as to your decision in this matter."[38]

The next day, April 16, Father T. D. Sullivan, chairman of the biology department at St. Michael's College in nearby Winooski, Vermont, sent a letter to Senator Welker commending Novikoff's work. Sullivan, who had retained Novikoff as a consultant on a cancer research grant from the U.S. Public Health Service, had been asked by Novikoff to write Welker. His somewhat restrained letter stated that he respected Novikoff "as a scientist with exacting ideals in research and as a colleague who has always been ready to give assistance and counsel."[39]

These letters were a final attempt by Novikoff to convince the Jenner Committee to accept that (1) he had not been a Communist while at Vermont, (2) he would not name other Communists, and (3) he therefore had nothing of importance to contribute to the investigation. He rested his hopes on Senator Welker, who pressed the need to talk about his past but seemed to be genuinely sympathetic to his plight. All of this was of no avail when a telephone conversation with Welker on April 21 and a letter from Morris on April 22 confirmed that he must appear in Washington on the 23rd.[40]

He was now faced with the certainty of going before the Jenner Committee in public and of seeing his case blared forth in the media. This was a daunting prospect for a man who over the previous six years had become a scientist of considerable national reputation. As he told Senator Welker, his commitment to his work was so complete that "I have had difficulty with my wife, who would like me to spend more time socially. . . . But I have had the data to calculate and evaluate in the evenings." For the first time, his hopes that he might escape—as unwarranted as those hopes may have been—were gone. He knew that all that he had built for himself in Vermont was in mortal danger.[41]

Chapter 6

EXPOSURE AND NOTORIETY

Vermont Responds to the Public Hearing

Novikoff boarded the train on Wednesday, April 22, to head for his unwanted appointment in Washington. At 10 A.M. the next morning he went to Chief Counsel Morris's office. After a phone call to the Capitol to confirm Novikoff's arrival, the file on the Novikoff case was retrieved, and a secretary took Novikoff and the file to the Old Supreme Court Room in the Capitol. Novikoff waited outside the hearing room while the Jenner Committee consulted in private about the handling of his interrogation.

At 10:45 Senator Welker came over to Novikoff and indicated that he was "disappointed" in his decision to remain silent about his past. In turn, Novikoff was chagrined to discover that neither his letter nor Father Sullivan's letter had been received by Welker. After Novikoff showed copies to Welker, Welker said that he would read the letters to the committee in an off-the-record session prior to the public hearing. He went on to say that there was "no way of showing you are not still a communist, except by naming others." Novikoff then stated that the FBI must know that he was not still a Communist. Welker replied that "in fact the F.B.I. thinks you still are, though I shouldn't tell you." Since a present-day reading of available FBI files does not establish this point, one wonders on what basis Welker made this statement.[1]

Finally, at 10:53, Novikoff had a seven-minute off-the-record session with the full committee. Welker read the two letters to the committee, told of his personal interest in Novikoff, and expressed his regret that Novikoff had not decided to "come clean." In reply to Novikoff's statement that he had expected that there would be no public hearing, Welker indicated that there had not been any promise to cancel the public hearing. He said that the only reason that Morris had permitted a postponement was that since Novikoff had agreed to come at his own expense, a delayed public hearing would not cost the committee any money. After some formalities about the handling of the transcript, the committee decided to move immediately to a public session.[2]

Reporters, photographers, and other observers swarmed into the hearing room. Senator Jenner, accompanied by four senators and committee staff, asked Novikoff to raise his right hand and swear to tell the truth. The chairman allowed photographers to take pictures and then turned the proceeding over to Morris.

Mr. Morris: Mr. Chairman, the purpose in calling this witness here today was because we had received evidence in executive session that he had been a member of the Communist Party while he was a teacher in New York City in the late thirties and the early forties, and we brought Mr. Novikoff here in executive session approximately a month ago to ask him about that evidence. . . . Mr. Novikoff, were you a member of the Communist Party while you were a member of the faculty at Brooklyn College?

For the next several minutes Novikoff sought to explain why he could not answer the question, citing potential damage to the cancer research program and the reputation of the University of Vermont. Novikoff cited recent national recognition of his work. The Subcommittee repeatedly pressed the question of communist affiliation.

Chairman Jenner: Doctor, we want to congratulate you upon your fine work in cancer research.
Mr. Novikoff: Thank you.
Chairman Jenner: And we would like to be able to congratulate you upon your being a fine citizen, as being an American.
Senator Johnston: Mr. Chairman, I have listened to this statement. We are all interested in cancer work, every one of us. But I would like to ask the witness the question, What does that have to do with whether or not he is a Communist?
Mr. Novikoff: I am not a Communist, if you are asking me that, sir.

After being asked whether he had seen Melba Phillips in recent years, Novikoff finally cited the Fifth Amendment as grounds for not testifying about activities prior to going to Vermont. Several minutes of dispute followed on several points, including what Novikoff had told President Borgmann about his Communist connections and the nature of his contacts with Melba Phillips. The core of the conflict was captured in the following exchange:

Senator Welker: I informed you, Doctor, that if you told the truth before the committee in private session that you could go forth with a clear conscious back to the University of Vermont, your testimony would remain private, and your reputation in no way hurt; am I correct in that?

Mr. Novikoff: Yes, sir. But I should make it clear what telling the truth really meant in concrete terms. You say telling the truth, but I had been told within the first five minutes that I spoke to Mr. Morris that meant naming names.

Senator Welker: Dr. Novikoff, how can this committee tell whether or not a man has severed his connections with the Communist Party unless he tells us all the truth? Can you tell me that?

Mr. Novikoff: I have thought of that as you know because I wished there was a way for you to examine my brain. There isn't. You have to take the sincerity of what I am saying; you have to look into what I am doing. I have been at the laboratory day and night. I have worked on the data from the laboratory every minute of the day.

The committee continued to press questions about possible contacts with Communists since 1948, and Novikoff asserted that whenever he was in New York "if it is at all possible, I go out to Brooklyn College." He admitted that he might have seen Melba Phillips in the corridors at Brooklyn College, and "if I saw her I surely talked to her."[3]

Novikoff volunteered that he had taught two biology courses at the Jefferson School in New York "probably in the period of 1945 or thereabouts."

Mr. Morris: Do you know that the Jefferson School had been a Communist training school?

Mr. Novikoff: I have seen it listed as connected to the Communists, and whatever the Attorney General's list is, I have seen it listed there in the newspaper. I think after that time, however, I think.

Senator Welker: Answer the question. Did you know that it was a Communist training school?

Mr. Novikoff: I don't know what a Communist training school is. If it is connected to the Communists, if it is on a subversive list or the Attorney General's list, then you may interpret it as a Communist training school, and if it is so, then of course it would be. I can only tell you that the courses I gave had nothing to do with communism. I gave courses that were strict objective scientific courses in introductory biology and in the evolution of living matter.

As to whether he knew that Howard Selsam was director of the Jefferson School, Novikoff refused to answer.

Mr. Morris: Mr. Chairman, I submit that when I asked him the question before, the only reason he would have any knowledge of the fact that the Jefferson School is a Communist school was that it was listed by the Attorney General. We have evidence in executive session that this man was in the same unit in the Communist Party as Howard Selsam.

Have I made an unfair statement there, Doctor? Were not you and Howard Selsam in the same Communist unit there?

Again Novikoff refused to answer, citing his privileges under the Fifth
Amendment. The hearing ended with Morris entering into the record
information showing that Novikoff was listed as a member of several
alleged Communist-front organizations during 1946. Morris presented
catalogs of the Jefferson School listing Novikoff's courses. Also, Morris
entered into the record a listing of books available for purchase from
the Communist-sponsored Workers Bookshop in New York City, including the listing of the biology book written for children by Novikoff,
From Head to Foot.[4]

The official transcript of the hearing shows that the persistent questioning, especially Morris's repeated suggestions that Novikoff had
maintained his Communist activities after 1948, led to several bitter
exchanges between Morris and Novikoff. Novikoff's notes on the hearing, which differ in several places from the official transcript circulated
later by the committee, contain the following:

> I repeatedly became indignant about Morris' behavior—interrupting me,
> introducing in sinister fashion material which I had cleared up for him
> in previous testimony. . . . [I] asked why he couldn't act as decidedly as
> Senators did . . . said I wished we could do without him here. Later, he
> referred to my "impertinence" as being "unparalleled." Mr. Jenner
> leaned over for quite a talk with Morris, to calm him down, I imagine.

The rancor of Novikoff's exchanges with Morris differed from his
more careful and respectful exchanges with Senator Welker. Although
Welker pressed his point that Novikoff must name other Communists,
Novikoff's notes show that Welker stated, "In my own heart, I believe
you [are telling the truth]." The notes show also, however, that Welker
stated, "But the Committee can believe it only if you tell the whole
truth." This exchange with Welker was not included in the official
transcript of the hearing.

After the hearing Welker came out into the corridor to see Novikoff.
Welker told Novikoff that "he still felt like a friend" to him even though
Novikoff "had made a mistake." Welker said that he hoped Novikoff
would continue his "important work." He mentioned that he could not
understand how the two letters to him could have been lost and said
he would look through his office. Later in the day Welker sent a letter
to Novikoff indicating that the letters were nowhere to be found. He
closed this correspondence by stating that "I trust that this finds you
well even though I am, as you know, unhappy about your testimony
this morning."[6]

In the end, despite their avowed respect for each other and the apparent belief that each was acting in good faith, the two men were firmly on opposite sides of the fundamental issue. Welker believed that for a person who had been a Communist the only route to exoneration—even for a truthful person carrying out important scientific research—was in the naming of other Communists from the past. Novikoff believed that his former Communist colleagues had been well-intentioned and sincere in their desire to improve social and working conditions in the 1930s and were in no serious way subversive to the security of the United States. He believed the decision to reveal his former associates would seriously and unfairly injure these individuals. Moreover, Novikoff believed that an inquisition of the kind carried out by the Jenner Committee fed on itself, and one could not be sure what further demands it might make on oneself or on those named. Welker and Novikoff parted ways on the central question of naming other Communists, and Welker's respect for Novikoff could not save Novikoff from the consequences of the disagreement. Without question, Welker's "disappointment" was surpassed by Novikoff's own disappointment and foreboding. He knew now that his life was about to be altered in a most complete and unhappy way.

Shortly after his closing conversation with Welker, Novikoff telephoned President Borgmann in Vermont. Novikoff's notes on this conversation, though probably not *verbatim*, are complete enough to reveal something of the relationship between Novikoff and Borgmann.

Novikoff: It's happened. Public hearing. Photographers, reporters. Same position as in private hearings. Would like to see you tomorrow. I can now come to your office.

Borgmann: What position?

Novikoff: Same as private. Answered all questions regarding time at Vermont. Used Fifth Amendment for all time prior to that. Got in a huff about insolence of Mr. Morris; maybe I shouldn't have. Senators were quite nice but Morris was mean. I inquired about the transcript, since I thought you'd want to know. Transcript available in a day, at a cost of about $20–$40. Printed record is free; it would be available in about three weeks.

Borgmann: I'll tell them that I'll go ahead as indicated and appoint a Faculty-Trustee Committee.

Novikoff: But you wouldn't appoint a committee until you'd seen record, would you? You can't act on newspaper stories, can you?

Borgmann: Well, I guess not.

Novikoff: You can tell them you will take appropriate action after you've seen the record.

Borgmann: Yes, Chin up, Alex.

Novikoff: I appreciate your friendship. It has made it possible for me to go through it all.

Borgmann: Okay, guy.

Not unlike the Welker relationship, it is apparent that Novikoff maintained respectful and friendly relations with his president. Whether Borgmann's positive feelings would ultimately benefit Novikoff in his time of crisis was yet to be seen.[7]

Novikoff returned home by train that day with unanswered questions, charges, and circumstantial evidence swirling around him. He had remained firm on his position against testifying about his Communist past, but even with the benefit of hindsight it is difficult to judge the wisdom and success of the decisions taken by Novikoff. In contrast to most witnesses, he did not have a lawyer when facing the committee in public and private. He stated later that he took this avenue because "I was not going to talk about anyone" and "I knew what my rights were and I didn't need a lawyer." It appears also that he believed that ultimately he would not have to appear in public. There are indications that Novikoff had hopes right up to 10 A.M. on April 23 that the hearing would be canceled. In any event, a review of the transcripts of his testimony suggests that the presence of a lawyer would have changed very little about the proceeding. Novikoff's best hope was to persuade Welker to help him, and a lawyer would not have improved his chances on that score.[8]

Novikoff decided not to name other Communists in executive session on the grounds that his former colleagues would be affected adversely and unfairly. Accepting that his refusal was a sincerely held moral position, how would his fate have been altered if he *had* named two Brooklyn College Communists? In April 1953 it was not at all clear how Vermont and, specifically, the University of Vermont would respond to the revelation of prior Communist activity and contact. Albaum had talked about his Communist past and named names, and he had survived the storm. Would Borgmann have protected Novikoff in the manner that Gideonse at Brooklyn College protected Albaum?

As events unfolded, reliance on Fifth Amendment privileges produced in the minds of many an even stronger presumption of guilt than identifying Communist associates. The Jenner Committee probably recognized this too. It is clear that Novikoff struggled prior to April 23 to persuade the subcommittee that his work and the reputation of the University of Vermont would be damaged by his public testimony. He dearly wanted to avoid the entire proceeding. Yet even when it was obvious to the subcommittee that Novikoff was not likely to name others or talk about his Communist past, they proceeded with the hearing and pressed the question of prior Communist activities.

Novikoff was trapped and, having turned away from the idea of naming former Communist colleagues, was forced to take the Fifth Amendment.

Given the tenor of the times and the popular assumption that the Fifth Amendment was a screen for hiding greater sins, the events of April 23 set in motion the next stage of the inquisition. Novikoff's name, testimony, and past became a focus of public recognition and debate. Novikoff's university and Vermont's political leaders moved quickly to assess the extent of his misdeeds and to determine an appropriate response.

VERMONT'S RESPONSE TO THE JENNER HEARING

Novikoff's testimony was covered on the inside pages of the national newspapers. The *New York Times* reporter recognized the animosity of Novikoff's exchanges with Morris and noted that Novikoff "turned on" the committee: " 'I cannot become an informer, and that is what you want me to be,' " he shouted angrily. " 'I promised to help this committee in its investigation and I will, short of that.' " Although the official transcript does not reflect it, the *Washington Times-Herald* reported that Novikoff "had considered co-operating with the subcommittee when questioned in executive session three weeks ago but had changed his mind."[9]

In Vermont the testimony was a front-page story, beginning with the afternoon *Burlington Daily News* on the day of Novikoff's appearance before the Jenner Committee. The *Daily News* ran a full headline saying, "UVM Prof Not a Red Now," and it carried a United Press dispatch on the testimony. The next morning, April 24, newspapers featured lengthy excerpts of his testimony and stories centering on his invoking of the Fifth Amendment. The stories contained several comments by President Borgmann. Borgmann indicated that the university would take no action until he had studied the "full transcript" of Novikoff's testimony. Borgmann reiterated the university policy first announced on March 26 but said that a faculty-trustee committee had not been set up. He said Novikoff would continue his research endeavors. The *Free Press* story briefly sketched Novikoff's career, identified his Burlington street address, and reported that "Associates of the biochemist describe him as a 'quiet scientist—completely wrapped up in his work.' "[10]

On the day following the hearing the governor of Vermont, Lee Emerson, told reporters that he would assure that the university conducts a "thorough investigation" of Novikoff. Emerson was in a position to exert influence since, according to University bylaws, the governor served as an *ex officio* member of the university board of trustees and held appointment power over six positions on the board. Furthermore, the conservative Republican was in a pivotal position to affect the share of the university's funding appropriated by the state legislature. The governor made funding recommendations to the legislature and was able to shape legislative decision-making. The *Free Press* article of April 25 noted Emerson's reply of "I don't know" to the question of whether a wider investigation of the university faculty should be conducted. The story noted also the possible connection between the Novikoff affair and state funding: "Speculation arose, meanwhile, in the General Assembly as to what effect, if any, the publicity will have on the university's bid for more than $4,000,000 in appropriations during the next biennium. UVM has requested increased grants amounting to approximately $2,000,000." The lead *Free Press* editorial of the 25th applauded the "reasonable course" of President Borgmann and noted that "it would seem that Dr. Novikoff has not made any converts to communism at UVM, even if he has tried."[11]

Shortly after his return to Burlington, Novikoff received a few expressions of sympathy and support. The former dean of the Medical College, William Brown, wrote on April 24, with a copy to President Borgmann.

> Today's paper gives me the unhappy news that you have been caught in the meshes of the witch hunt. . . . Whether or not you have been a communist in the past is no concern of mine because I have absolute confidence in your loyalty to our country and to the people with whom you have worked in your important research. I trust this unpleasant episode will not curtail your usefulness.

Benjamin Singerman, the Novikoff's family physician for several years, wrote Borgmann three days later, saying that "it is my duty as a humane person to stand beside another man who had dedicated his life to the welfare of mankind." He noted that "not once throughout this long period did Dr. or Mrs. Novikoff ever express an opinion that favored any foreign political ideology. . . . Never did they attempt to sway anyone from his own political beliefs." Anticipating the formation of a special university committee to investigate the charges against Novikoff, five of Novikoff's colleagues in the department of biochemistry expressed their support.

> During the five years of association with the Department of Biochemistry, Dr. Novikoff has never used the lecture hall, the class room or conference room for communist propaganda or any other subversive purpose. To the best of our knowledge, he has made no attempt either

in or out of school to proselytize student, faculty or any other person. Dr. Novikoff's teaching has been of the highest caliber.

Two of the signatories of this document, William Van Robertson and Arnold Schein, became rigorous and persistent supporters of Novikoff's cause.[12]

Meanwhile, Borgmann obtained a copy of the Jenner Committee transcript, consulted with the university counsel, Lisman, and others, and met privately with Novikoff. On April 28 the *Free Press*, noting that "an air of secrecy has surrounded the entire situation since Dr. Novikoff's return," complained that neither Borgmann nor Novikoff had made himself available to the press. On the same day Borgmann announced his decision to proceed with a faculty-trustee investigation in accordance with the policy statement issued on March 26. He appointed three trustees and, with advice from the policy committee of the faculty senate, three faculty members, as follows:

Trustees
Father Robert Joyce, chairman, pastor of St. Peter's Church in Rutland
Frederick Shepardson, businessman of Burlington
Charles Brown, lawyer and state representative of Brandon

Faculty
Paul A. Moody, College of Arts and Sciences
A. G. Mackay, M.D., College of Medicine
Thurston Adams, College of Agriculture

Borgmann did not reveal these names to the press on the grounds that he did not want to submit them to "outside pressure."[13]

Joyce, a University of Vermont graduate, was a figure of considerable respect who later would become bishop of the Roman Catholic Diocese in Burlington. Looking back on these events, Joyce wondered whether he had been made chairman because of the strong stand against communism of the Catholic Church and the assumption that he, as a Catholic priest, would be tough on this alleged Communist.[14]

On the same day that Borgmann appointed the investigating committee, Governor Emerson told reporters that he would not "embarrass the University by asking for a separate probe, but I will ask for a report on the University's findings." This statement by the governor led to a bold two-inch headline in the afternoon *Daily News*, "Gov. Emerson Leaves Novikoff Communism Probe Up To UVM." In addition, Emerson sent a letter to President Borgmann asking that he be informed "as soon as you reasonably can" of the university's decision on Novikoff. He added: "In your opinion, should the scope of the investigation be enlarged beyond the case of Dr. Novikoff? We do not want to intimate in any way that the University of Vermont has Communist professors, but we do want to be assured that everything is being done by the University authorities to see that the faculty is 100 percent pro-American and anti-Communist." Borgmann's response indicated that "you as a member of the Board will, of course, be notified of any meeting held for the purpose of receiving the report [of the faculty-trustee committee] and copies of the report will be sent to all trustees who are not able to attend that meeting." He also noted that he had sent a copy of the governor's letter to the investigating committee and "we can expect from them a recommendation with respect to the enlargement of the scope of the investigation."

The newly formed faculty-trustee committee met with Novikoff in Room 364 of the Waterman Building at 10:30 A.M. on April 30. The 5½-hour session was recorded on a dictaphone machine and transcribed later by a university secretary. Joyce, as chairman, opened the hearing and reported agreements reached at a planning meeting of the committee. The central question was posed at the outset: "The question which has been presented to the committee is: Will the University of Vermont and State Agricultural College terminate the appointment of Dr. Alex Novikoff as a member of its faculty?" Joyce indicated that (1) Novikoff would not be put under oath, (2) information obtained by the committee was meant only for the board of trustees and "possibly" the governor, and (3) Novikoff's "sincerity and frankness" and his attitude about communism especially for the present and for the future would be a major factor in the decision to be made.[16]

Novikoff endeavored in his first remarks to establish the basis on which he could be candid and open.

> I know what you are going to ask me about and I think you should ask it. I hope you can ask it in such a way that it won't be necessary for me to make a direct answer which will appear on the record which Governor Emerson and anyone else has a right to see if you so wish.
>
> Also, I don't want to put myself at the mercy of the committee in Washington. I think if we have a chance to talk about it you can see why I feel that way. So I will try to say what you would like in such a fashion that you will be satisfied with it and I can protect myself to the greatest extent that I see how.

Novikoff and the committee knew that Novikoff's claims about being free of communism since 1948 were credible only if there was some clarity and openness about the situation prior to 1948. Novikoff's dilemma was to tell about his Communist past in vague terms but in

such a way that the committee learned some facts and was convinced
of his candor for the period before 1948. Unlike the situation of the
hearing in Washington, where the slightest revelation about the pre-
1948 period would have led, he believed, to embarrassing disclosures
and probably self-incrimination, Novikoff sensed that he might be able
to hint the truth of his Communist past without stating it explicitly.
He knew that this small committee of colleagues and Vermonters was
a promising forum for making a convincing presentation of his position. Thus, in a manner that suggested a tacit understanding with the
committee, Novikoff alluded to his communist past at various points
over the next five hours.

Brown: So, if there ever was a time that you were connected with the
communist party, it wasn't coming to the University of Vermont that
dropped you from it, you had dropped long before that?

Novikoff: I had dropped from activities connected with the communists
before that, yes.

Brown: Then, Doctor, let's get this record very clear. If and when you
did become communist, and I use the word if and when, would it not have
been after you got into Brooklyn College?

Novikoff: Yes.

Brown: And all the association that you ever had with them would have
been with the fellow faculty members at Brooklyn College and their friends,
is that correct?

Novikoff: That's correct.

At the end of the hearing, the nature of the understanding was addressed again.

Mackay: What is the best assurance that you could give this committee
of your intent, of your future activities, if it should be the result of this investigation that you are not to be dismissed?

Novikoff: I tried to indicate that earlier. I think the very esteem I hold
you in, the very way in which I've answered questions, is the best answer I
can give to this.

Mackay: You mean to say by this that you've opened up your past much
more widely to us than you did in Washington?

Novikoff: Oh, yes, I mean I let you feel certain things here that I would
protect myself from there. I had to exercise some reserve here, simply because this was on the record. But I hope we understand each other, and all I
can say to you, is that if you don't believe me, I don't want to stay.[17]

The lengthy session addressed numerous issues, including details
of going before the Jenner Committee, Novikoff's family and educational background, contacts since 1948 with former Brooklyn College
colleagues, how a former Communist could be a loyal and patriotic

American, Novikoff's union activities, and his rationale for invoking the Fifth Amendment before the Jenner Committee. Novikoff identified several individuals who could speak about his work and his loyalty. He read the letter he had received from former dean, William Brown.

The transcript of the hearing (and of a subsequent brief session on May 7) indicates an atmosphere of mutual respect among the participants and efforts by the members of the committee to be fair. There was also an energetic attempt to examine Novikoff's Communist past and the likelihood that he might still be a Communist. Considering that Novikoff prided himself in never having directly admitted his Communist ties under committee pressure, his disclosures were the most candid of any he made before investigatory groups between 1940 and 1953.[18]

The most troubling issue for two members of the committee, MacKay and Brown, was the basis on which Novikoff had invoked the Fifth Amendment. Indeed, members of the committee did their own soul searching on the question as they pressed Novikoff to explain his reasons. Novikoff's rationale is expressed in the following exchange.

Joyce: I think I understand your answer to that—if you did talk, you would have to talk in such general terms that you would implicate people who may be innocent people or relatively innocent, but that you didn't want to implicate them, is that it?

Novikoff: Yes . . . I think under the present circumstances, it is virtually impossible to make the [Jenner] committee believe that there is a difference among communists, that there is a difference between a communist who would not stop at anything to overthrow our government, or do something that would put that in the realm of possibility, and the communists who out of confusion, out of sincerity, have seen only certain aspects of communist activity and who would never go that far. You cannot, it is my conviction, you cannot hope to draw that distinction before the committee. So when you say, name names, any name, your name is immediately put into the embrasive [sic] category of those who would not stop at anything.

Joyce: That would be reason for invoking the Fifth Amendment?

Novikoff: Well, my reason for invoking the Fifth Amendment was, well, I did not want to get involved in the mess at Brooklyn College. As I told you, my first reaction was to invoke it for the whole time, because I thought it was my principle to show opposition to what these committees were doing.

Following these statements, various members expressed their own perspective on taking the Fifth Amendment.

Brown: Each one of us has a different background, our activities have been different. If they were to call me before that committee now, I'd name anyone, because I have never been connected with the communist party whatsoever. But had I been, I might well invoke the Fifth Amendment. I don't know. That can't be answered.

Adams: Isn't the question here one of loyalty between your own con-science and the University, and perhaps some of the individuals you may have previously been associated with? I think it's a question of loyalty . . . particularly if they are willing to take your private testimony and keep your name out of the paper, and the name of the university out of the papers. Well, I think I wouldn't use the Fifth Amendment myself. I can't see any reason for it at all.

Mackay: Well, I can't either.

Shepardson: I can see a reason for it.

Joyce: I can too.

Shepardson: We mustn't forget there was a period when our government was very chummy with the Russian government and anything went. Our government at present is chummy with Yugoslavia, is it not, and the dictator of Yugoslavia has made an official visit to England. There is communism in many peoples' minds that is different than another kind of communism . . . So I can see where I might have invoked the Fifth Amendment . . .

At the second session, on May 7, Brown raised questions again with Novikoff about his reasons for invoking the Fifth Amendment.[19]

The committee interviewed four faculty members and two students from the School of Medicine, a Burlington rabbi, Max Wall, and the chairman of the biology department at St. Michael's College, who had retained Novikoff's assistance in conducting a cancer research project. During the month of May the committee conducted its interviews, discussed its conclusions and prepared a report. The committee uti-lized a transcript of the interviews prepared by Jean Wright, secretary to the dean of administration. Wright recalled her involvement in the Novikoff affair.

They had a dictaphone machine back then. . . . I had to do it on a weekend. I couldn't do it during working hours, and I was locked in a room and there was a guard outside. . . . It took me two days to do it, and I sat there and cried and cried and cried. It was terrible . . . what they were doing to him, because I started from the beginning thinking he was being abused and that he was not guilty of anything, and the more he talked, the more I was convinced.

Wright remembered that at one point Novikoff broke down during his session with the committee. "His voice caught and he had to take a few minutes to pull himself together during it. Well, it was terrible. I never cried so much for two days." Although she had deep misgivings about the university's treatment of Novikoff, Wright could not, for professional and personal reasons, share her thoughts. She guessed that "I wasn't supposed to talk about it," but she knew anyway that "there were very few people I could talk to." The ironic twist to Wright's role in the affair was that when Novikoff was forced to leave Burlington a few months later, her father bought Novikoff's house, and she moved into the house with her father. She has lived there ever since.[20]

During this same period public interest in the affair continued unabated. Nine scholars at Middlebury College, including two college deans, and a former state's attorney published a letter on May 4 in the *Free Press* expressing their fear of a "hasty reaction of a legislature sensitive to public opinion" and their desire that "this unfortunate circumstance will not prejudice the right of an individual to fair treatment or less public support of the University in its educational projects." The *Vermont Sunday News* featured an extensive front-page interview with one of the signers of the letter, the dean of the French School, who spoke about the dangers of the public hearings in Washington to academic freedom and to the university's position with the legislature. On May 8 the *Vermont Daily News,* a sister publication of the *Sunday News,* reprinted an article from the Vermont edition of *Our Sunday Visitor,* the newspaper of the Catholic Diocese of Burlington. The paper called on its readers to "pray for this troubled man that he and others may see their duty for the sake of our country, himself and his family." In calling on Novikoff to testify openly about Communists, the reader was reminded of the "cancer of communism" and the importance of "early detection and treatment."[21]

Various other papers around Vermont got involved editorially, but virtually the only editor to express support for Novikoff was Bernard O'Shea, the editor of the weekly *Swanton Courier.* He argued that "Senator Jenner has no right to inquire into your beliefs or ours; into anyone's politics" and urged that Novikoff's career as a cancer researcher be protected. The storm of reaction to this point of view brought the suggestion that the *Swanton Courier* was "communist minded" and that its editor was flawed by his education and by his out-of-state origins: "It is known that O'Shea has a college education and it is more likely that he received some instruction about Communism. He brings those thoughts here to Vermont."[22]

The fears of Novikoff, President Borgmann, and others were realized on May 28 when Fred Crawford, a state senator from Governor Emerson's home county of Orleans, introduced an amendment to the omnibus budget bill that would deny state funds for any institution or agency employing a person who has refused to say whether he ever belonged to the Communist party. The proposal sparked heated argument in the senate, with accusations of laxity in government matched by expressed fears of undermining First Amendment freedoms. Robert Babcock, a Democrat from Burlington's Chittenden County and a university faculty member, led the fight against the amendment. The *Free Press* featured one of Babcock's statements in its section on important daily "quotes": "Vermont is one state, in the last analysis, where a man can say his piece and not be punished for it." Although the amendment was defeated by a 17–10 vote, a rush of letters to the *Free Press* editor attacked the arguments of those against the amendment. Still, it is significant to note that the independent minds of the Vermont senate were not prepared to join the groundswell of anti-Communist sentiment.[23]

A May 15 story revealed the name of Representative Charles Brown as one of the members of the faculty-trustee committee. However, Borgmann refused to identify other members on the grounds that he did not feel that "any purpose will be served by announcing the names of the other members until a report has been made to the Board of Trustees." On May 28 Borgmann announced that the report of the committee was almost ready and would be presented to the trustees at the board's June 12 meeting.[24]

The report of the faculty-trustee committee, which was presented at the board meeting on June 12, contained several findings, including that (1) Novikoff had not been a Communist since coming to the University of Vermont, (2) he was "completely absorbed" in his scientific work, (3) he was respected as a person and as a scientist, (4) he did not advocate any subversive activities, (5) he had been candid and cooperative with the committee, (6) if he had ever been a Communist ("and we believe he might have been while at Brooklyn College"), he now renounces communism, and (7) he had taken various government oaths and registered for the draft. The three-page report described the circumstances under which Novikoff had invoked the Fifth Amendment and identified his reasons. The committee's discomfort with the Fifth Amendment issue was reflected in its conclusions:

> This committee would not hesitate to recommend retaining Dr. Novikoff on the faculty of the Medical College of the University of Vermont, if he had not invoked the Fifth Amendment, because we feel that he is, as of now a good citizen of the United States, together with being an excellent teacher and scientist, and of great value to the Medical College. We also feel that he might have had a good reason for invoking the Fifth Amendment, so that the Trustees may in absolute honesty feel that even though he did invoke the Fifth Amendment, he should be retained.

After indicating that "the use of the Fifth Amendment is a regrettable practice," the committee, with the exception of Representative Brown, endorsed the following conclusion:

> Since each case is judged on its individual merits, we the undersigned members of this committee recommend, in view of all the circum-

stances in the case of Professor Alex Novikoff, that he be retained on
the faculty, unless further evidence with regard either to his past or future activities should at any time give reason to alter this decision.

Brown's addendum to the report expressed the view that although
Novikoff was not a Communist, the invoking of the Fifth Amendment
was sufficiently serious that he could not endorse the view of the majority. Thus, by a 5–1 vote the committee recommended that Novikoff
be retained.[25]

In a 1984 interview Joyce recollected that the committee was convinced that Novikoff was not ever a "real communist" and concluded
that Novikoff's absorption in his research and obvious distance from
the Communist activities of the past meant that he was no longer active
in any way. The committee was alert to the anti-Communist "fever"
of the times and saw its dangers, according to Joyce. Joyce's major
regret was that the committee decided, after considerable discussion,
not to visit Brooklyn College to learn more about Novikoff's activities
and contacts both prior to and after 1948. He felt that although more
knowledge of Novikoff's past would not have changed the committee's
recommendations, it would have enhanced the credibility of the report
with the trustees. Joyce indicated that the committee was not aware
of the Rapp-Coudert investigation in the early 1940s and expressed
surprise that Novikoff might have been an active leader of Communist
activities at Brooklyn College.[26]

The trustees read and discussed the report on June 12 and 13 but
could not decide whether to retain or dismiss Novikoff. According to
unofficial reports, a straw vote was taken at one point, and it came
out overwhelmingly in favor of retaining Novikoff. Both aware of Novikoff's value as a teacher and a scientist and troubled by the Fifth
Amendment issue, the board finally decided that Novikoff should be
contacted and "strongly urged" to appear before the Jenner Committee
and speak openly about his past. An influential voice in the proceedings was that of Governor Emerson, who for the first time exercised
his ex officio status on the board and attended the meeting. In the
early evening, shortly after the June 13 board meeting, Borgmann and
two other trustees visited Novikoff at his house to inquire whether he
would be willing to return to Washington and answer all questions.
Novikoff recalled this meeting a few weeks later: "I explained why I
could not, in all conscience, do so. I asked whether I should resign at
this point, to make future difficulties for the University less likely. All
three committee members felt that I should not do so."[27]

News accounts of the June 12 board meeting were sketchy and
featured the disclosure that Father Joyce was chairman of the six-man

committee. The *Free Press* noted that the committee had completed "a lengthy, secret report" and that the identities of the members had been "kept in strict secrecy" except for the names of Brown and now Joyce. By Monday, two days after the June 13 meeting, the *Burlington Press News* editorial on Tuesday the 15th attacked the lack of information: "Then [after the June 13 meeting] the curtain of secrecy descended again. The trustees would not reveal the contents of the report although there was an unconfirmed rumor that Dr. Novikoff would be retained at UVM. . . . The people of Vermont will not be satisfied with any more secrecy in the Novikoff investigation." The same story carried the report that at an alumni gathering on the university campus green the previous Saturday (the day of the trustees meeting) a Boston area alumnus and lawyer had stated that those "who refuse to answer questions by any United States committee probing Communism do not belong in education."[28]

The trustees reconvened on Saturday, June 20, to consider Novikoff's negative response to their request that he testify freely and to ponder how to proceed. Again Governor Emerson was in attendance, and at this meeting he played a crucial role. Emerson put forth the following motion:

> That Dr. Novikoff be indefinitely suspended without pay from any further duties at this institution as of July 15, 1953, unless on or before that date he advises the president in writing of his willingness to go down and appear before the Jenner Committee and answer fully and freely any questions that the committee may see fit to put to him and that before that date he offers to the Jenner committee to do so.

With this stroke, Novikoff was cornered. The politically shrewd Emerson obtained an 11–5 vote in favor of the motion and at the same time produced a solution that would sit well with Vermont public opinion. Joyce and Shepardson, members of the faculty-trustee committee, were among those voting with the minority. In his remarks to reporters after the meeting, President Borgmann communicated the view of the board that "a member of an institution of higher education has special responsibilities with respect to his willingness to answer frankly the questions of a properly authorized investigating committee." Borgmann also indicated that if Novikoff were to testify, the board was willing to retain him "on the basis of his record at UVM."[29]

Thus, the Board rested its case on the Fifth Amendment issue. It is difficult to assess how many board members saw the Fifth Amendment issue as a convenient vehicle for punishing Novikoff for his Communist past. The trustees knew that Novikoff was not likely to testify and therefore knew that setting these conditions was tantamount to dismissing Novikoff. If the real motive of the board's action arose from the judgment that a Communist—or an ex-Communist—should not serve as a professor, Emerson's motion was an expedient and masterful ploy. On the other hand, the six-man faculty-trustee committee, which had voted to retain Novikoff, was genuinely concerned about the invoking of the Fifth Amendment. If the real motive arose primarily from concern about the Fifth Amendment issue, the legal and moral basis for mandating testimony must be examined. Was Novikoff legally justified in refusing to testify? Beyond the legal question, was there a moral basis for a definition of citizenship that required testimony about political activities that might or might not have been dangerous to the country? Although the deeper motivations of the board members are not evident from available sources, it is clear that neither the legal nor moral sides of the decision were discussed in depth or in explicit fashion by either the six-man committee or the full board. Furthermore, at no point did the trustees have before them a brief setting forth the legal or moral issues. Neither Lisman, as counsel, nor the several lawyers on the board felt compelled to set forth a coherent, written justification for their interpretation of the Fifth Amendment privilege. Those of a more philosophical bent did not feel compelled to set forth a coherent justification of the moral basis for the board's action. Although various articles from journals and newspapers of the time were distributed and discussed, there is no evidence to suggest that members of the board or the board as a whole engaged in a systematic analysis of the issues. Political logic prevailed, and the burden of action now was placed on Novikoff.

Shortly after the board meeting, Borgmann called Novikoff to notify him of the board's action. Novikoff's recollection of the conversation was as follows:

> When, in the telephone conversation, I asked Dr. Borgmann when I would be dismissed if I did not meet the Trustees request, he said that he "guessed" that indefinite suspension meant dismissal. When asked why I was not being given the month's vacation due me, he replied to the effect, "Aren't you on an 11-month basis?" When asked about the tenure provisions and severance pay regulations governing the University, he expressed ignorance of them.

The following Monday Governor Emerson told reporters that he approved the board's action and "in fact, I made the motion adopted by the board." Emerson saw the motion as "a very logical solution" and "it puts it right up to him." On the same day a *Free Press* editorial headline expressed the view: "UVM Trustees Act Logically on Novikoff." The editorial presented its analysis of the Fifth Amendment and

pointed out that an unwillingness to inform on others was not a justification with "recognized legal standing, as was the claim under the
Fifth Amendment for protection against self-incrimination." Novikoff's
choice was seen in the following terms: "Dr. Novikoff's decision may
not be an easy one. He may have to decide whether he will be completely frank about his past, even at the risk of being an informer, or
failing to do the work which he might do for humanity in scientific
research." The *Daily News* was almost ecstatic about the Board's action:

> This forthright and American type of action is in contrast to the dis-
> gusting vacillations and chicken-heartedness of the administration of
> Harvard University which allowed various members of its faculty to re-
> main at Harvard University after they had refused to answer reasonable
> questions propounded to them by various Congressional committees. . . .
> It is refreshing to see the trustees of UVM and President Borgmann
> react in the usual patriotic Vermont manner to the Novikoff situation.

Beginning Monday, the 22nd, the *Daily News* began to print daily front-
page installments containing the verbatim transcript of Novikoff's testimony before the Jenner Committee. On the 23rd, the *Daily News*
Washington correspondent reported a statement from the Jenner Committee pointing out that the committee "has had no situation where
a man has come back and requested a second chance to testify."[30]

A few days after the board meeting Novikoff returned from a trip
and went to see Lisman to discuss his situation. Novikoff's question
to Borgmann on June 20 about the tenure rules had sparked concern
about university statutes concerning the breaking of tenure, and the
subject came up again. Lisman reported to Borgmann that "Novikoff
stated that he did not desire the appointment of another committee
under the tenure rules." This was an important issue since Article X,
Section 14, of the bylaws of the university stipulated that the "final
decision concerning a termination for cause of a continuous appointment" should include the review and the recommendations of a board
of review consisting of the full board, the policy committee of the
faculty senate, and four of the faculty from the faculty member's college. Various other procedural requirements were included in the provision. Acting on Novikoff's statement to Lisman, Borgmann felt
comfortable in moving ahead. He brought the question of terminal pay
to the executive committee of the board on June 26. The group de-
ferred final action until the matter could be considered by the full
board.[31]

Shortly after the June 20 trustees meeting, William Van Robertson,
a faculty member in the department of biochemistry and a friend of
Novikoff's, submitted a letter of resignation in protest of the univer-

sity's handling of the Novikoff situation. Robertson was motivated by the discrepancy between his view of what a university should be and the pattern of action in the Novikoff affair. Robertson recalled that he "had a feeling for what the school should be and what it should stand for and what Vermont had stood for for a number of years, and it was on that basis that I really took a very firm stand on this. . . . I felt I didn't want to stay at a university that wouldn't consider the faculty." Although Robertson went so far as to consider seriously a job possibility at another institution, he was dissuaded from quitting by colleagues, the previous dean, William Brown, and the new dean, George Wolf. Wolf replied on July 1 to the resignation letter by presenting some rather tortuous reasoning.

> May I suggest that you consider your resignation for a moment from our standpoint? Although I do not question your loyalty to UVM, the College of Medicine nor the State of Vermont, will your resignation do more than take care of an environment where you fear the fate of your constitutional rights to another environment where your status in this regard may be even less clear cut? Obviously you are resigning in protest in an attempt to educate. I don't believe you are running away in fear. Although martyrism [*sic*] is a public educational technique used successfully for centuries it is not the only one. Possibly Christ could have done an even better job if he had lived another twenty years.

Wolf went on to argue that Robertson would be more influential if he were to set out to educate people about the "precise differences between national security and the security (constitutional rights) of the individual." Robertson quietly withdrew his resignation and shortly thereafter became an active leader of a petition campaign on Novikoff's behalf. There is no evidence that the resignation became a matter of public knowledge. Thus, it is impossible to know whether a public gesture of this kind might have had a decisive effect on the course of events.[32]

During late June the newspapers presented pictures of Novikoff at work in his laboratory and reported that he would not speak to reporters about his situation. Although Novikoff had until July 15 to indicate his decision on whether to testify, and news reports speculated on what he would decide to do, the resolution of the matter had aspects of a foregone conclusion. Novikoff's Medical College dean, George Wolf, was thinking along these lines when he suggested to Novikoff's department chairman that Novikoff's dismissal with one year's pay would "knock a hole in your budget." He recognized, however, some possible benefits of Novikoff's departure: "Will Dr. Novikoff's leaving in any way alter things so we will not need the space in Pomeroy Hall?

If so, I would like to stop them from working on it immediately. What I mean is will Dr. Novikoff's leaving release any space in this building." Wolf's administrative mind had calculated the problems and opportunities created by the event.[33]

With the trustees' deadline looming, Novikoff began for the first time to address the possibility that he might shortly be out of a job. His correspondence with former colleagues at the University of Wisconsin described events in Vermont and expressed bitterness about the role he believed Harry Albaum had played in causing his troubles with the Jenner Committee. Albaum, who had worked in Wisconsin in 1942 and 1943, was known by Novikoff's friends, and Novikoff was not at all reluctant to express his feelings about Albaum. He told Henry Lardy of the Institute for Enzyme Research that "thanks to Harry's ratting to the Jenner Committee, I am through here on July 15." He told Van Potter, the man who had recommended Novikoff to the University of Vermont, that "It may be tough for a while for us but I would a thousand times rather have lived through this period than have to live with myself if I did what Harry did." He added, "I have Harry to thank for the position I am in at the moment." Van Potter's reply reflected his distance from the reality of Novikoff's situation: "Most of us know nothing of the ramifications of your association with Albaum and others and would be inclined to think that if you answered all questions freely you would not be morally guilty of anything and that the list of names would soon be exhausted." Another former colleague, Philip Siekevitz of the McArdle Memorial Laboratory, expressed outrage about the trustees' action and asked if there was any way he could fight "this clear cut case of political intimidation by the Governor."[34]

In response to Novikoff's inquiries, each of Novikoff's Wisconsin friends offered suggestions and their own initiatives in helping Novikoff find a new job. Van Potter recommended that Novikoff apply to the American Cancer Society for a senior fellowship, which could be used anywhere Novikoff could find laboratory space. He was pessimistic, however, about Novikoff finding a place in the United States to do his work: "You would then (with a grant) write directly to heads of all groups carrying out relevant investigations asking for a position or space and if they are all negative as they probably will be, you could write to the relevant laboratories in England or elsewhere, but probably England would be the best bet." Siekevitz took Novikoff's case to Harold Rusch, president of the Cancer Association, who agreed to write a letter of recommendation.[35]

On June 30 Novikoff wrote letters of inquiry to professional associates at Brown University, the Institute for Cancer Research at the Lankenau Hospital in Philadelphia, and the Rockefeller Institute in New York City. The reply from Sidney Weinhouse in Philadelphia stated, "Knowing the makeup of our Board, and knowing their feelings and those of our Directors, I can assure you that there is no likelihood of a position in this Institute." Weinhouse suggested contacting acquaintances at the Detroit Cancer Institute and the Southern Research Institute. The reply from J. Walter Wilson, chairman of the department of biology at Brown University, indicated that "I am afraid I may be of little help if any to you, but rest assured that I shall do anything I can to help you." Wilson's letter included a comment that did little to raise Novikoff's morale: "I cannot tell you how dismayed I am that you are involved in this mess, and with the way things are going it seems possible that you may actually have destroyed your usefulness as a scientist."[36]

Novikoff's most consequential letter was penned on June 29 in response to a notice about a new medical school in New York City bearing the name of Albert Einstein. He addressed a letter to Einstein at Princeton University.

> I write to you about the situation in which I find myself because of your deep concern over anti-intellectual activities of Congressional investigating committees and because you may be able, in this particular instance, to help avert the end desired by the committees. Because I exercised my constitutional right in refusing to answer certain questions put to me by the Jenner Committee, about my activities in the late thirties and early forties, I am being dismissed. . . . Yet, if I find a position elsewhere, I can, despite the committee, continue to contribute to cancer research and to the teaching of medical students. Would any position be open to me at the new medical school bearing your great name?

Novikoff went on to discuss briefly the findings of the faculty-trustee committee and the intervention of Governor Emerson who "prevailed upon the Board of Trustees . . . to vote my dismissal."[37]

Novikoff's reference to Einstein's "deep concern" about the anti-Communist campaign was a result of recent news stories about Einstein. On June 12 the *New York Times* had reported Einstein's remarks to a New York schoolteacher who had invoked the Fifth Amendment: "The reactionary politicians have managed to instil suspicion of all intellectual efforts into the public by dangling before their eyes a danger from without." Einstein urged witnesses to refuse to testify by adopting "the revolutionary way of non-cooperation in the sense of Gandhi's." His remarks elicited the expected response from zealous anti-Communists. Senator Joseph McCarthy labeled Einstein an "enemy of

America." Novikoff's interrogator, Senator Welker, suggested that "the men in Korea would not agree" with Einstein's advice. Novikoff, however, was happy to hear this advice from a man who had long supported progressive organizations, including entities designated "subversive" by the government. It is pertinent to note that the news clippings on Einstein's remarks were duly entered into the FBI's huge file on his activities. Since at least 1940 the FBI had tried to determine whether or not Einstein was ever a Communist.[38]

Einstein's brief hand-written response to Novikoff, dated July 4, indicated that he would forward his letter to the head of the new medical school at Yeshiva University "drawing attention to your case in a favorable sense." He expressed his hope "for the college and for you that it will come out well" and expressed his respect for "your upright attitude." Novikoff received a letter on July 9 from the associate director of the new medical school, acknowledging Einstein's presentation of his case and assuring Novikoff that his papers would be considered when the task of staffing the school got under way. In December 1953, after the completion of the university's proceedings against him, Novikoff met with the associate director in New York. The significance of these interactions was that two years later they led to Novikoff's appointment to a position at Albert Einstein College of Medicine.[39]

As Novikoff's firing looked more and more certain, two worries tugged at his morale. He was concerned that his scientific work was about to be curtailed, perhaps permanently. The deeper pain, however, arose from the illness of his son. Kenneth's struggle with nephrosis was almost completely debilitating, and no cure was in sight. At a time when Novikoff was confronted daily by the trauma of the proceedings against him, the illness more than anything brought the family closer. Although Rosalind was more subdued than usual, she was firm in her support of Alex and of her son. For both Alex and Rosalind there was much to think about but little to do that would make things better.

Chapter 7

THE FIRST RIPPLES
OF DISSENT

Academic Freedom Emerges
As an Issue

In the first week of July, just a few days before the July 15 deadline
for Novikoff's response to the trustees, active interest in the case began
to surface among university faculty members. For the first time members of the campus chapter of the American Association of University
Professors (AAUP) took a serious look at the Novikoff case and its
implications for faculty rights at the University of Vermont. Andrew
Nuquist, a political scientist at the university and chapter president;
Arnold Schein, an associate professor of biochemistry and Novikoff's
friend from the New York days; and Novikoff conferred on July 1 or 2.
On July 3, Schein sent a letter to Ralph Himstead, general secretary of
the AAUP in Washington. Schein presented the facts of the case and
pointed out that the actions of the university were not consistent with
the bylaws of the university dealing with the procedure for dismissals.
Schein mentioned that he had discussed with President Borgmann the
inconsistency between the procedures established in March by the
trustees and the bylaws. He noted that Borgmann "stated that the
establishment of this new policy was an error of unknowing omission
rather than of commission." Schein urged immediate AAUP intervention: "I am in hopes that your committee (Committee A) can take
quick action to attempt to delay a final decision (dismissal) by the Board
of Trustees which would probably be irrevocable. . . . It is far better to
try to correct an iniquity *before* it becomes irrevocable than to lament,
when it is too late, about what should or might have been done."
Schein sent copies of his letter to Borgmann, Nuquist, Novikoff, and

George Wolf, dean of the Medical College. Schein's prediction that trustee action would be irrevocable turned out to be an accurate assessment of the momentum already gathered in the case.[1]

Because of Himstead's scheduled absence from the AAUP office until July 13, Schein's letter was reviewed by George Pope Shannon, associate secretary, and William Middleton, also on the AAUP staff. Shannon's telegram to Schein, dated July 8, stated that "in termination of appointments for cause no circumstances justify special procedures denying protection of due process. . . . Urgently important that special procedures be reconsidered." Shannon pointed out in an accompanying letter that he would bring the case to Himstead's attention and that "we are concerned about the situation with reference to Dr. Novikoff."[2]

On July 8, the day that he received Shannon's wire, Schein sent a response expressing the urgency of the situation.

> But as you know, chapters as such are not encouraged to approach the administration in local cases involving promotion or dismissal. Therefore, while I can (and did) supply information, I had hopes that the National Association would attempt to intervene in this situation involving gross violation of tenure, before it is too late. Have you contacted Dr. Borgmann? Have you tried to obtain their point of view (Trustees)? Can you obtain permission for representatives of Committee A to appear before the Trustees *before* they make their final decision? I need not emphasize that speed is of the utmost importance.

Indicative of the modus operandi of the Washington office, Schein's letter was logged in and routed to Himstead. In the margin of Schein's letter Shannon penciled a note to Himstead, saying that "we have received no communication from the professor concerned." The AAUP staff conferred after Himstead's return to the office, and Shannon sent a reply on July 14. Shannon's letter pointed out that in order for the AAUP to take action on behalf of a faculty member, the faculty member must make a direct request. Shannon asked that Novikoff be informed of this.[3]

Since, as Schein correctly stated, Novikoff's case was at an urgent stage, the turning to the AAUP for active support was an understandable step. The AAUP was widely perceived to be a prestigious and influential protector of the academic profession. A fundamental question with immediate implications for Novikoff's future was whether the AAUP in 1953 was prepared—organizationally and philosophically—to play a forceful role on his behalf. Unfortunately, the AAUP had slipped gradually over the years onto a condition of almost complete paralysis. Because the AAUP became involved in the Novikoff

case to an unusual degree and because its principles were invoked
frequently by Novikoff's defenders, it is useful to examine how the
organization arrived at this state of affairs.

DEMISE OF THE AAUP

The AAUP was created in 1915 in response to the firing of university professors such as Edward Ross at Stanford University in 1900
and John Mecklin at Lafayette College in 1913. Its creation reflected
also the growing professional self-consciousness of professors at leading eastern universities. John Dewey, a graduate of the University of
Vermont in 1879, was a charter member and the organization's first
president. A. O. Lovejoy, a Johns Hopkins University philosopher, became the organization's first secretary. Although the primary intent of
the organization was to codify standards of academic freedom and
employment and to strengthen the voice of the teaching profession in
American colleges and universities, these goals took a backseat almost
immediately. Requests flooded in from around the country to take up
the cases of professors then under siege by administrators and trustees.
Thus, in its first year the Association became actively involved in investigating situations of alleged violations of principles of academic
freedom and tenure.[4]

To a significant degree, the practices of the AAUP in investigating
incidents on campuses were established by the exceptional initiative
and resolve of Lovejoy in his role as secretary. Lovejoy had resigned
as an associate professor at Stanford University in 1901 over the firing
of Edward Ross and in early 1915 had reacted with alarm to a newspaper editorial reporting that seventeen faculty members at the University of Utah had resigned over the dismissals and demotions of some
colleagues. Lovejoy told Dewey that he would visit Utah at once if the
Association would put up the money. The next day Dewey withdrew
$300 from the bank, and Lovejoy made his visit to Utah on behalf of
the Association. On his return Lovejoy wrote an extensive report on
the Utah situation and submitted it to the newly formed committee on
academic freedom and tenure. This committee, which in early 1916
became Committee A, accepted the report, and the AAUP published it
during the summer of the same year. During the year several practices
were initiated by Lovejoy, including campus visits to gather information, the preparation of written reports documenting the facts about a
situation, requests to AAUP members to undertake visits, and the publication of the AAUP findings. Over the next few years these precedents
became part of the procedures of the Association, supplemented later

by formal censuring of an institution by the vote of the members of the Association at the annual meeting.[5]

During the 1920s and 1930s the Association grew in size, and despite continuing pressure from some quarters to focus primarily on goals of general reform and education, it became more responsive to the needs of professors who were not treated in accordance with accepted principles of academic freedom. As principles pertaining to tenure and procedures for dismissal became codified and accepted more widely among professors and administrators, the scale of the AAUP's activities grew. A consequence of these changes was the enhanced influence and prominence of the staff of the Association. In 1916 Lovejoy was succeeded by Harry Tyler, a mathematics professor at the Massachusetts Institute of Technology. He was designated general secretary and served in that capacity for fifteen years.

The Association set up an office in Washington, D.C., in 1929, and Tyler moved there in 1930. Following Tyler's retirement from the general secretary's position in 1934 and the interim leadership of Walter Cook in 1934–1935, the Association's leaders saw the need for a full-time general secretary. Rejecting a candidate who emphasized that he wished to continue his research activities, the Association selected Ralph Himstead, a law professor at Syracuse University, to be the new general secretary in December 1935. Himstead was a member of the AAUP council and had led a Committee A investigation the previous year. He indicated his willingness to resign his academic position and devote his full efforts to the work of the Association. According to one scholar, Himstead's appointment as full-time general secretary "signified the acceptance by the Association of a greater obligation to act in behalf of individual members of the profession who had been treated unjustly."[6]

Himstead's appointment coincided with growing agitation by many AAUP members for action to improve the AAUP standards and procedures pertaining to faculty employment. It was evident that the earlier statements (a 1915 AAUP report and a 1925 joint statement of the AAUP and the Association of American Colleges) needed to be improved. First, it was bothersome to the AAUP that very few institutions had actually adopted AAUP principles in their bylaws, probably because the proposed procedures and machinery were interpreted as mandatory rules. Few boards of trustees or presidents were prepared to adopt the whole package. Second, there was discomfort with the unsatisfactory statement about the probationary period necessary for attaining a tenured status. A recent AAUP investigation had been impeded by the lack of an explicit statement on what constituted a maximum length of time in a probationary status.[7]

After extended negotiations between representatives of the AAUP and the Association of American Colleges during the late 1930s, a new statement of principles was adopted by the AAUP in 1940. The statement established seven years as the maximum duration of a probationary period for faculty and defined policy in a number of other important areas. Two clauses had direct application to Novikoff's situation:

—After the expiration of a probationary period teachers or investigators should have permanent or continuous tenure, and their services should be terminated only for adequate cause, except in the case of retirement for age, or under extraordinary circumstances because of financial exigencies.

—Termination for cause of a continuous appointment, or the dismissal for cause of a teacher previous to the expiration of a term appointment, should, if possible, be considered by both a faculty committee and the governing board of the institution. In all cases where the facts are in dispute, the accused teacher should be informed before the hearing in writing of the charges against him and should have the opportunity to be heard in his own defense by all bodies that pass judgment upon his case. He should be permitted to have with him an adviser of his own choosing who may act as counsel. There should be a full stenographic record of the hearing available to the parties concerned. In the hearing of charges of incompetence the testimony should include that of teachers and other scholars, either from his own or from other institutions. Teachers on continuous appointment who are dismissed for reasons not involving moral turpitude should receive their salaries for at least a year from the date of notification of dismissal whether or not they are continued in their duties at the institution.

In addition to these statements about tenure and due process, a clause pertaining to academic freedom had relevance:

—The college or university teacher is a citizen, a member of a learned profession, and an officer of an educational institution. When he speaks or writes as a citizen, he should be free from institutional censorship or discipline, but his special position in the community imposes special obligations. As a man of learning and an educational officer, he remembers that the public may judge his profession and his institution by his utterances. He should at all times be accurate, should exercise appropriate restraint, should show respect for the opinions of others, and should make every effort to indicate that he is not an institutional spokesman.

After almost twenty-five years of effort, the AAUP, with the endorsement of most important higher education organizations, had established practical statements of policy and of "acceptable academic practice." Although the AAUP statements were not directly enforceable on any campus, the statements represented commonly understood standards for evaluating institutional behavior and in time came to be accepted by most campuses—virtually *all* institutions striving for academic prestige—as rules to guide their own conduct.[8]

Himstead served as general secretary until his death in 1955, and during this time the AAUP grew in membership from twelve thousand to almost forty-five thousand. He was an opponent of authoritarian administrators and a strong proponent of faculty preeminence in academic governance. He was not reluctant to negotiate directly with college presidents over faculty disputes.

Himstead's national prestige grew as he used the AAUP forum to educate others about the obligations set forth in the 1940 statement, participated in various national commissions and conferences, and came to dominate the AAUP council and the internal workings of the Association. As the years passed, however, the pitfalls of Himstead's domination of the AAUP national office became evident. Extensive interviews of AAUP staff conducted in 1960 and 1961 indicate that Himstead's perfectionism and failure to delegate responsibility meant that correspondence and drafts of reports were often late or never finished. He read all letters that came to the office and all drafts prepared by members of the staff, and he personally reviewed all submissions to the Association *Bulletin*. As a result, the *Bulletin* was frequently published many months late.[9]

The combined effects of a growing membership, Himstead's management style, and his resistance to criticism served to incapacitate the central office by the mid-1940s. The 1945–1950 period was the least productive period in the history of the Association, as measured by the percentage of complaints from faculty that received AAUP attention. The AAUP investigated 35 percent of faculty complaints and made an on-campus inquiry in only 6 percent of the cases. During this period the AAUP published only five reports; there were no reports published over the next five years, until Himstead's death. The lack of productivity coincided with the McCarthy period and efforts by universities to dismiss faculty with actual or alleged ties to the Communist party. Walter Metzger, who studied Himstead's role, observed that "the man who ran the central office with an iron hand was profoundly and irremediably incapacitated, yet determined to stay in charge." Although some AAUP members attributed AAUP inaction in these cases to a reluctance to meet the McCarthy challenge squarely, the major factor was probably the general ineffectiveness and inefficiency of the office, regardless of the nature of the case.[10]

Criticism of Himstead's leadership came to a head in the spring of 1953, when many members voiced complaints at the national meeting in Chicago. A Committee on Organization and Policy was charged to study the management of the central office, with the goal of improving communications between the office and members of the Association. The chairman of the committee visited Washington in June 1953 to discuss the problems of the office, but Himstead canceled subsequent meetings in the fall. Himstead complained frequently about his workload, but despite pressure from others to alter his management habits, he did little to reorganize the workings of the office.[11]

Thus, as the Novikoff case unfolded at the University of Vermont in early 1953, it is clear that the AAUP was not prepared to play a potent role on behalf of Novikoff. There was already a backlog of cases from the McCarthy era, and Himstead was under siege from within and engaged in energetic defensive maneuvers to retain his power. Furthermore, the AAUP's position on the Fifth Amendment was ambiguous. On April 24 the national office had sent to its chapters a copy of the resolution approved at its national meeting, which stated that invoking the Fifth Amendment as the reason for not replying to questions concerning a faculty member's views and affiliations was "a valid constitutional reason for not replying." The resolution went on to say, however, that "since a decision to invoke the Fifth Amendment involved complex legal and ethical considerations, this statement is not to be construed as advising or generally approving such action by teachers under investigation."[12]

COUNTERATTACK BY NOVIKOFF'S DEFENDERS

Although faculty members at the University of Vermont were unaware of the problems in the AAUP national office, they knew that the slightest delay there would erase any possibility of stopping the actions of the trustees. As Arnold Schein's communications with the national office on behalf of Novikoff stretched out over several days, the local chapter became impatient and decided to move ahead on its own. Nuquist sent a note on July 7 (before receiving the telegram outlining the AAUP's position) notifying chapter members of a meeting on July 9 to discuss "what action, if any, the Vermont chapter of AAUP should take with respect to the matter involving the future status of one of our members." The local AAUP may have restrained its activity prior to this time because of the AAUP bylaw stipulating that local chapters should not take a stand on individual cases; however, Nuquist told a reporter on July 10 that the language of the AAUP bylaw "might leave the last resort to us in that the national doesn't forbid, just frown [*sic*] on, stands in individual cases."[13]

During efforts on July 8 to prepare for the meeting the following day, Shannon's telegram arrived from the national office. With this telegram in hand the local AAUP leadership drafted a resolution that made two major observations: (1) procedures as stipulated in the university bylaws were not followed, with omissions with respect to the composition of the faculty-trustee committee of inquiry, the lack of written charges, the failure to provide a stenographic record to Novikoff, and "other possible deviations" that might have been "obscured by the secret nature of the proceedings," and (2) the action of the trustees "constitutes a serious threat to the principle of tenure." The resolution urged the faculty senate to recommend to the board that it "rescind its recent action and institute a complete rehearing of the case" in accordance with provisions of the university bylaws. At the same time the AAUP chapter petitioned Borgmann to convene a special meeting of the senate before any final action by the board. The AAUP resolution was approved overwhelmingly by the faculty in attendance. News reports on July 10 briefly mentioned the AAUP meeting, along with the rumor that there would be a move to seek a court injunction to prevent the board from "carrying out its ultimatum" to Novikoff. However, the *Daily News* reported that efforts "were made in various quarters today to obtain verification of the reports about the possible injunction action, but they were unsuccessful."[14]

Although the initiatives by the local AAUP chapter would shortly exert considerable influence over the course of events, the news story that received greater attention and larger headlines was the July 9 report that eighteen local clergy had sent a letter to the board of trustees urging the board to reverse its decision on Novikoff and retain him on the faculty. Following the trustees' decision to reject the recommendation of the faculty-trustee committee, several of the Burlington-area clergy had discussed the Novikoff case and then convened a meeting of about fifteen clergymen. Vedder Van Dyck, bishop of the Vermont Episcopal Diocese, serving as chairman, Rabbi Max Wall, and Reverend Harold Bucklin of the Methodist Church formed a subcommittee to develop a statement on the matter. The subcommittee met with the larger group at Burlington's St. Paul's Church on three occasions. It is not evident from available sources what contacts, if any, they made with the university staff or with trustees in gathering their information and forming their position. In any event, part of the uproar caused by the letter stemmed from the revelation that the vote of the faculty-trustee committee had been 5 to 1 to retain Novikoff and that this one-sided vote had been overturned by the board.

> It seems to be common knowledge that the Faculty-Trustee Investigating Committee, after long and careful investigation, voted 5 to 1 to recommend to the Board of Trustees of the university to retain the services of Dr. Novikoff. . . . We are concerned that the Board of Trustees of the University of Vermont reversed the report of the committee and offered Dr. Novikoff only one choice, that of violating his conscience, by returning to Washington to testify against others whose guilt has not yet been established. . . . We are further concerned with the facts that the Trustees of the University of Vermont never made public the vote of the Faculty-Trustees Investigating Committee to retain the services of Dr. Novikoff; that the records of the investigation are not made available to the public; and that interested parties have been refused permission to review the record of the hearing on the grounds that the Trustees voted to keep the whole matter secret.

The uproar was due in equal measure to the clergy's taking a public stand on political and educational issues that went against the obvious trend of public and editorial opinion.

> The action taken by your Board in the case of Dr. Alex Benjamin Novikoff seems to us to be a dangerous blow to academic freedom and opposed to the essential interests of a free educational institution and the larger interests of democracy and humanity. There is a growing conviction that the methods of the McCarthy, Velde and Jenner Committees do violence to our democratic traditions.[15]

Although the letter was signed by several Protestant and Catholic ministers, it did not, of course, include the signature of Father Joyce, the chairman of the faculty-trustee committee. However, speculation arose with respect to his vote on the Novikoff matter. Joyce reported that many people suspected that he, as a Catholic, had been the single vote against Novikoff. With hindsight and knowledge of Joyce's vote in support of Novikoff, one might speculate that it was Joyce who had revealed details of the committee's deliberations. Joyce, however, emphasized in an interview that he knew nothing of the clergy's letter until it appeared and recalled that he had virtually no discussion of the Novikoff case with outside people, including with other clergy.[16]

In the days following the publication of the clergy's letter, the leading Burlington newspapers and the governor reacted negatively. The *Free Press* editor found it difficult to "follow their thinking." A *Daily News* story noted that the paper's "streamer banner which we contribute free on Friday, in an attempt to increase church-going, is a demonstration of our support of the church and our cooperation with the clergy." The story went on to express its criticism: "It would seem that the good ministers had let their hearts very much run away with their heads. In times such as these, when the nation faces destruction by the sympathetic and very able plotting of Communist agents and spies, such judgment on the part of the clergy is very miserable indeed." The *Daily News* published a special section identifying the names and affiliations of each of the ministers. The *Free Press*, on the same day that the clergy's letter was released, headlined an Associated Press story with "Documentary Evidence Reported of Red Infiltration of Clergy." The governor issued a statement, prominently headlined in both Burlington papers, saying that he saw "no denial of academic freedom" and that the Jenner investigation "was highly proper and one to which every American should lend assistance when called upon to do so." According to the *Free Press*, "rumors circulated wildly through the UVM campus," but there were no statements forthcoming from President Borgmann, who was on vacation in New Hampshire, and no one in the administration was prepared to speak on his behalf. One paper reported that after his return Borgmann would convene the board to consider the clergy's letter, then later reported that Borgmann had indicated to a university spokesman that he had no plans to call a meeting of the board prior to the next regularly scheduled meeting set for August 15.[17]

On the morning of July 14, the day before Novikoff's deadline, the group of clergy met again, reaffirmed their stand, and "expressed the hope that the trustees would make public the report of the investigating committee." The afternoon *Daily News* reported the meeting as its lead story and included a front page picture of Novikoff's house on Bilodeau Court in Burlington. The *Free Press* reported for the first time the July 9 resolution of the AAUP and indicated that several Medical College faculty were becoming active in Novikoff's defense. Suggesting that pressure was mounting for a review of Novikoff's dismissal, the paper reported that reaction to the clergy's letter had switched toward the positive: "An unofficial poll last night revealed the majority reaction now favors the clergy's stand and it was reported one Catholic priest has received 'overwhelming endorsement' of his stand."[18]

On the same day Novikoff left a letter with Borgmann's secretary asking that it not be shown to anyone else. Indicating that he had received no communication in writing requiring an answer, Novikoff wrote that "I am assuming that the Board of Trustees may wish to learn my feelings concerning the resolution, passed on June 20, 1953, which you read to me over the telephone that day." The letter restated his views about the Jenner Committee and his unwillingness to commit an "immoral act" by naming former colleagues at Brooklyn College. For the first time, Novikoff invoked the bylaws of the university: "Should the Board proceed for my dismissal I trust it will be carried out in compliance with the established procedures contained in Section X, Paragraph 14, of the 'Organization of the University of Vermont and State Agricultural College.'" Because Borgmann was away and his secretary apparently told no one of the letter, reporters and the university director of public relations maintained a vigil until midnight on the 15th on the chance that Novikoff might indicate a willingness to testify. According to the news reports, Novikoff "remained silent to the end" and was automatically suspended. Borgmann, still on vacation, was on his way to Rhode Island for a two-day meeting with college and university presidents and was not available for comment. As usual, Novikoff refused to speak to reporters. In Washington, Senator Welker told a *Free Press* reporter that he was "truly saddened that Dr. Novikoff would not cooperate as an American" and that he would have been "so happy to see him come through for us." Novikoff's letter remained unread until Sunday, July 19, when Borgmann returned to Burlington.[19]

In the days following Novikoff's suspension, public and editorial interest reached its height. One subject of interest was Borgmann's absence from Burlington. The *Daily News* asked, "Why has Dr. Borgmann absented himself . . . when all the people of Vermont were looking in vain for the answers to the questions they are asking?" The *Brattleboro Reformer,* a southern Vermont daily, speculated: "On what basis has Dr. Carl Borgmann . . . felt that a vacation was more important than being on the scene helping clear up the confusion in the public mind?" Some of the persistent questions cited by the two papers included why the trustees had not accepted the recommendation of the faculty-trustee committee, what response there would be to the clergy's letter, what action would be taken in response to the AAUP resolution, and whether the "suspension" of Novikoff actually meant he had been "discharged." Other speculation centered on the possible implications for the University of Vermont of Novikoff's suspension (or dismissal), including whether the AAUP might censure the university for its conduct and whether its cancer grants might be jeopardized. On July 17 Novikoff's personal situation was further affected when St. Michael's College in Winooski reported that they had dropped Novikoff as a paid consultant on a cancer project at the college. A spokesman was careful to point out that Novikoff was not "on the payroll" of St. Michael's and had been paid from grant money received from the U.S. Public Health Service.[20]

On the Monday following his return, July 20, Borgmann called a special meeting of the faculty senate for July 30 and issued a statement reiterating the rationale for the board's decision. He indicated that, in the light of the AAUP's accusation that procedures had not followed university bylaws, he took "full responsibility for any deviation from established procedure in setting up a six-man committee." At the same time, William Van Robertson, who had submitted and withdrawn his resignation a few days before, joined Schein in initiating a petition on Novikoff's behalf. Robertson and Schein sought signatures of faculty across the campus. In an interview Robertson recalled that a conflict developed with a Medical College colleague, who signed the petition and shortly thereafter claimed that he had been misled by Robertson about its intent. This faculty member wrote a letter of complaint to President Borgmann about the incident. An apparent repercussion of this bitter exchange between Robertson and his colleague was that six years later, when Robertson was a leading candidate to become chairman of his department, his old antagonist may have been instrumental in denying him the position.[21]

Robertson remembered another repercussion of the petition drive.

> What was interesting was . . . to find out how many people whom I'd heard of as being liberal and pretty intellectual had one reason or another for not signing it. . . . I have a feeling my relations with some of my colleagues from then were strained because . . . after Alex was fired and then after McCarthy was fired essentially, they became ashamed of what they'd done. And I think that made a worse relationship than if we'd really been at odds with each other. Because there were some I argued with, you know, on the whole principle of the thing, and it never spoiled or changed our relationship.

An additional result of these events was that Robertson soon joined the AAUP because "I saw without a forum, without something like that, we couldn't have done a damn thing." Robertson later became a member of the AAUP national council, and after leaving Vermont in 1961 following his failure to gain the chairmanship, he became president of the AAUP chapter at Stanford University.[22]

In the days before the senate meeting, Borgmann received two petitions, one signed by thirty-one faculty across the campus and another signed by faculty of the Medical College. According to Robertson, Borgmann "was kind of glad to get the petition; I don't think he resented it at all." Moreover, the local AAUP chapter forwarded a new resolution, endorsed at its July 21 meeting. Each document criticized the handling of the Novikoff case and asked that the board's decision be rescinded.[23]

By this time the academic freedom issue and the role of the AAUP had surfaced and become matters of public discussion. *Free Press* editorials rejected the suggestion that academic freedom was at issue in the Novikoff affair and saw no threat to academic freedom principles. The paper stated that "the great majority of loyal teachers in the United States" did not feel that academic freedom was endangered by the McCarthy era. On July 21 the *Free Press* expressed doubts that the reputation or status of the University of Vermont would be adversely affected by any actions undertaken by the AAUP.

> The fact is that as of last winter, only six institutions were listed by the AAUP as having administrations that had acted counter to "the generally recognized principles of academic freedom and tenure, endorsed by this association," and six other collegiate bodies. The last time an institution was so listed was in 1950. In no case has the listing of an institution followed suspension of an individual for failure to co-operate with authorities against Communist Party activities. . . .
>
> Judging from the past actions of the AAUP, there appears small likelihood that the rating of the University will be affected by the present case.

Although probably unaware of the circumstances that had gradually paralyzed the AAUP under Himstead's leadership, the *Free Press* accurately assessed the capacity for action of the AAUP. Nevertheless, Novikoff and his colleagues continued to seek AAUP support. Novikoff replied on July 22 to the letter seeking his intentions by "respectfully requesting that the Association intervene in the situation." Novikoff added the following:

> From remarks made to me yesterday by President Borgmann, I gain the impression that they may try to rush through a procedure on one day (August 15) which would satisfy the superficial requirements of the tenure provisions, but not their spirit, and have the Board of Trustees vote on the same day. Any chance for reinstatement, under these conditions, would be virtually nil, despite the very strong feelings of the local chapter of the American Association of University Professors, individual faculty members, possibly the University Senate (the major faculty body, which is to have a special meeting on "the Novikoff case" on July 30), the committee of clergymen and other interested individuals in the State.

He suggested that, unless "persuaded to do otherwise," on August 15 the board would probably change his "suspension" to dismissal.[24]

On July 27 Schein wrote Himstead registering his alarm over the *Free Press* editorial.

> Not having the available facts I am unable to refute the statements contained in this newspaper article yet I believe such dogmatic assertions (which may emanate from the administration itself) which imply that effective action by the AAUP is usually lacking and is at best feeble must be answered. I hope the national office will do so. . . . What has been the action of the AAUP in cases similar to Dr. Novikoff's? Has there been any censure of an administration when a faculty member has been fired for invoking the Fifth Amendment or for suspected Communist party membership?

Schein did not know that he was dealing with a paper tiger and that the AAUP had censured no one. One can understand why Himstead failed to answer Schein's embarrassing plea.[25]

The following day Novikoff sent to Shannon, as requested, a detailed summary of the events of his case. This six-page, single-spaced document, which Novikoff labeled as "confidential," contained insights into his personal experience to that point and several revelations about events. For example, he pointed out that the report of the faculty-trustee committee had not been shown to him until "only this week . . . unofficially, by one of the Trustees." He reported that "it has been rumored recently that (at the June 13th meeting of the Board) the Board of Trustees voted, by a margin of better than 2 to 1, to retain me." These various communications produced no response from the AAUP national office until Novikoff sent a more urgent letter prior to the trustees' meeting on August 15.[26]

On July 28 Novikoff issued his first public comments on his situation. They were contained in a letter to the Burlington Lion's Club, in which he explained his reasons for not accepting an invitation to speak at the Lion's Club on the subject of academic freedom. He reviewed the important events of his case and suggested that the board's action had been a "violation both of generally accepted principles of academic freedom and of constitutional liberties." Noting the publicity given to his initial rejection of the invitation to speak (the *Daily News* headline read, "Lion's Club Disappointed As Novikoff Balks at Talk"), Novikoff stated that "I assume that you will also release my reply to the public."[27]

In preparation for the senate meeting, various parties worked to reconstruct the crucial events of the previous weeks and to get their facts in order. Novikoff copied his summary for use by the Vermont AAUP chapter. Borgmann prepared a lengthy review of events since March for presentation to the senate. Despite the fact that the university was not officially in session, approximately two hundred faculty turned out for the July 30 senate meeting. No newsmen were allowed in the meeting. Borgmann's opening statement ended with the observation that Novikoff's "indefinite suspension" did not amount to a "dismissal."

> At this point, I want to say that I have assumed that the "indefinite suspension" of the Board was to be interpreted as dismissal. I have been informed recently by the University's attorney that such an interpretation is an improper one. It seems clear to me that the procedure outlined in Article X, Section 14 . . . ought to be followed in arriving at a final determination of Dr. Novikoff's future status.

Borgmann assured the faculty that he would present to the trustees all communications he had received regarding the Novikoff matter. Nuquist, the AAUP chapter president, then presented a motion recommending a "complete rehearing" of the case, which, after discussion, passed with only two dissenting votes. Nuquist's second resolution proposed a stronger message to the trustees:

> BE IT RESOLVED that until evidence is presented and sustained which in a court of law would lead to a conviction the University Senate records its judgment that Doctor Novikoff has been wrongly suspended from this University, and requests that the Board of Trustees follow the usual American custom of assuming that a member of the faculty like any other person is innocent until proved guilty, and, in consequence rescind its action of June 21, 1953.

This resolution produced the longest and most heated discussion of the meeting, with the faculty divided on the question of whether Novikoff had rightly or wrongly invoked the Fifth Amendment. The senate secretary noted that those who took the negative side of the issue argued that "if the welfare of the country is at stake and a duly authorized investigating committee is seeking facts that a witness can give, he is morally and patriotically bound to answer the questions of the committee." The disagreement with Nuquist's motion was sufficiently strong that a motion to table the resolution was approved by a vote of 70 to 57. Recognizing that Nuquist's motion dealt primarily with the Fifth Amendment question, William Huber, an AAUP member, moved that "no faculty member be suspended or dismissed on the grounds of refusing to answer questions under the Fifth Amendment." Two amendments, adding "legally" and "solely" to the sentence, weakened the motion but permitted the following resolution to pass with only six dissenting votes: "That the University Senate recommend to the Board of Trustees that no member of the University staff be suspended or dismissed solely on the grounds of legally refusing to answer questions under the Fifth Amendment." As in the deliberations of the Joyce committee, the Fifth Amendment issue was again the area producing the strongest questions about Novikoff's behavior. Because it appeared that in some instances witnesses had used the Fifth Amendment to hide misdeeds, many of the faculty were not prepared to grant absolute privileges under the Fifth Amendment. Whether or not this point of view was constitutionally correct, the faculty—like most Americans—was not in a mood to protect those who might have participated in "un-American" activities. In this situation, principles of due process argued by the AAUP or strict principles of constitutionality argued by civil libertarians were weak defenses against the prevailing mentality.[28]

The Senate meeting closed with Borgmann's suggestion that the College of Medicine elect four faculty members to serve on a board of review, in accordance with the bylaws. The next morning's news reports indicated that the university "will begin all over again" in its action against Novikoff because of several "mistakes" and that "no real decision" has been reached on his fate. Borgmann used the afternoon *Daily News* to correct these impressions by pointing out that the suspension of Novikoff was a "definite action" and that there had been no violation of tenure regulations since no action of dismissal had occurred. Borgmann responded to reports that the meeting was "secret" (the *Free Press* showed a picture of "a scowling faculty member" who barred newsmen from the meeting) by pointing out that the meeting was conducted in its usual fashion and that Senate meetings were never open to the public.[29]

Having now determined that it was necessary for the Board to carry out a hearing according to the bylaws, Borgmann wrote to each member of the Board on July 31. His letter began with a mea culpa: "I regret more than I can say the continuous uproar over the Novikoff affair. A good part of the blame for this lies with the fact that I failed to take cognizance of the established rules of procedure some months ago. Had the faculty-trustee committee been tied into the rules, as it should have been, much confusion would have been prevented. But that is water over the dam." He indicated that it "will be my strong recommendation that before the Board takes final action, the rules on tenure be completely followed." He revealed that he was taking steps so that if the board were to agree with his recommendation, faculty representation would already be selected and be ready to take part in deliberations as early as the August 14 board meeting. Borgmann enclosed a copy of his remarks at the senate meeting and transmitted the resolutions approved by the faculty. He also sent a copy of a legal brief prepared by University Counsel Lisman outlining the bylaw procedures and suggesting specific modes of operation. Lisman recommended that the newly constituted board of review meet at the close of the board of trustees meeting on August 14 to choose a chairman, receive the charges against Novikoff approved by the trustees, decide whether Novikoff could have a counsel present, determine its policy with respect to the calling of witnesses by Novikoff, and set a date for a final hearing.[30]

With events coming to a head, Novikoff decided to take action on several fronts. One step resulted from fear. In early June he had received an unsigned letter, postmarked in Newport, Vermont, from "an alumnus of U.V.M." The writer stated: "You are just a damned good for nothing rat and thats [sic] the way most of us feel. . . . Get back to Russia and stay there—your usefulness is nil." A second, more abusive letter from Newport arrived on July 31:

> "Violating Academic Freedom" is a joke when related by a RED GYP
> like you. Just get out and stay. . . . You have no "constitutional liberty"
> in trying to undermine a nation that allows rats like you to really
> amount to something. . . . If you don't *get out*—you may rest assured
> your light will go out one of these days and you will be one good Communist—not a live one—you bastard!

The death threat produced almost unbearable tension for Novikoff and his wife, and he decided to report the letters to the police. Because of the possibility of a federal offense (extortion), the matter was transferred to the FBI for investigation. FBI laboratory tests determined that the letters had come from different individuals. Eventually, the U.S. Attorney in Vermont, Joseph McNamara, and FBI representatives concluded that the letters did not constitute a "positive threat" to Novikoff's life, and the investigation was curtailed. Novikoff's anxiety was eased by the investigation and its findings.[31]

In the days after the senate meeting, Novikoff consulted with Nuquist, Schein, and other members of the Vermont AAUP about strategy for the next stage of the proceedings. One result was that for the first time since his entanglements had begun in April, Novikoff decided to contact a lawyer. Novikoff recalled in an interview that "I needed a lawyer and I wanted to be sure to have a lawyer who smelled right." Novikoff's inquiries led to a neighbor in the insurance business with excellent connections in Burlington, who suggested that he try the law firm of a friend of his, Leon Latham. Latham's partner at the time, Francis Peisch, recalls that he will "never forget" receiving a phone call from Novikoff: "walking in there (to get the phone) and there was this low, pleasant voice. 'This is Dr. Alex Novikoff. I'd like to come and see you.'" Peisch and Latham met with Novikoff the next day and discussed the advisability of his retaining an attorney. According to Peisch's notes from that meeting, the "conclusion taken that day was at that stage there was no necessity for him to retain an attorney."[32]

Rather than turning to a lawyer, Novikoff embarked on a political strategy. During late July and early August he carried out an effort to lobby members of the board of trustees who might support his position. He set appointments with several trustees living in Vermont, including Chester Eaton of Rutland. Eaton mentioned at the time that he appreciated "Dr. Novikoff having come to Rutland for a lengthy conversation with me . . . because I cannot treat lightly the part I must necessarily have in this matter." Novikoff met with Eaton on July 29 and brought with him four articles for Eaton's reading. Eaton recalled the visit:

> And he came down [to Rutland] and arrived in mid to latter part of the morning and visited at home over on Ash Street until noontime and then we went to lunch together downtown and back to the house. And the principal thing that stayed in my mind over the years was that we gave him a big basket of very delicious blackberries which we grew to take home for himself and his family. We must have spent at least three or four hours together that day, visiting about everything he was willing to talk about.

It is evident that Eaton did not find that Novikoff's visit was an inappropriate attempt to influence his opinions. Unfortunately for Novikoff, later events would show that the visit did nothing to alter Eaton's opinions. It is not clear who inspired Novikoff's visits (Eaton suggested that it was likely that President Borgmann played a role) or whether anyone expected them to change minds, but the discussions did provide Novikoff with an opportunity to talk face-to-face with the trustees in an informal setting. After the recent actions of the trustees, this was a small step in the right direction for Novikoff.[33]

Novikoff's other move was to seek the active support of the national AAUP. On August 8 Novikoff wrote Shannon in Washington with "an important request." After reviewing in detail the recent events in Vermont, Novikoff indicated that he would "like very much to have either Mr. Ralph Himstead or yourself act as my advisor in the hearing, if held." Novikoff indicated that the AAUP's participation in this fashion "may have a very favorable effect on the Trustees action on August 14, and it may even make a hearing unnecessary." Novikoff anticipated that the AAUP would have a positive influence on events, but his concluding paragraph suggests that he was well aware that the course of events might not be altered: "I sincerely hope that it will be possible for the Association to take the action I am requesting. It may well gain my reinstatement. But even if it fails to do so, it will put the Association in a fine position to consider further action."[34]

While Novikoff's request helped move the AAUP to action, a quite unexpected occurrence was important in persuading the Washington staff to get involved. Howard Prentice, a member of the board of trustees and a resident of Washington, D.C., made an appointment to meet with the AAUP staff on August 12. Available sources do not indicate whether Prentice made this visit as an individual decision or whether it was a product of discussions with Borgmann and others in Vermont. Prentice met with Himstead, Shannon, and Middleton at 2:00 P.M. in the AAUP offices. Immediately following the session Shannon prepared a confidential summary of the discussion for the use of the AAUP office. This internal memorandum, addressed to Himstead, reveals the extent to which trustee sentiment had hardened against Novikoff. Shannon summarized at length Prentice's point of view, especially his objection to Novikoff's invoking of the Fifth Amendment.

> Mr. Prentice stated that, after giving long consideration to the problem, he is convinced that the case does not involve a question of academic freedom and tenure. He emphasized, first, his opinion that it is improper for a teacher to invoke the Fifth Amendment, because of the duty of assisting the government to uncover a dangerous threat; and secondly, the harm that has been done and will be done to the University by the present situation. Mr. Prentice does not grant the validity of objections, on grounds of conscience, to revealing the name of fellow members during a period of former Communist Party membership. . . . Mr. Prentice grew emotional on the obligation of a citizen to cooperate with the government.

Prentice expressed his doubt about Novikoff's behavior since his arrival at the University of Vermont.

> Mr. Prentice held some doubt that Novikoff has been entirely clear of the Communist party since coming to the University of Vermont in 1948. He stated that Novikoff refused to say whether, within this period, he had seen certain specified Communists. He also mentioned the reported attendance of Novikoff at a discussion group at which "anti-Semitism" was discussed. GPS [Shannon] tried, without success, to obtain from Mr. Prentice a precise statement of what was objectionable in the action thus indicated. Mr. Prentice seemed to feel that, since Communists use discussion groups to disseminate their views, and since they make an issue of anti-Semitism, anyone in a discussion group on this subject is suspicious.

The meeting produced the following conclusions:

> GPS and WCM [Middleton], on the basis of this conference, felt rather

certain that the Board's decision will be unfavorable to Novikoff. Mr. Prentice's sincerity and desire to do the right thing seems evident, but he is unable to appreciate a man's reluctance to name other persons who have participated with him in an enterprise which he did not feel to be criminal. To GPS, Mr. Prentice's position on discussion groups and the discussion of certain topics, and his apparent feeling that a Senator's conscience is more significant than the conscience of another individual, seemed alarming.

Although Prentice's visit may have caused pessimism among the AAUP staff about Novikoff's situation, it helped the staff focus on the Vermont situation and on what the AAUP could do on Novikoff's behalf.[35]

On the evening of August 12, Himstead sent a telegram to Borgmann urging a hearing in accordance with the tenure rules and asking that an AAUP representative be present at such a hearing. Borgmann wired back asking for a clarification on several points concerning the AAUP role. Himstead's reply stated that the work of the AAUP "is judicial in nature, strictly judicial. . . . Because of this fact Association does not publicize situations currently under consideration." He noted that the AAUP was invited frequently by universities "to provide representatives at hearings and conferences to determine professional fitness of teachers." Himstead went on to reiterate the AAUP position on the Fifth Amendment and the need to "uphold and honor the Constitution of the United States."[36]

At about this time Borgmann received a letter from thirty-two scholars associated with the Woods Hole research facilities. The letter indicated that they were "deeply disturbed" by the reports of Novikoff's dismissal, that they held Novikoff in "high regard" as a scientist, and that they agreed with previous statements of the national AAUP, which they quoted. Going back to his first years at Brooklyn College, Novikoff had been a regular summer participant in the research activities at Woods Hole and was a personal acquaintance of many of the outstanding scientists in the country. Novikoff's first interest in political issues grew partly out of interactions with fellow scientists during his summer sojourn at Woods Hole. The Woods Hole letter came at the height of summer research activities and at a time of concern for scientists under institutional pressure.[37]

Governor Emerson returned a day early from the National Governors' Conference in Seattle to attend the board meeting on August 14. After several items of routine business, Borgmann reviewed events in the Novikoff case and pointed out that "through inadvertence" the regulations had not been followed. Upon the motion of trustee Brown, seconded by Father Joyce, the board authorized the formation of a

board of review to consider the charges against Novikoff and to recommend whether he should be retained on the staff. Frederick Shepardson, a member of the previous faculty-trustee committee and a
supporter at that time of Novikoff's retention, then moved that the act
of invoking the Fifth Amendment was in and of itself cause for dismissal. Shepardson's motion was unanimously defeated. At this point
Borgmann said that the board needed to formulate the charges against
Novikoff. After considerable discussion the four lawyers present (Governor Emerson, a lawyer, had not yet arrived at the meeting) were sent
off to prepare the charges.[38]

The lawyers returned to the meeting at about 3 P.M. and presented
three charges for discussion and revision. In the midst of the discussion, Emerson arrived and asserted that there was no need to set up a
board of review. He argued that the suspension did not amount to a
dismissal and that Novikoff at any time could clear himself by offering
to testify before the Jenner Committee. The governor's reasoning did
not persuade the other lawyers, and they assured him that indefinite
suspension without pay would actually constitute dismissal.

Although the minutes of the board meeting do not indicate as
much, a news story the next day reported that Cornelius Granai, a
legislative trustee from Barre and a Democrat, had "stomped out" of
the meeting about thirty minutes after the governor's arrival and had
told a reporter that Emerson was calling for the immediate dismissal
of Novikoff. Unquestionably, Emerson wanted to end, one way or another, the continuing process of adjudicating the Novikoff case. Acting
as a politician and as one who believed that the McCarthy era was
alerting "thinking people of the country" to the dangers of the communism threat, he sensed a growing public impatience with the university's inability to move decisively against Novikoff.[39]

After considerable discussion the following charges were approved
with three negative votes, including those of Father Joyce (who believed that Novikoff was innocent of wrongdoing) and Governor Emerson (who believed that the board of review was unnecessary):

> 1. That Dr. Alex B. Novikoff is guilty of conduct which justifies his
> discharge, in that when summoned to testify before a sub-committee of
> the United States Senate Judiciary Committee, investigating the subver-
> sive influence in the educational process, he testified freely concerning
> his activities since coming to the University in 1948, but when ques-
> tioned concerning his connections with the Communist Party, if any,
> prior to 1948, he claimed privilege under the Fifth Amendment.
> 2. That Dr. Novikoff is guilty of conduct which justifies his dis-
> charge, in that when summoned to testify . . . he improperly invoked

the Fifth Amendment for the protection of others and not for his own protection.

3. That Dr. Novikoff was guilty of conduct which justifies his discharge in that he has refused to disclose fully his connections with the Communist party prior to 1948, if any.

The trustees then voted to convene immediately a meeting of the board of review, including the twenty-person board of trustees, the five faculty members on the Senate Policy Committee and four faculty members elected by the College of Medicine. The previously designated faculty had been waiting on the sidelines for the notice to join the meeting.

The board of review convened at 4 P.M. and took several actions in accordance with the suggestions contained in Lisman's brief of July 31. In a gesture of fairness to Novikoff's position, Paul Evans, a history professor with personal prestige throughout the university, was elected chairman. Evans had spoken eloquently on Novikoff's right to due process at the senate meeting. It was agreed that Novikoff would be notified of the charges by registered mail and that Novikoff would be able to defend himself against them, with both sides free to present evidence. A hearing was set for Saturday, August 22, subject to a one-week delay at the request of Novikoff. It was noted that "the hearing will be a public one, meaning that representatives of the press will be admitted, witnesses, and a representative of the American Association of University Professors, but not the general public." Finally, it was agreed that Lisman would represent the review board at the hearing.[40]

Later on the day of the August 14 board meeting, the secretary of the newly formed board of review sent a letter to Novikoff containing the charges and the arrangements for the hearing. The letter stated that the testimony and report of the previous faculty-trustee committee would be available for Novikoff's inspection in the president's office. Novikoff responded on August 19, saying that he did not object to a public hearing but wanted it to be held on August 29. He asked that two copies of the faculty-trustee report be sent to him. His request for two copies fueled speculation that he would have an advisor, perhaps a lawyer, at the hearing.[41]

Developments at the August 14 board meeting, particularly the formalizing of the charges and the designation of Lisman to represent the board of review, led Novikoff to contact Peisch and Latham. The three men met on Saturday, August 15, and on the following Thursday the firm was retained by Novikoff. Peisch's recollection was that he told Latham that they had to take the case, and Latham replied, "That's right, Francis, but I wish to Christ he'd go someplace else." It was decided that Peisch, then thirty-five years old and struggling to make $68-a-month mortgage payments and feed four young children, would handle the case.[42]

With the designation of Peisch as Novikoff's lawyer, the opposing forces were now fully arrayed in preparation for the final hearing. Lisman, the university's prosecutor, believed at first that Novikoff was falsely accused and sought in April and May to help Novikoff avoid the Jenner hearing. When Novikoff told the Jenner Committee that he disagreed with Lisman's account of the conversations at his home in April and then took the Fifth Amendment, Lisman felt betrayed. With the public spotlight on him, he was emotionally committed to punishing Novikoff's perfidy. His subsequent behavior would incur the wrath of Novikoff's supporters (one would call Lisman a "reptile") as well as the discomfort of his allies, including President Borgmann.[43]

As for Borgmann, he was a new president, inexperienced (like almost every other college president) in a political arena of this kind, and socialized into the state university model of the Midwest, one in which university and state government usually operated in an atmosphere of friendly consensus about goals, money, and public policy. The short-term political pressures to go along with the proceedings against Novikoff were immense. He did not yet know well the politics of Vermont, and even if he had, an action to oppose Emerson and public opinion, while courageous, might have been an act doomed to failure. Furthermore, his position was weakened by his unfortunate error in initiating an investigation of Novikoff (the Joyce committee) that was inconsistent with the process stipulated by university bylaws. Compounding all of this, Borgmann was almost certainly influenced by the point of view that invoking the Fifth Amendment was unjustified, an opinion expressed by the higher education establishment. He "hated" the Novikoff affair and had wanted the trustees to accept the recommendation of the Joyce committee but "couldn't figure a way out." So he was swept along by events and, with Lisman, was committed to carrying out the proceedings against one of his faculty members.[44]

Pressing from the outside were the political spokesmen of Vermont. Governor Emerson had taken unusual interest in the case and had forced the hand of the trustees. Although the self-described "country lawyer" was physically unimposing (he was barely over five feet in height), his tenaciousness was legendary. He was known in the state capitol as "only a ten watt light but on all the time." Considering the traditional respect for the office of governor in Vermont, it is not surprising that Emerson was listened to by the trustees as well as by Vermonters at large.[45]

In private, political figures such as former U.S. Senator Warren Austin argued against Novikoff. Austin had served as counsel to the university while serving in the Senate and, in an arrangement of questionable ethics, had drawn a considerable retainer from the university over those years. Austin was the country's first ambassador to the United Nations and after years of confronting the Russians had become a hard-line anti-Communist. Slowed by illness, Austin retired to Vermont in January 1953 and became honorary chairman of the Committee of One Million, which was committed to keeping the People's Republic of China out of the United Nations. He was a man of immense prestige and, according to one faculty member, was "adamant about Novikoff." His private opinions made their way through the Burlington community.[46]

The incumbent Vermont congressmen were publicly silent on the Novikoff case but, in the case of Senator George Aiken, worked behind the scenes to help Lisman gather information in Washington. Senator Ralph Flanders finally saw enough of the excesses of Senator Joseph McCarthy and led the effort in the U.S. Senate to bring a censure motion. He did not, however, raise a hand to defend Novikoff.

We have seen evidence of the rabid anti-Communist stance of the William Loeb–led *Burlington Daily News.* Although milder in its rhetoric, the more middle-of-the-road *Free Press* was equally damaging to Novikoff's cause. The business manager, David Howe, shaped the editorial policy of the paper and pressed an anti-Communist point of view in public and private. At the height of the Novikoff controversy, Howe rejected for publication a pro-Novikoff letter written by George Little, a University political scientist and AAUP member. On the editorial pages, there was no room for an opposing point of view.[47]

Against this unified front of university officials, politicians, and editorial writers was a small, isolated minority. The inexperienced Peisch was saddled with a case confused by numerous extralegal issues. Novikoff was committed to remain silent about his Communist past, which was a widely unpopular position. The national AAUP would finally make its presence felt, but Himstead operated from a position of weakness. His academic freedom arguments, which were distant from common experience and knowledge, paled before the opposition. As it turned out, the most influential advocates of Novikoff's case were the few faculty members and local citizens who saw an injustice and were motivated to take action. Although limited by his low institutional status (he was not a full professor and did not hold an administrative position), Schein stood strong throughout. Schein knew that he could not play an effective public role because he lacked "impeccable WASP credentials," and "I was too much like Alex in background—Jewish, leftist, working class." He endured criticism from Borgmann and his department chairman but continued his agitation and letter-writing. When the FBI investigated Schein in 1961 at the time he sought a passport to attend a scientific meeting in the Soviet Union, an FBI source in Burlington reported that Schein had "constantly" pleaded for Novikoff and was "pro-communist."[48]

Other defenders among the faculty included Van Robertson (he actually played a more important role at the time the AAUP reviewed the Vermont case in 1958); Paul Evans and Sam Bogarad (both spoke for Novikoff at the senate meeting); and Ethan Allen Sims (who was a descendant of a famous Vermonter and a faculty member in the Medical College). Working behind the scenes was a local citizen, Martha Kennedy, who was deeply involved in progressive causes. Her involvement in the Wallace campaign and the Progressive party had "thoroughly tainted" her among most politically active women in Burlington. Nevertheless, her friendship with the wives of several of the actors in the Novikoff case—Florence Schein, Florence Wall, Virginia Little, and Rosalind Novikoff—impelled her to participate in the defense. Alex and Rosalind had been to her house for dinner on at least one occasion. As one might expect in a small city, Kennedy also knew President Borgmann's wife, Mabel. Kennedy and her women friends knew that Mabel was an outspoken liberal and had been a vocal supporter of Adlai Stevenson during the 1952 presidential election. Kennedy typed letters and stencils, printed and collated the minutes of hearings, sent a letter and an article on the Fifth Amendment to each trustee, and contributed money to cover costs.[49]

Supporting Novikoff was a lonely business. The group of clergymen, led by Vedder Van Dyck, Rabbi Max Wall, and Harold Buckland, had discovered this when their statement unleashed a torrent of criticism from the editorial writers. Although the faculty senate had voted to overturn the first action of the trustees and an occasional editorial outside Burlington resisted the proceedings, few other voices were heard. There may have been many Vermonters, on and off the campus, who had serious doubts about what was unfolding before their eyes, but they were silent. This was the situation faced by Peisch as he took on the case in mid-August.

Peisch began to familiarize himself with what had already happened. Since he had followed events only to a limited degree and knew little of what had occurred up to that time, Peisch began by visiting the editorial offices of the *Daily News* to study the news coverage. His first meeting with Novikoff to plan the defense led to the conclusions that the August 22 hearing date was too soon to prepare a case and that the transcript and report of the faculty-trustee committee might contain information favorable to Novikoff. Novikoff sent a letter on August 18 with a request on these two points. Although Peisch was curious about Novikoff's possible connections with the Communist party, they discussed the subject only briefly. Peisch stated: "I felt that I had better begin this job on the basis that, yes, he had been a communist. It was never against the law to be a communist in this country. It's not against the law today. . . . I did realize that the Fifth Amendment was something that was available to everybody." Although Novikoff and Peisch had at once moved the hearing date to August 29, Peisch thought about trying to delay the hearing until mid-September when the students and faculty would be back on campus. However, he decided against this tactic. He recalled that "I thought about it [the decision] over and over over the years . . . and concluded that having a bunch of young kids outside beating their drums wouldn't have helped."[50]

Peisch explored with Novikoff who might be called as witnesses to support his position. They settled on two leaders of the group of clergy who had raised questions in early July about the Novikoff proceeding, Rabbi Max Wall and Protestant Bishop Vedder Van Dyck. William Brown, former dean of the Medical College, and Professor William Van Robertson, who had submitted and retracted his resignation in June, were also approached. Each man agreed to testify, and Peisch visited their offices to discuss strategy for the hearing. Although it was clear to Peisch that the witnesses' testimony would establish Novikoff's professional and personal integrity and raise forcefully the academic freedom issues at stake, Peisch soon became convinced that his chances for success were weak: "These witnesses were the biggest piece of plumage there ever was. They didn't amount to anything. You see, the charges that were brought against Novikoff were crap. Nothing to them. If we had been in a justice court, they would have been thrown out. It was awful." When Peisch and Novikoff looked to see who might be their allies among the trustees on the board of review, they "never came up with anything but the horsecollar." Because Peisch "thought of them as the judges," he made no contact with any member of the board of review.[51]

Novikoff's selection of Peisch as his counsel made political sense. Peisch, a Catholic, would not be seen as part of any "Jewish communist conspiracy," and he had strong ties to Burlington Republican politics. At the time Peisch was chairman of Burlington's Ward Four Republican committee and was a member of a newly appointed parking authority. His father had been well known in Vermont as an auditor and was acquainted with state and university officials. His parents knew the governor, going back to the time that Emerson ran for lieutenant governor in 1945.

> [Emerson] came to the house in Norwich. My father and mother were still living. And he walked to the door. My mother invited him in and she knew him slightly because my father had done some work for the state. "Well," he said, "I'm running for lieutenant governor." My mother said, "That's interesting. Who's your opposition?" He said, "Asa Bloomer." So mother said, "What are the issues?" "There aren't any," he said. "He wants it and I want it, and I hope to God I get it." My mother said, "That's the best campaign speech I ever heard. I'm going to vote for you."

Although Novikoff might have been able to find a lawyer with more legal experience or better political connections, Peisch—a Harvard Law School graduate—was not a poor choice.[52]

In their first conversations Novikoff and Peisch discussed what role, if any, the AAUP might play in the proceedings. As agreed on August 14, the trustees had extended an invitation to Himstead in Washington to have a representative at the hearing. On August 19 Novikoff sent a letter to Himstead with copies of the complete testimony of the faculty-trustee committee and the final report. On the same day Himstead sent a telegram to Professor Carl Shoup, an economist at Columbia University, requesting his attendance at the hearing.

> Following Association intervention in serious situation University of Vermont have succeeded in getting hearing for faculty member concerned. Board of Trustees University has invited Association to have representative at hearing August 29 Burlington. Question at issue: Whether invoking Fifth Amendment Constitution United States is, in and of itself, justifiable cause for dismissal. Extreme pressure work this office involving continuous conferences and staggering volume of correspondence makes it difficult for me or for either my professional associates to serve Association at hearing. Will you represent Association at this hearing? Teacher concerned will have legal counsel. Your role at hearing will be to observe proceedings, to make a statement presenting and clarifying views, and to present argument for acceptance of these views by hearing committee. Your acceptance this assignment will be deeply appreciated. Wire reply collect today.

Himstead's telegram demonstrated several aspects of the situation: (1) Himstead and the other AAUP staff saw the situation in Vermont as a serious one, (2) Novikoff's invoking of the Fifth Amendment was perceived as the central issue, (3) Himstead's problems within the Association over the running of the central office were not forgotten, and he took this occasion (and many others) to point out the administrative burdens he faced, and (4) Himstead expected that the AAUP would play an advocacy role in the Vermont proceeding.[53]

A second telegram reached Shoup in New York City and produced a negative reply. Himstead wired back expressing his disappointment and asking for suggestions for other AAUP possibilities: "Invite your suggestions members profession, preferably members Association's Council, who concur our views on question at issue Vermont hearing, who are competent to present these views convincingly, and who would probably accept assignment." These interactions led to identical August 21 cables to Professor Fred Millett, vacationing on Cape Cod, and to Professor Ralph Perry, a philosopher at Harvard University. Millett, a professor of English literature at Wesleyan University, was then serving as president of the AAUP. Himstead's cable included the information that he had "conferred at length with teachers legal counsel" and that "you should plan to arrive Burlington Friday, August 28 to confer with teacher and his legal counsel." These messages did not bring an immediate response, and a day later Himstead's delay in locating an AAUP representative inspired an urgent cable from Peisch: "As attorney for Alex Novikoff I most strongly urge that you be present in Burlington for hearing before University of Vermont Board of Review set August 29. Your legal background, prestige as an individual and as representative of the Association make your presence essential. Please confirm by Western Union." Himstead cabled Millett again, indicating that Peisch's telegram and communications from "chapter officers urging that I personally represent Association at hearing" had persuaded him to take on the assignment himself. He informed Millett that he regarded the situation "sufficiently important to justify your attendance also as observer if your work permits." Millett agreed to join Himstead in Vermont, and Himstead cabled on August 25 notifying him of his hotel reservation at the Hotel Vermont and indicating also that "if time permits" he wished to discuss "some crucial personal and Association matters."[54]

Himstead's decision to go to Vermont on behalf of Novikoff points up some unique circumstances of the Vermont situation. From a review of AAUP files it appears that Himstead did not attend any other hearings of professors under siege during the McCarthy era. No other campus produced such a volume of letters and telegrams seeking AAUP intervention. Himstead was under great pressure from the AAUP council over the administrative bottleneck in the central office and the failure to actively support professors as the number of McCarthy-era cases increased in 1952 and 1953. Whether it was the unique aspects of the Vermont case or the political need to demonstrate to the AAUP his ability to respond, or both, that moved Himstead to intervene personally, his impending visit added significance and drama to the preparations under way for the final hearing.

SUPPORT FROM WASHINGTON

While Novikoff and Peisch were working to strengthen their case, Borgmann and Lisman were seeking information to reinforce the charges against Novikoff. Prior to the board meeting on August 14, Borgmann telephoned Governor Emerson to request that the governor ask the FBI to supply its file of information on Novikoff's Communist connections. Borgmann had learned from another university president about the willingness of the FBI to supply information about Communist faculty to state governors. Emerson telegraphed FBI headquarters on August 13 to request the file on Novikoff "re communistic connections and views."[55]

Coincidentally, on the same day that Emerson's telegram arrived at FBI headquarters, a memorandum from the Albany field office arrived reporting on an editorial in the *Brattleboro Daily Reformer,* a newspaper in southern Vermont. The editorial asserted that whereas the FBI had supplied information to the Jenner Committee, the FBI had withheld crucial information from the University of Vermont that "apparently linked Dr. Novikoff with Communist activities." Noting that important information had "languished" in FBI files during Novikoff's five years in Vermont, the editorial argued that "there is something wrong in our system of fighting Communism." The Albany office requested permission to tell the publisher of the *Reformer* that "the FBI does not furnish information to the Jenner Committee." The Emerson telegram and the Albany memorandum produced discussion and a flurry of memos at headquarters. FBI Assistant Director D. Milton Ladd decided to give Emerson the requested information but elected to make no contact with the *Reformer.*[56]

On August 18 a special agent of the Albany office visited Emerson in Montpelier and reported the following episode:

> . . . he immediately asked "Have you brought the file?" I told him that I had not brought a file and explained to him the confidential nature of the Bureau's files. I thereupon pointed out to him that information in possession of the Bureau had been furnished to him confidentially by ASAC Earl E. Brown on April 16, 1952. It was obvious that for the first

time he realized the significance of his conversation with ASAC Brown
and had completely forgotten that information had been previously furnished to him. He immediately left his office in an effort to find his file
and eventually returned to his office with a file which contained only
three newspaper clippings relating to NOVIKOFF.

FBI files show that in late 1951 the Albany field office requested and
received permission to contact Emerson about Novikoff, who "has
been engaged in subversive activities sufficient to warrant placing his
name in the Security Index." Despite Emerson's somewhat humorous
lapse of memory about the prior FBI contact, the agent conveyed ver-
bally a summary of information about Novikoff. The agent pointed out
"on three occasions the fact that none of the information could be
attributed to the FBI, the the information was furnished in strictest
confidence and that no reference could be made to the FBI in connection with any action which he might take based on the information
which we furnished."[57]

Providing confidential information to Governor Emerson was in
keeping with the FBI's so-called Responsibilities Program. This program was started in early 1951 following a meeting at the National
Governors' Conference between J. Edgar Hoover and a committee
headed by Governor Frank Lausche of Ohio. The governors sought
cooperation between the FBI and state authorities in the field of internal security. Hoover believed that "responsible officials of state gov-
ernments should have knowledge of dangerous Communists and other
subversives" employed by the states and, consequently, set up procedures whereby "information regarding the subversive activities of that
person is volunteered orally to the Governor of the state in which he
is employed." As the campaign against alleged Communists in higher
education proceeded, FBI records show that on numerous occasions
the FBI supplied governors with derogatory information about faculty.
The information was then transmitted to university officials.[58]

Shortly after his meeting with the FBI, Emerson wrote President
Borgmann to describe the meeting (he neglected to mention his lapse
of memory) and to convey a one-page resume of information about
Novikoff. The summary covered the following areas:

1. Novikoff's role as an editor of *Staff*, which was identified as a
Communist publication.

2. Novikoff's leadership role in the College Teachers Union local,
which was discharged from the American Federation of Teachers "because of its Communist tendencies."

3. A 1944 report that Novikoff and his wife were members of a
"Communist Party Club" in New York City.

4. Novikoff's activities at the Jefferson School of Social Science, which was "cited by the Attorney General as a Communist organization within the purview of Executive Order 9835."

5. Novikoff's name on a letter of the Council for Pan-American Democracy, which was also cited by the Attorney General as a Communist organization.

The significance of the FBI information was that if there was any question in Borgmann's, Lisman's, or Emerson's minds about Novikoff's Communist connections, this probably removed any doubt. Convinced of Novikoff's "guilt," it surely became easier to press rigorously for Novikoff's dismissal and to see the invoking of the Fifth Amendment as a smokescreen for covering the truth of his prior activities. Unquestionably, the information was self-justifying for the central actors in the case.[59]

Lisman, with Borgmann's backing, sought confidential information on another front, the Senate Internal Security Subcommittee. Lisman received assistance from Vermont Senator George Aiken, who received Lisman in his office and communicated on Lisman's behalf with Senator Jenner. According to Lisman, four individuals, whose names had been provided by Robert Morris and by Senator Welker, were interviewed and invited to come to Burlington to testify against Novikoff. Actually, the FBI helped in this undertaking also. An FBI memorandum, dated August 25, reported that Governor Emerson called the Albany field office to get addresses of potential witnesses. Emerson stated that "he has appointed an attorney, Louis Lisman, to investigate Novikoff for the purpose of seeing whether Novikoff can be fired from the University of Vermont." FBI headquarters provided the address of a potential witness staying at the Hotel Harrington in Washington.[60]

According to an interview with Lisman, he planned to call witnesses at the board of review hearing *only* if Novikoff denied having been a Communist. Lisman stated that on the eve of the hearing the witnesses were lodged at the Hotel Vermont in Burlington. A search of records and interviews with the main actors offer no evidence to support Lisman's assertion; indeed, other participants have expressed serious doubt about the veracity of his claim. As matters turned out, Novikoff remained consistent with his stance of neither confirming nor denying Communist activities prior to 1948, and Lisman had no reason to call witnesses to the hearing.[61]

With information from the FBI and from Lisman's travels to interview witnesses, Lisman and Borgmann now knew a great deal more about Novikoff's past. They decided, however, that much of the information, as well as the sources of it, could not be divulged to the board of review. When the trustees became aware at a later time that Lisman and Borgmann possessed information about Novikoff that they had not revealed, there was considerable consternation.

SETTING THE GROUND RULES

Peisch, Lisman, Trustee Dunbar Bostwick, and Professor Evans, chairman of the panel, met on August 22 to make decisions about the conduct of the hearing. Peisch's summary of the understandings reached at the session (and mailed, as agreed, to each participant) indicated that the "square question to be decided by the Board of Review is the question of what constitutes 'conduct which justifies his discharge.'" He pointed out that no "clear understanding was reached at this meeting as to the standard on which evidence would be judged." He recorded that Bostwick "stated that his understanding of the matter was that Dr. Novikoff was expected to disclose fully to the Board of Review his prior connections with the Communist Party." Peisch's summary shows that there was a brief discussion of the meaning of the charges against Novikoff. Lisman indicated that evidence of Communist activity would be the first piece of evidence to prove the first charge (that Novikoff refused to testify about the pre-1948 period before the Jenner Committee). On this point he indicated that he planned to call four witnesses who "will testify as to Dr. Novikoff's prior connection with the Communist Party." Lisman said that the second charge (that Novikoff improperly invoked the Fifth Amendment) was clear. The third charge (that Novikoff had not disclosed anything about the pre-1948 period) referred to Novikoff's refusal to be forthcoming with the faculty-trustee committee or to authorized university representatives, including Lisman and Borgmann.[62]

An informal conversation following this meeting may have had a significant impact on how Peisch and Novikoff handled themselves at the hearing. In a memorandum that Peisch typed for his own records later that afternoon, he recorded the following: "After the conference with the Executive Committee of the Board of Review, Louis Lisman asked me to step into another room where he could talk to me privately. While there he told me that he wanted to record the fact that Dr. Novikoff should understand clearly that he no longer had a friend in Louis Lisman." According to Peisch, Lisman saw the AAUP as a negative influence on events.

> He said that the AAUP had been more active in this case than in any other case. He mentioned a number of other cases such as Rutgers and

NYU where the AAUP, according to him, has sat quietly and done nothing. . . . [H]e thought the Trustees would have accepted the report of the (Faculty-Trustee) Committee. At this point the AAUP intervened, first in terms of its local chapter and then in terms of the National Chapter. Mr. Lisman indicated that the Board of Trustees was extremely offended by the vigorous action of the AAUP and pointed out that this was not really the action of the local AAUP but Dr. Novikoff's friends who were really making this motion.

Peisch's memo alluded to another serious charge against Novikoff: "Mr. Lisman also stated that a most serious allegation which I will not record here will be brought. . . . He told me that the FBI had permitted him to bring this before the Board of Review where it had not even permitted it to come before the Genner [sic] Committee." Peisch told Novikoff later that the charge mentioned by Lisman was "germ warfare," an accusation vehemently denied by Novikoff.[63]

According to Peisch's memorandum, Lisman talked about his efforts to gather evidence: "Louis Lisman went forward to tell me that all the traveling he has been doing recently has been to interview witnesses; that he is interviewing a witness in Wilmington and expected to see one in Boston; although he did not tell me this I assume he has been in close touch with the Genner [sic] Committee." Lisman stated that Novikoff's wife "had been in some way connected with the Communist Party" and that "Dr. Novikoff's brother-in-law had been fired for similar reasons to Dr. Novikoff's case."[64]

Accepting Peisch's memo as genuine, it is likely that Lisman's statements caused Peisch and Novikoff to take a cautious approach in the hearing. Whether or not Lisman was bluffing about his intention of calling witnesses to testify or about raising the charge of germ warfare, it was obvious that Lisman had ammunition that would be devastating to Novikoff. The trustees and Vermont public opinion were not likely to view Novikoff's past activities as "innocent" or as permissible behavior for a faculty member.

It was possible, however, that Lisman and Borgmann did not actually *want* to have the out-of-town witnesses appear at the hearing. Certainly, their presence as witnesses would have raised an element of risk for Lisman in a situation where the facts themselves were less important than the aura of a Communist conspiracy and the assumption that the Fifth Amendment was used to cover one's guilt—ideas that were already established in the minds of Vermont newspaper editors and many of the trustees. The witnesses would have created a different kind of hearing, one where evidence (of Communist activities, conspiracy, etc.) was central to establishing Novikoff's guilt. Perhaps influenced by this logic, Peisch and Novikoff did not engage in the elaborate preparations that would be necessary to counter the potential witnesses from Novikoff's past.

On August 25, the day that Peisch sent his summary of the planning meeting to the executive committee of the board of review, Novikoff wrote a letter to Himstead notifying him of his accommodations in Vermont and reviewing the status of preparations for the hearing. Himstead was informed that when he arrived on the 28th, he should ride in by bus from the train station in Essex Junction and get off at the downtown terminal, which was across the street from the Hotel Vermont. Novikoff went on to report the results of the August 25 meeting.

> At the pre-hearing meeting last Saturday, Mr. Lisman, the attorney who will argue for the charges brought against me by the Board of Trustees, indicated that I will be his first witness and he will then follow with four witnesses whom he is bringing to Burlington to testify to my activities prior to 1948. He said that he had been working with the Jenner committee, FBI, and possible witnesses. He indicated privately to my attorney what some of his contentions will be, but because of his complete unreliability we doubt very much whether he will do as he says. We have some doubt even that he will have four witnesses as he stated at the pre-hearing meeting.

Although Peisch and Novikoff doubted that Lisman would actually present witnesses, they knew that Novikoff's activities prior to arriving in Vermont in 1948 presented potential problems.

> We have not yet determined upon the best policy to follow at the hearing concerning these pre-1948 activities. We will, of course, stress their irrelevance to the charges before the Board of Review and to the issue of my retention. But we do not yet know if it is best for me to take the position that since these are irrelevant issues I will not discuss them or answer questions concerning them, or the position that, despite the dangers this may expose me to before the Jenner committee again, I will speak candidly about my past, irrelevant though it is, in order to make absolutely clear that the issue is not communism but academic freedom, the right of a teacher to use the Fifth Amendment and the insistence that he be judged by the traditional standards of competence.

This paragraph in Novikoff's letter is a concise expression of the dilemma facing the defense team and of the logic of Novikoff's position. The passage is the only available evidence that Novikoff may have seriously considered talking about his past. Ellen Schrecker's study of the national picture shows that none of the faculty who refused to talk about their political past was retained. By this time in the anti-Communist campaign, Novikoff may have perceived this pattern and been tempted to discuss these matters. It appears, however, that this strategy was considered only remotely. Novikoff's worst fear was that the details of his Communist past—which he knew to be in the possession of the FBI and perhaps Lisman—might come forth in public. Even without naming others, these revelations would be acutely embarrassing, potentially fatal to his professional reputation, and a repudiation of his avowed position against testifying before an "immoral" proceeding. He had come this far, and he was not ready to change his stance.[65]

Novikoff closed his letter with a reference to the Fifth Amendment question.

> In connection with the Fifth Amendment issue, you should know that the Board of Trustees on August 14th approved the resolution that no member of the staff should be dismissed for the use of the Fifth Amendment, in and of itself. One interpretation of this resolution has been that it cuts the ground completely from charge 1 against me. Another interpretation is that the Trustees were saying it is all right to use the amendment, but not in any instance connected with communism!

Novikoff's doubts about the actual intent of the trustees' resolution were well founded. As events unfolded, Novikoff's invoking of the Fifth Amendment was the most serious problem he confronted with the review board.[66]

As both sides finished their preparations, there was confusion about the charges and an obscurity in the logic behind them. This state of affairs would create problems at Novikoff's final hearing. In essence, the three charges said that Novikoff refused to talk about his past and took the Fifth Amendment, and that warranted dismissal. The legal and moral basis for the connection between Novikoff's actions—about which there was no disagreement—and dismissal was not directly addressed. Therefore, the kinds of evidence or standards to be employed in the hearing could not be made explicit. As the hearing later showed, Peisch could not mount an effective defense strategy because the prosecutorial position contained no consistent stream of logic connecting Novikoff's behavior, the charges, and the penalty of dismissal. That Peisch did not attack this problem more forcefully is unfortunate, but the quasi-legal nature of the proceedings and the political forces at play probably meant that Peisch's objections would have been overwhelmed in short order. The paranoia about communism, the suspicions of individuals connected in any way with communism, the cynicism about the motives of those invoking the Fifth Amendment, and the pragmatic impulse that finds virtue in expedient action produced the logic of the situation. More esoteric issues pertaining to legal due process, the purpose of the constitutional protection against self-incrimination, and the concept of academic freedom could not stand up to the popular will. Emerson, Lisman, most of the trustees, newspaper editors, and Borgmann moved with and shaped the stream of public events. Against this, the youthful lawyer defending Novikoff brought ideals and courage but very little legal or political ammunition.

Chapter 8

THE FINAL HEARING
Vermont Renders Its Verdict

The days before the August 29 hearing set the scene for the final confrontation between Novikoff and the board of trustees. Editorial opinion registered renewed impatience with the proceedings against Novikoff. The *Burlington Daily News* stated that it was "tired of reading about" Novikoff and pointed to the university's "inept handling" of the case. WCAX, a Burlington radio station, took out a newspaper advertisement to protest the board's decision to prohibit instantaneous or recorded broadcasts of the proceeding.[1]

Several faculty members submitted letters to the board of review in support of Novikoff, including one from Arnold Schein, who criticized Lisman's serving as both confidant to Novikoff (in March and April) and then as prosecutor. Louis Joughin, executive officer of the Academic Freedom Committee of the American Civil Liberties Union, submitted a lengthy brief focusing mainly on Fifth Amendment issues. On August 26 a university spokesman announced that the faculty of the university would not be able to attend the hearing.[2]

On the 26th, Himstead sent telegrams to Novikoff and Millett, his fellow AAUP representative, confirming the arrangements for his visit. He asked Novikoff to inform Professor Andrew Nuquist, president of the Vermont AAUP chapter, that he would "be available Sunday afternoon for any service I can be to chapter provided hearing will then be concluded." He told Millett that "attorney for Professor Novikoff has requested me to work with him Friday, in preparation for hearing Saturday." On Thursday, Peisch left a note at the Hotel Vermont telling Himstead that as soon as he had "rested and washed some of the Central Vermont roadbed off," Peisch stood ready to discuss the case. Following his arrival in Burlington on Friday morning, Himstead went to Peisch's office at 115 Bank Street:

> Himstead walked in. . . . He said, "I'm here. Is there anything I can do
> in this case?" And I said, "Yes, stay out of the way." And Himstead,
> who was a hell of a nice man, said, "Well, Mr. Peisch, I'm not a lawyer
> and, if I were you, that's what I would say to a guy that showed
> up.". . . He never lifted his hand. He was there. He had a lot of stuff
> with him. . . . My memory was that he thanked me, we shook hands, I
> saw him at the Waterman Building, and that was that.

The ready agreement that Himstead and Millett would play no direct
role in the hearing contradicted Himstead's apparent expectation when
he telegraphed Professor Perry on August 21 and Professor Millett on
August 24. In these telegrams Himstead indicated that Peisch and Novikoff wanted the AAUP's "help" and wanted the AAUP representatives to clarify the Association's views and "to present argument" at
the hearing for accepting those views. After all of Schein's, Novikoff's,
and Peisch's efforts to get Himstead actively involved, the role played
by the AAUP turned out to be a passive one. Despite the shift in tactics,
Peisch remembered that "I was glad to see him here . . . because I
wanted to make Borgmann nervous." He added, "It didn't do any
good."[3]

By the eve of the hearing members of the board of trustees had
accumulated a considerable amount of material and had engaged in
extensive dialogue about the issues at meetings on March 26, June 12,
June 20, and August 14. The rejection of the Joyce committee recommendation and the ultimatum to Novikoff were, thus far, the major
policy decisions of the body in the Novikoff case. On the surface these
decisions were consistent with the political orientation of the trustees.
Overwhelmingly, the twenty-member board was republican, living in
Vermont, and inclined to listen to the warnings of Communist subversion in America. A majority of the members were businessmen or
lawyers. The wife of a former governor was the only woman on the
board. The two ex officio members, Governor Emerson and President
Borgmann, were the most important actors and had already staked out
positions that did not favor Novikoff.

On the basis of their backgrounds, the decisions of the board members may have been predictable, but a general analysis of this kind tells
us little of substance about the thinking of the board. What specific
principles and rationales, if any, were behind the actions in the Novikoff
case? What were the issues and what did they believe was at stake?
Unfortunately, the minutes of the trustee meetings provide little insight
into the thinking of the trustees or the specific basis for the conclusions
they had reached by this time. The minutes of meetings were primarily
summaries of decisions and individual statements and included almost

no verbatim dialogue. At the time of this research only five of the twenty trustees in 1953 were still living, and this also hampers a reconstruction of their thinking. Moreover, the passage of time and old age had impaired the memories of four of the survivors.

Fortunately, the fifth living trustee, Chester Eaton, retained mental alertness at age seventy-one and an exceptional ability to recall the events of 1953. Eaton, who in 1953 was a resident of Rutland and a sales executive for the Vermont Public Service Corporation, is an organized and precise man. Characteristically, he retained intact his file on the Novikoff affair, which he put away in the 1950s. The Eaton file and commentary are important for several reasons: it is the only available collection of this kind; the file contains the correspondence received by each trustee; and it appears that Eaton's decisions and thinking were in the mainstream of trustee thinking during the Novikoff proceeding.[4]

The Eaton file contains considerable material on the Novikoff case, including the normal flow of minutes and agenda items, letters and documents from persons attempting to influence his opinion on the case, and his own hand-written and typewritten notes on the case. His own notes include a three-page document typed on June 19 just prior to the trustees' "talk or walk" ultimatum to Novikoff. Certainly, there were sources of information and influence that were unique to Eaton, such as the newspapers he happened to read, conversations with his fellow trustees, and personal interactions with friends and casual acquaintances. The significance of the file, however, derives from six documents sent to each trustee. One surprise, perhaps, is that there were so *few* documents mailed to the trustees for the express purpose of influencing their opinion. A more pertinent issue is whether these documents disposed the trustees in one direction or the other on the Novikoff case. The Eaton file includes the following:

1. A two-page typewritten transcript of remarks made on June 13 by a distinguished University of Vermont alumnus at the fiftieth reunion of the class of 1903. The essence of his message was that "academic freedom is not a constitutional right" and faculty members can not "invoke the Fifth Amendment against legitimate procedures to protect us from the Communist conspiracy."

2. A letter on July 13 from Martha Kennedy, Novikoff's advocate, with an attached article, "Does Silence Mean Guilt," taken from the June 6, 1953, edition of *The Nation*. The essay's lengthy analysis of the Fifth Amendment asserted the "clear command of the English common law: 'No man shall be a witness against himself.'" (Inspection of Mar-

tha Kennedy's private papers reveals that she received responses from Governor Emerson, President Borgmann, and trustees Eaton, Mower, Shepardson, Granai, and Prentice. Mower pointed out in his July 16 letter that "I too am most concerned about the action thus far taken by the Trustees with respect to Dr. Novikoff. . . . I felt at the time and still feel that it was wrong." Mower, who was probably referring to the June 20 ultimatum to Novikoff, went on to be an aggressive and antagonistic interrogator of Novikoff at the board of review hearing and voted against Novikoff on each occasion.)

3. A copy of a July 14 letter from Bradley Soule, a professor of radiology in the Medical College, to President Borgmann, urging reconsideration of the case. Soule emphasized that he had come to think differently about the Fifth Amendment question and now hoped that "the Board of Trustees, like myself, will give themselves the privilege of changing their minds."

4. A pamphlet containing remarks by Lewis W. Jones, president of Rutgers University, where two professors, Simon Heimlich and Moses Finley, were dismissed on December 31, 1952, for invoking the Fifth Amendment. The position taken by Jones was known to have influenced many administrators across the country. Eaton carefully marked and underlined the pamphlet in 1953, including the following important passage: "Legitimate and 'non-hysterical' criticisms of the methods of such inquiries [of congressional committees] are in order; ways must be found to protect loyal people from irresponsible charges. But improvement is not likely to come from negative attitudes of non-cooperation." (Eaton emphasized in an interview that the phrase "negative attitudes of non-cooperation" had been influential in shaping his conclusions.)

5. A copy of the report of the Jenner Committee, entitled "Subversive Influence in the Educational Process," sent on August 7 by David Howe, business manager of the *Burlington Free Press*. This report contained summary conclusions about the "communist conspiracy" in education and a list of witnesses who had taken the Fifth Amendment before the committee. The list, which included Novikoff's name, became a valuable source for presidents and other employers intent on keeping out "disloyal" faculty.

6. A letter on August 7 from Vedder Van Dyck, Max Wall, and Harold Buckland, leaders of the clergy group in support of Novikoff, with two enclosed articles critical of the activities of the House Un-American Committee. (Eaton's handwritten response to each of the clergymen expressed his appreciation for the two articles and pointed out that "I had already read both of them, as I have everything I could

find expressing opinions and giving analyses on all sides of the many interlocking questions involved in the Novikoff case.")[5]

One suspects that this flow of documents had very little effect on the majority of trustees already committed to punishing Novikoff for his transgressions. The documents favoring Novikoff's position (from Kennedy, Professor Soule, and the three ministers) were from persons with limited political influence in the Burlington community. The documents undercutting Novikoff's position (the speech of the prestigious alumnus, the widely disseminated views of the Rutgers president, and Novikoff's congressional testimony sent courtesy of the *Burlington Free Press*) conveyed the "establishment" point of view. It is clear that there was no concentrated campaign of political pressure—either for or against Novikoff—brought to bear on the trustees. Novikoff's supporters were scarce, with little clout, and they had thrown in their lot with the AAUP. Novikoff's antagonists were omnipresent in government and the media and had no need for a focused initiative.

Looking beyond what was common to the trustees, Eaton received a letter in mid-August from Francis Colburn, an art professor at the university and a classmate of Eaton's at the university in the class of 1934. Colburn argued that "we seem to have forgotten that in the 1930's thousands of thinking and sincere people saw the left wing as the only articulate group protesting the growing horror of Fascism and Nazism." He told Eaton that "To condemn them now, in 1953, as dangerous and un-American would . . . be a thoughtless, hysterical and silly act." Colburn closed by apologizing for "burdening you" and pointing out that "it is being done by me personally in, I need hardly to say, strictest privacy." Eaton's agreement with Colburn's point of view is suggested by a document that he typed on June 19. This document represented Eaton's effort to record his observations and conclusions prior to the June 20 trustees meeting. He noted the "basically innocent origin of Dr. Novikoff's present dilemma," which he attributed to a "below-moderate-income home in Brooklyn as a child, in the depression 30's in New York as a student and young teacher, and at Brooklyn College during the war years when our country was an all-out ally of communist Russia."[6]

Eaton's acceptance of the past, however, did not bring him to accept Novikoff's refusal to testify:

> . . . there seems to be general agreement [by the faculty-trustee committee] that had Dr. Novikoff not invoked the Fifth Amendment, and even though he had been a communist, he should be retained on the faculty of the UVM College of Medicine. . . . Therefore the sole question at issue (assuming that the full Board of Trustees agrees with the points

stated above) is whether, under all the circumstances as they exist in this country and the world today and under the circumstances pertaining to his individual case, Dr. Novikoff has an obligation to answer the questions of a legally constituted investigatory body concerning his knowledge of communists and communism. . . . I believe that he has that obligation, if he is to remain on the faculty of the University of Vermont.

On August 11 he added that "at the time of above notes, I had not weighed fairly, in my thoughts on the subject, the so-called moral issue or the academic freedom issue because refusal to testify for so-called moral reasons is not sanctioned by law or legal interpretation and seemed to be a secondary factor and because the case did not seem to me to involve academic freedom." He indicated that "since June 19th, I have weighed both these factors carefully, including lengthy conversations with Dr. Novikoff himself regarding both of them." That Eaton did not waver from his position of June 19 is evidenced by his votes against Novikoff and by his penciled comments on this document on August 31. He asserted that "academic freedom is not involved in this case and . . . I have become increasingly convinced that Dr. Novikoff is not sincere [on this issue]."

If these sentiments are an accurate reflection of Eaton's point of view, they lend credibility to his assertion that Novikoff's probable ties to Communist activities were not a controlling factor in his belief that Novikoff should be fired. Other issues, primarily Novikoff's failure to cooperate with "legally constituted" committees, were at the core of his position. The willingness to cooperate, not whether or not one had been a Communist, was the test of one's patriotism. Eaton did not revise his judgment, expressed in the June 19 document, that Novikoff should be fired "unless he is willing to demonstrate under these difficult circumstances that his loyalty to his country transcends all other considerations, and that his faith in his country's institutions is so firm that he will expose himself to the hazards of retaliation or other risks that may be in his mind."

Although it is impossible to distinguish, with complete confidence, self-justification and rationalization from sincere positions of principle, the consistency and thoughtfulness of Eaton's point of view throughout the proceedings suggests strongly that these views were arrived at honestly and in good conscience. It is telling that even a four-hour conversation between Eaton and Novikoff did nothing to alter Eaton's position on the case. The similarity between Eaton's statements and the statements and votes of a majority of trustees is a strong indication that Eaton was in the mainstream of the thinking of the board during the summer of 1953.

By this time in a proceeding stretching over five months, there is little doubt that the trustees were wedded to a position with ominous consequences for Novikoff: he should talk about the past or be prepared to lose his job. After extensive public debate and several points of decision, it is not surprising that the trustees had already worked out their conclusions and justifications. On the eve of Novikoff's hearing the only serious question was whether the event itself might loosen a few of the trustees from their already determined position.

NOVIKOFF'S HEARING

The board of review—numbering twenty-three persons, including Governor Emerson—convened in the Waterman Building on the university campus at 10 A.M. Six trustees were missing. The room was packed, with the board of review, university officials, witnesses, and newsmen in attendance. It was a sweltering August day, and the water cooler was emptied and refilled on four occasions. A stenographer was present to record the dialogue. Peisch remembered his own discomfort: "I got ready the day of the hearing. I didn't have any money and didn't really have a summer suit. If I had a summer suit, I got mixed up and put on a wool suit. I got down there; I thought I was going to die I was so hot. And I knew I was dead. The weather was awful and . . . I got no place as I expected. What the hell, I was only thirty-five."[7]

In the opening minutes the chairman turned to Lisman, and Lisman asked that Novikoff take the stand to answer his questions. Peisch objected immediately, arguing that "this Board of Trustees has preferred charges against the man. . . . I think he is entitled to have some evidence not out of his own mouth as to these charges." The ensuing discussion among the lawyers on the panel was inconclusive, and Peisch finally stated that "my client declines to take the stand; he declines to put himself in a position to be questioned." Peisch then made an important offer, one that indicated a softening of Novikoff's position. He indicated that Novikoff would be willing to testify in private about all of his past activities. The offer, however, was rejected unanimously by the board.[8]

One can surmise why the offer was made and why it was rejected. Although talking in private would have led inevitably to revelations about his Communist party activities, it would have satisfied the trustees' desire for full disclosure from Novikoff. Novikoff was ready now to go this far. The danger was that the Jenner Committee might decide that candid private testimony compromised Novikoff's right to invoke the Fifth Amendment; Novikoff might be called back to Washington for another grilling. The trustees feared a similar eventuality: if they were privy to secret disclosures about communism, *they* might be subpoenaed to testify before the Jenner Committee. As remote as this event was, the trustees were fearful of the possibility. The more significant factor in the board's rejection of the offer, however, was the realization that hearing about Novikoff's past, especially his Communist past, would create a serious dilemma. A major stated reason for the firing would be removed, and it would be more difficult to fire Novikoff for his other transgressions: his invoking of the Fifth Amendment and his past involvement with Communists. At this point in the deliberations a majority of the trustees believed that these were sufficient grounds for the firing. If they commanded the political and moral high ground (as they believed they did), and if they had the proceedings under control, why make the inevitable more difficult? Politically, it was an astute decision, and it removed any real chance for Novikoff to shift the political forces at play in the hearing.[9]

Lisman attempted to conclude this phase of the hearing by stating that Novikoff's refusal to testify fully in the public session proved the third charge and sustained the first two. This impelled Trustee Granai to pursue again the possibility that the board might go into a private session to hear Novikoff: "Now the question is would your client give us a full and complete disclosure of any connection that he might have had in the past with the Communist Party if we give him the privilege of going into private session?" Novikoff answered, "Most assuredly, yes." Again the board voted against a private session, this time by an 11 to 8 tally. Granai, who became an active protector of Novikoff's interests during the hearing, noted that not everyone had voted and asked for a voice vote. The new vote came to 15 to 8 against, with Granai and Borgmann voting with the minority.[10]

As the session continued, the board heard witnesses called by Peisch, including William Brown, retired dean of the Medical College; Rabbi Max Wall of Burlington, who had participated in the effort to develop the clergy's letter; Protestant Bishop Vedder Van Dyck, who had led the clergy's undertaking; and William Van Robertson, the Medical College colleague of Novikoff's. Two highlights of the testimony were the following:

> Dean Brown said that when Novikoff was hired in 1948, he had not made an attempt to contact Novikoff's department chairman at Brooklyn College. Brown went on to say that even had he known at that time of Novikoff's Communist party connections, that fact would not have changed his mind about Novikoff's qualifications to serve as a university faculty member.

Both Rabbi Wall and Robertson indicated that they thought that Novikoff was "probably a communist" before he came to Vermont. Both expressed their strong support of Novikoff.

The consistent theme of the witnesses was that available evidence did not alter their view that Novikoff was fit to remain a faculty member. Granai was instrumental in leading the witnesses to this conclusion, which, on the face of it, was the fundamental question being addressed by the board.[11]

Robertson's testimony was followed by a lunch break. By this point in the hearing, Peisch recognized the difficulty of his situation: "I was in a forum that was no place. There were no rules. There was no evidence. There was nobody you could talk to. Nobody was ruling on evidence." His mental state was not improved by an incident at lunch.

> So it came time for lunch. . . . Now I'm not a major figure in Vermont, but a hell of a lot of these people knew my father and mother. My father had never been elected auditor but he used to audit the state. He knew about all these people. And this woman said, "You're invited to come down and have lunch. And so I went down in the cafeteria of the Waterman Building and picked up, I guess, a glass of water and a saltine, and she said, "Come sit with us." So I walked over to sit down at the table and [a trustee] was at the other corner of the table, and he picked up his plate and went away.

A couple of weeks later a mutual friend told Peisch that "I understand that Dunbar was disagreeable to you in the course of this hearing. . . . I want you to know that Dunbar was doing the best he could in the situation in which he found himself." This trustee, a member of a wealthy Vermont family with estates along Lake Champlain in Shelburne, voted down the line against Novikoff in the course of the proceedings.[12]

After the board of review convened at two o'clock, examination of the witnesses continued. Then Peisch said that "I am troubled as an attorney by the unwillingness of this Board to hear Dr. Novikoff in private." However, Peisch continued, he was now willing to have Novikoff speak publicly about all events since 1948. The Board voted 13 to 9 to bring Novikoff to the stand. Lisman stated that "it would be a waste of time to ask the Doctor any questions about his activities since 1948"; consequently, until his final presentation, Lisman chose to play only a minor role in the dialogue. Peisch asked that the report of the faculty-trustee committee, including the transcript of the interviews, be entered into the public record. There was discussion about whether the transcript should be open to the public, and Peisch indicated that his request on this point was a spur-of-the-moment action. After rethinking the question, Peisch then decided that he wanted to review the transcript before deciding whether it was to his client's best interest to have the transcript released.[13]

Novikoff discussed at length his reasons for invoking the Fifth Amendment. He cited his legal right against self-incrimination; his refusal to name others, which he saw as a moral issue; and the procedures of the Jenner Committee, which were outside the "Democratic traditions of our country." Trustee Mower, a Boston lawyer, pressed Novikoff to tell what there was that would incriminate him if he were to testify openly. Peisch objected that this question was leading Novikoff into the pre-1948 period. The following exchange demonstrates the confusion and disagreement prevailing at this point in the hearing:

> *Mower*: He stated that he was afraid he would incriminate himself. I want to know [why he is] afraid he would incriminate himself of what. Mr. Chairman, may I have a ruling on the propriety of my question?
>
> *Chairman Evans*: Well, obviously I am not in a position to give such a ruling. All we can do, therefore, is to leave it to the Board to pass such a ruling. You are the first person we would normally appeal to, one of the lawyers in the group. That is the anomalous status of a group like ourselves. I have no doubt whatever of Mr. Mower's belief that this is a proper question and this is fair play. It is up to the group as a whole to rule on this.
>
> *Granai*: Mr. Chairman, of necessity if the question is answered he will incriminate himself and will make void what he sought to protect himself from at that time. There is no question about it. As the question is now framed he will, if he has to answer this, answer what the Committee wanted to know at the time he invoked it. That is just what it amounts to.
>
> *Mower*: I don't think so, at all.

Peisch ended the discussion by saying that he would advise his client not to answer the question.[14]

Novikoff's testimony included the disclosure that he had visited Brooklyn College on several occasions since 1948 and had seen his former colleague, Harry Albaum, more than once. After further discussion about releasing the report and transcript of the faculty-trustee committee (Peisch agreed to allow the transcript to be released), Peisch asked Lisman to "sum up a little bit." As promised in the planning session of August 22, Lisman cited information about Novikoff's Communist activities as evidence of guilt on the first charge. His primary example was Novikoff's leadership of a "Communist dominated union." He alluded to suspicions of sinister activities by Novikoff:

> He is being discharged because, having knowledge, particular knowledge, knowledge not available to the ordinary Communist, even of activities inimical to the security of this country, nevertheless refuses in an investigation of the subversive influence in the educational process to

give to a Congressional Committee the benefit of his knowledge. . . . In my opinion such conduct constitutes moral turpitude. In my opinion you are not only justified in discharging Dr. Novikoff under the first charge, but further you are justified in discharging him on the ground of moral turpitude under the first charge.

Lisman's raising of "moral turpitude" as an issue became a source of bitterness for Novikoff and for many of his partisans. The use of the term was tied to language found in standards established by the American Association of University Professors as grounds for curtailing a continuous appointment (i.e., tenure) of a faculty member. However, the term had historically referred to behavior such as overt criminal acts, sexual misconduct, or similar kinds of gross misconduct. The term had not previously been used to denote political or moral acts of the kind attributed to Novikoff. In the minds of many, Lisman's introduction of the term was mean-spirited and indicative of an obtuseness about the academic environment. In addition, the term had particular relevance for Novikoff since a faculty member found guilty of moral turpitude was not eligible to receive severance pay.[15]

Lisman went on to reject the basis on which Novikoff had invoked the Fifth Amendment. He asserted that Novikoff "did not claim his privilege in good faith" and that "his evasiveness, his loss of memory tend to show that he had a reason which was not a good reason, whatever it may have been." After mentioning the instances where Novikoff had failed to cooperate with duly constituted authorities, including the board of review, Lisman concluded by stating that "when you have given this matter due consideration you will decide that Dr. Novikoff is guilty of conduct which justifies his discharge." He then added, "And I am inclined to think you will go further and find that that conduct constitutes moral turpitude."[16]

Peisch then presented a brief summary. His argument centered on the Fifth Amendment question and its basis in legal tradition. He read from the 1781 King's Bench case in England, in which the government attempted to compel Lord George Gordon to answer whether he was a Roman Catholic. Peisch pointed out that the court ruled that Lord Gordon "was not obliged to answer it because, if he were to say he was, his declaration would be evidence against him and might subject him to penalties." This argument was designed to rebut charges one and two, that Novikoff had refused to testify before Congress about his pre-1948 activities and that he had improperly invoked the Fifth Amendment. Peisch dealt with the third charge, that Novikoff had refused to testify fully before "duly authorized authorities of the State of Vermont," by pointing out that there "isn't a syllable of evidence that anybody, that anybody connected with the University of Vermont ever asked him anything that he refused to answer, and I have already read and you are all familiar with the report of your own committee as to what he did there." Given the point of view of many of the trustees on the pre-1948 limitation set by Novikoff and the long debates during the day about going into an executive session to hear Novikoff on the earlier period, one can surmise that this was an unpersuasive statement. Peisch closed by saying, "I think that regardless of what has been said you'd be firing a man for exercising a right."[17]

During the course of his argument, Lisman stated that "we now know something that we never knew before, that he was a leader in this movement; that he was a leader of the Communist conspiracy; he was a leader of a Communist dominated union." Prior to adjourning the panel at the end of the day, Father Joyce returned to this statement by Lisman and wondered "if I have missed a point somewhere."

Joyce: Mr. Lisman said that it has been shown today that Dr. Novikoff was a leader in the Party and so forth. Perhaps that is in some of the documents that were submitted.
Lisman: No.
Joyce: I just wondered where that came up.
Lisman: I was referring to Dean Brown's testimony and I think that you will find it in his testimony in answer to some questions that I asked him.
Chairman Evans: I'm afraid it must be an implication that I didn't catch.

This exchange opened up an extensive debate about Lisman's interrogation of Dean Brown, and Dean Brown was recalled to the stand. Brown denied having asserted or known that Novikoff was a leader of a Communist union and stated that "if I were tricked into that assertion I certainly was very stupid to be caught by that because I never even knew of it." He then accused Lisman of employing "heresay and rumor," and Lisman entered the fray to defend his position. However, the board denied Lisman's request to introduce additional information about Novikoff's past activities. The board then voted to adjourn the public session and "proceed to consider the matter."[18]

Before the members of the board of review left the room, the chairman of the session, Professor Evans, asked the group whether they wished to hear the views of the national AAUP as expressed by Ralph Himstead. He indicated that "we have made no commitments to him." The sharply worded response of one trustee, endorsed by the group, was that they had decided to go into executive session, and they should now do it. With that, the group adjourned and reconvened again at 4:45 P.M. in executive session to decide whether Novikoff was to be dismissed.[19]

During the three-hour executive session, the basis for the 5-to-1 recommendation of the faculty-trustee committee was discussed at length. Many members of the board conveyed their assumption that it was Father Joyce who had voted against the motion to retain Novikoff. Joyce responded by discussing his background as an army clergyman and his broad view of the issues of the case. He expressed his continued support of the conclusions of the faculty-trustee committee.[20]

Finally, the board moved to take a vote. According to the recollection of Joyce, the board might have supported Novikoff if Governor Emerson had not been present and had not played a forceful role. Instead, influenced by the arguments of the governor, the board voted at 7:30 P.M. to recommend that Novikoff "is guilty of conduct which justified his dismissal." The vote was 14 to 8. This recommendation was then to be taken up by the board of trustees at a special meeting called for the following Saturday, September 5.[21]

After he was informed of the verdict, the shaken Novikoff left Waterman Building and walked across the campus to his home. Since it was unlikely that any of the trustees would change their minds in the next few days, he knew that the vote sealed his fate. Alex and Rosalind were joined at home by Peisch and Paul Evans, who had chaired the hearing. Other than expressions of sympathy, there was not much to be said.[22]

The vote of the board of review and extensive excerpts of the testimony were reported in Vermont newspapers the following Sunday and Monday. Numerous photographs of the proceeding were printed. The papers noted that the recommendation did not include any specific reference to the three charges brought against Novikoff. In addition, there was mention that if moral turpitude was applied in the situation, Novikoff might lose his severance pay.

Bernard O'Shea, who was the editor of the weekly *Swanton Courier* and who had been attacked by other editors back in May for his support of Novikoff, published a lengthy assessment of the hearing. He expressed the opinion that if Novikoff had spoken publicly about his Communist connections before 1948, it was likely the board "would have respected this" and "might even have voted to keep him on the faculty." He pointed out that the board would not accept testimony in private because "they did not want to take responsibility for such a hearing." He added: "Charles Brown of Brandon hit this sentiment on the nose when he said that if they voted to bar the press they would in fact be subjecting each member of the Board to subpoena before Senator Jenner to tell what Dr. Novikoff refused to tell the Senator. Few like a trip to Washington, D.C. that well." Although this line of reasoning is not evident from reading the transcript of the hearing (O'Shea pointed out that the "Waterman lounge was too hot for any real debate on this issue"), Chester Eaton confirmed in my interview with him that this was indeed a concern of the Trustees.[23]

O'Shea also reported that he had asked Lisman by what precedent he had raised the charge of moral turpitude. " 'None,' he answered. It was his idea and he hoped to make it stick with the trustees, he said; so UVM would not have to pay Novikoff the usual yearly terminal salary. I doubt the trustees will go along with this rather fantastic extreme position." O'Shea went on to point out that the "low point of the hearing was reached when Edmund Mower, Trustee of Braintree, Mass. paced up and down the hot room questioning Novikoff at length on dates, times, trains and people he remembered on his trips to New York and biochemistry conferences." Eaton confirmed that "Mower was tremendously aggressive. . . . I can recall very clearly my own feeling that he was far more prosecutorial than he should have been." Eaton noted, however: "I think he was the one we trustees did ask to be principal spokesman for or questioner on behalf of the trustees." O'Shea concluded his summary by offering his judgment about who had performed best among the members of the board of review. "I would say in conclusion that the most impressive men on the Board were Representative Granai of Barre, Father Joyce of Rutland and Dr. Paul Evans, presiding, who seemed to me very fair men, and trustees Chester Eaton and Shepardson. In retrospect no one else stood out except witnesses and counsel." A reading of the hearing transcript from a distance of thirty years confirms O'Shea's assessment. Some thirty years later Chester Eaton recalled O'Shea's positive assessment of his performance.[24]

President Borgmann and Ralph Himstead met for an hour on the Sunday after the hearing. According to a letter from Borgmann to the trustees, Himstead "was completely understanding concerning our action in turning down the suggestion by Professor Evans that he say a few words." Borgmann said that he had accepted Himstead's offer to return to Burlington the following Saturday "to discuss with the Board the general AAUP attitude on problems similar to the one we have faced." Borgmann told the board: "If you feel such [a presentation] is not wise, I am certain we can reach Mr. Himstead in time to save him the time and trouble of coming here." Apparently, no trustees had an objection because plans went forward for Himstead to lead off the meeting on Saturday. In Washington, Himstead wired Fred Millett to tell him about his next trip to Vermont and to express his worries about his deepening problems within the AAUP:

Dr. Borgmann, President University Vermont, has invited me by telegram today to meet with Board of Trustees University, Saturday,
September 5 in Burlington to advise the Board concerning case Professor Novikoff. In view apparent inability some members Association's
Council to understand volume and time consuming nature professional
work this office and its importance, or their refusal to accept my word
concerning volume, nature and importance of this work, I should, as
regards my personal welfare, decline this invitation. However, in view of
paramount importance of observance principle involved in Novikoff
case, as regards objectives of Association, it is my decision to accept Dr.
Borgmann's invitation.

Himstead's seeming misrepresentation of the situation—Borgmann's
letter indicated that Himstead, not Borgmann, had initiated the visit;
his remarks were to be general in nature and not addressed to the
particulars of the Novikoff case—suggests that Himstead saw his involvement as a possible means of strengthening his position in the
AAUP. He wanted to impress on the AAUP council the significance of
his role in the "important" Vermont case.[25]

Although the identities of those voting for Novikoff's dismissal
were not revealed, news reports over the next few days disclosed several names. Charles Brown, who had been the single dissenter on the
faculty-trustee committee, released a statement indicating that Novikoff's invoking of the Fifth Amendment was the sole basis for his vote
to dismiss Novikoff. He stated that "I feel had he not invoked the Fifth
Amendment, and even though he had been a Communist, that he
should be retained." Governor Emerson told reporters at a news conference that he "certainly approves the decision of the board of review"
and "I feel it is fully justified." In answer to a reporter's question about
severance pay, Emerson said, "I wouldn't be inclined to be too stiff on
that."[26]

George Wolf, dean of the Medical College, took up the severance
pay question in a letter to Borgmann on September 2. Citing the dic-
tionary definition of turpitude as "inherent baseness; depravity," Wolf
pointed out that Novikoff "has a family and one child was seriously ill
for a long period" and that he had not received any income since
August 15. He pointed out that in the event that Novikoff was not
helped financially, it was likely that some of the faculty would be inclined to take up a collection on his behalf.[27]

William Van Robertson, Novikoff's colleague in the Medical College, wrote to Chester Eaton asking that a compromise solution be
examined. He offered a proposal "which would to some extent assuage
the many faculty members who share my feelings" and allow the
university to continue to benefit from Novikoff's research abilities.

Robertson proposed that once Novikoff had been dismissed (which "appears inevitable"), he be provided laboratory space at the university and that his salary be paid by grants from the American Cancer Society and other funding agencies. The letter indicated that Robertson had reason to believe that Novikoff might accept such an offer. However, there is nothing in available resources that suggests that this proposal was ever seriously considered.[28]

Although the simple task of the trustees on Saturday was to vote on the board of review's recommendation that Novikoff "be dismissed inasmuch as he was found guilty of conduct which justified such action," Eaton believed that the specific grounds for the dismissal should be articulated by the trustees. Thus, without a mandate from or consultation with his fellow trustees, Eaton devoted considerable effort in the days before the meeting to drafting a statement of rationale for the trustees' action. The original of Eaton's three-page document remains in Eaton's Novikoff file and includes many penciled changes based on suggestions from Eaton's brother, a Boston lawyer. Eaton was determined that "every single person who voted must know at the moment of their vote precisely what the words were that were going to be finally on paper." Eaton drove from Rutland with Father Joyce for the September 5 meeting and read the draft to Joyce during the trip.[29]

The board of trustees, with sixteen of twenty members in attendance, convened on Saturday at 10 A.M., and the session had the aura of an anticlimax. News reports in the previous days contained unattributed statements from university officials suggesting that it was very unlikely that the trustees would reverse the recommendation of the board of review. Obviously too, the same trustees who sat as members of the board of review and voted against Novikoff were now sitting as members of the board of trustees.[30]

The meeting opened with the presentation by Himstead, who "gave a brief history of the AAUP, its aims, policies, and principles, and ended by requesting the Board of Trustees to retain Dr. Novikoff." According to the minutes of the meeting, the weeks of effort to bring to bear the AAUP's influence on the course of events ended in the following manner: "Upon motion of Mr. Prentice, seconded by Mr. Granai, it was voted to express to Dr. Himstead the thanks of the Board for his very fine talk on academic freedom and tenure." There was no discussion of the points raised by Himstead. The board, impatient to get on to the business at hand, ended this phase of the meeting.[31]

Trustee Shepardson then stated that certain actions at the hearing indicated that some members of the panel, as well as Lisman, had information on the case that had not been available to all members.

He asked that all information be made available now and that Lisman join the meeting. However, after extensive discussion the board decided that the recommendation of the board of review should be accepted on the basis of the evidence presented and that Lisman should not be invited to the meeting at that point. The motion was made to dismiss Novikoff in accordance with the recommendation of the board of review. Thirteen trustees voted for dismissal, including Emerson, Borgmann, and Eaton, to whom Robertson had addressed his letter. Only Joyce and Shepardson voted negatively. Granai abstained on the grounds that the university attorney had not given the trustees all of the facts on the case. Shortly thereafter, on the motion of Eaton, the board of trustees voted unanimously that Novikoff should receive terminal salary through September 5, 1954.

Lisman was invited to join the meeting and was asked whether he had information bearing on the case that had not been transmitted to the board of trustees. Lisman acknowledged that he had received information from confidential sources that he could not divulge. According to the minutes of the meeting, Lisman revealed the following:

> [Lisman] stated that he had interviewed certain people to whom he had been directed by Mr. Morris, Counsel for the Jenner Committee, and Senator Welker, and had received information about Dr. Novikoff which could not be used at the hearing because he could not reveal the source because he could not persuade the individuals to come to Burlington to testify. He did say that the Jenner Committee were [sic] convinced that Dr. Novikoff was still under Communist party discipline; that Dr. Novikoff had been called to testify before an investigating committee of the State of New York in 1940–1941; that he had sponsored a teachers union local which later was expelled from the national federation because of its communist activities; and that he had been a prominent member of the staff of the Jefferson School which was considered a Communist training center. Mr. Lisman also stated that known Communists had visited Dr. Novikoff in Burlington but it would be difficult to prove that they did not come to consult on scientific questions.

Evidence for the belief of the Jenner Committee that Novikoff remained a committed Communist was not presented. Ironically, the conclusions of the FBI on this point would have been helpful to Novikoff. FBI investigators had decided that Novikoff had disengaged himself from Communist activities. It is pertinent to note that Lisman kept the governor's side of the bargain made at the time the FBI came to the governor's office: he did not reveal that the FBI was the source of some of his information. Another noteworthy point was Lisman's statement that his witnesses had refused to come to Burlington. This directly contradicted his statement to Peisch in the days prior to the hearing.[32]

The assertions of Lisman were not pursued by the trustees. Nevertheless, Shepardson then indicated that he wished to change his vote because he now felt that Novikoff was guilty of misconduct. Granai also indicated his desire to go on record as voting with the majority. Father Joyce did not change his vote and became the only negative vote. Thus, after the many months of controversy and deliberation, Joyce stood alone in opposition to Novikoff's firing.

The board then approved, with amendments, Eaton's lengthy statement representing the official action of the board. The statement included a review of the significant facts of the case in the form of several "whereas" statements and ended with a short "therefore" clause indicating that Novikoff was dismissed and that he would receive terminal pay. The rationale for the board's decision was expressed in the summary judgment that Novikoff was "guilty of conduct which justifies his dismissal from the faculty." However, a brief statement prepared for release to the press was more explicit. The statement indicated that the second charge, that he had improperly invoked the Fifth Amendment before the Jenner Committee, was not a factor in the final action of the board. It was emphasized that the dismissal was based on the special circumstances of Novikoff's case and did not represent a repudiation of the board's stance that invoking the Fifth Amendment was not, in and of itself, cause for dismissal. The judgment of the board was expressed as follows:

> That the dismissal of Dr. Novikoff represents the considered opinion of the Board of Trustees that he has failed to display to a sufficient degree in his actions and statements during the past five months, both before the committee of Congress and before the University bodies, the qualities of responsibility, integrity, and frankness that are fundamental requirements of a faculty member. The actions referred to include, but are not limited to, his invoking of the Fifth Amendment.

Although the board did not rule on whether or not Novikoff's use of the Fifth Amendment was "improper," it is clear that several members judged the failure to cooperate with the Jenner Committee to be part of a larger pattern of noncooperation with various panels.

The meeting was adjourned at 1:00 P.M., and Novikoff was notified of the decision shortly thereafter. After the press was notified of the decision and received the board's statement, Novikoff was contacted by reporters. Novikoff was "openly crestfallen" and stated, "I am sorry it went that way; I had hoped it would be otherwise." He told reporters that he had no plans for the future. News reports pointed out that the trustees had ignored Lisman's urging that Novikoff be found guilty of moral turpitude.[33]

REACTIONS AND CONSEQUENCES

Support for the action against Novikoff came from the editorial writers of the *Free Press* and the *Daily News,* who commended the "soundness" of the trustees' decision. The *Daily News* invoked a patriotic theme by stating that the "American decision rendered by the trustees of UVM is in bright and patriotic contrast to the muddled thinking that goes on at Harvard and some of the other universities which have retained on their faculties professors who have done what Novikoff has done." Letters to the papers presented more positive than negative opinions of the university's action. University alumni got into the act a few weeks later when the Greater Boston UVM Alumni Club heard a presentation about the Novikoff case by the assistant to the president for university development. The sixty alumni in attendance unanimously endorsed a resolution commending the dismissal of Novikoff and condemning the invoking of the Fifth Amendment in investigations of communism in education.[34]

Persons closer to the situation, however, were worried about aspects of the case. On September 10 Borgmann sent a letter to the policy committee of the faculty senate asking that this group study the procedures by which faculty appointments are terminated. Borgmann referred to the "long and tortuous" attempt to follow existing guidelines and proposed a September 23 meeting to plan the study. Andrew Nuquist, head of the local AAUP chapter, was concerned that university faculty were not sufficiently informed about the events of the summer and sent a letter to the faculty indicating that important documents pertaining to the case were now available. Nuquist conveyed his personal judgments about the case in a letter to a colleague on the staff of Fresno State College in California: "The procedures followed were entirely farcical and of complete ineptness on the part of the administration. . . . It has left considerable bitterness in the minds of some of the faculty, and a feeling on the part of many that civil liberties and academic freedom are neither well understood nor particularly supported at least by some members of the administration." Developments over the next two years did not change Nuquist's assessment. A 1955 letter to the same individual contained the statement that the "President seems to have washed his hands of the whole affair and as far as I can tell was not cognizant of all the issues involved in the case at all." Nuquist pointed out that it is "the one thing in which people on campus feel disappointed in what Borgmann has been doing."[35]

Shortly after his dismissal Novikoff received a letter from Ralph Fuchs, an officer of AAUP and a faculty member in the Indiana University School of Law. Fuchs noted that he had followed Novikoff's case with interest "both because of my professional concern as a teacher and lawyer, and because my daughter, Martha Ferger, has naturally spoken of you often." Fuchs's daughter was a student of Novikoff's at the University of Vermont. Fuchs asked Novikoff's permission to review the record of the proceedings and to publish a report. After Novikoff sent information to Indiana, Fuchs wrote a carefully worded letter to Himstead saying he was "considering the possibility of reviewing the record in Dr. Novikoff's case, if I can obtain a copy, for the purpose of preparing a critique and submitting it for possible publication either in the AAUP Bulletin or elsewhere." Fuchs explained his interest in the case:

> My interest is aroused especially because I think maybe the case makes possible a realistic appraisal of the adequacy or of possible weaknesses in the test of "fitness" which we had been advocating for use in such cases. Since it is a vague test, it may be possible for an institution, after all of the procedures have been gone through, to come out with a predetermined conclusion, whether or not it is adequately supported by the evidence. I do not know whether there was abuse of this sort in Novikoff's case, but I am interested in finding out. If there should have been or if the case indicates that there is substantial danger of such abuse, it is important, I think, to initiate a process of subjecting such decisions to professional appraisal.

Fuchs closed by telling Himstead that he did not wish to duplicate anything that Himstead had in mind, adding "I would deeply appreciate a few words from you, telling me what you think of my idea and what its relationship may be to any plans the AAUP may have." Himstead did not respond to this overture from Fuchs. Fuchs discovered in mid-November that the American Civil Liberties Union had decided to review the case and therefore temporarily shelved the idea. In 1955 Fuchs succeeded Himstead as general secretary of the AAUP and at once began a review of the Novikoff case.[36]

In early October, Arnold Schein sent a letter to Himstead with copies of the material sent by the Vermont AAUP chapter to each faculty member before the meeting of the faculty senate on September 25. Schein mentioned that the mailing had had no effect on the faculty and that the "natural timidity of the University Professor was never more apparent." Distinctly pessimistic about matters, he noted that the local AAUP had not met and that "I haven't the faintest idea if any faculty group will disassociate itself from the action of the trustees." Despite the failure of his efforts on Novikoff's behalf over several months, Schein's tenacity did not abate. When the AAUP undertook to study the case in 1955, Schein's letter writing and lobbying resumed.[37]

Over the next few weeks the senate policy committee worked on (1) a revision of the university policy on Communist activities, which had been approved by the board of trustees on April 10, 1953, just as the Novikoff case was surfacing, and (2) new dismissal procedures. Various drafts of a proposed new policy on communism and the Fifth Amendment were studied and debated, with the common themes being the guarantee that the procedures for a board of review enunciated in the bylaws be followed in every case and the stipulation that "disloyalty should be regarded as the overt illegal act toward the government; not criticism of it, no matter how unpopular the criticism." The proposed policies were discussed at a senate meeting on January 21, 1954, but were tabled for further discussion in March. At the March meeting the Senate approved new and more explicit procedures for taking a dismissal action against a faculty member on continuous appointment. The procedures provided for extensive guarantees of due process and appeal. A revised statement on communism was not acted upon, however, because of various parliamentary tangles, lengthy debate, and the invoking of the traditional 6 P.M. adjournment of the senate. Most important, differences of opinion surfaced about whether a statement should present specific definitions and procedures or propositions of a more philosophical nature. Many faculty members expressed the view that procedural safeguards were now guaranteed, and a more general statement of principles was needed. As it turned out, this course was pursued, and a revised statement was developed that was presented for faculty action the following fall. On September 23, 1954, the senate took up a statement containing four sections: "The Necessity of Academic Freedom in Higher Education," "Academic Freedom and Special Responsibilities of Faculty Members," "Responsibility of the Institution to the Faculty," and "Academic Freedom and Tenure." The statement emphasized the right of dissent of faculty and the duty of universities to "maintain an independence of judgment in the face of public opinion." The statement concluded as follows: "In the interpretation and the application of these principles we shall expect the university authorities to be quick to protect its heritage of academic freedom, in doubtful cases remembering that an excess of freedom is always less dangerous than an excess of constraint." Borgmann sent a letter to the faculty supporting the statement and pointing out that the specific provisions of the present policy were no longer needed because Congress had passed legislation outlawing membership in the Communist party. Borgmann's letter quoted Section 4 of the Communist Control Act of 1954: "Whoever knowingly or willfully becomes or remains a member of . . . the Communist Party . . . shall be subject to all the provisions and penalties of the Internal Security Act of 1950, as amended, as a member of a 'Communist-action' organization." The senate and then the board of trustees approved the statement as proposed.[38]

During the fall of 1953, as the university was acting to improve its policies and procedures, the logistics of Novikoff's departure were being carried out. A squabble developed over the possibility that Novikoff's severance pay would not include the regular university contributions to Social Security and to the retirement fund for teachers. In a letter to Governor Emerson, Peisch noted that a proposed agreement between the university and Novikoff ignored these payments. Peisch also expressed his "outrage" that Novikoff was required to sign a "release of any and all rights, claims or demands, which he may now have" against the university. The situation was resolved to Peisch's satisfaction when the board of trustees, on October 17, approved the Social Security and retirement payments and required that Novikoff sign only a "receipt" for having received his payments.[39]

A series of incidents occurred over the disposition of Novikoff's scientific equipment, personal effects, and grant funds. On September 22 the chairman of Novikoff's department, Bjarne Pearson, wrote the Medical College dean expressing his impatience with Novikoff's not having removed his personal effects from his office and not having returned his keys to the building and to various laboratories. In the following days Pearson monitored Novikoff's activities and submitted a detailed chronology of developments to the dean. The chronology noted that Novikoff had taken data books from the Cancer Research Laboratory, had broken open a deep freeze, and had exterminated with ether seventy-five infected rats used for experimental purposes. The extermination of the rats and the removal of the test tubes used in Novikoff's experiments caused an angry exchange between Novikoff and his chairman. All of this made its way into newspaper reports, and Dean Wolf finally had to address the "rumor" that Novikoff had wantonly destroyed laboratory specimens and records. He told a reporter that the test tubes "contained tissues which had tumors in them and the rats had artificially created tumors in them . . . and were items on which Novikoff alone would have worked." He pointed out that there had been agreement all along that the test tubes and rats should be destroyed. Novikoff's departure from the Medical College occurred with a minimum of further problems.[40]

The more important issue for the Medical College dean concerned the disposition of Novikoff's grant from the American Cancer Society. The dean wrote Pearson on September 14 suggesting that he contact the Cancer Society about keeping Novikoff's grant in Vermont, or even better, securing a new grant "though you might be working on the same topic." Inquiries by Pearson on this issue did not lead to any resolution until the following spring.[41]

Once Novikoff's plans to join the Waldemar Research Foundation in New York became known, there was a flurry of letters between the College of Medicine and the American Cancer Society about the disposition of research equipment purchased under the grant received by Novikoff in April 1953. Although university officials wished to retain the equipment purchased under the grant, the conditions stipulated by the Cancer Society in issuing the grant provided the basis for transferring the equipment to Novikoff's new laboratory. The firm resolve of the Cancer Society to continue support of Novikoff's work, regardless of the outcome of the proceedings against him, had been evident since the previous August. During the period of Novikoff's suspension from the university, the executive vice-president of the Cancer Society notified Dean Wolf that Novikoff's grant would be continued and urged that Novikoff be permitted to transmit instructions to his laboratory assistant "so that research progress will not be adversely affected."[42]

On May 11, 1954, Novikoff arrived at the university with a truck and took possession of six items of equipment, including an M-3361 International Centrifuge and a Dubnoff Metabolic Incubator. On May 18 a letter from the Cancer Society to Novikoff's former chairman expressed appreciation for his "excellent administration" of the transfer of Novikoff to Waldemar and stated that the "matter is therefore closed." The letter ended with the observation that "I know that Novikoff was personally very happy at Burlington, Vermont, and only time will tell whether it would have been more desirable to have the situation different from what has happened." At a time when his scientific career was in the balance, the American Cancer Society provided crucial professional support to Novikoff. Novikoff felt deeply the trauma of his trial and dismissal, but as he recalled later, there existed just enough support to provide for his personal and professional survival.[43]

Chapter 9

REMAKING A LIFE AND A CAREER

From Blacklist to Redemption

The Novikoff house was not a happy place in the days and weeks after the dismissal proceeding. The expected had happened, but the firing was now a harsh reality. Although he believed that he had taken a principled stance in refusing to talk about others and that he had been treated unjustly, Novikoff was now unemployed with no immediate prospects for a job. Inevitably, he struggled with feelings of rejection and self-doubt. He had been cast aside by his university and by his community, and it was easy for him to imagine the self-satisfaction of a few political leaders, the editorial writers, and Lisman, the university's lawyer. Struggle as he might against such negative thoughts, there was unmistakably a sharp hurt. After weeks of publicity and effort focused on the board's proceedings, a somber quiet and a period of mourning settled on the small bungalow on Bilodeau Parkway.[1]

Novikoff's state of mind was helped, however, by the letters he received from his active supporters as well as other Vermont citizens. Two of Novikoff's students wrote to express their sense of "personal loss." A note from a University of Vermont alumnus in Brattleboro stated that he was "out of sympathy" with the university's board of review and expressed the hope that "if you are a bit discouraged, this will help cheer you up." At Father Joyce's suggestion a woman wrote to say "how sorry we are for all you've been through, for the immediate outcome." She felt compelled, however, to express her ambivalence about Novikoff's past: "You will, perhaps, forgive my saying that it is difficult for me to understand anyone's being deceived by Communism, even momentarily." Novikoff received a copy of a statement by the director of Christian education and evangelism of the Vermont

Baptist State Convention, who was urging his fellow clergy to join again in action on behalf of Novikoff. The statement asserted that the university "in the long run will suffer far more than the Doctor and his family" and that the trustees "did not dare to do what they must have believed to be right, for fear of what certain prominent people, and a large segment of the general public, might say or do." At Christmas, Father Joyce, the one dissenter on the board of trustees, sent holiday greetings, saying "I hope you will have peace, happiness and the best of God's gifts after this past unpleasant year."[2]

Inevitably, the University of Vermont was a target of recriminations. Novikoff, Dean Brown, and others vented their criticism of the behavior of several individuals at the university, especially President Borgmann and University Counsel Lisman. Brown told a colleague at Harvard that Borgmann had "bungled" the case and enumerated Borgmann's misdeeds throughout the affair. Novikoff stated in a letter that in mid-July Borgmann was "all on my side, but did not express himself; had he done so, I am sure that the trustees would have gone along with the committee's recommendation; instead they voted 12 to 5 against me." Novikoff was especially harsh on Borgmann's role in the final hearing:

> But I regret that President Borgmann, finally breaking his silence, voted against me. He subsequently issued a statement to the University Senate expressing his views. It was both pathetic and vicious, pathetic because of the lack of understanding and immature logic, vicious because, without stating it openly, he was saying by innuendo that I was an "underground" communist who was "lying."

Borgmann, who was at first friendly and helpful to Novikoff, had, under great political pressure from the governor and Vermont public opinion and in the face of complex, fast-moving circumstances, gone along with the majority. Immediately after his dismissal Novikoff was in no mood to forgive Borgmann. As years passed, Novikoff softened his judgment and concluded that Borgmann was a fine human being who had been unprepared to handle the situation. At the moment, however, the criticism had a useful therapeutic effect on Novikoff's morale.[3]

Novikoff's penchant for action probably did more than anything to deter any serious bouts with depression and pessimism. Within days of his dismissal he was in correspondence with professional colleagues around the country seeking information about job openings. These letters expressed how he had come to view his situation. On September 12 he told a friend that he would "stay put until I get something." He told a colleague at Harvard that "if despite all my efforts, I find no suitable connection in my fields, I may try editorial work or other science writing." He also mentioned that "Were it not for our two boys, age 5 and 7, I would be ready to go to a nation like Israel where my research and teaching abilities would be utilized." In January he told his friend, William Van Robertson, that he had decided to put his house up for sale and leave for New York whenever it was sold. He thought this move would help him "pursue more effectively the possibilities which may exist in hospitals, etc." In February he assessed the impact of his travails on his family:

> Rosalind has come through this year heroically, as she did with our
> boy's illness. But there are scars, and for all of us the sooner we leave
> Burlington and get settled elsewhere, the better. The boys (Kenneth, 7,
> and Larry, 5), are doing well in school, despite emotional and speech
> difficulties stemming from Kenny's long hospitalization. Between letters,
> I manage to keep at my work (at home).[4]

Thirty years later, Novikoff spoke for the first time about the personal side of his months of controversy and sadness. Tears came to his eyes when he discussed Kenneth's illness and the long search for a medicine that would ameliorate his condition. He described the coldness of neighbors who avoided him, such as the woman on Bilodeau Parkway who was so terrified of the "communist" that she avoided the sidewalk in front of his home. He told of the emotional shock of seeing newspaper headlines and half-page pictures addressed to his case. As a "Russian" and a member of the small Jewish community in a state not accustomed to Jews, he had faced an overwhelming consensus of public opinion that he should be fired; and he expressed his dark feelings about the sources of this unanimity of opinion, including an intuition that anti-Semitism lurked beneath the attitudes of many. He remembered that, following the final hearing and his dismissal, there was a sharp emotional letdown as his life subsided back to a degree of privacy and solitude. Nevertheless, from the evidence of comments by associates, his correspondence and his own testimony, it appears that Novikoff never lapsed into serious melancholy or pessimism about the future. In the end, his energy and his ingrained systematic approach to problem-solving—an aspect of his scientific training and experience—led him to focus on the particulars of his situation and to seek concrete solutions. Principally, this meant finding a new job that would preserve his career as a researcher into the causes of cancer.[5]

Because Novikoff was so conscientious in maintaining the records and correspondence of his search for a new position, one is able to trace the progress of his efforts. In the months after his dismissal, Novikoff wrote letters to twelve universities, fourteen cancer research laboratories, ten industrial research laboratories, and eight hospitals. He contacted his many scientific colleagues, responded to advertisements in professional publications, and wrote prominent people known to have liberal leanings. For the first five months the results were uniformly poor. Robert Hutchins, then at the Ford Foundation, said that he was "deeply sympathetic" but referred Novikoff to another foundation. His letter to a Canadian diamond prospector, who had made a fabulous diamond strike in Tanganyika, was not answered. Novikoff concluded quickly that his more promising prospects were among his colleagues.[6]

The responses to Novikoff's inquiries of scientists across the country were consistently sympathetic to his situation but contained few promising leads. The director of the Biological Research Laboratory at Cold Spring Harbor on Long Island told Novikoff that "in view of the fact that more than ninety percent of the research going on at this Laboratory is supported by government funds, the opinion I obtained was that your presence here might expose the Laboratory to pressures to [sic] which neither you nor we would enjoy and which all of us would wish to avoid." Two contacts at the University of California cited the oath controversy still brewing there. One, a professor of zoology, wrote the following:

> . . . I have long admired your scientific publications. As you have no doubt read in the daily press we have had a good deal of trouble on the campus and at Berkeley with members of the faculty in connection with their signing a loyalty oath. Although I was fairly certain that the authorities would look with great disfavor on the matter of employing a person in your situation, I talked the matter over with several persons. They agree that there is no probability of your gaining employment here despite your recognized scientific accomplishments and ability.

A response from a professor at the University of Buffalo, an institution that retained a professor who had taken the Fifth Amendment, was not encouraging:

> On the basis of what I know about this region, as well as Harvard, I am not optimistic about your prospects. The institutions which stand by those invoking the Fifth Amendment are not likely to engage a scholar who has done so elsewhere. Thus, it is quite certain that Dr. Parry could not find academic employment elsewhere. He has lost tenure, as you have probably heard, and is on probation for at least three years. This is a most difficult period, and it is unusual to be retained at all under such conditions.

For these individuals and others with whom Novikoff corresponded, there was a clear disinclination to open up the possibility of a controversy over someone's Communist past. Senator Flanders had not yet taken to the floor of the Senate, and the McCarthy era was still in full swing. Furthermore, invoking the Fifth Amendment remained a *bête noire* for those in authority. On this score, Van Robertson reported from Wisconsin that his dean "takes the position that 5th Amendment and guilt go hand in hand and he simply won't listen to any reasonable arguments on the subject, and his reasoning is enough to make me very surprised while he probably feels the same way about me." The conclusion of one correspondent was that a foreign country offered better prospects:

> The question arose in my mind—have you ever considered moving to England? Of course, there might be difficulties thrown in your way, but the climate of opinion there is certainly at the present time more free than here. As an American citizen of several generations' standing, I have the humiliating thought—how much better it would have been for your parents to have moved to England in their search for greater opportunities than in coming to this country!

Although Novikoff did have overseas contacts, and he knew that some other scientists under fire during the McCarthy era had moved to Europe, Novikoff never thought seriously of leaving the United States.[7]

Four places raised hopes that a position might be forthcoming. There were serious interactions with individuals at a research laboratory in New York City; the Jackson Memorial Laboratory in Bar Harbor, Maine; the Kirksville College of Osteopathy and Surgery in Missouri; and the Beth-El Hospital in Brooklyn. In each case, discussions came to a halt. From all appearances, Novikoff's political background was not a controlling factor in the outcome at the first three institutions. Officials went out of their way to say that financial and staffing considerations were the overriding factors. The director of the New York research lab was sensitive on this point: "For the sake of your peace of mind you must believe that what I am about to say is the truth." He went on to say that an anticipated gift from a former patient, which would have funded a research position, had been withdrawn, and "I deeply regret having evoked these false hopes." The director of the Jackson Laboratory told Novikoff that "I am sorry that you have had the experience which you have, and I want to be of assistance" but said that no opening existed. He hinted at political considerations when he stated that he was "not at all certain . . . that, all things considered, this is the best place for you to work." Novikoff's letter of rejection from Kirksville College emphasized that "the question of your non-scientific convictions would never be an issue. . . . We have finally reached the stage at this college where only competence

matters." There was a promise to "survey the possibilities of creating
an appropriate position if the funds can be found," but nothing ever
developed on this score.[8]

On the recommendation of a professional colleague in New York,
Novikoff began shortly after his firing to pursue a research position in
the Biochemistry Division of Beth-El Hospital. Although at first nothing developed, a possible position emerged in December. The discussions went well, and Novikoff went to New York at the end of the
month for a final interview. Things looked so good at this point that
he paid a deposit on an apartment in New York. Dr. I. J. Greenblatt,
the chief of the division, wanted to appoint Novikoff and, in order to
bring matters to resolution, requested a formal letter of application.
Novikoff's letter of January 3, 1954, described his professional qualifications as well as the circumstances of his firing. He spoke candidly
about his decision to invoke the Fifth Amendment:

> Last spring I was called before the Jenner committee in Washington. I
> answered all questions concerning the five years during which I have
> been here in Vermont, stating that I have had no connection whatever
> with communist activities during this period. I was willing to speak of
> my former connections with the Communist Party while at Brooklyn
> College, but they insisted upon my naming my former colleagues. This I
> could not do because to my knowledge not one of them was guilty of
> subversion or disloyal activities, and by informing on them I might be
> subjecting them to the same difficulties which I faced.

It appears that this was the first and only time that Novikoff admitted
in writing, with a potential for wide dissemination, his prior membership in the Communist party. Clearly, he had decided that open
disclosure at the beginning might save embarrassing difficulties later.[9]

Although his scientific credentials were impressive and he had the
strong support of Greenblatt, opposition arose almost immediately. He
learned on January 6 that the superintendent of the hospital opposed
the appointment. After consulting with his allies at Beth-El, Novikoff
requested letters of support from Father Joyce, Rabbi Wall, ex-dean
Brown, and Bishop Van Dyke. The letters provided glowing testimony
about Novikoff's loyalty, professionalism, and morality. Meanwhile,
Greenblatt, who admitted to Novikoff that his wife "made him realize
how important the issue really is," renewed the fight for Novikoff's
appointment with the hospital administration. The issue became sufficiently heated that the question of Novikoff's appointment was
brought before the hospital's board of trustees for resolution. On
January 15 the board voted to reject the appointment. Novikoff's letter
of acknowledgment to Greenblatt indicated his appreciation for the

efforts "to convince the Board that the Hospital stood to gain far more than it could lose." His frustration surfaced when he pointed out, "How narrow-minded fear makes so many people!" The matter was closed officially when the hospital sent Novikoff $130 to cover the deposit on the New York apartment. Although other institutions may have misrepresented their reasons for rejecting Novikoff, there was no doubt that Beth-El's decision was a result of Novikoff's political past.[10]

By February 1954 Novikoff saw that his prospects of attaining an academic position in a university or a research position in a hospital were poor. He turned at this point to a friend in New York from whom he had received advice for several months. Norman Molomut was director of research and guiding spirit of the Waldemar Medical Research Foundation, Inc., located in Brooklyn prior to a recent move to Port Washington on Long Island. This small enterprise included only Molomut, another researcher, and a lab assistant but was prolific in its output of scientific publications. Aided in its work by grants from the National Institutes of Health and the American Cancer Society, Molomut's name went on twelve publications during 1952 and 1953. A government security investigation conducted in 1966 revealed that from its inception the Waldemar facility attracted donors and scientists with leftist political connections, many of whom had ties to the Communist party.[11]

Novikoff began corresponding with Molomut in October when he wrote that he was "beginning to get just a little bit itchy about getting a new job." Over the next few weeks, Novikoff's most serious job prospects developed from suggestions and contacts initiated by Molomut. Finally, on February 3 Novikoff wrote saying that he was seriously interested in joining Molomut's laboratory. Novikoff acknowledged that "you have, several times, indicated that you would make room available to me were I to need space to carry on my work for a while."

> Needless to say, I'd much rather be working with a person who understands things, whom I know and who knows me, than I would with General Foods or Pfizer or Jackson Memorial. And I'd rather continue in cancer research than go into unknown work at General Foods, etc. And I'd rather live near Port Washington (and New York!) than near Hoboken, or Bar Harbor, or Pearl River. In fact, Dave Spain may have told you that when I thought the Beth-El job was mine, we took an apartment (and paid a month's rent!!!) in Roslyn, NY, where we have several friends and where we would like very much to live. . . . If I had reasonable prospects of being able to continue to work in your laboratory, with a modicum of security, there is nothing I would like better. (Except what is not a possibility for me, for some time; working in an academic institution, with students by whom I am stimulated and whom I, in turn, stimulate.)

So Novikoff recognized that his fondest wish, to return to academe, was not a realistic possibility, and he was now ready to accept the offer of Molomut.[12]

Novikoff traveled to New York a week later, and the two men agreed on the arrangements for Novikoff's work, including the transfer of his Vermont Cancer Society grant, lab space, and fund-raising effort designed to bring a $10,000 annual salary. When Novikoff suddenly got some qualms about the arrangement a few days later, Molomut brought to bear his keen sense of humor. He told Novikoff that his "disturbed letter of Feb. 23 made me smile. . . . You make several inductive leaps. . . . You can sustain a fracture from a leap—say a fracture of the front lobes." Novikoff's final question arose when he heard that the Kirksville College of Osteopathy was interested in his services, but that possibility soon died. During March he made final arrangements for his departure from Vermont, and in early April he moved his family to Roslyn, New York, and began work at the Waldemar Foundation. Despite the diminished nature of his professional situation, Novikoff recognized that "I had my lab and my centrifuge" and could continue scientific work. Novikoff remained at Waldmar for eighteen months, until a better professional opportunity finally emerged.[13]

In 1955 Novikoff's letter to Albert Einstein produced the best possible result. The new medical school associated with Yeshiva University had become a reality, and the school was committed to moving into the front rank of medical research. The impulse for its creation was the dream of Jewish-sponsored research as well as the desire to overcome problems arising from the exclusion of Jews from many medical schools. It was not planned, however, that the school would play a role as a haven for refugees from the harsh realities of American politics. Yet Novikoff's application for employment presented just this challenge. Not only were administrators at the medical school aware of Novikoff's promise as a scientist, but they knew well his problems with the Jenner Committee and the circumstances of his firing. They were aware also that Novikoff was the only candidate for a faculty appointment with the personal endorsement of Albert Einstein. Alfred Angrist, head of the new department of pathology, wanted to name Novikoff to the faculty and was supported by Samuel Belkin, president of Yeshiva University. The potential difficulties created by the appointment were recalled by an Einstein faculty member:

> . . . when Alex, seeking to end his exile, applied for a position in our Department of Pathology, the College of Medicine faced its first challenge of principle. It was not the kind of challenge that the founders had conceived would arise. In essence, what do you do when a refugee from

American political injustice asks for asylum—more properly, for the right to continue a career in science and teaching? And the College of Medicine and Yeshiva University met that challenge head on.

The appointment, however, did not go forward without controversy. In order to sooth the objections of the trustees, Novikoff was made a "research professor." Despite this reminder of the McCarthy era, arrangements were acceptable to Novikoff and his new employers, and he became one of Albert Einstein's founding faculty. It is noteworthy that, having established this precedent, the medical school went on to hire other victims of the McCarthy era, including Helen Deane Markham, whose contract had not been renewed by Harvard University.[14]

Novikoff joined a faculty of superb medical scientists, and the medical college went on to acquire an outstanding reputation, as did Novikoff. Novikoff had righted himself professionally, and as the years passed, he slowly put the unpleasantness in Vermont behind him. He remained on the faculty of the Albert Einstein College of Medicine until his death thirty-two years later.

POLITICAL CONCERNS

During the months that Novikoff struggled to reestablish himself professionally, there were other worries. In the light of his past affiliation with the Communist party and his unemployed status, his worst foreboding was that the government might try to deport him. Early in 1954 he began paperwork to certify his derivative American citizenship. Problems arose because many of his family's official documents had been lost or were unauthenticated copies. After Novikoff was interviewed by the St. Albans, Vermont, office of the Immigration and Naturalization Service (INS), the INS decided to interview Novikoff's parents, who were living in Florida. A particularly thorny issue arose because the Novikoff family had changed their first names upon their arrival in America in 1912 and 1913: Zelig, his father, became Jake; Hinda, his mother, became Anna; Sose, his sister, became Sophie and then Sonia; Elje, Alex's Russian name, had been dropped. The directive to the Miami INS office took note of the fact that Novikoff "was discharged from the University of Vermont for failure to testify before a congressional committee, claiming exemption under the Fifth Amendment." Fortunately, the interviews with Novikoff's parents and other inquiries, including attempts to verify the arrival of Alex's ship in 1913, went successfully. In late April a certificate of citizenship was issued, and a month later Novikoff swore his oath of allegiance to the United States of America.[15]

Without his knowledge, Novikoff was the subject of another official review. In the early years of the Eisenhower administration there had been a concerted effort to dismiss security risks from federal employment. The FBI's Security Index, on which Novikoff was listed, was a convenient tool for identifying potential security risks. In this atmosphere of extreme vigilance about subversion, the number of persons listed on the Security Index rose from 19,577 in November 1952 to 26,174 in December 1954. In due course there was considerable debate about the criteria used to place a name on the index. To head off criticism, J. Edgar Hoover decided to tighten the FBI's criteria and to evaluate names already on the list. In 1955 Novikoff's file was reviewed. On the basis of this review and the previous finding that Novikoff had separated from Communist party activities, his name was deleted from the list in September 1955. The review found "no information indicating activity or membership in a basic revolutionary organization during the past five years . . . [or] in a front organization during the past three years." If Novikoff had known about all of this, it is doubtful that he would have been elated. The FBI kept his name on its unofficial Communist Index and, of course, kept intact the large file in his name. We will find shortly that the FBI's interest in Novikoff would continue to have negative consequences for his scientific career.[16]

In October 1953 the American Civil Liberties Union (ACLU) undertook an investigation of the Novikoff case, and Counsel Lisman's role came under scrutiny. ACLU members in Vermont asked the national office how Lisman, as Novikoff's prosecutor, could remain the Vermont correspondent for the national ACLU. Lisman made a personal visit to the national office on October 9 and was interviewed by a staff member. The staff member heard Lisman's version of the events in Vermont, including the assertion that Novikoff had "reneged" on a promise to tell all to the Jenner Committee. He concluded that Lisman "is a very decent guy" and reported to Louis Joughin, the ACLU research director, that he had persuaded Lisman to remain as the state correspondent. In due course, Lisman stepped down, but the feeling against him remained strong, especially among Novikoff's allies who had followed events closely. Novikoff eventually lost the will to harbor bitterness against anybody in Vermont, except for Lisman. Novikoff did not forget Lisman, and the indications are that Lisman continues to reciprocate animosity toward Novikoff.[17]

The effort by the ACLU to investigate the Novikoff case led to a review of the formal proceedings but did not lead to a comprehensive report. Since at that time the ACLU had an anti-Communist leaning, it is not surprising that the undertaking lacked enthusiasm. By 1955 it was clear that the best possibility of achieving a serious assessment of the case would be through the long dormant AAUP. Events were brewing within the AAUP that would make such a review possible.

THE AAUP REVIEWS THE VERMONT CASE

Shortly after the conclusion of the Novikoff case, the national AAUP office fell into even greater confusion and conflict. Himstead delayed the work of the special committee appointed to study the central office until, without his sanction, the committee met in December in St. Louis. The committee developed and circulated proposals designed to reduce the authority of the general secretary. A meeting of the AAUP council in February 1954 produced bitter debate but had the effect, temporarily at least, of sustaining Himstead's leadership. However, in the weeks before the annual meeting of the AAUP membership in April, the pressures on Himstead resumed, and he took the step of offering his resignation to the council. In doing this, he expressed his desire to remain as editor of the *AAUP Bulletin*. In his letter to the council he noted the litany of unfair charges made against him: "I have been subjected to the charges of not knowing how to delegate work, of inefficiency and of remissness [sic] in the handling of the work of the office, particularly the correspondence of the office." This was probably a fair statement of his deficiencies as an administrator. Although Himstead may have hoped that the council would not accept his offer to resign, shortly after the annual meeting the council approved Himstead's request and appointed a committee to find a successor. Himstead engaged in various delaying tactics over the next few months and disputed several of the actions of the council and the AAUP president. Finally, in August 1954, Himstead had a serious heart attack, which kept him out of the office for two months. At the annual meeting the following spring, his planned retirement was announced. After extensive negotiations between the Council and Ralph Fuchs, the man with whom Novikoff had corresponded in late 1953, Fuchs agreed to become temporary general secretary until such time as AAUP finances would permit a permanent appointment. Himstead, who had been instructed by the AAUP president to announce the appointment of Fuchs to the AAUP membership, delayed such action for several weeks. In June 1955, while working at his desk on the news release about Fuchs's appointment, Himstead suffered a cerebral hemorrhage and died the following day.[18]

The consequence of the almost two years of crisis in the central

office was that the AAUP had taken virtually no steps to appraise the
events of the early 1950s and to determine whether censure was warranted for institutions that had fired professors. The failure to undertake reviews of the many cases of the McCarthy era frustrated and
incensed many AAUP members, including Fuchs. Thus, immediately
following his appointment, Fuchs moved to rectify the situation by
naming a special committee to investigate those cases where professors
had been fired, many of them involving the invocation of the Fifth
Amendment. Novikoff, still at the Waldemar Medical Research Foundation on Long Island, heard of the AAUP's interest in the Vermont
case from Arnold Schein, and he wrote to Fuchs on November 16.

> I wonder if anything you are planning may involve further publicity for
> me. If so, you will want to know that my present position might be
> jeopardized by any widespread publicity, and even more important, an
> important research grant virtually assured for next year, and two dis-
> tinct possibilities of attractive offers at academic institutions would
> probably be endangered by even limited publicity, in the Bulletin or
> other national organ, at the present time. Of course I realize the impor-
> tance to academic freedom that the Association express publicly its con-
> demnation of behavior such as that of the University of Vermont when it
> dismissed me. Can this be done in some manner not involving publicity
> and further hardship for me personally?

Fuchs's response to Novikoff indicated his awareness that the problem
of publicity was "a difficult one" but pointed out that any written
material would be submitted for review by the affected institution and
individuals in the case. He suggested that "we let it rest until you
receive the material." He assured Novikoff that "we would be loath to
proceed contrary to your wishes, and I am confident matters can be
worked out satisfactorily."[19]

The AAUP proceeded with preparing a report on the Vermont case
with an intended release date of March 15, 1956. On February 6 and
9, respectively, Fuchs sent confidential drafts of the report to Novikoff
and President Borgmann. Borgmann was not surprised by the arrival
of the report because he knew of the AAUP special committee of investigation and had, at Fuchs's request, sent to Fuchs the transcript of
the public hearing before the board of review. However, one can surmise that he was not happy that, two and a half years after the final
action of the board of trustees, the affair was about to become again
a matter of public debate and critique. His own role, about which he
had admitted personal error and misjudgment, would become again a
subject of discussion. Moreover, he knew the animosity of the local
media toward the AAUP, and he remembered the predictions in 1953
that the university would *not* become a candidate for censure. The *Free*

Press at the time had expressed the view in an editorial that the local AAUP chapter was mistaken and that it "appears improbable that the suspension of Dr. Alex Novikoff will involve the University in loss of rating" by the AAUP. The editorial pointed out that 1950 was the last year an institution had been censured and that there had been no cases of censures as a result of situations similar to Novikoff's. Now, with renewed conviction and new leadership, the AAUP was determined that the transgressions of the McCarthy era would not fade quietly from memory.[20]

The three-page draft report reviewed by Borgmann and Novikoff traced the events and circumstances of 1953. The essence of the committee's judgment was presented in a lengthy concluding paragraph, which included the following statements:

> In the entire case the Committee finds that the formal obligations of due process in relation to a public hearing were adhered to in this proceeding. It is nevertheless impossible to condone the outcome or the insistence of the Trustees that the faculty member must testify in public. The duty of candor to representatives of the employing institution does not include a duty to make public disclosure; and the insistence that the faculty member in this instance speak in public deprived him, in effect, of a hearing appropriate to an academic proceeding.

The committee argued that there was an insufficient basis to conclude that Novikoff had not met his professional duty of candor. The report closed with a call for censure.

> In spite of the measure of due process that was accorded by the administration here and the evident effort on the part of a minority of Trustees to obtain the facts needed for a full and fair treatment, the committee is of the opinion that a grave violation of academic freedom and tenure occurred. It recommends that the administration of the University of Vermont be visited with censure by the American Association of University Professors.

The report honored Novikoff's request that his name not be used by employing such phrases as "a professor of biochemistry" and "the faculty member."[21]

Borgmann's response to the draft raised a question about the "dilemma" of public testimony by Novikoff. He pointed out that Novikoff had insisted that if he were to testify publicly, no record was to be kept. Borgmann emphasized that such a stipulation was contrary to the bylaws of the trustees and, he argued, to the desires of the faculty. Fuchs's brief response to Borgmann on February 24 carried the welcome news that the AAUP committee was withholding a recommendation on the University of Vermont, and therefore only the basic facts of the case would appear in the spring 1956 edition of the *AAUP Bulletin*. Fuchs stated that Borgmann's "point that Novikoff insisted additional testimony be off the record is important."[22]

As matters turned out, the draft report was the closest that the University of Vermont would come to being visited with censure. Borgmann's perceptive statement of the board's quandary over accepting public off-the-record testimony, Fuchs's careful legalistic mind, and the tightness of the deadline for preparing material for the spring 1956 edition of the *Bulletin* combined to postpone decisive action by the AAUP. It is likely also that Fuchs realized that an investigation based on available documents, new reports, and long-distance communication—the method used by the AAUP committee—was insufficient to penetrate the details and the complexity of the Novikoff case.

Fuchs set in motion further study of the Novikoff case so that a recommendation could be made by the AAUP council on April 5 in St. Louis. He requested comments from Novikoff and Borgmann and on March 30 invited Borgmann to send a representative to the council meeting in St. Louis. When Borgmann indicated that the timing was too tight to have anyone go to St. Louis, it became clear to Fuchs and the council that they were not ready to proceed with a final recommendation. At its April 5 meeting the council decided that a supplementary investigation should include a visit to Burlington by a subcommittee. When it became impossible to organize a visit before the end of the academic year, it was decided to schedule it for next fall. With these various delays, the gap in time between the firing of Novikoff and AAUP action became greater, and it became much less likely that the AAUP would sustain a censure recommendation against the university.[23]

During October and early November 1956 arrangements were completed for the visit of the AAUP review team. Fuchs recruited Bentley Glass, professor of biology at Johns Hopkins University; Fred Millett, professor of English at Wesleyan University and an observer at Novikoff's final hearing; and Bertram Willcox, professor of law at Cornell University, to serve on the team. The importance of the Vermont case was evidenced by the appointment of Glass. Glass was the committee chair and primary author of a special AAUP report on the impact of McCarthyism on the campuses, which was issued in 1956 under the title *Academic Freedom and Tenure in the Quest for National Security.* He knew Novikoff from the 1940s, when he had enthusiastically reviewed Novikoff's two books on science for children. Borgmann and Samuel Bogorad, new president of the Vermont AAUP chapter, worked together in setting up an interview schedule with participants in the events of 1953. The schedule for November 19 and 20 included meetings with seventeen individuals, including Borgmann, Peisch, Lisman, several faculty members, and at least one trustee. Novikoff wrote Fuchs informing him that he was too busy to come to Burlington but would be glad to meet with an AAUP representative in New York.[24]

Despite the best efforts of all parties to keep the visit a confidential matter, a *Burlington Free Press* reporter learned of the impending review and sought detailed information about the visit. Bogorad told reporters that the visit was not a local AAUP matter, and therefore he could not be helpful. A prominent *Free Press* story on November 20 discussed the visit in a sketchy fashion and reported that "newsmen and photographers who attempted to learn details of the interviews and take photographs of the AAUP committee members were told the meetings were not public." An accompanying editorial, headlined "What Purpose Secrecy in Novikoff Review," argued that a secret review would not add to the AAUP's "dignity or stature in this part of the country." Both the business manager, David Howe, and the city editor, Robert Beaupre, of the *Free Press* wrote letters protesting the secrecy of the review. Beaupre asked Fuchs for a "collect wire on the findings." Fuchs replied that "I am unable to follow the reasoning which asserts that professional interviews and communications regarding such a case should be a matter of public knowledge at the time they take place." He pointed out that the committee's report, including its methods and reasoning, would be made public when it was completed. In spicy language that suggested that ultraconservative segments of the Vermont press were in a mood similar to that which prevailed in 1953, the *Vermont Sunday News* editorialized as follows:

> With blood running in the streets of Budapest, even such a near-sighted individual as premier Nehru of India is on the verge of realizing that Communism should be known as "Murder Incorporated" rather than a liberal philosophy . . . The AAUP, of course, mumbles the usual nonsense about academic freedom being involved. Somehow, though, it ignores the academic freedom that allows academic authorities to insist on reasonable conduct by teachers and professors. . . . It might be noted that the AAUP, which goes to hysterical lengths about academic freedom, has no similar qualms about star chamber proceedings. The current session is behind closed doors with the public and the press banned. A shameful exhibition of split standards.

A November 22 letter to the *Free Press* from Bogorad was published with an editor's note pointing out that Bogorad had been called four times for information about the review, and he had "refused even to confirm that the review was scheduled."[25]

As suggested by the press response to the AAUP review, feelings still ran strong in Vermont about the Novikoff case. However, Bentley Glass wrote Fuchs a relaxed letter on November 24, shortly after his return to Johns Hopkins.

> We had a very interesting and in fact pleasant trip to Burlington, and I think the situation became sufficiently clear to us that we are unanimous in our appraisal of it. We intend to report that although certain aspects of the hearing were censurable at the time, nevertheless the very commendatory efforts to improve procedures and to take a firm stand to protect academic freedom since the admittedly (by the university administration) unfortunate aspects of the hearing make a censure at this time definitely unwarranted.

The group's twelve-page report was completed in March 1957 and circulated to Borgmann, Novikoff, and the members of the AAUP Committee A on Academic Freedom and Tenure. From their analysis of the suspension and dismissal decisions and the conduct of the two hearings, the committee of inquiry reached the conclusion that "the actions taken by the University of Vermont in this case were grave offenses against recognized principles of tenure and academic freedom; and at the time they would have merited censure by the American Association of University Professors." To the relief of the University's leaders, the committee refrained from making a censure recommendation.

> Nevertheless, it is also our conviction that this case has come to be recognized by the administration of the University, as well as by its faculty, as a deplorable stain upon an institution otherwise devoted to intellectual freedom; and that earnest efforts have been made to redress the situation and to prevent any future abuses of a like kind. . . . The committee of inquiry is unanimous in believing that the evidence of an increased freedom of mind and improved safeguards for tenure which the foregoing statement supplies, renders censure of the University of Vermont inappropriate at this time.

The evidence cited by the committee for improved procedures and safeguards included the new bylaw procedures for dismissal proceedings and the statement on academic freedom and tenure endorsed by the faculty senate and the board of trustees.[26]

Editing changes were made in the Vermont report over the next few weeks. In October the new General Secretary of the AAUP, Robert Carr, sent revised copies to Novikoff, Vermont, and the visiting committee. Carr's note to Novikoff indicated that after extensive debate in Committee A they had decided to use his name in place of the previous vague references to a "faculty member." Carr pointed out that "the contrary practice seems artificial and lacking in substantial justification" and that all reports to the committee would use names. Novikoff's reply expressed his "regret" about the use of his name. Bertram

Willcox, a member of the visiting team, wrote to urge that the report show "that what happened when Doctor Novikoff was discharged did merit censure at the time." Letters circulated among these parties during October and November until a final version went to press in December for publication in the spring 1958 edition of the *AAUP Bulletin*.[27]

The March 1958 edition of the *Bulletin* contained a change that produced confusion back in Vermont. The statement that recent developments "renders censure of the University of Vermont inappropriate at this time" was revised as follows: "The committee of inquiry is unanimous in believing that the evidence of an increased freedom of mind and improved safeguards for tenure which the foregoing statement supplies, coupled with the present posture of the dismissal case itself, modify significantly the situation at the University of Vermont." The significance of these final changes was that when the report was published in March, the recommended action in the Vermont case was not communicated. The reader could not tell for sure whether the committee of inquiry or its parent, the Committee on Academic Freedom and Tenure, would recommend for or against a censure action at the AAUP annual meeting scheduled for April 25 and 26 in Denver.[28]

The *Bulletin* included reports on cases at nine institutions, each alleging a violation of academic freedom during the McCarthy era. The Vermont report, which appeared first in the volume, was one of four (including cases at New York University, the University of Michigan, and Reed College) continued from 1956. The *Free Press* telephoned Novikoff for his reaction to the report's assertion that his dismissal had been "unjustified." Novikoff expressed the hope that the University of Vermont would in the future be able to "spare itself all of this embarrassment and difficulty" and stated that "I am naturally pleased that they feel as I did about the basic nature of the action." He expressed his willingness to "let the issue drop." Borgmann's comments to reporters noted the report's favorable comments about the university's newly adopted procedures and raised again the problem of off-the-record testimony. The *Free Press* story noted that the Novikoff case would come before the Committee on Academic Freedom and Tenure at the AAUP annual meeting, where the committee "may recommend" to the full AAUP that the university be censured.[29]

In anticipation of the Denver meeting, faculty in the University of Vermont AAUP chapter expressed concern that their institution might be censured by the national organization. Although memories of the Novikoff case remained bitter for many, there was also worry about the stigma that would be attached to the university and its faculty if a censure action were to be taken. Influenced by the new chapter

president, William Van Robertson, the chapter endorsed by written
ballot the following resolution:

Resolved:
    a) that the University of Vermont Chapter of the American Associa-
tion of University professors strongly urges the Board of Trustees of the
University of Vermont to formally accept the report of Professor Glass's
committee (March 1958 Bulletin of the AAUP, Vol. 44, No. 1) dealing
with the proceedings and dismissal of Professor Alex B. Novikoff.
    b) that if such action is taken by the Board of Trustees before
April 23, the date of the National Convention of the AAUP, the delegate
of the University of Vermont Chapter to that meeting be instructed to
press against visitation of censure on the University of Vermont Administration and the Board of Trustees.

Robertson wrote President Borgmann on April 17 to convey the resolution. Borgmann decided to place the matter on the agenda of the
previously scheduled April 19 board of trustees meeting.[30]

Noting that only four members of the board of trustees had been
members during the 1953 proceedings against Novikoff, Borgmann
took considerable time at the April 19 meeting to review the history
of the 1953 proceedings and to review the contents of the AAUP report
published in the March *Bulletin*. After preliminary discussions of the
AAUP resolution, Professor Robertson was invited into the meeting to
speak on the resolution. Robertson said that thirty-three chapter members had voted by mail to present the resolution to the board. There
were no dissenting votes. According to minutes of the meeting, he
stated that "it was his desire to be in as strong a position as possible
as the chapter's delegate to the AAUP meeting in Denver on April 23
to urge that the University not be censured by the AAUP." Shortly after
Robertson's presentation, the trustees approved the following motion:
"This is to acknowledge receipt of the report of the Special Investigating Committee of the AAUP Committee on Academic Freedom and
Tenure. In view of the present administrative procedures adopted by
the Trustees and now in effect, further comment is inappropriate."[31]

In Denver on April 25 Bentley Glass, chairman of the AAUP Committee on Academic Freedom and Tenure, made an oral report to the
group's annual meeting. He reported that his committee recommended
censure against six institutions, including the University of Michigan,
and recommended that censure be withheld in five cases, including
the Vermont case. The full text of the Vermont recommendation read
as follows:

Committee A holds that the summary suspension of professor Alex B.
Novikoff at the University of Vermont in 1953 and his subsequent dis-

missal on charges unsupported in the hearing were unjustified, although mitigated by the payment to him of a year's severance pay. In view of the complex procedural difficulties which arose, the subsequent lapse of time, and the adoption by the University since that date of satisfactory new regulations governing dismissal and an admirable statement of adherence to the highest standards of academic freedom and tenure, and because of formal cognizance of the Association's report on the University of Vermont taken by the Trustees on April 19, 1958, Committee A refrains from making any further recommendations in the matter.

The full AAUP accepted this report without action and effectively closed the Novikoff case as an issue of immediate concern to the AAUP and the University of Vermont. After two and a half years of scrutiny by the AAUP, extending almost five years after the dismissal proceedings against Novikoff, the primary parties to the affair, including Novikoff, seemed ready to let the case subside quietly. The University of Vermont had made amends with its new policies; the AAUP had asserted publicly that the dismissal was unjustified; Borgmann had suffered public and private criticism but had guided the university away from censure; and Novikoff, although he wanted a censure recommendation, had survived professionally and personally and was ready to look to the future.[32]

The actions of the local AAUP chapter in 1958 exemplified the attitude that had emerged among Novikoff's former colleagues. While continuing to condemn the dismissal, these faculty members believed that a censure action would do unnecessary and perhaps permanent damage to the institution. The chapter's success in bringing the board of trustees to "receive" the AAUP report helped assure a noncensure recommendation in Denver, which in turn permitted the university to go forward with a minimum of lingering bitterness. As the McCarthy period receded into the past, there was a readiness to move ahead to new challenges and commitments.

EMERGENCE OF A BRILLIANT SCIENTIST

In the years following the proceedings in Vermont against Alex Novikoff, the careers of the important actors—Borgmann, Emerson, Joyce, Peisch, Lisman, and Novikoff—went in different directions. Carl Borgmann succeeded in changing the charter of the University of Vermont by persuading the new governor and legislature to make the university an "instrumentality of the State." He achieved this step, his foremost strategic goal as president, by immersing himself in Vermont politics and traveling the state from end to end. It is difficult to deter-

mine for certain whether Borgmann's "sensible" position on the Novikoff case helped persuade Vermonters to his point of view on the
charter question. He left the University of Vermont during the summer
of 1958 and went on to professional accomplishment with the Ford
Foundation and the University of Colorado. His professional reputation,
however, never fully recovered from his involvement in the dismissal
of Alex Novikoff.[33]

Governor Lee Emerson left the governorship voluntarily in 1955
and thereafter worked primarily as a lawyer in his home county in
northeast Vermont. In 1987 the state legislature voted to name a nearby
courthouse in his memory. The *Rutland Daily Herald,* however, diminished the gesture when it noted that the Emerson administration had
signaled the end of Republican dominance in Vermont politics. Emerson's efforts to undo the progressive legislation of previous governors
and his "jingoism" at the time of the Novikoff firing were cited as
contributing factors in the weakening of the party.[34]

Father Robert Joyce, who cast the solitary vote to keep Novikoff
on the faculty, was elevated to auxiliary bishop and then bishop of the
Burlington Diocese. At Joyce's invitation, Novikoff traveled from New
York for the ceremonies. As bishop Joyce demonstrated a capacity for
farsighted, albeit not always popular, leadership. In 1962 he took the
step of changing the Mass from Latin to English, an action that earned
disapproval in some quarters of the church. In 1967 he was instrumental in the merger of two hospitals, one affiliated with the Catholic
Church, and the creation of a major medical center affiliated with the
University of Vermont. He retired in 1972 and was still active in the
Burlington community at the age of ninety.

Thirty-five years later, the two lawyers, Francis Peisch and Louis
Lisman, still maintained their law practices in Burlington, although at
a much reduced scale to accommodate the effects of old age. Because
of his involvement in a financial irregularity involving a gift of funds
to the University of Vermont, Lisman's connection to the university
was ended not long after the Novikoff affair. From the testimony of
many of his contemporaries, it is evident that Lisman's actions against
Novikoff irretrievably damaged his reputation among segments of the
Burlington community.[35]

Among the cast of characters, only Novikoff—forty years old at the
time of his firing—went on to achieve a career of national prominence.
At the very moment that Novikoff's life was thrown into turmoil by
the dismissal proceeding, the seeds of an exceptionally promising future were planted. In the spring of 1953 Novikoff published an article
in the *Journal of Histochemistry and Cytochemistry* that reported some of

his last experiments at the University of Vermont. The research demonstrated a biochemical approach to the study of enzymes that broke new ground. Entitled "Biochemical Heterogeneity of the Cytoplasmic Particles Isolated from Rat Liver Homogenate," the article was later described by Nobel laureate Christian de Duve as "truly innovative . . . as well as prophetic." At the time, de Duve was himself working along similar lines at the University of Luvain in Belgium. When he read Novikoff's paper, he wrote to him and included an account of his findings. De Duve recounted later that it was "the beginning of a fruitful collaboration and of a long, enduring, and deep friendship, inaugurated, as I remember, by an interminable discussion in Central Park, on a lovely day in the spring of 1953." In de Duve's estimation, the paper that sparked this relationship made several crucial contributions:

> Instead of isolating the classical "nuclei, mitochondria, microsomes, and supernatant," Alex and his girls [his research assistants], as he called them, had modified the fractionation scheme so as to isolate six, and even ten, fractions. Each fraction was examined by phase-contrast microscopy and analyzed for protein, RNA, DNA, and seven distinct enzymes. The choice of these enzymes was almost prophetically insightful, as they included markers for half a dozen different cytoplasmic organelles, several of which were still waiting discovery at that time.

A collaboration between Novikoff and de Duve flowered two years later when Novikoff visited de Duve's lab in Belgium.[36]

Now established at the Albert Einstein College of Medicine, Novikoff accepted de Duve's invitation to give a paper at the Third International Congress of Biochemistry in Brussels in the summer of 1955 and to spend several weeks working with his research team. At the time, de Duve was developing his lysosome theory, which became the basis for his 1974 Nobel Prize for Medicine. He saw that Novikoff's research techniques and his gifted eye through a microscope would complement his own work nicely.

> I will always remember his arrival in our laboratory. His first question . . . was, "Where is the microscope?" I can still see the look of shocked disbelief on his face when I told him there was none. This difference was to remain between us for all subsequent years. Alex, although trained as biochemist, had a special love and gift for morphology [the study of the form and structure of organisms]. He belonged to the "seeing is believing" school, whereas I was a member of the "grind and find" coterie. This made us ideally complementary for collaborative work.

Because there was no electron microscope in de Duve's lab, Novikoff spent considerable time traveling with an ice bucket of prepared cell material to Albert Claude's lab in Brussels and later to a lab in Paris. With the use of the microscope, the research team got its historic first look at lysosomes on the day that Novikoff returned with a photograph showing "a cluster of particles . . . having the morphological features of the pericanalicular dense bodies seen by Rouiller." As de Duve said, "We felt like Le Verrier after the planet Neptune was discovered." Novikoff reported the findings the next year at an important conference in the United States. A jointly authored article appeared in the *Journal of Biophysical and Biochemical Cytology* in 1956 which, in de Duve's words, "presented the lysosome for the first time to a select American audience, both as a biochemical concept and as a morphological entity."[37]

Novikoff's work with de Duve, only two short years after the problems in Vermont, established solidly his reputation in the scientific world and set the groundwork for a long career of accomplishment. The collaboration culminated in 1963 when the two jointly sponsored a symposium on lysosomes that drew many eminent scientists, including Albert Claude, George Palade, and Lewis Thomas. Over the years Novikoff made additional contributions to the lysosome field, including chapters on the subject in medical texts. Eventually, his research interests went in new directions, and he began serious studies of a complex structure known as GERL. In this field, too, he broke new ground and in time gained converts to his theoretical insights.[38]

There were many marker events in a career that lasted until his death in early 1987. In 1958, the year that the *New York Times* printed a long article on his research, Novikoff was promoted to full professor. His first research grant from the National Institutes of Health covered the 1957–1959 period. The grant that secured his professional career was a "lifetime" annual award of $25,000 to cover a period of twenty-five years. This prestigious award, which was noted in various newspapers, began in 1962. Novikoff served as president of the American Society for Cell Biology and as editor, reviewer, and contributor for the *Journal of Cell Biology* and the *Journal of Histochemistry and Cytochemistry.* In 1974 he was elected to America's oldest academic society, the National Academy of Sciences. With a colleague he wrote what has been called a classic textbook, *Cells and Organelles.* In 1982 he was awarded the prestigious E. B. Wilson Medal by the American Society for Cell Biology. Wilson, who was a pioneer in the field of cell biology, was at Columbus University while Novikoff was a student there and had taken an active interest in Novikoff's work. In his acceptance speech Novikoff noted that "in the 1930s at Woods Hole, Dr. Wilson used to come to see me in the Columbia lab every day, to learn what I had done with the eggs of a beautiful sea-worm, *Sabellaria.*" Indicative of the

impact of his work, his 1961 paper on the Golgi apparatus was identified recently as a "Citation Classic," for having been cited in more
than 695 publications.[39]

It is noteworthy that over the years several colleagues mentioned
Novikoff as a worthy candidate for a Nobel Prize. In 1974 three of
Novikoff's professional associates—Albert Claude, George Palade, and
Christian de Duve—were awarded the Nobel Prize for their discoveries
concerning the structural and functional organization of the cell. When
Novikoff heard the news on the radio, he tried to reach de Duve at
Rockefeller University in New York, Because de Duve was busy with
television interviews, he called Claude in Belgium to offer his congratulations. Still flushed with his own excitement, Claude recovered
and cursed the absence of Novikoff from the award list: "Damn, you
should have shared it." Novikoff acknowledged later that "maybe I
could have shared it." He noted that de Duve himself had stated that
although he (de Duve) had articulated the lysosome concept, Novikoff
had "shown him the existence of the thing." Immersed in the excitement of his own work and confident of its importance, however, Novikoff showed no sign that he harbored any bitterness about the matter.
Indeed, it was Novikoff who wrote the essay on de Duve's award for
the November 8, 1974, edition of *Science*.

Although Novikoff's career seemed to unfold in a pattern of un-
broken success, a few troubling developments arose. By the 1960s his
marriage to Rosalind had deteriorated badly. After the departure from
Vermont, Rosalind took a job as a librarian in New Rochelle, New York.
In the view of one of Alex's relatives, the "mousy" Rosalind could not
stand up against Alex's forceful and sometimes overbearing behavior.
Over the years she became more withdrawn and resentful of Alex.
Certainly, his single-minded devotion to work, with long hours in the
laboratory, contributed to the rupture. After a while Rosalind began
to go out with a man who was energetically pursuing her. The relationship became an open secret when Alex's sister saw the two together at a movie theater, and Alex realized that "some bastard [was]
after her, and even in my presence." Despite the warning signs of
trouble, he was stunned and wounded when Rosalind left him. The
damage to his pride was sufficiently great that he felt bitterness toward
Rosalind for the rest of his life. The marriage was irretrievably broken,
and they were divorced in Juarez, Mexico, on May 30, 1967.[41]

Like that of other productive scientists, Novikoff's work was supported by collaborations with colleagues. Among his many close relationships over the years, one of the most important was with Phyllis
Iaciofano, whom he had hired as a laboratory technician shortly after

his arrival at Albert Einstein. At the time of the divorce Phyllis had left Novikoff's lab for a job with the Sloan-Kettering Cancer Institute. Not long after the divorce Novikoff called Phyllis to ask for a date, and "I was amazed that she said, 'yes.'" The relationship blossomed and eventually Phyllis returned to his lab. Their subsequent marriage began a remarkable partnership that, according to Novikoff, was the most "beautiful" part of his life. After Phyllis earned her PhD, she became an equal partner with Alex, gaining numerous credits in her own right. Almost all of Novikoff's papers in the 1980s were co-authored with Phyllis.[42]

QUESTIONS ABOUT NOVIKOFF'S LOYALTY

Even after his dismissal from the University of Vermont and the closing of the McCarthy era, Novikoff's Communist past remained a concern of various authorities. When he was invited to deliver a paper at the Seventh International Cancer Congress in London in 1958, he needed to renew his passport. This presented a dilemma because the standard application form contained questions about Communist party affiliation. He answered affirmatively to the question of whether he had ever been a member, stating that he was a member from "approximately 1937" to "approximately 1945." Rosalind, who planned to travel with him, stated that she had been a member from 1939 to 1945. Novikoff's cover letter described his scientific work and emphasized that "I am not now, nor is my wife now, nor have we been since 1945, members of, or in any way sympathetic to the Communist party. Since the Communist phobia had diminished somewhat in the Department of State, he and Rosalind were issued passports on June 13 after a normal lapse of time. Novikoff's admission, however, produced a flurry of activity at the FBI. After notification by the Passport Office, an FBI special agent visited the State Department on July 15 to look at Novikoff's passport file. FBI headquarters then sought a report on Novikoff's activities from the New York office. The subsequent report, dated August 14, summarized Novikoff's security history and was conveyed to the embassies in London and Paris. Additional inquiries and investigations occurred over the next three years, but no new derogatory information was found. Novikoff kept his passport, and it was renewed on several subsequent occasions.[43]

Novikoff came to the attention of the Senate Internal Security Subcommittee in 1962 when he received his lifetime grant—$25,000 per year for twenty-five years—from the U.S. Public Health Service. Two New Jersey residents read of the award in the August 3 *New York World*

Telegram and complained to Senator James Eastland, the chairman of the Senate Internal Security Subcommittee (SISS). One of the letter writers recited the charges against Novikoff in the 1953 report of the SISS and asked whether this "misuse of tax money" could be rescinded. At the direction of Jay Sourwine, the SISS counsel, the committee staff tried to find out whether Novikoff was still a Communist and, in either case, whether the government could take back the grant. When the SISS research director, Benjamin Mandel, suggested that they might get a "rather negative reaction if we raised the Communist issue in this connection" and suggested that they should drop the matter, Sourwine replied sarcastically, "This does not answer the question." On September 12 the American Law Division of the Library of Congress transmitted a report to the committee affirming that there was a statutory basis for firing a Communist from a research contract of the type held by Novikoff. The concluding paragraph of the ten-page brief, however, placed the burden of proof on the government: "It is for the scientist to initiate an action for breach of contract if he deems it advisable. However if he does institute such action the burden is on the Government to prove its allegations." Sourwine labeled the report "impudent" and asked Mandel, "What proof is there Novikoff is CP?" Since Sourwine had a long-established relationship of mutual assistance with the FBI, it is likely that he contacted this source and heard the FBI's assessment that Novikoff had left any Communist-connected activities. In any event, the committee dropped the matter, and Novikoff's grant remained in effect until December 1986.[44]

The last time the FBI paid serious attention to Novikoff was in the early 1970s when Novikoff's appointment to a research review panel for the National Institutes of Health (NIH) came under review. Despite Novikoff's prestige as a scientist and the NIH grants in support of his research, he had been excluded previously from NIH research advisory groups. He was not alone in this situation; as many as two hundred scientists, including the Nobel laureate Salvador E. Luria, were victims of an unofficial blacklist at NIH. The exclusion of scientists was an anachronism from the McCarthy years, when no federal agency wanted to risk the wrath of Congress over the appointment of a possible security risk. Most agencies eventually revised their review procedures, but the Department of Health, Education and Welfare (HEW) and its constituent agencies maintained their tight security system through the 1950s and 1960s. By 1970 HEW was known to have one of the "most rigid security operations in Washington."[45]

The standard practice was to examine every name suggested for appointment to an HEW advisory panel. Prior to approaching a candidate to determine his or her availability, the name was submitted by the HEW Office of Internal Security to a "National Agency Check," which included a check of FBI files. When derogatory information was reported, HEW quietly excluded the scientist from the panel, usually without an explanation to the HEW official suggesting the appointment. Thus, scientists were excluded without their knowledge and without any opportunity for presenting an appeal. An iniquitous development was that the system encouraged bureaucrats in the appointing agencies to develop a list of unappointable scientists—a blacklist—in order to avoid the embarrassment of rejections by the Office of Internal Security. Common sense as well as information leaked by insiders told most blacklisted scientists, including Novikoff, of their plight.[46]

The situation at HEW finally changed in 1970 as a result of pressure from several scientific groups. For the first time, a few scientists—including some who had invoked the Fifth Amendment in the early 1950s—came forward to tell about their exclusion. Mainly, the scientists talked about the harm done by the security procedures, especially the potential damage to a career. Appointment to an advisory group was seen to be a mark of professional accomplishment as well as an opportunity to learn about the status of current research in a discipline. For a scientist excluded from review groups. "it looks like you haven't really made it in your field." Prodded by this lobbying effort, an internal study of the system was commissioned that led to a decision by HEW Secretary Robert H. Finch to make changes. The new arrangements dropped a preappointment investigation and instead called for three character references and a signed affidavit stipulating whether one belonged to an organization advocating the violent overthrow of the U.S. government. The affidavit would then be reviewed by the FBI to determine whether perjury had been committed. In the event that derogatory information was unearthed, the scientist had the right to challenge the findings.[47]

Two years after the easing of the security procedures, Novikoff was appointed to a four-year term on Pathology Study Section B in NIH. Six months later his appointment papers came across the desk of Nathan Dick, the director of security at HEW. Dick's check of HEW files disclosed that a name check in 1963 had revealed Novikoff's problems with the Jenner Committee as well as his 1958 admission of former Communist party membership. On December 15, 1972, Dick wrote Acting FBI Director L. Patrick Gray to request a full field investigation of Novikoff. In turn, FBI headquarters ordered its New York, Washington, St. Louis, and Albany offices to carry out investigations of Novikoff's loyalty. The FBI's sensitivity about its reputation on university campuses was reflected in its instructions: "You are authorized to conduct necessary investigation involving persons connected with educational institutions unless your office is aware of a possible problem at a particular school. . . . It is encumbent upon each office to insure that such investigations . . . are handled by mature personnel to avoid possible embarrassment to the Bureau." The reports that flowed into headquarters over the next two months reviewed in detail Novikoff's earlier problems with the authorities but contained no new information about possible Communist activities. A special agent of the Washington field office interviewed the executive secretary of the NIH Pathology B study section, who reported that "Novikoff is an outstanding authority on Cell Biology and his study section is extremely happy to have him as a member." The FBI sent copies of its field reports to the Civil Service Commission on February 8, March 5, and March 12. Shortly thereafter, security officers at the Civil Service Commission and HEW decided that Novikoff should keep his part-time position as a member of the pathology study section. For all practical purposes, this determination removed the last vestiges of the blacklisting of Alex Novikoff.[48]

The last entry in Novikoff's FBI file, March 1973, came thirty years after the FBI's first documented interest in him. This last investigation came almost thirty-five years after the Dies Committee interrogated Novikoff's department chairman about communism at Brooklyn College and almost twenty years after his most severe punishment, his firing by the University of Vermont. Although a Novikoff file of 822 pages remains today in the possession of the FBI, Novikoff lived the last fourteen years of his life knowing that his loyalty to the United States was no longer in serious doubt. At age sixty, there was for the first time a peace of mind and a sense of security about his existence. The inquisition was over.

CLOSING THE CIRCLE

In April 1968 Novikoff returned for the first time to the University of Vermont campus to give an invited seminar sponsored by the zoology department. The visit was the occasion for a prominent story in the *Burlington Free Press*, which included a review of the chronology of events in 1953. One faculty member quoted in the story said that the invitation was designed "to demonstrate how some faculty members feel about him." Another said that "a lot of faculty members were unhappy at the time about the treatment Dr. Novikoff received but many of them felt they couldn't do anything to prevent it, what with the possibility that their own jobs might be on the line."[49]

In November 1982, as a result of a petition organized by a faculty member in the College of Medicine, the University of Vermont board of trustees voted to present Novikoff with an honorary doctor of science degree at the May 1983 commencement proceedings. Novikoff told a reporter that although he had no bitterness against anyone or the university, he saw that the honorary degree "redresses an old grievance." The *Free Press*, whose editorials had supported the university's action against Novikoff, recalled the "sinister" McCarthy and the "infection" that had reached Vermont. Failing to remember its own role in reinforcing prevailing public opinion of the time, the *Free Press* pointed out that it was "not one of the cheerful chapters in the annals of the University," and now "university officials will take a slight step toward righting that awful wrong." On May 21, 1983, President Lattie F. Coor presented Novikoff with his honorary degree, saying that "we welcome you back to the campus" and the university "salutes your integrity and courage." The citation did not refer to the circumstances of the dismissal but instead cited Novikoff's contributions to science. The initiators of the petition, however, emphasized that Novikoff's firing was an important reason for pushing for the honorary degree.[50]

Novikoff accepted happily the spontaneous applause of the commencement audience and the outpouring of feeling following the ceremony. He was surrounded by former students, lab assistants, and faculty colleagues as well as other well-wishers. For Novikoff the day of recognition and adulation closed the circle on a life that had been so directly affected by the events in 1953.

Curiously, stories in several newspapers the next day, including the *New York Times*, reported incorrectly that the University of Vermont had been censured by the AAUP. The *Times* closed its story with a reference to an AAUP official who, after reviewing the AAUP archives of the period, "concluded that there might not be any comprehensive record of the number of victims of those years, much less what has become of them." We know, however, that one such person, Alex Novikoff, survived, prospered and eventually returned in honor to the scene of the darkest period of his life.[51]

Although Novikoff suffered a heart attack in the 1970s, he continued his work at the usual feverish pace. As always, his work was his recreation and his relaxation. During the summer of 1986 he became seriously ill and was operated on for the replacement of his abdominal aorta. Within days he was reading scientific papers and talking on the phone with his laboratory staff. In six weeks he was back in the lab preparing grant proposals and writing papers. One day in early 1987 he sensed something amiss with his heart and walked from his lab to the hospital. Two days later, shortly after talking with his wife, his heart gave out and he died in his sleep.

Novikoff's former colleagues at the University of Vermont sent a statement of condolences, concluding with the observation that his passing "becomes part of the great history of biochemistry and the UVM faculty of biochemistry feels proud and privileged to have been associated with him in making some of this history." The Albert Einstein College of Medicine held a memorial service on January 29 at which former colleagues, including Christian de Duve, spoke about him. These men who knew him best talked candidly about his politics, his sometimes excessive behavior, his science, and his influence on their work. The chairman of the biochemistry department at Albert Einstein described the time that Novikoff walked the picket lines: "When interns and residents went out on strike, Alex joined their picket lines, not because he believed all their demands and tactics, but because they spoke sufficient truth to be shown solidarity." At the end, Novikoff's colleagues recognized that politics and science were inseparable in understanding his past. As one former colleague observed, the destructive potential of McCarthyism would always be a part of the story:

> Unfortunately, [the McCarthy committees] were successful in destroying some careers, and we shall never know the magnitude of loss of those actions imposed on our country. But fortunately they could not destroy and remove Alex, because he fought indomitably, would not give up, and because he found a refuge in the Albert Einstein College of Medicine.[52]

In his lifetime Alex Novikoff engaged himself passionately in politics and science. Unquestionably, his political activities were harmful to his life and work. He had few regrets, however. He was a man of considerable accomplishment, and in the final analysis he was a fortunate man. Unlike so many others, he overcame the consequences of America's anti-Communist inquisition. His good fortune—and ours—was that he had the opportunity to pursue his destiny in the halls of academe. He was a scientist, and that, ultimately, was the life he lived.

EPILOGUE

Alex Novikoff's life was affected by his involvement in left-wing politics, particularly the Communist party, by America's powerful and seemingly unending anti-Communist campaign, and by the government's national security program, particularly that of the FBI. He was subpoenaed, interrogated, investigated, and blacklisted. His history as a subject of loyalty review (see Appendix B) extended for thirty-five years, and a massive file remains in the possession of the FBI. Moreover, he was a scientist and a university man, and at the moment of truth in 1953 his university dismissed him from its faculty.

Novikoff's life story poses some fundamental questions. To what extent are we as a society prepared to tolerate dissent, even when that dissent may be damaging to the perceived "national interest"? In the eighteenth century Jefferson urged that we not punish rebellion too severely on the grounds that this "would suppress the only safeguard of the public liberty." He argued that the "spirit of resistance" should be "always kept alive." We know that Jefferson's message has been ignored frequently in our nation's history, especially in the matter of the Communist party. Expedient action has often prevailed, and McCarthyism was an example of political expedience on a national scale. Novikoff's life provides insight into the damaging consequences of a program to enforce conformity in thinking and behavior. Only by the most farfetched logic were Novikoff and his colleagues risks to national security. Certainly in Jeffersonian terms, they were loyal Americans. This book demonstrates that, among academic Communists, the anti-Communist campaign was unnecessary and, moreover, was damaging to the fabric of our society and our intellectual culture.[1]

The role of the universities is another issue of consequence. To what extent is higher education prepared to tolerate and defend dissenters on its faculties? At the University of Vermont the initiative of Governor Emerson was the crucial influence on the board of trustees. He took the unusual step of exercising his ex officio status and forced

through the "talk or walk" ultimatum. President Borgmann was in
the best position to protect Novikoff and academic freedom at the University of Vermont, but he did not oppose the popular sentiment and
the political pressure. He was a well-intentioned, moral man caught
in a situation that ultimately overwhelmed him. In hindsight, we see
that Borgmann and his university colleagues were unprepared by experience and knowledge to act with greater philosophical clarity and
moral courage. This is little solace, however. We cannot avoid the harsh
outcome: considerable harm was done to one of President Borgmann's
faculty members.

Academic freedom, then, is a fragile concept that demands protection from the inside and the outside. The challenges and threats to the
academic enterprise take different form today, but the special mission
of the universities—the search for truth, the elevation of the human
spirit—is no less vulnerable. The current generation of political and
educational leaders needs to absorb the lessons of the past if our universities are to flourish.

Never again do we want to hear a man of President Borgmann's
fiber and goodwill lament, as he did to Novikoff a few years later, "I
have lost more than you did." Never again do we want college teachers
such as Novikoff to become the victims of a political campaign that
ignores the principles of due process, rational discourse, and the time-
honored principles of academic freedom. In this circumstance each of
us is diminished, and so too is our freedom.[2]

APPENDIX A

Important Names in Novikoff
Life Story

New York

Harry Albaum — Faculty member at Brooklyn College
L. G. Barth — Faculty member and Novikoff's doctoral advisor at Columbia University
William Boylan — President of Brooklyn College
Frederic Ewen — Faculty member at Brooklyn College
Harry Gideonse — President of Brooklyn College
Bernard Grebanier — Faculty member at Brooklyn College
Earl Martin — Chairman of biology department at Brooklyn College
Howard Selsam — Faculty member at Brooklyn College
Paul Windels — Counsel to the Rapp-Coudert Committee

Washington

Bentley Glass — Professor of biology at Johns Hopkins University and active in American Association of University Professors (AAUP)
Ralph Himstead — General Secretary of the AAUP
William Jenner — Chairman of the Senate Internal Security Subcommittee (Jenner Committee)
Robert Morris — Counsel to the Jenner Committee
Herman Welker — Senator, member of Jenner Committee

Vermont

Carl Borgmann — President of the University of Vermont
Lee Emerson — Governor of the state of Vermont
Paul Evans — Faculty member and chairman of the board of review at the University of Vermont
Robert Joyce — Catholic priest and chairman of faculty-trustee committee at the University of Vermont
Louis Lisman — Counsel to the University of Vermont

Francis Peisch	Novikoff's attorney
Arnold Schein	Faculty member at the University of Vermont
William Van Robertson	Faculty member at the University of Vermont

Other

| Christian de Duve | Nobel laureate and collaborator in research with Novikoff |
| Albert Einstein | Recommended Novikoff to Albert Einstein College of Medicine |

APPENDIX B

Security History of
Alex Novikoff

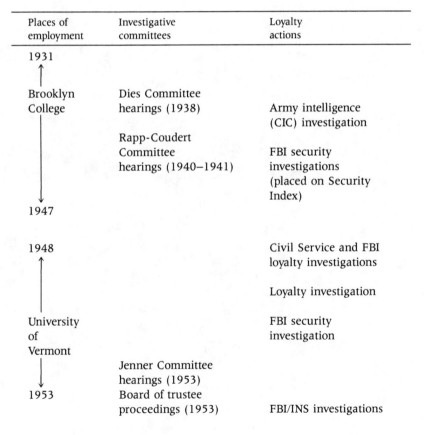

Places of employment	Investigative committees	Loyalty actions
1931 ↑		
Brooklyn College	Dies Committee hearings (1938)	Army intelligence (CIC) investigation
	Rapp-Coudert Committee hearings (1940–1941)	FBI security investigations (placed on Security Index)
1947		
1948 ↑		Civil Service and FBI loyalty investigations
		Loyalty investigation
University of Vermont		FBI security investigation
	Jenner Committee hearings (1953)	
1953	Board of trustee proceedings (1953)	FBI/INS investigations

Places of employment	Investigative committees	Loyalty actions
1954–1955 Waldemar Foundation		
1955 ↑ Albert Einstein College of Medicine │ │ │ │ ↓ 1987	Senate Internal Security Subcommittee inquiry (1962)	FBI investigation (removed from Security Index) State Department/FBI passport investigation NIH/FBI loyalty investigation

APPENDIX C
Special Sources

Interviews and correspondence with the author

Carl Borgmann, February 22, 1985
Dunbar Bostwick, August 8, 1985
Chester Eaton, July 10, 1985
Frederic Ewen, November 13, 1984
Frederic Ewen, December 17, 1987
Frederic Ewen, letter, January 9, 1988
Bishop Robert Joyce, June 29, 1984
Martha Kennedy, July 2, 1987
Sonia Novikoff Klein, September 22, 1987
Louis Lisman, February 7, 1986
George Little, May 21, 1987
Alex Novikoff, March 12, 1984
Alex Novikoff, May 18, 1984
Francis Peisch, May 30, 1985
Arnold Schein, letter, April 12, 1987
Oscar Shaftel, letter, May 20, 1986
Oscar Shaftel, March 20, 1987
Ethan Allen Sims, May 21, 1987
William Van Robertson, June 4, 1985
Rabbi Max Wall, August 14, 1986
Charles Weaver, by telephone, September 15, 1986
Jean Wright, May 21, 1985

Other interviews

Harry Albaum, October 10, 1979 (interviewed by Murray Horowitz, Special
    Collections, Brooklyn College Library)
Paul Evans, June 21, 1975 (interviewed by Priscilla Welsh, Special Collections,
    Bailey-Howe Library, University of Vermont)
Frederic Ewen, November 7, 1980 (interviewed by Ellen Schrecker)
Harry Gideonse, February 23, 1961 (Columbia University Oral History Project)
Bernard Grebanier, April 22, 1974 (interviewed by Marvin Gettleman)
Alex Novikoff, April 4, 1978 (interviewed by Ellen Schrecker)

Alex Novikoff, May 12, 1983 (interviewed by Harriet Zuckerman)
Alex Novikoff, May 23, 1983 (interviewed by Lester Wallman, Special Collections, Bailey-Howe Library, University of Vermont)
Francis Peisch, March 19, 1985 (interviewed by Michael Sarvak)
Harry Slochower, December 29, 1980 (interviewed by Ellen Schrecker)
Paul Windels, 1950 (Columbia University Oral History Project)

Manuscript collections

American Association of University Professors, Committee A and Committee H files, Washington, D.C.
Brooklyn College Archives, Special Collections, New York City
National Archives, Legislative Archives Division, Senate Committee on Internal Security files, Washington, D.C.
New York State Archives, Rapp-Coudert Committee files, Albany, New York
University of Vermont Archives, Waterman Building, Burlington, Vermont
University of Vermont Special Collections, Bailey-Howe Library, Burlington, Vermont
Vermont State Archives, Redstone Building, Emerson papers, Montpelier, Vermont
Wayne State University, Archives of Labor and Urban Affairs, American Federation of Teachers files, Detroit

Private papers

Chester Eaton, private papers
Sonia and Sidney Klein, private papers
Alex Novikoff, private papers
Arnold Schein, private papers, including FBI file
Ethan Allen Sims, private papers

Federal documents released through Freedom of Information Act

Department of the Army, Novikoff file
Department of Health and Human Services, Novikoff file
Department of the Navy, Novikoff file
Immigration and Naturalization Service, Novikoff file
Federal Bureau of Investigation
   Communist Party in Education file
   Albert Einstein file
   Alex Novikoff file
U.S. Civil Service Commission, Novikoff file

NOTES

Introduction

(pages 1–7)

1. Ellen Schrecker, *No Ivory Tower: McCarthyism and the Universities* (New York: Oxford University Press, 1986), 3–11.

2. Several books discuss individual cases in the context of more general analyses, including David Gardner, *The California Oath Controversy* (Berkeley: University of California Press, 1972); Vern Countryman, *Un-American Activities in the State of Washington* (Ithaca, N.Y.: Cornell University Press, 1951); Jane Sanders, *Cold War on Campus* (Seattle: University of Washington Press, 1979); and Schrecker, *No Ivory Tower.*

3. Valuable sources for this book included recently opened archives of the Rapp-Coudert Committee (which investigated alleged Communist activities in New York City schools) at the New York State Archives, Albany, N.Y. and of Committee A of the American Association of University Professors, Washington, D.C. Schrecker, *No Ivory Tower,* 25–26, interviewed about seventy former Communists.

4. Walter Metzger, *Academic Freedom in the Age of the University* (New York: Columbia University Press, 1955).

5. See Richard Hofstadter, *Anti-intellectualism in American Life* (New York: Alfred Knopf, 1962).

Chapter 1. Origins of Political Activism

(pages 8–24)

1. The best general treatments of political activity on the New York campuses are Robert Iversen, *The Communists and the Schools* (New York: Harcourt, Brace, 1959) and Ellen Schrecker, *No Ivory Tower,* chaps. 2 and 3. Another useful source is an essay by Marvin Gettleman: "Communists in Higher Education: C.C.N.Y. and Brooklyn College on the Eve of the Rapp-Coudert Investigation, 1935–1939," presented at the 70th Annual Meeting of the Organization of American Historians, Atlanta, April 9, 1977.

2. See Kenneth Keniston, *Young Radicals* (New York: Harcourt Brace Jovanovich, 1968), 20, 106.

3. Ibid., 35, 113.

4. Alex Novikoff, interview with author, March 12, 1984; Sonia Klein, interview with author, September 22, 1987.

5. Klein, interview.
6. Private papers of Sidney and Sonia Klein.
7. Klein papers; Klein, interview.
8. See, for example, Irving Howe, *World of Our Fathers* (New York: Harcourt Brace Jovanovich, 1976).
9. Klein papers.
10. Oscar Shaftel, letter to author, May 20, 1986; Novikoff, interview, March 12, 1984.
11. Klein, interview.
12. Klein, interview; Alex Novikoff, interview with Harriet Zuckerman, May 12, 1983.
13. Klein, interview; Novikoff, interview, March 12, 1984.
14. A comprehensive discussion of Columbia's handling of Jewish admissions may be found in Harold Wechsler, *The Qualified Student: A History of Selective College Admission in America* (New York: John Wiley and Sons, 1977), 65–111.
15. The mutual concern among the eastern elite colleges is discussed by Wechsler, *The Qualified Student,* and by Marcia Graham Synnott, *The Half-Opened Door: Discrimination and Admissions at Harvard, Yale, and Princeton, 1900–1970* (Westport, Conn.: Greenwood Press, 1979).
16. Wechsler, *The Qualified Student,* 164–68, 206, 170; Heywood Broun and George Britt, *Christians Only: A Study of Prejudice* (New York: Vanguard, 1931), 102.
17. For a discussion of Jewish enrollments at various colleges and universities, see Synnott, *The Half-Opened Door.* Jewish enrollment at City College in 1918–1919 was 78.7% of the total.
18. Klein, interview; Novikoff, interview, March 12, 1984.
19. Academic transcript of Alex Novikoff at Columbia University, private papers of Alex Novikoff.
20. Novikoff, interview, March 12, 1984; Wechsler, *The Qualified Student,* 170, 206.
21. Novikoff, interview, March 12, 1984.
22. Novikoff, interview, March 12, 1984; Novikoff's salary history is shown in *Report on Novikoff Case, 1938,* Novikoff papers, 4.
23. Letter from Frederick Keppel to Nicholas Murray Butler, October 4, 1912, Columbia University Files, Dean Frederick Keppel, 1910–1913 file, cited in Wechsler, *The Qualified Student,* 192; for a discussion of the origins of Brooklyn College, see Wechsler, 192–93, and Thomas Coulton, *A City College in Action: Struggle and Achievement at Brooklyn College, 1930–1955* (New York: Harper and Brothers, 1955), 17–18; Coulton, 18.
24. Coulton, *A City College in Action,* 9.
25. Ibid., 10.
26. Ibid., 13.
27. Ibid., 13–14.
28. Memorandum from Earl A. Martin, *Report on Novikoff Case,* 80.
29. Novikoff, interview, May 18, 1984; *Report on Novikoff Case,* 80.
30. Harry Albaum, interview with Murray Horowitz, October 10, 1979; Novikoff, interview, May 18, 1984.
31. Novikoff, interview with Zuckerman; Novikoff, interview, May 18, 1984.
32. *Report on Novikoff Case,* 3.

33. Albaum, interview, October 10, 1979.

34. Novikoff, interview, March 12, 1984.

35. "A Statement Regarding the Cooperation of Mr. Alex B. Novikoff While Teaching with Me in Vertebrate Zoology," B. R. Coonfield, *Report on Novikoff Case*, 81.

36. "Delinquency of Alex B. Novikoff While Teaching Biology 31," Paul R. Orr, *Report on Novikoff Case*, 82; "Report of Laboratory Assistance in Biology 24 (Embryology) from September 1934 to June 1938," Leonard G. Worley, *Report on Novikoff Case*, 62–67; Martin Memorandum, *Report on Novikoff Case*, 80.

37. There is a paucity of studies that examine the internal dynamics of academic departments. There are several general studies of twentieth-century higher education, however, that describe the forces that have shaped the formation of departments and the movement toward specialization among faculty, including Christopher Jencks and David Riesman, *The Academic Revolution* (New York: Doubleday, 1968); Laurence Veysey, *The Emergence of the American University* (Chicago: University of Chicago Press, 1965); Clark Kerr, *The Uses of the University* (New York: Harper and Row, 1963).

38. Novikoff, interview, May 18, 1984. The December 1938 edition of *The Staff*, the paper of the Brooklyn College branch of the Communist Party, compared the scholarly output of Earl Martin with that of Novikoff. The story, which may have been written by Novikoff, indicated that Martin had one published paper over a career of eighteen years.

39. *Report on Novikoff Case*, 3.

40. L. G. Barth to Brooklyn College, July 1938, Novikoff papers.

Chapter 2. Consequential Acts

(pages 25–54)

1. See Thomas Coulton, *A City College in Action: Struggle and Achievement at Brooklyn College, 1930–1955* (New York: Harper and Brothers, 1955); Harry Albaum, interview with Murray Horowitz, October 10, 1979.

2. Oscar Shaftel, interview with author, March 20, 1987; Alex Novikoff, interview with author, March 12, 1984.

3. The term *political ghetto* is used by Ellen Schrecker, *No Ivory Tower: McCarthyism and the Universities* (New York: Oxford University Press, 1986), 34; testimony of Edward I. Fenlon, "Investigation of Un-American Propaganda Activities in the United States," Special House Committee to Investigate Un-American Activities (Dies Committee), August 23, 1938, 950; Albaum, interview.

4. The political agenda of the Association of Tutors, Fellows and Instructors is discussed in the May and June 1935 issues of *The Staff*, the paper of the Brooklyn College branch of the Communist Party.

5. Theodore Draper, *The Roots of Communism* (New York: Viking, 1957), 94, 101; John Reed, *Ten Days That Shook the World* (New York: Boni and Liverright, 1919).

6. Draper, *The Roots of Communism*, 388–90.

7. Robert Iversen, *The Communists and the Schools* (New York: Harcourt, Brace, 1959), 14–18, 20, 21–22, 76–77; *Investigation of Communist Propaganda: Hearings before a Special Committee to Investigate Communist Activities in the United States,*

71st Congress, 2nd Session (Washington, D.C.: U.S. Government Printing Office, 1930), Part 1, Vol. 4, 358–59, 380, 384; Draper, *The Roots of Communism*, 395.

8. Harvey Klehr, *The Heyday of American Communism* (New York: Basic Books, 1984), 38, 153, 172.

9. Iversen, *The Communists and the Schools*, 32–36.

10. Ibid., 46–57.

11. Ibid., 125–27; also, see Coulton, *A City College in Action*, 104–5.

12. Klehr, *The Heyday of American Communism*, 309–23; Iversen, *The Communists and the Schools*, 139–40, 146–47.

13. Novikoff, interview, March 12, 1984; Iversen, *The Communists and the Schools*, 142.

14. Iversen, *The Communists and the Schools*, 157, 160–62.

15. Testimony of Bernard Grebanier before the Rapp-Coudert Committee, January 30, 1941, files of the Joint Legislative Committee to Investigate the State Education System, 1940–1947, New York State Archives, Albany, N.Y., RC Subject file, 135, 212–14, 246–47; *Staff*, Vol. 3, May 1, 1935, RC File 91, 3, files of the Joint Legislative Committee.

16. Testimony of Bernard Grebanier, 244–45.

17. Testimony of Bernard Grebanier, 138, 254; Novikoff, interview, March 12, 1984.

18. Testimony of Bernard Grebanier, 135–42, 150; Novikoff, interview, March 12, 1984, Schrecker, *No Ivory Tower*, 37.

19. Ellen Schrecker estimated that at least half of the academic Communists were scientists; see *No Ivory Tower*, 44. Novikoff, interview, May 18, 1984.

20. *Report on the Novikoff Case, 1938*, private papers of Alex Novikoff, 7, 21. In 1938 Novikoff conveyed his suspicion that "racial considerations" played a part in his problems in the biology department.

21. Schrecker, *No Ivory Tower*, 37; Harry Slochower, interview with Ellen Schrecker, December 29, 1980.

22. See Schrecker, *No Ivory Tower*, chap. 2, for an excellent discussion of the environment in New York City during the 1930s.

23. Novikoff, interview, May 18, 1984.

24. Novikoff, interview, March 12, 1984; testimony of Bernard Grebanier, 211—14; testimony of Abraham Goldfield, Joint Legislative Committee, undated, RC Subject file.

25. Testimony of Bernard Grebanier, 213–14; Novikoff, interview, May 18, 1984; Frederic Ewen, interview with author, November 13, 1984; Frederic Ewen, interview with Ellen Schrecker, November 7, 1980; the December 10, 1940, *Brooklyn Eagle* carried a front-page story about Lifshutz's problems in Oklahoma.

26. The June 1, 1935, edition of *Staff*, for example, contained a plea for "regular monthly contributions" to pay for the publication of the paper.

27. *Staff*, May 1, 1953, 1; *Staff*, June 1, 1935, 4; *Staff*, May 1936, 3.

28. The praise from Moscow was noted by Henry Klein in an interview with Marvin Gettleman, April 24, 1976, cited in "Communists in Higher Education: C.C.N.Y. and Brooklyn College on the Eve of the Rapp-Coudert Investigation," presented at the 70th Annual Meeting of the Organization of American Historians, Atlanta, April 9, 1977. Coulton, *A City College in Action*, 125.

29. Testimony of Bernard Grebanier, 136, 155.

30. See testimony of Bernard Grebanier.

31. Testimony of Bernard Grebanier, 145–46. Selsam's role as advisor to the Karl Marx Society is noted in a report prepared by the Rapp-Coudert Committee, "Summary of Facts re Karl Marx Society," Joint Legislative Committee, RC File 50. Robert Iversen, *The Communists and the Schools*, 139–40. A summary of *Vanguard* stories was prepared by the Rapp-Coudert Committee investigators, dated October 21, 1941, Joint Legislative Committee, RC File 54.

32. Frederick Ewen, interview with Ellen Schrecker, November 7, 1980.

33. Testimony of Bernard Grebanier, 143. See Lawrence Chamberlain's assessment of the teaching performance of the Communists in *Loyalty and Legislative Action* (Ithaca, N.Y.: Cornell University Press, 1951), 122–28; also, Schrecker, *No Ivory Tower,* 43–44.

34. Novikoff, interview with Harriet Zuckerman, May 12, 1983; summary of Novikoff's publications is contained in his private papers.

35. *Staff,* May 1, 1935.

36. This document is quoted in Coulton, 111–12. Testimony of Edward Fenlon, August 23, 1938, Dies Committee; testimony of Earl Martin, August 23, 1938, Dies Committee.

37. Testimony of Harry Albaum, January 31, 1941, Joint Legislative Committee, RC Subject file, 8–9.

38. See testimony of Edward Fenlon and Earl Martin before the Dies Committee, August 23, 1938.

39. See the Dies Committee testimony of Edward Fenlon for a description of the Klein campaign. Novikoff, interview with Harriet Zuckerman.

40. *Staff,* February 1938, 1; *Staff,* March 1938, 1, 4.

41. Testimony of Earl Martin, Dies Committee, 958; *Brooklyn Eagle,* May 15, 1938, 1–2.

42. *Brooklyn Eagle,* May 22, 1938, 2.

43. Harry Gideonse, interview with Donald Shaughnessy, February 23, 1961, Columbia University Oral History Collection, 5–8.

44. Ibid.

45. A. J. Schechter (M.D.), letter to Brooklyn College, June 23, 1938, Novikoff papers.

46. Alex Novikoff to B. R. Coonfield, May 28, 1938, carbon copy in Novikoff private papers; B. R. Coonfield to Alex Novikoff, June 10, 1938, Novikoff papers.

47. *Report on Novikoff Case,* 1; "Conversation with Prof. Coonfield—April 5, 1937," Novikoff papers.

48. *Report on Novikoff Case,* 10–11.

49. Ibid., 2–8, 33–46.

50. Alex Novikoff to L. G. Barth, June 21, 1938, carbon copy in Novikoff papers; L. G. Barth to Alex Novikoff, June 24, 1938, Novikoff papers; Alex Novikoff to L. G. Barth, June 26, 1938, carbon copy in Novikoff papers; L. G. Barth to Alex Novikoff (five-page letter of advice), undated, Novikoff papers; Alex Novikoff to L. G. Barth, July 21, 1938, carbon copy in Novikoff papers; Alex Novikoff to L. G. Barth, July 28, 1938, carbon copy in Novikoff papers.

51. "Chronology of Novikoff Case," undated, Novikoff papers.

52. *Staff,* November 1938, 2, 4; *Report on Novikoff Case,* 34–42.

53. *Report on Novikoff Case*, 47–55; letter to *Staff* from Edwin Burgum and Arnold Shukotoff of the New York College Teachers Union, undated (approximately December 1, 1938), files of Joint Legislative Committee, RC File 91; *Staff*, December 1938, 3.

54. Minutes of executive board of the Brooklyn College branch of the New York College Teachers Union report the "successful termination of the Novikoff case," April 21, 1939, Joint Legislative Committee, RC File 91.

55. Summary of campus activities prepared by Rapp-Coudert Committee, October 21, 1941, Joint Legislative Committee, RC File 54; program brochure, "Society and Education," December 17, 1938, Novikoff papers; minutes of executive board of Brooklyn College branch of College Teachers Union show Novikoff in attendance at meeting, September 29, 1939, Joint Legislative Committee, RC File 91.

56. Testimony of Harry Albaum, Committee on the Judiciary, Subcommittee to Investigate the Administration of the Internal Security Act and Other Internal Security Laws, U.S. Senate, 83rd Congress, *Subversive Influence in the Educational Process*, Part 1, September 25, 1952, 213.

57. Sonia Klein, interview with author, September 22, 1987.

Chapter 3. Confronted by the Anti-Communists

(pages 55–79)

1. See Kenneth O'Reilly, *Hoover and the Un-Americans* (Philadelphia: Temple University Press, 1983), 36–74, for an excellent overview of the Dies Committee and its mode of operation.

2. Ibid., 43.

3. *Brooklyn Eagle*, August 15, 1938.

4. *Brooklyn Eagle*, August 16 and 18, 1938.

5. Testimony of Edward Fenlon, Earl Martin, and Martin Meyer, "Investigation of Un-American Propaganda Activities in the United States," Special Committee to Investigate Un-American Activities (Dies Committee), August 23, 1938, 943–73.

6. The September–October 1938 edition of *Staff* printed Tead's statement; *Brooklyn Eagle*, August 25, 1938, 1; *Staff*, September–October 1938, 1, 3; *Staff*, December 1938, 2; the Teachers Union resolution is located in the files of the Joint Legislative Committee, RC File 91 (Novikoff's name appeared at the bottom of the union resolution).

7. O'Rielly, *Hoover and the Un-Americans*, 41–74.

8. Ibid., 48.

9. Oscar Shaftel, interview with the author, May 20, 1987.

10. Harry Slochower, interview with Ellen Schrecker, December 29, 1980; Novikoff, interview, May 18, 1984.

11. *The New York Times*, June 2, 1939; Shaftel, interview. On a passport application in 1958 Rosalind Novikoff stated that she was a member of the Communist party from 1939 to 1945. A draft of this document is contained in the Novikoff papers.

12. Bernard Grebanier, interview with Marvin Gettleman, April 22, 1974. Grebanier's letter was submitted by Grebanier to the Rapp-Coudert Committee during his public testimony, December 2–4, 1940. The letter is quoted in Coul-

ton, *A City College in Action: Struggle and Achievement at Brooklyn College, 1930–1935* (New York: Harper and Brothers, 1955), 123–24.

13. See summary of *Vanguard* stories prepared by investigators of the Rapp—Coudert Committee, RC File 54, Joint Legislative Committee, RC File 376. The circular is contained in RC File 376.

14. *Staff,* November 1938, 3.

15. Harvey Klehr, *The Heyday of American Communism* (New York: Basic Books, 1984), 409.

16. Harry Gideonse, interview, 3–8.

17. Peter Cacchione, chairman of Kings County Committee of the Communist Party to "Friend," May 25, 1939, RC 91, Joint Legislative Committee; Coulton, *A City College in Action,* 115–16; Iversen, *The Communists and the Schools* (New York: Harcourt, Brace, 1959), 208.

18. See summary of *Vanguard* stories prepared by investigators of the Rapp-Coudert Committee, RC File 54, Joint Legislative Committee. The *Vanguard* reported rallies and speeches on February 9, March 8, and May 31.

19. Jacob R. Fischel, *Harry Gideonse: The Public Life,* unpublished doctoral dissertation, University of Delaware, 1973, 198–99.

20. Joint Resolution of the Senate and Assembly of the State of New York, March 29, 1940; Fischel, *Harry Gideonse,* 200.

21. Paul Windels, interview, Columbia University Oral History Collection, 145–50.

22. Lawrence Chamberlain, *Loyalty and Legislative Action* (Ithaca, N.Y.: Cornell University Press, 1951), 83. It is relevant to note that the committee accumulated hundreds of letters from citizens, both supporting and condemning the committee's work. Many letters named alleged Communists for follow-up by the committee. One note asked, "Why don't you investigate the activities of H. Slochower and his chief—Kenneth Burke—a well-known communists lecturer. Both are landowners in Byra township, Sussex County, N.J. This is the Summer rendezvous of those 'Reds.'" (See RC File 608.) A telegram on August 28, 1941, indicated that "Harry Albaum of Brooklyn College Biology Department may give important testimony on communism." (See RC File 588.) A letter from "An American Mother" named a high school English teacher, Bernard Malamud: "My boy had told me many times of this teacher's communist views." Mr. Malamud emerged later as one of America's most distinguished novelists. (See RC File 608.) Letters of accusation from Brooklyn College faculty members Edward Fenlon and Earl Martin appear in committee files. Both individuals testified at the 1938 Dies Committee hearings in Washington, D.C. (See RC File 587.)

23. Author not identified, "Memorandum of Trip to Washington," Joint Legislative Committee, RC File 600, 1; undated document in the files of the Joint Legislative Committee, RC File 600, 3.

24. Bernard Grebanier, "Memorandum of All the Circumstances Connected with my One and Only Conversation with Mr. Mulligan," dated January 4, 1941, files of the Joint Legislative Committee, RC File 593, 1–3. Grebanier's suspicions of Mulligan's motives may have been misplaced. Mulligan was a respected lawyer, a member of the legal staff of a previous New York State investigation, and an expert on the legal basis for legislative investigations. Chamberlain stated that Mulligan was excluded from the daily strategy sessions of the union and never received the "full cooperation from those he was

attempting to represent." See Chamberlain, *Loyalty and Legislative Action*, 133–34.

25. Bernard Grebanier, interview with Marvin Gettleman, April 24, 1974. Grebanier stated, "I hadn't supplied a name that they didn't have." See Schrecker, *No Ivory Tower: McCarthyism and the Universities* (New York: Oxford University Press, 1986), 78–79.

26. *Brooklyn Eagle*, November 13, 1940, 1.

27. Chamberlain, *Loyalty and Legislative Action*, 90.

28. Hearing transcript, November 27, 1940, Joint Legislative Committee, RC Subject file, 1–2.

29. *Final Report*, Legislative Document (1942), No. 49, released April 23, 1942, 234; Paul Windels, interview, 148–50.

30. Quoted in Thomas Coulton, *A City College in Action*, 120.

31. *Brooklyn Eagle*, December 2, 1940, 1.

32. Grebanier's testimony was reported in detail in the New York newspapers. See Coulton, *A City College in Action*, 121–25, for a summary of the testimony.

33. Grebanier said the following to the committee counsel: "Mr. Windels, I think you ought not to ask me such a question." On the basis of a 1974 interview with Grebanier, Marvin Gettleman concluded that the request to name Communists in public was unexpected. See "Rehearsal for McCarthyism: The New York State Rapp-Coudert Committee and Academic Freedom, 1940–1941," paper presented at the 97th Annual Meeting of American Historical Association, Washington, D.C., December 28, 1982, 7–8. *Brooklyn Eagle*, December 2, 1940.

34. Testimony by Harry Gideonse on December 4, 1940, quoted in Coulton, *A City College in Action*, 119; *College Newsletter*, the New York College Teachers Union, Vol. 4, No. 5, December 9, 1940, 3, Joint Legislative Committee, RC File 91, 3.

35. For an excellent description of the controversy over committee procedures, see Chamberlain, *Loyalty and Legislative Action*, 82–88. *College Newsletter*, December 9, 1940, 1.

36. *The New York Times*, December 5, 1940, 29.

37. Sonia Klein, interview with author, September 22, 1987.

38. *Brooklyn Eagle*, December 6, 1940; *The New York Times*, December 7, 1940, 19.

39. A copy of this letter is in the private papers of Alex Novikoff.

40. *College Newsletter*, December 9, 1940, 1–3.

41. Hearing transcript, January 30, 1941, Joint Legislative Committee, RC Subject File, 150, 239.

42. Hearing transcript, January 31, 1941, Joint Legislative Committee, RC Subject File, 1–11.

43. Schrecker, *No Ivory Tower*, Introduction; Schrecker, "Academic Freedom: The Historical View," in *Regulating the Intellectuals*, ed. Craig Kaplan and Ellen Schrecker (New York: Praeger, 1983), 26–27. Board of Higher Education response is quoted in Chamberlain, *Loyalty and Legislative Action*, 159. A copy of the board resolution was sent by the board's administrator to teachers under suspicion. A copy is contained in the private papers of Alex Novikoff. A cover letter from the board's administrator, dated January 21, 1941, is contained in the private papers of Alex Novikoff.

44. The Stone letter is in private papers of Novikoff. Novikoff made careful notes on his exchange with the committee and then typed a transcript. He demonstrated on this circumstance and later that he had the ability to keep detailed notes without seriously disrupting the interview. The transcript from his private hearing with the Rapp-Coudert Committee is contained in Novikoff's private papers.

45. Hearing transcript, March 6–7, 1941, Joint Legislative Committee, RC Subject File, 9–18, 59–78.

46. Quoted in Marvin Gettleman, "Communists in Higher Education: C.C.N.Y. and Brooklyn College on the Eve of the Rapp-Coudert Investigation, 1935–1939," paper presented at the 70th Annual Meeting of the Organization of American Historians, Atlanta, April 9, 1977, 16.

47. Canning's private testimony about Communist activities of Brooklyn College teachers, including Novikoff, probably reinforced the Rapp-Coudert Committee's desire to learn more about the college's Communist organization. It may be, however, that the Board of Higher Education was not privy to Canning's testimony about Brooklyn College.

48. A transcript of this interchange was made by Novikoff and is contained in his private papers.

49. See Schrecker, *No Ivory Tower,* 25–26.

50. *Interim Report and Conclusions of the New York City Subcommittee Relative to Subversive Activity among Students in the City of New York,* December 1, 1941, 132 pages; contained in *Final Report,* Legislative Document (1942), No. 49, 394 pages. Coulton, *A City College in Action,* 125–26.

51. Coulton, *A City College in Action,* 126; Jacob Fischel, *Harry Gideonse: A Public Life,* 376; Novikoff, interview, March 12, 1984.

52. Lawrence Chamberlain, *Loyalty and Legislative Action,* 126–27.

53. Ibid., 126.

54. Joint Legislative Committee, RC File 560. Entry 418 is in the records of the Senate Internal Security Subcommittee, undated, "Education—New York State, Individuals, 1953–1959" file, Legislative Archives Division, National Archives.

Chapter 4. Disengagement and Retreat

(pages 80–115)

1. Harry Gideonse, interview with Donald Shaughnessy, February 23, 1961, Columbia University, Oral History Collection, 56–57, 92.

2. Ibid., 90, 95.

3. Alex Novikoff, interview, March 12, 1984; Gideonse, interview, 61.

4. Bernard Grebanier, interview with Marvin Gettleman, April 24, 1974; Frederic Ewen, interview with Ellen Schrecker, November 7, 1980.

5. Ewen, interview, November 7, 1980; Grebanier, interview, April 24, 1974.

6. Harry Albaum, interview with Murray Horowitz, October 10, 1979, Special Collections, Brooklyn College Library, 6.

7. W. J. Agnew to Alex Novikoff, October 27, 1942, Novikoff papers; R. G. Morrill to Alex Novikoff, October 26, 1942, Novikoff papers; ONI reports on Novikoff, dated June 6, 1942/June 26, 1942/December 1, 1942, FBI file number 65-4309-13824.

8. This letter, under the heading of the War Department, Headquarters of the Army Air Forces, was dated November 12, 1942. The letter is contained in Novikoff's private papers.

9. Assistant to the Chairman of the Second Service Command Advisory Board, Office of the Commanding General, Governors Island, New York, to Miss Brown of the Legislative Committee to Investigate Education, December 18, 1942, Joint Legislative Committee, RC File 588.

10. A report of these activities was sent by Harold Smith, Special Agent, CIC, to "Officer in Charge" on February 20, 1943, and subsequently transmitted to the FBI on April 12, 1943, FBI file 100-19815-1.

11. A copy of the letter from the chairman of Local Board 213 to headquarters of the Army Air Force is contained in the private papers of Alex Novikoff. The letter of rejection is quoted in a chronology of events pertaining to Novikoff's attempt to attain a position in the military. The chronology was prepared by Novikoff during October 1943 and sent to Kirtley Mather of Harvard University on October 15, 1943. A copy of the chronology is contained in the private papers of Alex Novikoff.

12. Chronology of events prepared by Alex Novikoff, October 1943, Novikoff papers. The text of Professor Carman's letter is contained in the chronology of events prepared by Novikoff.

13. See Frank Donner, *The Age of Surveillance* (New York: Random House, 1980), 290–93.

14. Ibid. See Smith report, February 20, 1943, FBI file 100-19815-1. The text of letter from Ralph Luten, Captain, Air Corps, Appointment Unit, Military Personnel Division, dated March 16, 1943, is contained in the chronology of events prepared by Alex Novikoff, Novikoff papers.

15. Irwin Stewart, Executive Secretary, to Alex Novikoff, October 2, 1943, Novikoff papers; Kirtley Mather, Department of Geology and Geography, Harvard University, to Alex Novikoff, October 20, 1943, Novikoff papers; Alex Novikoff to Kirtley Mather, October 25, 1943, carbon copy in Novikoff papers.

16. E. E. Conroy, Special Agent to Thomas Quinn, November 21, 1944, FBI file 100-48011-16-1; E. E. Conroy to FBI Headquarters, November 21, 1944, FBI file 100-198015-1.

17. E. E. Conroy, memorandum, September 13, 1944, FBI file 100-198015-1; Conroy to FBI Headquarters, November 21, 1944 and Conroy to Quinn, November 21, 1944, FBI file 100-198015-1.

18. Athan Theoharis, *Spying on Americans: Political Surveillance from Hoover to the Huston Plan* (Philadelphia: Temple University Press, 1978), 40–64.

19. FBI files include several reports on Novikoff during 1944–1945. The summary report of investigation was prepared by E. E. Conroy on February 2, 1945. His recommendation to FBI headquarters to place Novikoff on the Security Index was sent on the same day. See FBI file 100-198015-1.

20. A resumé of Novikoff's publications is included in his private papers.

21. "The Concept of Integrative Levels and Biology," *Science* 101 (1945): 209–15, 212.

22. "Continuity and Discontinuity in Evolution," *Science* 102 (1945): 405–6; F. R. Moulton to Alex Novikoff, March 5, 1945, Novikoff papers.

23. Copies of the contracts for Novikoff's books, signed by Novikoff and Trachtenberg, are contained in the private papers of Alex Novikoff. Trachtenberg is featured prominently in Theodore Draper's history of the American

Communist party. See Draper, *Roots of Communism* (New York: Viking Press, 1957), 98–99, 142–43, 330. See *Climbing Our Family Tree* (New York: International Publishers, 1945), 58–59. A promotional brochure sponsored by International Publishers contained excerpts from a review by the *Saturday Review of Literature* and a letter from Kirtley Mather at Harvard. The promotional brochure is contained in the private papers of Alex Novikoff. Harry Gideonse to Alex Novikoff, February 5, 1946, Novikoff papers. See *The Quarterly Review of Biology* 21 (March 1946): 75–76. See invitation (and personal note from Esther Johnston) for opening on November 13, 1945, of the Thirty-Fifth Annual Exhibit of Children's Books sponsored by the New York Public Library, Novikoff papers.

24. Bentley Glass, *The Quarterly Review of Biology* 22 (September 1947): 227; Harry Albaum, Alex Novikoff, and Maurice Ogur, "The Relationship Between Cytochrome Oxidase and Succinoxidehydrogenase in the Developing Chick Embryo," *Federation Proceedings* 5 (1946): 119; Harry Albaum, Alex Novikoff, and Maurice Ogur, "The Development of the Cytochrome Oxidase and Succinoxidase Systems in the Chick Embryo," *Journal of Biological Chemistry* 165 (1946): 125–30.

25. Catalog of the Jefferson School of Social Science, Fall Term, September–December 1954, file on Education—New York State—Individuals, 1953–1959, National Archives, 4; report of Committee on Un-American Activities, dated 1959, 965.

26. Enrollment figure was cited in *Time,* December 6, 1956, 25; see catalog of Jefferson School, September–December, 1954; *Daily Worker,* November 10 and 27, 1945. Before the Senate Internal Security Subcommittee in 1953, Robert Morris, committee counsel, asked Novikoff whether he knew that the "Jefferson School has been a Communist training school." See testimony of Alex Novikoff, hearing transcript, Committee on the Judiciary, Subcommittee to Investigate the Administration of the Internal Security Act and Other Internal Security Laws, *Subversive Influence in the Educational Process,* U.S. Senate, Part 2, April 23, 1953, 807.

27. Robert Morris introduced into the record at Novikoff's 1953 hearing a January 29, 1946, article in the *Daily Worker* listing Novikoff as treasurer of the American Association of Scientific Workers, *Subversive Influence in the Educational Process,* 809. Novikoff claimed that he was an officer of the council but not of the Association. Morris's line of questioning presumed that these were Communist-front organizations. A brochure for the March 1946 conference is contained in the private papers of Alex Novikoff.

28. Novikoff made this statement on a passport application in 1958. A copy of his application is in his private papers.

29. Oscar Shaftel, interview, March 20, 1987; Novikoff, interview, May 18, 1984.

30. Hearing transcript, Special Trustee-Faculty Committee of the University of Vermont to Investigate Charges against Alex Novikoff, April 30, 1953, University Archives, University of Vermont, 26; Novikoff, interview with Lester Wallman, May 23, 1983, Special Collections, Bailey-Howe Library, University of Vermont.

31. Resumé of Novikoff's publications, Novikoff papers.

32. Alex Novikoff to Raymond Dart, October 3, 1949, Novikoff papers; fifteen FBI documents between March 17 and December 23, 1949, trace the

Novikoff loyalty investigation, FBI file 121–8951; the date of Novikoff's termination was reported in a letter from Guy Hottel, Special Agent, to "Director, FBI," November 7, 1949, FBI file 121-8951-36.

33. Raymond Dart to Alex Novikoff, October 24, 1949; Edward Gunn to Alex Novikoff, October 17, 1949. Novikoff was a consultant on two films, *Inside the Cell* and *Inside the Cell, Part II*. After he left the project, he suggested that the Institute on Pathology turn to Harry Albaum at Brooklyn College as a substitute. The chief of the Medical Illustration Service of the Institute commended Novikoff's work on "these two pioneering film projects." Correspondence between Novikoff and the Institute of Pathology is contained in Novikoff's private papers.

34. A copy of Novikoff's curriculum vitae at the time is contained in Novikoff's private papers.

35. Comments by Dean Brown in 1953 suggested that the subject of Novikoff's involvement in political activities in New York City and in the Rapp-Coudert investigation never came up for discussion. However, the counsel to the University in 1953, Louis Lisman, stated in an interview with the author (February 7, 1986) that Dean Brown knew of Novikoff's troubles in New York and chose to ignore them at the time Novikoff was hired.

36. Schein's recollections of these events are contained in letter to author, April 12, 1987.

37. Schein letter; Alex Novikoff to Bjarne Pearson, June 3, 1948, carbon copy in Novikoff papers.

38. *The Vermont Sunday News*, May 1, 1949, 10-B; *The Vermont Sunday News*, April 29, 1951.

39. Schein letter.

40. Shaftel, interview; Schein letter.

41. Novikoff's work on the St. Michael's College grant was noted in the August 21, 1952, edition of the *Burlington Free Press*. The *Free Press* four-part series began on January 29, 1953.

42. M. F. Forgione, acting chief of the Investigations Section, to Alex Novikoff, April 10, 1952, Novikoff papers; Novikoff notes on meeting, Novikoff papers.

43. Robert Griffith, *The Politics of Fear* (Lexington: University Press of Kentucky, 1970), 102.

44. David Oshinsky, *A Conspiracy So Immense: The World of Joe McCarthy* (New York: The Free Press, 1983), 53; Griffith, *The Politics of Fear,* 12.

45. Griffith, *The Politics of Fear,* 13, 33–34.

46. Ibid., 40, 42.

47. Ibid., 44, 46; David Caute, *The Great Fear: The Anti-Communist Purge under Truman and Eisenhower* (New York: Simon and Schuster, 1978), 31.

48. Schrecker states that the March 22, 1947, Executive Order 9835 of President Truman established anticommunism as the nation's official ideology, which was several years before Senator McCarthy entered the scene. See Schrecker, *No Ivory Tower: McCarthyism and the Universities* (New York: Oxford University Press, 1986), 4–5. Whether it was Truman's executive order or the McCarran Act of 1950 that best defined American policy, the two actions together leave no doubt as to the political consensus that had arisen on the subject of communism.

49. See Griffith, *The Politics of Fear,* for an excellent portrayal of McCarthy's

involvement in congressional controversies, beginning with his entry into the Senate in 1946.

50. Richard Hofstadter, *Anti-Intellectualism in American Life* (New York: Vintage Books, 1962), 3, 6.

51. See Vern Countryman, *Un-American Activities in the State of Washington* (Ithaca, N.Y.: Cornell University Press, 1951) and Jane Sanders, *Cold War on Campus: Academic Freedom at the University of Washington, 1946–64* (Seattle: University of Washington, 1979).

52. Jane Sanders, *Cold War on Campus*, 62–63, 71.

53. Caute, *The Great Fear*, 407, 605–6. See Committee A case file on the University of Miami, American Association of University Professors, Washington, D.C. This case file contains correspondence between the AAUP and the three faculty members, Daniel Ashkenas, Leonard Cohen, and Charles Davis. An internal memorandum of the AAUP, dated September 30, 1948, conveyed the "sober conclusion that we probably cannot be of any great service, that effort on our part to ascertain facts and reach conclusions would be incommensurately burdensome, and that we had better drop the case with a frank admission of our lack of ability to give it adequate handling." For a discussion of warnings to Wallace supporters, see Charles Davis to George Pope Shannon, Associate Secretary, American Association of University Professors, September 9, 1948, Committee A case file on the University of Miami, AAUP, Washington, D.C.

54. Caute, *The Great Fear*, 424.

55. Ibid., 410, 420. See summary of University of Colorado controversy in Robert MacIver, *Academic Freedom in Our Time* (New York: Columbia University Press, 1955), 298. See Robert Hodes to Ralph Himstead, executive secretary, AAUP, October 16, 1952, Committee A case file on Tulane University, AAUP, Washington, D.C. The Hodes case is discussed in an internal AAUP memorandum from George Pope Shannon to Ralph Himstead, April 30, 1953, Committee A case file on Tulane University, AAUP, Washington, D.C.

56. For a description of the Rutgers case and President Jones's influence on other campuses, see Schrecker, *No Ivory Tower*, 185–86.

57. The works of Caute and Schrecker are the most comprehensive treatments of the national scope of the anti-Communist campaign. The estimate of the number dismissed is derived from examination of the case files of the AAUP and interviews with faculty who were Communists. Schrecker's research is the most valuable on this point.

58. Various sources, especially the case files of the AAUP, provide insight into the procedures used by universities across the country.

59. See Clark Kerr, *The Uses of the University* (New York: Harper and Row, 1963). Ellen Schrecker, "Academic Freedom: The Historical View," in *Regulating the Intellectuals*, ed. Craig Kaplan and Ellen Schrecker (New York: Praeger, 1983), 25, 37.

60. Zechariah Chafee and Arthur Sunderland, letter to editor, *Harvard Crimson*, January 8, 1953, quoted in Schrecker, *No Ivory Tower*, 184.

61. Lewis Webster Jones, *Academic Freedom and Civic Responsibility*, Board of Trustees of Rutgers University, January 24, 1953.

62. Association of American Universities, "The Rights and Responsibilities of Universities and Their Faculties," Princeton, N.J., March 25, 1953; Schrecker, *No Ivory Tower*, 189.

63. Robert Morris, *No Wonder We Are Losing* (New York: The Bookmailer, 1958), 135–36.

64. Robert Iversen, *The Communists and the Schools* (New York: Harcourt, Brace, 1959), 266–67, 317–23; Frederic Ewen, interview with the author, November 13, 1984; letter from the Board of Higher Education is quoted in Thomas Coulton, *A City College in Action: Struggle and Achievement at Brooklyn College, 1930–1955* (New York: Harper and Brothers, 1955), 143–44; Schrecker, *No Ivory Tower,* 169.

65. Harry Albaum, interview with Murray Horowitz, October 10, 1979, Special Collections, Brooklyn College Library.

66. *New York Herald Tribune,* September 26, 1952, 1; hearing transcript, Committee on the Judiciary, Subcommittee to Investigate the Administration of the Internal Security Act and Other Internal Security Laws, U.S. Senate, 83rd Congress, *Subversive Influence in the Educational Process,* Part 1, September 25, 1952, 213–14, 221.

67. According to an interview with Novikoff by the author (May 18, 1984), Novikoff and Albaum spent the summer together at Lake Mahopac. A report on Albaum from New York FBI field office to FBI headquarters, April 24, 1953, noted that he was "presently furnishing this office with the names of numerous associates which he knew while he was in the Communist Party." See SAC, New York, to Director, FBI, April 24, 1953, FBI file 100-94031. Novikoff, interview, May 18, 1984.

68. Victor Navasky, *Naming Names* (New York: Viking Press, 1980), 20-24; hearing transcript (Albaum), *Subversive Influence in the Educational Process,* September 25, 1952, 228; hearing transcript (Harry Gideonse), *Subversive Influence in the Educational Process,* March 11, 1953, 547.

69. Navasky, *Naming Names,* 28–29; hearing transcript, *Subversive Influence in the Educational Process,* March 11, 1953, 547.

70. The dating of the transmitting of the Albaum testimony to the FBI is contained in a summary prepared by the Senate Internal Security Subcommittee, Executive Hearings—New York Education Hearings file, National Archives.

Chapter 5. Inquisition and the Unraveling of a Life

(pages 116–37)

1. See H. Nicholas Muller III and Samuel Hand, *In the State of Nature: Readings in Vermont History* (Montpelier: Vermont Historical Society, 1982); Appendices A, B, and D contain useful information about population trends.

2. Ibid., 329–30, 333.

3. See Robert Griffith, *Politics of Fear* (Lexington: University Press of Kentucky, 1970), 271–317, for a description of Flanders's gradual emergence as the leader of the anti-McCarthy forces in the Senate.

4. Frank Bryan, *Yankee Politics in Rural Vermont* (Hanover, N.H.: University Press of New England, 1974), 61, 98.

5. *The Burlington Free Press,* March 30, 1948.

6. Ibid., March 1, 1948, and March 27, 1948; *The Caledonian Record,* March 27, 1948.

7. Letter to FBI, signature not shown, July 21, 1950, FBI file 61-7558-492;

Special Agent, Albany, to Director, FBI, December 20, 1950, FBI file 61-7558-492.

8. Chester Way to Lee Emerson, November 13, 1950, Emerson papers, Series II-1-7, Vermont State Archives; copy of Emerson inaugural address, January 1951, Series II-1-8, Emerson papers.

9. Martin Trow, *Right-Wing Radicalism and Political Intolerance: A Study of Support for McCarthy in a New England Town*, unpublished doctoral dissertation, Columbia University, 1957. A summary of public response to McCarthy reported by the Gallup Poll in 1954 showed a gradual decline of his favorable rating during 1954, from a 50% favorable rating in January to a 36% rating in August. See the *Washington Post*, November 12, 1954.

10. Trow, *Right-Wing Radicalism*, 18, 25–28. The 42% figure is calculated from information provided in Table 2, p. 18, of Trow's dissertation.

11. Trow, *Right-Wing Radicalism*, 15, 17, 20–21.

12. Summary of undergraduate enrollments, 1935–1970, prepared by Michael Lapides, assistant dean of men, *Enrollment Reports*, Appendix A, 1969, University of Vermont; *The Burlington Free Press*, May 22, 1952.

13. See the Minutes of the Board of Trustees, Treasurer's Office, University of Vermont. Except for Governor Harold Arthur's attendance at five meetings in 1950, Vermont governors attended no meetings for the period 1948–1952.

14. Minutes of the University of Vermont Board of Trustees, April 19, 1952; remarks of Carl Borgmann on the occasion of the 175th anniversary of the University of Vermont, April 15, 1967, personal papers of Carl Borgmann, Boulder, Colo., 4–6, 9.

15. Robert Griffith, *The Politics of Fear*, 189–95.

16. Ibid., 209.

17. Quoted in Emmet John Hughes, *The Ordeal of Power: A Political Memoir of the Eisenhower Years* (New York: Atheneum, 1963), 38; Griffith, *The Politics of Fear*, 209.

18. Entry 418 was copied for mailing to the Senate Internal Security Subcommittee on March 16, 1952, SISS files, "Education—New York State, Individuals, 1953–1959," Legislative Archives Division, National Archives.

19. Louis Lisman, interview with author, February 7, 1986.

20. Hearing transcript, testimony of Alex Novikoff, Committee on the Judiciary, U.S. Senate, *Subversive Influence in the Educational Process*, Part 2, April 23, 1953, 800-801; hearing transcript, testimony of Alex Novikoff, April 2, 1953, Executive Hearings, Senate Internal Security Subcommittee, Committee on the Judiciary, National Archives, 29.

21. Lisman, interview.

22. Hearing transcript, *Subversive Influence in the Educational Process*, April 23, 1953, 800-1.

23. A copy of Novikoff's letter to the law firm is contained in the private papers of Alex Novikoff. Notes made by Alex Novikoff on or about March 28, 1953, described these actions by Lisman. The notes are contained in the private papers of Alex Novikoff.

24. Lisman's role in arranging for Novikoff's Washington testimony is noted in a document prepared by Novikoff on July 28, 1953. The document, entitled "Outline of events at the University of Vermont and State Agricultural College and related facts pertaining to the Novikoff case," is in the Novikoff file, Uni-

versity of Vermont Archives, Burlington, Vermont. See Minutes of the University Senate, March 26, 1953, University of Vermont Archives, 2–3.

25. *The Burlington Free Press*, March 26, 1953; Minutes of the University Senate, March 26, 1953, 2; *The Burlington Free Press*, March 31, 1953.

26. L. B. Nichols to Clyde Tolson, February 11, 1953, FBI file 61-7558; F. J. Baumgardner to A. H. Belmont, March 3, 1953, FBI file 61—7558.

27. Director, FBI, to SAC, Washington Field Office, January 26, 1953, FBI file 61-7558.

28. See Sigmund Diamond, "The Arrangement: The FBI and Harvard University in the McCarthy Period," in *Beyond the Hiss Case: The FBI, Congress and the Cold War* (Philadelphia: Temple University Press, 1982), ed. Athan Theoharis, 362–64, for excerpts of the Hoover memorandum and useful discussion. SAC, New York, to Director, FBI, April 20, 1953, FBI file 61-7558; SAC, New York, to Director, FBI, April 24, 1953, FBI file 61-7558.

29. SAC, Albany, to Director, FBI, April 30, 1953, FBI file 61-7558; transcript of hearing with Lewis Feuer, March 20, 1941, Joint Legislative Committee, RC Subject file.

30. A. H. Belmont to D. M. Ladd, July 17, 1953, FBI file 61-7558; L. B. Nichols to Clyde Tolson, July 21, 1953, FBI file 61-7558.

31. Oscar Shaftel, interview, March 20, 1987; L. B. Nichols to Clyde Tolson, March 19, 1953, FBI file 61-7558.

32. Alex Novikoff, "Outline of events at the University of Vermont"; notes on discussions with Senate Subcommittee on Internal Security in executive session on April 2, 1953, private papers of Alex Novikoff.

33. Testimony of Alex Novikoff, April 2, 1953, Executive Hearings, 17–20.

34. Ibid., 33–36.

35. Notes on discussions with Senate Internal Security Subcommittee, April 2, 1953, Novikoff papers.

36. *The Burlington Free Press*, April 4, 1953.

37. Ibid., April 13, 1953.

38. Ibid.; Alex Novikoff to Senator Herman Welker, April 15, 1953, Novikoff papers.

39. T. D. Sullivan, SSE, Ph.D., to Senator Herman Welker, April 16, 1953, carbon copy in Novikoff papers.

40. Robert Morris to Alex Novikoff, April 21, 1953, Novikoff papers.

41. Alex Novikoff to Senator Herman Welker, April 15, 1953, Novikoff papers.

Chapter 6. Exposure and Notoriety

(pages 138–60)

1. Notes on discussions with the Senate Internal Security Subcommittee, April 23, 1953, private papers of Alex Novikoff.

2. Ibid.

3. Hearing transcript, Committee on the Judiciary, U.S. Senate, *Subversive Influence in the Educational Process*, April 23, 1953, 796, 798, 799, 803, 805.

4. Ibid., 807, 816.

5. Notes on discussions with Senate Internal Security Subcommittee, Novikoff papers.

6. Ibid.; Senator Herman Welker to Alex Novikoff, April 23, 1953, Novikoff papers.

7. Notes on discussions with Senate Internal Security Subcommittee, April 23, 1953, Novikoff papers.

8. Alex Novikoff, interview with Harriet Zuckerman, May 12, 1983.

9. *The New York Times*, April 24, 1953, 12; *Washington Times-Herald*, April 24, 1953.

10. *Burlington Daily News*, April 23, 1953; *The Burlington Free Press*, April 24, 1953.

11. *The Burlington Free Press*, April 25, 1953.

12. W. E. Brown, M.D., to Alex Novikoff, April 24, 1953, Novikoff papers; Benjamin Singerman, M.D., to Dr. Carl Borgmann, April 27, 1953, Novikoff papers; "Memorandum to the Trustee-Faculty Committee considering the case of Dr. A. B. Novikoff," April 28, 1953, Novikoff papers.

13. Carl Borgmann, "Written Summary Prepared for University Senate Meeting, July 30, 1953," University of Vermont Archives, Novikoff file; *The Burlington Free Press*, April 28, 1953.

14. Robert Joyce, interview with author, June 29, 1984.

15. *Burlington Daily News*, April 28, 1953; Lee Emerson to Carl Borgmann, April 28, 1953, University of Vermont Archives, Novikoff file; Carl Borgmann to Lee Emerson, May 1, 1953, University of Vermont Archives, Novikoff file.

16. Hearing transcript of Trustee-Faculty Committee to Investigate Alex Novikoff, University of Vermont Archives, 1.

17. Ibid., 1–2, 20–25, 34–35.

18. Ibid., 11–12. These pages show the committee's attempt to understand Novikoff's position on testifying before congressional committees.

19. Ibid., 11–13.

20. Jean Wright, interview with author, May 21, 1985.

21. *The Burlington Free Press*, May 4, 1953; *Vermont Sunday News*, May 10, 1953; *Burlington Daily News*, May 8, 1953.

22. *Swanton Courier*, May 14, 1953; *Suburban List*, May 21, 1953.

23. *The Burlington Free Press*, May 29, 1953.

24. Ibid., May 15, 1953, May 29, 1953.

25. Report of the Findings of the Trustee-Faculty Committee to Investigate Alex Novikoff, June 12, 1953, University of Vermont Archives, Novikoff file.

26. Robert Joyce, interview.

27. The minutes of the board of trustees meeting do not show that such a vote took place. Other sources, however, suggested that a straw vote had taken place: (1) *The Burlington Free Press* of June 15, 1953, mentioned the vote and (2) Novikoff reported the "rumor" in his "Outline of events at the University of Vermont," prepared July 28, 1953. Minutes of the University of Vermont Board of Trustees, June 13, 1953, University of Vermont Treasurer's Office; Alex Novikoff, "Outline of events at the University of Vermont," prepared July 28, 1953, Novikoff papers.

28. *The Burlington Free Press*, June 12, 1953; *Burlington Daily News*, June 15, 1953.

29. Minutes of the University of Vermont Board of Trustees, June 20, 1953, University of Vermont Treasurer's Office; *Burlington Daily News*, June 21, 1953.

30. Alex Novikoff, "Outline of events at the University of Vermont"; *The*

Burlington Free Press, June 23 and 24, 1953; *Burlington Daily News,* June 23 and 25, 1953.

31. Carl Borgmann, a chronology of events prepared approximately July 25, 1953, University of Vermont Archives, Novikoff file, 3.

32. William Van Robertson, interview with author, June 4, 1985; George Wolf, Jr., M.D., to Dr. W. V. Robertson, July 1, 1953, University of Vermont Archives.

33. *The Burlington Free Press,* June 25 and June 26, 1953; George Wolf, Jr., to Bjarne Pearson, June 29, 1953, University of Vermont Archives.

34. Alex Novikoff to Dr. Henry A. Lardy, Institute for Enzyme Research, The University of Wisconsin, June 26, 1953, carbon copy in Novikoff papers; Alex Novikoff to Dr. Van R. Potter, McArdle Memorial Laboratory, University of Wisconsin, June 26, 1953, carbon copy in Novikoff papers; Van R. Potter to Alex Novikoff, July 8, 1953, Novikoff papers; Dr. Philip Siekevitz, McCardle Memorial Laboratory, University of Wisconsin, to Alex Novikoff, June 30, 1953, Novikoff papers.

35. Van R. Potter to Alex Novikoff, July 8, 1953, Novikoff papers; Dr. Philip Siekevitz to Alex Novikoff, June 30, 1953, Novikoff papers.

36. Copies of June 30 letters are contained in Novikoff papers; Sidney Weinhouse to Alex Novikoff, July 8, 1953, Novikoff papers; J. Walter Wilson to Alex Novikoff, July 3, 1953, Novikoff papers.

37. Alex Novikoff to Albert Einstein, June 29, 1953, carbon copy in Novikoff papers.

38. *The New York Times,* June 12, 1953. McCarthy and Welker were quoted in the *Daily Worker,* June 15, 1953. The FBI investigated allegations about Einstein's loyalty in the 1950s. It appears that the final investigation during his lifetime was closed in March 1955 at the recommendation of the Newark Field Office: see report to FBI Headquarters, March 9, 1955, FBI file 61-7099.

39. Albert Einstein to Alex Novikoff, July 4, 1953, copy of letter in Novikoff file, University of Vermont Archives; Abraham White, Associate Director, Albert Einstein College of Medicine, to Alex Novikoff, July 9, 1953, Novikoff papers.

Chapter 7. *The First Ripples of Dissent*

(pages 161–96)

1. Comments by individuals acting on Novikoff's behalf in the following days, including a letter written by Schein on July 3 to the AAUP, indicate that Nuquist, Schein, and Novikoff consulted with each other before approaching the AAUP. The July 10 edition of the *Burlington Free Press* reported that Nuquist "knew of several letters by UVM members asking the association to take a definite stand [on the Novikoff case]." Arnold Schein to Ralph Himstead, July 3, 1953, Committee A case file on the University of Vermont, AAUP.

2. Western Union telegram from George Pope Shannon to Arnold Schein, July 8, 1953, copy in the Committee A case file on the University of Vermont; George Pope Shannon to Arnold Schein, undated, copy contained in Committee A case file on the University of Vermont.

3. Arnold Schein to George Pope Shannon, July 8, 1953, Committee A case file on the University of Vermont; Shannon's letter to Schein with the information that Novikoff must request AAUP assistance is referred to in a letter

on July 22 from Novikoff to Shannon (Committee A case file on the University of Vermont).

4. See Loya Metzger, *Professors in Trouble: A Quantitative Analysis of Academic and Tenure Cases,* unpublished doctoral dissertation, Columbia University, pp. 41–46. Chapter 2 of Metzger's dissertation presents a useful overview of the early history of the AAUP.

5. Loya Metzger, *Professors in Trouble,* 42, 44–53. Lovejoy told of his trip to Utah in an interview in 1960 at which Metzger was present.

6. Ibid., 59–60.

7. Loya Metzger, *Professors in Trouble,* 62–67.

8. "1940 Statement of Principles on Academic Freedom and Tenure," *Policy Documents and Reports,* AAUP, 1984.

9. Loya Metzger, *Professors in Trouble,* 76.

10. Ibid., 77–78, 334; Walter Metzger, "Ralph Fuchs and Ralph Himstead: A Note on the AAUP in the McCarthy Period," *ACADEME* 72 (November–December 1986): 30.

11. Loya Metzger, *Professors in Trouble,* 78–81.

12. "Invoking the Fifth Amendment," Chapter Letter No. 3, April 24, 1953, AAUP, Washington, D.C.

13. AAUP document, Novikoff file, University of Vermont Archives; *The Burlington Free Press,* July 10, 1953.

14. "A Resolution Adopted by the University of Vermont and State Agricultural College Chapter of the American Association of University Professors at a Meeting on July 9, 1953," Novikoff file, University of Vermont Archives, 3; *Burlington Daily News,* July 10, 1953.

15. *Burlington Daily News,* July 9, 1953. Harold Bucklin described for reporters the "spontaneous nature" of the clergymen's effort. "To the Board of Trustees of the University of Vermont," text printed in the *Burlington Daily News,* July 9, 1953.

16. Robert Joyce, interview, June 29, 1974.

17. *The Burlington Free Press,* July 10, 1953; *Burlington Daily News,* July 12, 1953; *The Burlington Free Press,* July 9, 1953; *Burlington Daily News,* July 9, 1953.

18. *Burlington Daily News,* July 14, 1953; *The Burlington Free Press,* July 14, 1953.

19. Alex Novikoff to Carl Borgmann, July 14, 1953, Novikoff file, University of Vermont Archives; *The Burlington Free Press,* July 16, 1953.

20. *Burlington Daily News,* July 16, 1953; *Brattleboro Reformer,* July 22, 1953; *The Burlington Free Press,* July 18, 1953.

21. *The Burlington Free Press,* July 21, 1952; William Van Robertson, interview, June 4, 1985.

22. William Van Robertson, interview.

23. Ibid. Letter to Carl Borgmann, signed by University of Vermont faculty, July 27, 1953, and memorandum to members of university senate from University of Vermont AAUP chapter, July 27, 1953. Both documents are contained in the Novikoff file, University of Vermont Archives.

24. *The Burlington Free Press,* July 15 and July 21, 1953; Alex Novikoff to George Pope Shannon, July 22, 1958, Committee A case file on the University of Vermont, AAUP.

25. Arnold Schein to Ralph Himstead, July 27, 1953, Committee A case file on the University of Vermont, AAUP.

26. Alex Novikoff, "Outline of events at the University of Vermont and State Agricultural College and related facts pertaining to the Novikoff cae," Novikoff file, University of Vermont Archives.

27. *The Burlington Free Press*, July 28, 1953.

28. Carl Borgmann, a chronology of events prepared approximately July 25, 1953, Novikoff file, University of Vermont, 5; Minutes of the University of Vermont Faculty Senate, July 30, 1953, Faculty Senate Office, University of Vermont.

29. *The Burlington Free Press*, July 31, 1953; *Burlington Daily News*, July 31, 1953.

30. Carl Borgmann to Lee Emerson (with similar copies to other members of the board of trustees). A copy of this letter is contained in the Novikoff file, University of Vermont Archives. Louis Lisman to Carl Borgmann, dated July 31, 1953, Novikoff file, University of Vermont Archives.

31. The two letters were sent by SAC, Boston, to Director, FBI, on August 31, 1953, FBI file 9-24714-1. J. Edgar Hoover to FBI field office (addressee is not clear on decaying document), September 3, 1953, FBI file 9-24714-1. Hoover's telegram refers to Novikoff as "victim, extortion." SAC, Boston, to Director, FBI, September 24, 1953, FBI file 9-24714-3.

32. Alex Novikoff, interview, March 12, 1984; Francis Peisch, interview with author, May 30, 1985; Francis Peisch, "Battle Plan," notes prepared by Peisch for board of review hearing, Novikoff papers.

33. Chester Eaton to Harold Buckland, August 10, 1953, carbon copy in private papers of Chester Eaton; Chester Eaton, interview with author, July 10, 1985.

34. Alex Novikoff to George Pope Shannon, August 8, 1953, Committee A case file on the University of Vermont.

35. George Pope Shannon to Ralph Himstead, August 12, 1953, Committee A case file on the University of Vermont, AAUP.

36. Ralph Himstead to Carl Borgmann, telegram, August 12, 1953, copy in Committee A case file on the University of Vermont, AAUP; see telegram from Ralph Himstead to Carl Borgmann, August 13, 1953, thanking Borgmann for his reply. A copy of this telegram is contained in the Committee A case file on the University of Vermont, AAUP.

37. Letter to Board of Trustees, University of Vermont, August 10, 1953, Novikoff file, University of Vermont Archives.

38. Minutes of the University of Vermont Board of Trustees, August 14, 1953, Treasurer's Office, University of Vermont.

39. *The Burlington Free Press*, August 15, 1953. Emerson expressed this view of McCarthy in an interview with Thomas Bassett in July 1975. See Emerson file, Special Collections, Bailey-Howe Library, University of Vermont.

40. Evans's role at the July 30 senate meeting was noted by a faculty colleague, Ethan A. H. Sims, in a letter to the editor, *The Burlington Free Press*, November 15, 1982; Minutes of the Board of Review, August 14, 1953, Treasurer's Office, University of Vermont.

41. Thurston Adams to Alex Novikoff, August 14, 1953, Novikoff file, University of Vermont Archives; *The Burlington Free Press*, August 18, 1953.

42. The meetings of Novikoff with Peisch and Latham are noted in Peisch's

"Battle Plan" for the Board of Review hearing. The decision to take the Novikoff case was described by Peisch in his interview with the author on May 30, 1985.

43. Louis Lisman, interview with author, February 7, 1986; Arnold Schein to the author, April 12, 1987.

44. Carl Borgmann, interview with author, February 22, 1985.

45. Lee Emerson to Angelo Spero, September 2, 1950, Emerson papers, Series II-1-7, Vermont State Archives. Emerson used the phrase "country lawyer" in this letter, which served as the basis for an introduction of Emerson for an appearance on a radio program. Francis Peisch, interview with author, May 30, 1985.

46. George Little, interview with author, May 21, 1987.

47. Ibid.

48. Schein to author, April 12, 1987; SAC, Albany, to Director, FBI, April 13, 1961, FBI file number missing, private papers of Arnold Schein.

49. Martha Kennedy, interview with author, July 2, 1987; Schein to author, April 12, 1987.

50. Alex Novikoff to Carl Borgmann, August 22, 1953, carbon copy in Novikoff papers; Francis Peisch, interview.

51. Francis Peisch, interview.

52. Ibid.

53. Alex Novikoff to Ralph Himstead, August 19, 1953, Committee A case file on the University of Vermont, AAUP; telegram from Ralph Himstead to Carl Shoup, August 19, 1953, copy in the Committee A case file on the University of Vermont, AAUP.

54. Telegram from Ralph Himstead to Carl Shoup, August 20, 1953, copy in the Committee A case file on the University of Vermont; telegram from Ralph Himstead to Carl Shoup, August 20, 1953, copy in the Committee A case file on the University of Vermont; telegrams from Ralph Himstead to Fred Millett and Ralph Barton, August 21, 1953, copies in the Committee A case file on the University of Vermont; telegram from Francis Peisch to Ralph Himstead, August 22, 1953, Committee A case file on the University of Vermont; telegram from Ralph Himstead to Fred Millett, August 24, 1953, copy in the Committee A case file on the University of Vermont; telegram from Ralph Himstead to Fred Millett, August 25, 1953, copy in the Committee A case file on the University of Vermont.

55. SAC, Albany, to Director, FBI, August 19, 1953, FBI File 100-198015-33; telegram from Lee Emerson to FBI headquarters, August 13, 1953, FBI File 100-198015; Lee Emerson to Carl Borgmann (letter and "resume" of Novikoff's FBI file), August 18, 1953, Novikoff file, University of Vermont Archives.

56. SAC, Albany, to Director, FBI, August 12, 1953, FBI File 100-19015-30; A. H. Belmont to D. M. Ladd, August 14, 1953, FBI File 100-198015-29; *Brattleboro Daily Reformer,* August 8, 1953.

57. SAC, Albany, to Director, FBI, August 19, 1953, FBI File 100-198015-33; SAC, Albany, to Director, FBI, November 27, 1951, FBI File 100-198015-19.

58. The history of the Responsibilities Program and FBI procedures were summarized by J. Edgar Hoover in a memorandum to Attorney General Herbert Brownell, July 22, 1954, FBI File 61-7558.

59. Lee Emerson to Carl Borgmann (letter and "resume"), August 18, 1953.

60. Louis Lisman, interview; Charles Weaver, telephone interview with the author. Weaver was an aide to Senator Aiken at this time.

61. Louis Lisman, interview; Francis Peisch, interview; Alex Novikoff, interview, May 18, 1984.

62. Francis Peisch to Executive Committee of the Review Board, August 25, 1953, Novikoff file, University of Vermont Archives.

63. Francis Peisch (personal memorandum), August 22, 1953, Novikoff papers. Novikoff denied Lisman's charge of "germ warfare" in a letter to Ralph Fuchs, general secretary of the AAUP, dated March 9, 1956, Committee A case file on the University of Vermont.

64. Francis Peisch, August 22, 1953, Novikoff papers.

65. Alex Novikoff to Ralph Himstead, August 25, 1953, Committee A case file on the University of Vermont; Ellen Schrecker, *No Ivory Tower,* 218.

66. Ibid.

Chapter 8. The Final Hearing

(pages 197–219)

1. *Burlington Daily News,* August 21, 1953. The advertisement appeared in Burlington papers on August 29, 1953.

2. Arnold Schein to Paul Evans, August 20, 1953, Novikoff file, University of Vermont Archives; Louis Joughlin, "In the matter of Professor Alex. B. Novikoff: Brief Submitted by Academic Freedom Committee of the American Civil Liberties Union," August 27, 1953, Novikoff file, University of Vermont Archives; *The Burlington Free Press,* August 26, 1953.

3. Telegram from Ralph Himstead to Alex Novikoff, August 26, 1953, copy in the Committee A case file on the University of Vermont, AAUP; telegram from Ralph Himstead to Fred Millett, August 26, 1953, copy in the Committee A case file on the University of Vermont; Francis Peisch to Ralph Himstead, August 27, 1953, Committee A case file on the University of Vermont; Francis Peisch, interview with the author, May 30, 1985; telegrams from Ralph Himstead to Fred Millett and Ralph Perry, August 21, 1953, copies in the Committee A case file on the University of Vermont.

4. Private papers of Chester Eaton.

5. Chester Eaton, interview with author, July 10, 1985; Edmund Mower to Martha Kennedy, July 16, 1953, Martha Kennedy papers, Special Collections, Bailey-Howe Library, University of Vermont; see, for example, Robert Iversen, *The Communists and the Schools* (New York: Harcourt, Brace, 1959), 341, on Jones's influence.

6. Francis Colburn to Chester Eaton, August 7, 1953, private papers of Chester Eaton papers; Eaton papers.

7. The verbatim record of the hearing, running to 118 pages, *In Re: Dr. Alex Novikoff before Board of Review,* was made by Eda Calcani, a stenographer, and is located in the University of Vermont Archives. Quotes from the hearing are taken from this source. See interview with Francis Peisch, May 30, 1985.

8. *In Re: Dr. Alex Novikoff,* 12–18.

9. See Eaton, interview, and Bernard O'Shea, *The Swanton Courier,* September 3, 1953, on trustee fears about being called to Washington to testify.

10. *In Re: Dr. Alex Novikoff*, 22–23, 29–30.

11. Ibid., 34–61.

12. Peisch, interview.

13. *In Re: Dr. Alex Novikoff*, 62–73.

14. Ibid., 74–78.

15. Ibid., 78–94, 102–103.

16. Ibid., 104–106.

17. Ibid., 106–108.

18. Ibid., 105, 109–116.

19. Ibid., 116–117.

20. Ibid.; Joyce, interview.

21. Joyce, interview.

22. Francis Peisch, interview with Michael Sarvak, March 19, 1985.

23. *The Swanton Courier,* September 3, 1953; Eaton, interview.

24. *The Swanton Courier,* September 3, 1953; Eaton, interview.

25. Carl Borgmann to Lee Emerson, September 1, 1953, carbon copy in Borgmann file, University of Vermont Archives; telegram from Ralph Himstead to Fred Millett, September 1, 1953, carbon copy in the Committee A case file on the University of Vermont.

26. *The Burlington Free Press,* September 2, 1953.

27. George Wolf, Jr., to Carl Borgmann, September 2, 1953, Novikoff file, University of Vermont Archives.

28. William Van Robertson to Chester Eaton, September 3, 1953, Novikoff file, University of Vermont Archives.

29. Eaton, interview.

30. *The Burlington Free Press,* August 31, 1953.

31. Minutes of the University of Vermont Board of Trustees, September 5, 1953, Treasurer's Office, University of Vermont.

32. See, for example, SAC, Albany, to Director, FBI, October 19, 1950, FBI File 198015-16, for finding of "no communist activity on the part of this subject in the recent past." The various FBI investigations in the late 1940s and early 1950s found no new derogatory information.

33. *The Burlington Free Press,* September 7, 1953.

34. *Vermont Sunday News,* September 13, 1953; Alumni Newsletter, January 1954, Novikoff file, University of Vermont Archives.

35. Carl Borgmann to Policy Committee, September 10, 1953, Novikoff file, University of Vermont Archives; University of Vermont AAUP Chapter to Members of the Faculty Senate, September 18, 1953, Novikoff file, University of Vermont Archives; Andrew Nuquist to Chester Cole, December 17, 1955, Novikoff file, University of Vermont Archives; Andrew Nuquist to Chester Cole, January 11, 1955, Novikoff file, University of Vermont Archives.

36. Ralph Fuchs to Alex Novikoff, September 14, 1953, Novikoff papers; Ralph Fuchs to Ralph Himstead, October 2, 1953, Committee A case file on the University of Vermont.

37. Arnold Schein to Ralph Himstead, October 6, 1953, Committee A case file on the University of Vermont.

38. *The Burlington Free Press,* March 22, 1954; *The Burlington Free Press,* March 27, 1954, and Minutes of the Faculty Senate, March 26, 1954, Faculty Senate Office, University of Vermont; Minutes of the Faculty Senate, September 23, 1954, Faculty Senate Office, University of Vermont; Carl Borgmann to mem-

bers of the Faculty Senate, September 22, 1954, Faculty Senate file, University of Vermont Archives.

39. Francis Peisch to Lee Emerson, October 7, 1953, carbon copy in Novikoff file, University of Vermont Archives.

40. This document covers the period September 22 to September 24, 1953, Novikoff file, University of Vermont Archives; press release, dated October 6, 1953, by WCAX radio station of "item broadcast on a WCAX News Report" on October 1, 1953. Novikoff papers.

41. George Wolf, Jr., to Bjarne Pearson, September 14, 1953, Novikoff file, University of Vermont Archives.

42. M. R. Runyon to George Wolf, Jr., August 6, 1953, Novikoff file, University of Vermont Archives.

43. J. Edward Spike, Jr., to Bjarne Pearson, May 18, 1954, Novikoff file, University of Vermont Archives.

Chapter 9. Remaking a Life and a Career

(pages 220–248)

1. Alex Novikoff, interview, March 12, 1984.

2. Cristina Schweiker and Betty La Grange to Alex Novikoff, September 8, 1953, Novikoff papers; Claude Tate to Alex Novikoff, September 13, 1953, Novikoff papers; L. F. Sanborn to Alex Novikoff, September 22, 1953, Novikoff papers; Carroll Tripp to Rt. Rev. Vedder Van Dyck, September 10, 1953, and attached statement signed by Carroll Tripp, Novikoff papers; Robert Joyce to Alex Novikoff, undated, Novikoff papers.

3. William Brown to Arthur Hertig, October 13, 1953, copy in Novikoff papers; Alex Novikoff to Kirtley Mather, October 7, 1953, carbon copy in Novikoff papers; Novikoff, interview, March 12, 1984.

4. Alex Novikoff to "Ed," dated September 12, 1953, copy in Novikoff papers; Alex Novikoff to Kirtley Mather, October 7, 1953, copy in Novikoff papers; Alex Novikoff to William Van Robertson, January 11, 1954, copy in Novikoff papers; Alex Novikoff to Irwin Korr, February 19, 1954, copy in Novikoff papers.

5. Novikoff, interview, March 12, 1984.

6. Novikoff kept in his private papers a list of the letters he wrote and the responses he received. The three lists covered universities, cancer research laboratories, and industry. Robert M. Hutchins to Alex Novikoff, February 3, 1954, Novikoff papers; Alex Novikoff to James Thorburn Williamson, December 12, 1953, copy in Novikoff papers.

7. M. Demerec to Alex Novikoff, November 4, 1953, Novikoff papers; A. M. Schechtman to Alex Novikoff, January 21, 1954, Novikoff papers; Marvin Farber to Alex Novikoff, January 25, 1954, Novikoff papers; William Van Robertson to Alex Novikoff, January 6, 1954, Novikoff papers; Jean Oliver to Alex Novikoff, February 3, 1954, Novikoff papers.

8. Milton Friedman, M.D., to Alex Novikoff, November 14, 1953, Novikoff papers; C. C. Little to Alex Novikoff, November 9, 1953, Novikoff papers; Irvin Korr to Alex Novikoff, January 18, 1954, Novikoff papers.

9. Alex Novikoff to I. J. Greenblatt, January 3, 1954, copy in Novikoff papers.

10. Notes and chronology prepared by Alex Novikoff, Novikoff papers; Ved-

der Van Dyke, to I. J. Greenblatt, January 14, 1953, Novikoff papers; Max Wall to I. J. Greenblatt, January 11, 1953, Novikoff papers; William Brown to I. J. Greenblatt, January 11, 1953, Novikoff papers; Robert Joyce to I. J. Greenblatt, January 11, 1953, Novikoff papers; Alex Novikoff to I. J. Greenblatt, January 18, 1953, Novikoff papers.

11. Minutes of the Annual Membership and Board of Directors Meeting of the Waldemar Medical Research Foundation, Inc., May 19, 1953, Novikoff papers.

12. Alex Novikoff to Norman Molomut, October 2, 1954, copy in Novikoff personal papers; Alex Novikoff to Norman Molomut, February 3, 1954, copy in Novikoff papers.

13. Letters from Molomut to Novikoff on January 29, 1954, and February 25, 1954, elaborated on the arrangement for Novikoff's work, Novikoff papers; Norman Molomut to Alex Novikoff, February 27, 1954, Novikoff papers; Novikoff, interview, May 23, 1983, Special Collections, Bailey-Howe Library, University of Vermont.

14. Transcript of remarks by Sam Seifter, chairman of department of biochemistry, Albert Einstein College of Medicine, at memorial convocation for Alex Novikoff on January 9, 1987, *The Einstein Quarterly Journal of Biology and Medicine*, 5 (1987): 77–79; Ellen Schrecker, *No Ivory Tower: McCarthyism and the Universities* (New York: Oxford University Press, 1986), 298.

15. A. G. Jones to District Director, INS, Miami, March 8, 1954, INS File 0100-27575; transcripts of interviews with Jake Novikoff and Anna Novikoff, March 31, 1954, INS File 0100-27575.

16. Athan Theoharis, *Spying on Americans: Political Surveillance from Hoover to the Huston Plan* (Philadelphia: Temple University Press, 1978), 44; SAC, New York, to Director, FBI, August 30, 1955, FBI File 100-198015-44; Director, FBI, to William Tompkins, Assistant Attorney General, September 30, 1955, FBI File 100-198015.

17. George Rundquist to Louis Joughlin, October 9, 1953, American Civil Liberties Union Archives, Box 84, 1953 General Correspondence, Vol. 7, Princeton University Library, Princeton, N.J.; interviews with Alex Novikoff on March 12, 1984, and May 18, 1984, and with Louis Lisman on February 7, 1986, revealed these sentiments.

18. See Loya Metzger, *Professors in Trouble: A Quantitative Analysis of Academic and Tenure Cases*, unpublished doctoral dissertation, Columbia University, 78–83; Council Letter III, March 10, 1954, Council Letters 1954, American Association of University Professors files.

19. Alex Novikoff to Ralph Fuchs, November 16, 1955, Committee A case file on the University of Vermont, AAUP; Ralph Fuchs to Alex Novikoff, November 23, 1955, copy in the Committee A case file on the University of Vermont, AAUP.

20. Fuchs indicated to Novikoff that "I hope to hear from you before I write President Borgmann." Copies of both letters are contained in the Committee A case file on the University of Vermont, AAUP. *The Burlington Free Press*, July 21, 1953.

21. "Confidential Draft," attachment to letter sent by Ralph Fuchs to Carl Borgmann, February 9, 1956, Novikoff file, University of Vermont Archives.

22. Carl Borgmann to Ralph Fuchs, February 21, 1956, copy in Novikoff

file, University of Vermont Archives; Ralph Fuchs to Carl Borgmann, February 27, 1956, Novikoff file, University of Vermont Archives.

23. Ralph Fuchs to Carl Borgmann, April 19, 1956, copy in Committee A case file on the University of Vermont, AAUP.

24. Samuel Bogarad to Ralph Fuchs, November 14, 1956, Committee A case file on the University of Vermont, AAUP; Alex Novikoff to Ralph Fuchs, November 8, 1956, Committee A case file on the University of Vermont, AAUP.

25. *The Burlington Free Press*, November 20, 1956; Robert Beaupre to Ralph Fuchs, November 23, 1956, and letter from David Howe to Ralph Fuchs, March 18, 1957, Committee A case file on the University of Vermont, AAUP; Ralph Fuchs to Robert Beaupre, November 29, 1956, copy in the Committee A case file on the University of Vermont, AAUP; *The Vermont Sunday News*, November 21, 1956; *The Burlington Free Press*, November 22, 1956.

26. Bentley Glass to Ralph Fuchs, November 24, 1956, Committee A case file on the University of Vermont, AAUP; Carl Borgmann to Ralph Fuchs, April 16, 1957, copy in Novikoff file, University of Vermont Archives.

27. Robert Carr to Alex Novikoff, October 17, 1957, copy in the Committee A case file on the University of Vermont, AAUP; Alex Novikoff to Robert Carr, October 30, 1957, Committee A case file on the University of Vermont, AAUP; Bertram Willcox to Ralph Fuchs, October 30, 1957, Committee A case file on the University of Vermont, AAUP.

28. "The University of Vermont," *AAUP Bulletin* 44 (March 1958): 20–21.

29. The volume also reported on cases at Dickinson College, the University of Southern California, Alabama Polytechnic Institute, Texas Technological College, and Livingstone College. *The Burlington Free Press*, March 29, 1958.

30. Robertson's letter and the AAUP resolution are included in the minutes of the April 19, 1958, meeting of the University of Vermont board of trustees, which are located in the Treasurer's Office, University of Vermont.

31. Minutes of the University of Vermont Board of Trustees, April 19, 1958.

32. *AAUP Bulletin* 44 (1958): 665; Novikoff's attitude about the future was conveyed in his correspondence at the time and recalled in an interview with the author on March 12, 1984.

33. Carl Borgmann, interview with the author, February 22, 1985.

34. *Rutland Daily Herald,* April 28, 1987.

35. Peisch, interview; Little, interview; Novikoff, interview, May 18, 1984.

36. A. B. Novikoff, E. Podber, J. Ryan, and E. Noe, "Biochemical Heterogeneity of the Cytoplasmic Particles Isolated from Rat Liver Homogenate," *Journal of Histochemistry and Cytochemistry,* 1953, 1, 27; Christian de Duve, memorial convocation, *Einstein Quarterly Journal* 5 (1987): 75.

37. De Duve, memorial convocation, *Einstein Quarterly Journal* 5 (1987): 76; de Duve, "The Lysosome in Retrospect," in *Lysosomes in Biology and Pathology,* (Amsterdam: North-Holland, 1969), eds. J. T. Dingle and H. B. Fell, 16; A. B. Novikoff, H. Beaufay, and C. de Duve, *Journal of Biophysical and Biochemical Cytology* 2 Suppl. (1956): 179.

38. De Duve, memorial convocation, *Einstein Quarterly Journal* 5 (1987): 76–77.

39. Recollections of E. B. Wilson from remarks by Alex Novikoff on the occasion of receiving the E. B. Wilson Medal Award, December 1, 1982, Novikoff papers.

40. Alex Novikoff, interview with Harriet Zuckerman, May 12, 1983; "The

1974 Nobel Prize for Physiology or Medicine," *Science* 186 (8 November 1974): 516–20.

41. Sonia Klein, interview with author, September 22, 1987; Novikoff, interview with Harriet Zuckerman, May 12, 1983; Oscar Shaftel, interview with author, March 20, 1987.

42. Novikoff, interview with Harriet Zuckerman.

43. Draft copy of passport application, Novikoff papers; Alex Novikoff to Director, Passport Division, Department of State, May 23, 1958, carbon copy in Novikoff papers; SAC, New York, to Director, FBI, August 14, 1958, FBI File 198015-46.

44. Anne Stommel to James Eastland, August 3, 1962, and Henry Strack to James Eastland, August 9, 1962, Novikoff file, files of the Senate Internal Security Subcommittee, National Archives; Ben Mandel to Jay Sourwine, August 21, 1962, Novikoff file, SISS files, National Archives; Mollie Margolin, Library of Congress, to Benjamin Mandel, September 12, 1962, Novikoff file, SISS files, National Archives; Jay Sourwine to Ben Mandel, undated, Novikoff file, SISS files, National Archives.

45. Bryce Nelson, "Scientists Increasingly Protest HEW Investigation of Advisers," *Science* 164 (27 June 1969): 1499–1504; Nelson, "HEW Security Checks Said to Bar Qualified Applicants to PHS," *Science* 165 (18 July 1969): 269.

46. Nelson, "HEW: Blacklists Scrapped in New Security Procedures," *Science* 167 (9 January 1970): 154–56.

47. Nelson, "Scientists Increasingly Protest HEW Investigation of Advisers," *Science* 164 (27 June 1969): 1499–1504; Nelson, "HEW: Blacklists Scrapped in New Security Procedures," *Science* 167 (9 January 1970): 154–156.

48. Nathan Dick to L. Patrick Gray III, December 15, 1972, FBI File 121—8951—39; Acting Director, FBI, to SAC, New York, January 2, 1973, FBI File 121-8951-39; report of Washington Field Office, January 29, 1973, FBI File 121-8951-43; Acting Director, FBI, to Director, Bureau of Investigations, Civil Service Commission, February 8, 1973, FBI File 121-8951-47; Acting Director, FBI, to Director of Investigations, Civil Service Commission, March 5, 1973, FBI File 121-8951-53; Acting Director, FBI, to Civil Service Commission, and Acting Director, FBI, to Director of Investigations, Civil Service Commission, March 12, 1973, FBI File 121-8951-55.

49. *The Burlington Free Press*, April 23, 1968.

50. Ibid., November 7, 1982, November 9, 1982, and May 22, 1983.

51. *The New York Times*, May 22, 1983.

52. Kenneth Mann to Phyllis Novikoff, January 26, 1987, private papers of Phyllis Novikoff; Sam Seifter, memorial convocation, *Einstein Quarterly Journal* 5 (1987): 78; Seifter, memorial convocation, 78.

Epilogue

(pages 249–50)

1. Thomas Jefferson to Edward Carrington, January 16, 1787, and Thomas Jefferson to Abigail Adams, February 22, 1787, cited in Dumas Malone, *Jefferson and the Rights of Man* (Boston: Little, Brown, 1951), 158.

2. Alex Novikoff, interview with author, May 18, 1984.

INDEX